MY HOME, MY MONEY PIT

MY HOME, MY MONEY PIT

Your Guide to Every Home Improvement Adventure

Tom Kraeutler
and Leslie Segrete

Hosts of ***The Money Pit***
Home Improvement Radio Show

Guilford, Connecticut
An imprint of The Globe Pequot Press

For our parents,

who helped us build big dreams

Text design by Sheryl P. Kober

Illustrations by Robert L. Prince

Cover photos by Phillip Friedman

Library of Congress Cataloging-in-Publication Data

Kraeutler, Tom.
My home, my money pit : your guide to every home improvement adventure / Tom Kraeutler and Leslie Segrete.
p. cm.
Includes index.
ISBN 978-1-59921-287-6
1. Dwellings—Remodeling—Popular works. 2. Dwellings—Maintenance and repair—Popular works. I. Segrete, Leslie. II. Title.
TH4816.K686 2008
643'.7--dc22

2008012810

Printed in the United States of America

10 9 8 7 6 5 4 3 2 1

CONTENTS

ACKNOWLEDGMENTS

It takes many hands to build a house. And it took many hands to help us write this book.

We're blessed with the opportunity to work with an amazing team who help us create a fun, inspiring, and entertaining radio program every week. Without Team *Money Pit,* we'd have neither a show, nor a book.

Our deepest gratitude goes out to Nora DePalma and Aimee Oscamou, who served as our researchers, coaches, and taskmasters throughout the entire project. Good thing our last joint venture crashed in the dot-com bomb, or we'd be doing something else right now. We'd be tan. We'd be rich. But we'd definitely be doing something else. Sheetal Werneke, our brilliant Executive Producer, who shares a birthday with Tom and was the first producer to ever put him on television. Now look what you did. Skip Joeckel, the world's best affiliate manager. We have no idea how you find us all those new stations while stretched out on the couch watching soaps. Don't ever change.

Lisa Vitale, our efficient office manager, who somehow keeps the office rolling every day, as well as kids, a dog, goldfish . . . and Tom. He's the hard part. Ivo Kurvits and Pamela Del Hierro, Web god and graphic goddess. Your brilliance and creativity are truly amazing, even if you do live in Canada. Ehh? Jim Kenzie, our head engineer, and Amy Zarend, our screener. Thanks for laughing with us, and at us, as we wrote this book between the callers that punctuate our radio lives. Holland Cooke, our top-notch talk radio consultant. Thanks for being our ears, even when we don't listen to you.

Ian Heller and Jeff Schwartz of Media Management Group, LLC, our business managers, agents, and trusted colleagues. Your guidance helped us shape this project with the hands of expert craftsmen. Glad the new air conditioner recommendation worked out, despite all that hot air. Maura Teitelbaum, our talented literary agent of Abrams Artists Agency, your enthusiasm has been electrifying. Electricity, however, is not something we'd recommend you tackle, after learning that you tried to put up a shelf with Gorilla Glue.

And thanks to our families. Of all the things we have in common, it is the love and support of our families that provided both of us the foundations we've built upon.

To both our parents, thanks for all the cool power tools. Although you probably should have held off on the circular saw and wood-burning set until we got out of elementary school. Our friends were impressed, and the scars have just about healed.

Tom: To my loving wife Sue and children Thomas, Sara, and Trevor. Without you there'd be no me. Thanks for the gift of time you give me every day to do what I do. And I promise I'll fix the porch light soon. To my Mom and Dad, JoAnn and Ken, and Lisa, Mary Beth, Ken, Jason, Elizabeth, and Christopher, your love, strength, and support are an inspiration.

Leslie: To my amazingly supportive husband Edward. You give me the confidence to build my dreams, thank you. To my Mom and Dad, Pauline and Dominick, and Stephanie, Elyse, and Craig. I cannot thank you enough for making me feel so loved and blessed in so many ways.

And last but not least . . . thank *you*, our readers and listeners, for allowing us to come into your homes, your cars . . . and your earbuds every week to share our passion for great home improvement and fabulous design. It's our privilege to hold the nail for you each week.

Good thing it's only on the radio, though, because we've seen you swing a hammer.

INTRODUCTION:
Adventures in Home Improvement

What do we really mean by a Money Pit?

A Money Pit is not a house. It's a home.

A Money Pit home is not a disaster. It's an asset. It's an asset that can sometimes feel like an endless pit into which money is thrown. If you have kids, you know that feeling.

And, much like raising kids, owning a Money Pit is a combination of love, pride, and heart-stopping fear—the latter most often occurring when it's time to remodel.

No one knows that better than we do. We're Tom Kraeutler and Leslie Segrete, and *The Money Pit* is also the name of our radio show and website, where we take calls and emails every day from homeowners across America trying to figure out how to manage their Money Pit. We'd say their questions fall into three different categories:

- People who haven't started their home improvement project yet, looking for a little advice.
- People who are in the middle of their project and wish they had called us sooner.
- People who have completed their project and *definitely* wish they had called us sooner.

People in the first group are excited. People in the second group are stressed. People in the third group are getting a divorce.

We're just kidding, pretty much. But it got us thinking: someone ought to do a book that people can read *before* they do home improvements that tells you all the stuff no one ever tells you.

It's the stuff we learned years ago, from our parents. Growing up in his family's 1886 New Jersey[1] shore homestead, Tom got his start by getting in his parents' way. Like all good parents in mid-20th-century America, they sent him out to play with all kinds of dangerous things, like nails, a hammer, and a block of wood to occupy him. There he banged away dreaming of the day he could put all that nervous home improvement energy to good use, before riding off on his bike without a helmet.

Years later, it all seemed to work as Tom graduated college with a degree in Industrial Arts Education, taught high school, and was named Teacher of the Year after his first year on the job. He eventually worked as a home inspector for almost 20 years, literally the CSI of Money Pit management, learning how homes are put together and how they fall apart during more than 6,000 inspections. From there, Hollywood came calling,[2] with Tom's insider knowledge making him a highly sought-after expert for television and radio programs. Finding out that being on TV and radio was a lot more pleasant than those early-morning crawl spaces he used to belly through, Tom founded *The Money Pit* and grew it into the largest home improvement radio program in America.

Leslie had a similar start growing up during the 1970s on Long Island, where her dad kept her busy at his architectural design office cutting out wallpaper and carpet samples, and encouraging her eye for color, line, and detail. Leslie remembers searching through all of the samples within the design library, creating mini design boards for her dream home. If you're catching a theme here about parents using home products to keep little ones occupied,

---

1.) If you are about to make a joke about NJ, know that Tom is very proud of his Garden State roots. Tramps like him were born to run.
2.) Actually, it was a small radio station in Toms River, NJ. 3.) She did—and still does—wear a bike helmet. Just kidding.

that would be Tom and Leslie's parents. Leslie also learned how to be comfortable using tools ranging from a sewing machine to a power saw.[3]

Where Tom took to the classroom, Leslie formed a love affair with the stage, and graduated college with a degree in theater and a dream to design theatrical sets. Her years spent behind the camera and backstage creating scenery were about to change when a friend asked her to step in for a carpenter on a new show on TLC called *While You Were Out*. While she was there, the show producers noted that she could do both carpentry *and* design. Leslie went on to construct dream rooms for over 250 families, up close and personal with the full range of human emotion that accompanies a home improvement project.

There's no doubt home improvements are stressful. Any time you put money and emotion together, you're pretty much guaranteed an extreme time of it. It gets the adrenaline pumping. That's why we call home improvement an adventure: it gets the blood going, it's good exercise, and it can't be beat when it comes to gaining a sense of accomplishment. People pay good money for adventure vacations, so why not look at the money you're pouring into your Money Pit as an ongoing adventure?

You say hiking in Peru. We say remodel your kitchen.

You say parachute jump. We say remodel your kitchen just weeks before Thanksgiving.

You say Seven Summits. We say get credit accounts at all home improvement centers.

We're your guides for this adventure. It's all those things you wish someone would have told you before doing it yourself, not doing it yourself, not doing it all, or doing each other in.

Dive in.

Warming Up: Getting Ready for Home Improvements

So, what's the first thing you do for an adventure? Jump out of a plane? We suppose you could, but we'd probably start by putting on a parachute. And learning how it works.

Every adventure is different, but nearly all start out the same way: getting the right gear and learning how to use it. When it comes to home improvement, getting the right gear is about the products—the ones you need to do the project and the ones you are going to install. Learning how to use them may mean not using them at all, but rather hiring a professional.

The process of figuring that all out is the same for all home improvements. *We call it the warm-up.*

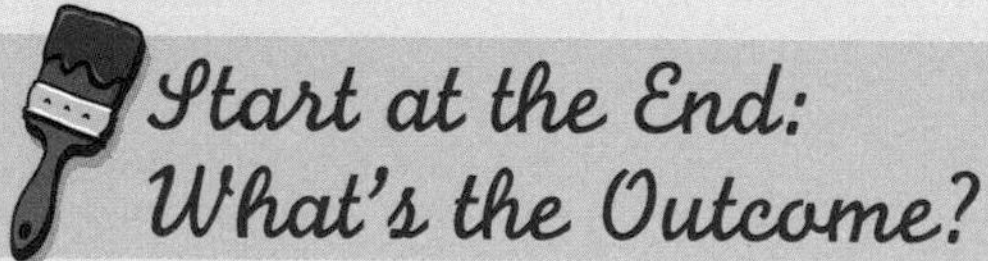

Start at the End: What's the Outcome?

We get a lot of questions on *The Money Pit* about whether a specific product, technology, or technique will achieve the desired results. The decisions can seem overwhelming if you don't start at the end: what do you want out of this home improvement? How many people (and/or pets) use the space, and how often? How much maintenance and upkeep can you tolerate?

Most important: Are you doing this for your use and enjoyment, or for resale or investment? Dr. Donald Moliver, Director of the Kislak Real Estate Institute at Monmouth University in West Long Branch, New Jersey, says the number one reason consumers buy homes is resale value, so it makes sense that the more you invest in home improvements—or the closer you are to selling—the more important it is for your home improvement adventures to be selected with an eye on resale value.

The same project may require completely different approaches, depending on the big picture. Understanding your objectives helps you narrow down choices and be more confident in your decisions.

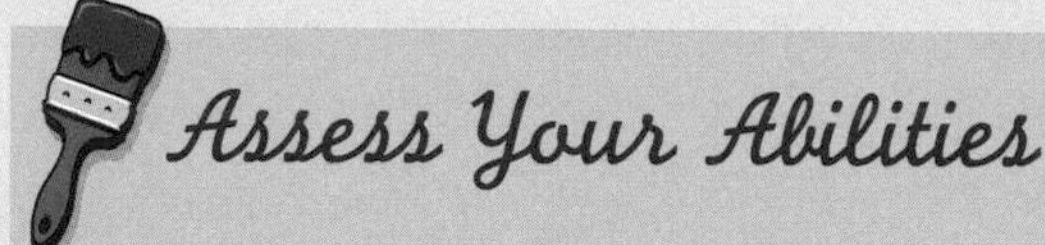

Assess Your Abilities

Once you know what you're doing, the next question is: Is there any part of the remodel you can do yourselves? Do you want to stay married? Just kidding, pretty much.

Most home improvers fall into these three categories:

- **Do-it-yourselfers:** These are the fearless folks who tackle most of the projects themselves. Do-it-yourselfers include those who tackle everything from simple to complex projects.

- **Direct-it-yourselfers:** Home improvers who like to do the research and then hire folks for all or part of the job are known as direct-it-yourselfers. Direct-it-yourself projects could include small remodeling projects like baths or bigger projects like additions.

- **Do-it-for-me:** If you're the type that has neither the time, desire, or ability to do your own home improvement projects, then do-it-for-me is for you. Go ahead and get knowledgeable about the improvement you want to accomplish. Then, select a pro to do the entire job, write a check, and take a vacation until it is complete.

Cash or Credit?

Most of us sink the money into our Money Pits using savings or short-term debt. If you're a regular at home centers and hardware stores on Saturday mornings, a store credit card is a convenient way to pay for smaller-ticket items as well as helping to finance larger projects with regular same-as-cash or delayed payment schedules. Plus, some store credit cards come with store-based sign-up discounts that wouldn't be available with more generic major cards. For example, Tom bought his last big table saw at a home center using that store's card and saved 50 bucks on the spot! Just be very aware of the interest rates for store cards, which are sometimes higher than major credit cards, and remember to use those cards strategically.

Many retailers and some professionals offer finance programs, an option when you have to do significant work but don't have enough equity in your home to qualify for a bank-issued loan. A finance program is kind of like a private loan that helps you pay for the purchase over time. Retailers and pros offer them because they free up a source of cash to help you pay for their products or services. But like any loan, the devil is in the details. Be sure you are fully aware of the interest rate and late-payment penalties before diving in.

Your home's equity, the difference between your Money Pit's fair market value and the mortgage balance you have yet to pay, can be used to finance home improvements through a line of credit or a loan obtained through a bank, credit union, or other lending institution. A home equity line of credit provides access to funds as needed. Repayment is flexible (some people may choose to pay only the interest for a certain period of time), with interest rate variable and the amount of interest paid being up to 100 percent tax-deductible.

With a home equity loan, you receive your funds in a lump sum. You repay the loan over several years, preceded by loan fees and closing costs. Because of that long-term, big-ticket factor, a home equity loan is suited to home improvement purchases that will have a long-time impact, such as a new roof.

While many folks think that doing or directing the project themselves can result in cost savings, it's important to note that a single costly mistake can quickly eliminate the savings, impact your ability to borrow money for the project, or even void homeowner's insurance coverage if errors cause serious damage to your home.

Honest self-assessment is a good thing. You probably wouldn't exaggerate your ability to rappel down a sheer cliff. Good home improvements gone bad can theoretically have the same catastrophic outcome.[4]

Even confident DIYers like us call in the pros. Some tasks require a level of detail we won't have time to do until we're retired. Others are simply too risky for anyone but professionals to tackle: gas lines, central heating and air, structural changes. For each project, we start by figuring out what we can do and what we like to do, and then contract out the rest. We give you some tips on how to hire and work with professionals in Section 3.

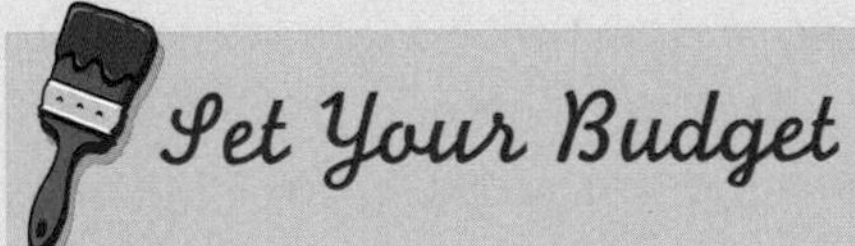

Set Your Budget

Once you know what your labor needs are, you can start planning your budget. Always include a reserve of about 20 percent, since part of the thrill of home improvements is to expect the

4.) Living with "I told you so" forever.

Songs to Work By:

Tunes to help you get through your projects.

- *Start Me Up*—Rolling Stones
- *Sweet Home Alabama*—Lynyrd Skynyrd
- *Our House*—Crosby, Stills, Nash & Young
- *Burning Down the House*—Talking Heads
- *Take the Long Way Home*—Supertramp
- *Can't Find My Way Home*—Blind Faith
- *Bring It on Home to Me*—Sam Cooke
- *Homeward Bound*—Simon & Garfunkel
- *If I Had a Hammer*—Peter, Paul, and Mary
- Anything by The Carpenters

unexpected, because (a) houses are never perfectly square, and (b) you don't know what's going on behind those walls. Then there's "while we're at it," the four most expensive words of owning a Money Pit.[5]

Getting the Right Gear

Choosing products can be the most fun part of home improvement adventures, especially in the realms of kitchens, bathrooms, decks, and outdoor living. It almost becomes a lifestyle, checking out new looks, styles, and performance everywhere from hotels and restaurants to store displays. You find yourself offering to clean up at dinner parties just to get a look in the fridge and dishwashers. You rejoin the table after taking a powder and blithely ask the host if she's happy with her toilet.

Beauty is only skin deep, and for your Money Pit, both form and function matter when it comes to product selection. Function is a matter of reliability, maintenance, resource conservation, safety, and comfort.

Some manufacturers offer quite generous warranties, although they typically don't include labor replacement costs. As a rule, we never recommend extended warranties except in a few cases you'll see throughout the book.

The Green Scene

You won't get too far in researching home products these days without encountering tips for going green. We certainly encourage you to consider improved operating efficiencies with every home improvement adventure. At the very least, you'll save yourself some green in utility costs.

In general, green products tend to cost more than others, for one of two reasons. The first relates to appliances and other mechanical or hydraulic systems that can be breathtaking in their engineering detail. These modern marvels will pay for themselves through reduced resource consumption. The second, well, has more to do with the fact that they have green on their packaging. How to tell the difference? A little Google research can go a long way, but you can also turn to federal labeling programs such as Energy Star and WaterSense to help find the best buys, as will our Green Scene suggestions throughout this book.

Access Everyone

Yes, we know. You're never going to get old. Neither are we. But here's why we recommend accessible design. It's easier for everyone, no matter what your ability or age. How about when you come home with arms full of groceries? It's

5.) The three most expensive are "might as well."

easier to flick a light with a paddle switch than a toggle switch, or open a door with a lever knob versus a round knob. Who hasn't reached out for something to hold getting in and out of a bath or shower? Wider doorways make sense whether it's your parents or your toddler with the walker.

A smart, well-planned space enables anyone who uses it to enjoy comfort and convenience, and you can ensure that your addition or remodel does just that by applying the principles of universal or accessible design. This inclusive, multigenerational approach combines safety, accessibility, and convenience to accommodate changing needs and enables homeowners to continue enjoying their homes as they age—a pretty significant benefit, considering recent AARP research reporting that over 90 percent of homeowners over the age of 50 plan to stay in their present abodes rather than retire elsewhere.

Survival Skills

Home improvement is a heart-pounding, extreme sport that pretty much won't kill you.[6] No one is saying it's a cakewalk, or the title of this book would have been different. It builds mental toughness to tame your Money Pit. Here's just a short list of what to expect:

- Your spouse exaggerates his abilities
- Your spouse exaggerates her credit limit
- Products arrive late
- Products never arrive
- Products arrive damaged
- Contractor arrives late
- Contractor never arrives
- Contractor was damaged in childhood
- It rains
- It doesn't rain
- Behind your wall are very bad things
- Behind your wall is your cat, accidentally drywalled
- We're out of that color
- It's the wrong color
- What possessed you to pick that color?
- The kid that you gave wedgies to in high school is now your local building inspector.

This is why we recommend the 20 percent budget reserve. Double that when it comes to a reserve of patience and a sense of humor. Keep it in perspective as we step inside.

6.) Although human vs. electricity is one that tends to end badly.

MY HOME, MY MONEY PIT

Designing Confidence

If first impressions count, your home's walls, floors, and ceiling are the canvas for your personal expression of style and comfortable living. For most of us walking into a home for the first time, our first impression is the décor. What does your Money Pit say about you? What would you prefer it to say?

We love décor projects. Think of the dramatic makeovers you see us do on TV and in magazines with something as simple as paint. These are like the bunny-slopes improvement: ratcheting down the skill requirements so you can learn good form and build the confidence to tackle bigger adventures in and around your Money Pit.

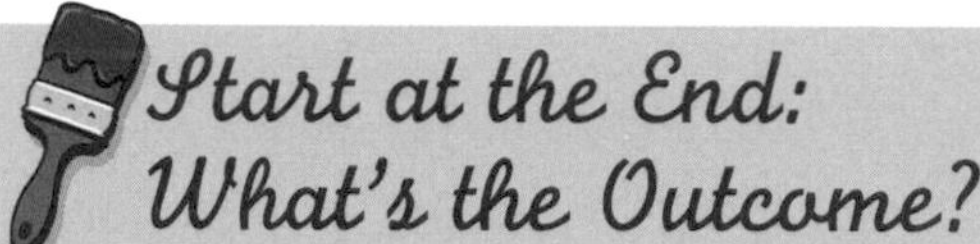

Start at the End: What's the Outcome?

So you know you want to redo that room, but aren't sure where to start, what to keep or junk, or what parts to tackle, right? You may have started with a pretty simple, livable room years ago, but then as furniture, pictures, and collectibles found their way into the space, it became the kind of living area of last resort it is now.

Wiping the decorating slate clean, so to speak, is usually the best way to tackle a room makeover. Begin with a checklist of what you have. Identify what you like most about the space, as well as the "keepers" among the room's surfaces, something like a hardwood floor or walls with great texture. This will help you start defining a palette.

Songs to Work By:

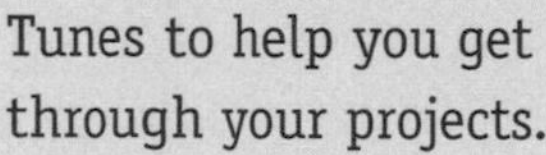

Tunes to help you get through your projects.

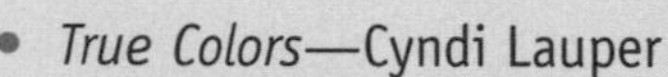

- *True Colors*—Cyndi Lauper
- *Paint It Black*—Rolling Stones
- *In My Room*—The Beach Boys
- *Color My World*—Chicago
- *Fashion*—David Bowie
- *Seven Rooms of Gloom*—Four Tops
- *Handy Man*—Jimmy Jones or James Taylor
- *Like Red on a Rose*—Alan Jackson
- *White Room*—Cream
- Anything by Simply Red

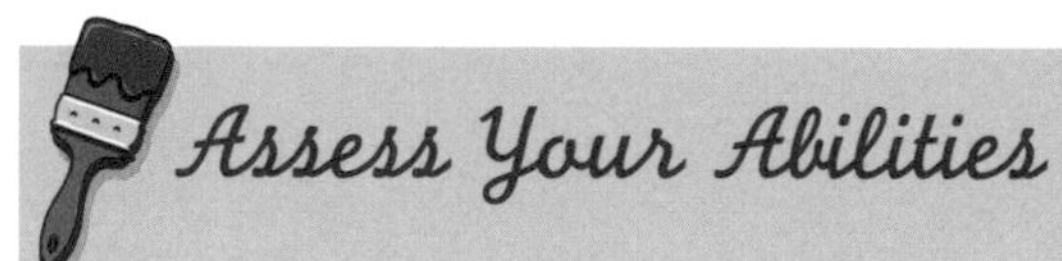

Assess Your Abilities

Painting should really rank up there as one of the great American pastimes. You don't have to be a rocket scientist or Michelangelo to paint a room.[7] It's literally something you can do by yourself, with your spouse, even with your kids. Most of the projects in this chapter are attainable for do-it-yourselfers with novice to moderate skill levels.

Credit goes in part to manufacturers who have become much more innovative with products that are easier to install and easier to maintain, such as installing a hot-looking, easy-care new floor by snapping together laminate boards or carpet tiles.

A few projects related to walls, floors, and ceilings are best left to the pros. Hardwood floor sanding is definitely one, given the value of hardwood

7.) Or the ceiling, for that matter.

floors and how easy it is to cause permanent damage to your asset. While light-duty floor sanding is a DIY project, badly worn floors must be sanded with a heavy-duty floor belt sander, a tool best left to the hands of professionals who work with it every day.[8] Vinyl flooring is also a tricky job where the unskilled may unwittingly damage the product and add costs to the job.

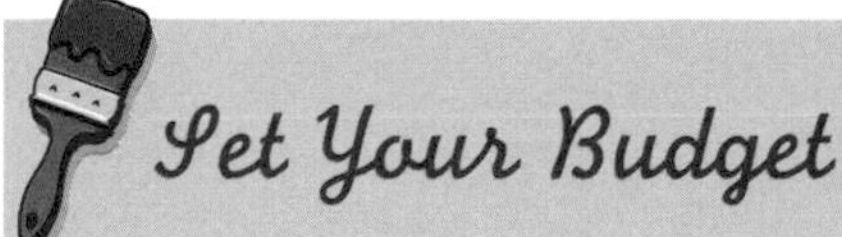

Set Your Budget

The projects in this chapter are among the least expensive your Money Pit will consume during your time together. That's one of the things that makes décor projects so much fun. For the cost of a can of paint, you can add loads of color to your life. But if your newfound color confidence went a bit too far fuchsia, you can dial it back for another 20 bucks' worth of paint.

Color Crazies

Color is one of those things it's just too easy to get neurotic about. When it comes to decorating, the number one question we get is about the "right" color. As if there is some book of color rules that only the cool kids have.[9]

There's only one rule, and we'll let everyone in the lunchroom in on it: Choose the one thing that you love the most. It may be a paint color, or a fabric, a floor swatch, or that great couch you can get with no payments for 18 months. Then let everything fall in around it.

Maybe your color scheme and texture cues come from what you already have. Maybe you've found a certain fabric or a must-have piece of furniture or find inspiration in one that is already in your home. Maybe you're inspired by Mother Nature's palette as seen on a favorite hike or camping trip . . . or maybe you're a strict adherent to the wonders of the basic color wheel (a smart source for double-checking complementary colors).

Or maybe your husband just brought home a big-screen TV and you need a color to match "gray" when the TV is in off position.

Where to Begin

Now you have a starting point. A color, a texture. As far as the actual order of business, we always recommend leaving the floor for last, whether it'll be replaced or simply touched up. Gravity being what it is, your flooring will serve as the project drop cloth, even if it's protected. No matter how great the plastic or sheeting, we've learned from experience[10] that if something has even the slightest possibility of getting damaged in any way, it will, so don't let that something be a brand-new floor.

Plan for Care, Maintenance, and Your Indoor Environment

When selecting new room finishes, think about their formulations, quality, and what they'll con-

> **Green Scene**
>
> 
>
> *Now's your chance to create a space that not only looks great but offers a healthful, VOC-free environment. VOC stands for volatile organic compounds, which are found in many building and decorating products, as well as in the adhesives and other chemicals used in their installation. Renewed awareness of the dangers that VOCs pose to consumers as well as the environment in general has inspired a range of products created without harmful chemicals. Shop for these as you design your new space, and you'll be making an important investment in the long-term enjoyment of it.*

8.) Unless you like the "distressed" look, which will develop very quickly, first on the floor and then on you. 9.) Actually, that's not quite true, there are people called color forecasters who often do put out books on color, and all the ones we've known have been quite cool. 10.) Like the time Tom's son knocked over an open can of paint, which then fell from the second floor hall down the steps to the first floor. He learned from that experience. His son also learned some new words that daddy had to promise mommy he'd never, ever, say again.

tribute to a space beyond a great new look. Rooms such as kitchens and bathrooms call for moisture-resistant finishes and flooring to keep mold, mildew, and rot at bay. Easy-care finishes can make life much easier and more pleasant through limited upkeep, and green products whose ingredients forgo the toxins and allergens that can impact indoor air quality are smart choices for better health as well as great design (see Chapter 8 for more details).

On the Walls: Solutions for Surfaces

What you put on your walls can have the biggest impact in a room's décor scheme. There's a wide range of products and treatments out there, with selection tied into the way a room is used, what moisture and other environmental factors are involved, and the existing condition of the walls themselves.

Wall Covering Material	Pros	Cons
Paint	One of the most affordable wall covering solutions, offered in a wide range of colors and sheens. Moisture-resistant and easy-clean formulations are widely available.	Meticulous surface preparation required; fumes generated during and after application can be harmful (although greatly reduced if a low-VOC formulation is used).
Faux Finishing	Custom look adds texture and dimension to wall surfaces.	Can be difficult to remove faux finishing effects in preparation for a new finish. Some are hard to achieve.
Wood Paneling	Durable material adds texture and scale to a space, and can be painted or stained.	Difficult to remove or resurface, and is not very moisture resistant.
Synthetic Paneling	Durable option is moisture-resistant and can be painted; other looks such as metal, stone, and leather are available.	Can be difficult to remove.
Wallpaper & Borders	Available in a wide range of patterns, colors, and textures. Reasonably easy to install and clean.	Not always moisture-resistant (except for vinyl wall covering) and can be time-consuming to remove.
Tile & Stone	Rich, luxurious look combined with durability and moisture resistance.	Difficult to remove or repair; requires periodic sealing and regrouting.

Out with the Old, In with the New

If you've got a tricky-to-remove treatment such as paneling, tile, or textured drywall, a little creativity and flexibility go a long way toward solving the problem. Before you swing into demolition mode, a little surface assessment is needed so you can determine what can go, what you can (or will have to) work around or over, and what can be transformed.

Paneling

Old paneling is one of the trickiest wall coverings to change, and there's still a heck of a lot of it around today.[11] It's possible to remove it, but not without a lot of effort and possible damage to the surface underneath if glue has been used in addition to easy-to-remove paneling nails.

If that falls within your adventure confidence zone, determine whether or not your paneling is glued to the wall. Remove a small piece of paneling, which may involve pulling off some molding to access an open edge, or remove an outlet or switch plate cover and see if you can determine its application there. If the paneling isn't glued down, go ahead and rip it all out.

If it is glued down, know that you will probably need to replace the drywall. When you rip out the paneling, glue will peel away the papered surface of the drywall underneath. Spot-patching of damaged drywall is a major job, not always successful when the area to be repaired is extensive.

Attempts at paneling camouflage generally aren't successful, either, as we've told many a *Money Pit* caller who has considered plastering the grooves in existing paneling to create a smooth surface. Instead, if you're going to keep paneling in place, play into its texture and graphic elements by priming it and giving it a fresh coat of paint. You can either use one color for a simpler backdrop, or make the most of paneling's built-in vertical guidelines by painting subtle stripes on the surface in contrasting tones or sheens.

Plaster

Once again, your first step in the rip-out-or-live-with-it evaluation is determining the condition of the plaster. Plaster is generally durable unless it gets wet, at which point it can lead to dangerous sags, especially if it's of the early-1900s variety that was installed over wood lath. If yours is in good shape, you're best off leaving it as is and installing new drywall over the plaster for a super-smooth remodeling canvas. It requires retrimming the doors and adjusting the electrical outlets, but it beats the massive amounts of dust and dirt that'll fill the air if you attempt a time-consuming demolition.[12]

Wallpaper

When it comes to wallpaper removal, we recommend using a rented steamer over other gadgets on the market (and believe us, there are a zillion gadgets out there). A steamer will work with either paper or vinyl-based coverings. Make the going easier with vinyl by lightly scoring it with a utility knife from floor to ceiling beforehand to allow the steam to get underneath the surface for a smoother lift-off.

When you're ready to go, work one small area at a time (generally the width of one roll of the wallpaper), moving from the top down and heavily saturating the wall surface as you go. As the steam loosens the adhesive, you'll be able to pull it back and away for easy removal. Once your walls are unpapered, use a mixture of distilled white vinegar and water to remove any remaining adhesive, and be sure to prime walls before applying a new finish.

For the record, this is one of those projects that both of us can do, yet both of us would hire a professional to do it. It's just not pleasant, especially when it comes to wallpaper that's been up a long time, which we realize is usually the most hideous and, therefore, most in need of a change. We would recommend giving up a few lattes and investing in a pro who can get your wall paint-ready for you to take it from there.

11.) There is still a lot of disco around, too. Paneling is easier to remove. 12.) Unless you like that sort of thing.

Texture

It's possible to minimize the effects of wall texturing with a good sanding, but texture is almost always related to a stucco application that isn't really designed to come off before the turn of the next century,[13] so your results may be mixed. A better bet is to cover textured walls with an altogether new surfacing material, such as drywall, paneling, or wainscoting.

Another option is to use fabric to upholster a textured wall. This can instantly change the appearance of the room and be an easy do-it-yourself project. The fabric can cover the entire height of the wall or work very nicely with paneling and trim work on the lower portion of the wall. Choose a fabric in a durable cotton or upholstery weight and look for width of 54 inches to cover the most wall with the fewest seams. Attach the fabric to pieces of foam core or ¼-inch lauan plywood using a spray adhesive or contact cement that will not bleed through the fabric (try a test area just to make sure and wrap the fabric around the back to create clean edges). Be sure to keep the fabric straight to avoid wavering patterns. Affix the panels to your wall using brads and attach the panels into studs when possible; or, if attaching the panels into the studs is not an option, drive nails at a slight angle to hold the panels into the drywall.

Tile

Removing tile is a doozy of a job—difficult, involved, and like glued-down paneling, requiring some wall reconstruction after it's removed. You can replace damaged tiles on an individual basis using a tool like the RotoZip, a little wonder that looks like a drill bit but cuts sideways like a router. Otherwise, the makeover options are few. Painting or retexturing of the surface doesn't usually make for a great result. You'll have to look into either regrouting the tile or sprucing it up with adhesive embellishments, like IdeaStix, a series of peel-and-stick décor accents (see www.ideastix.com). Short of that, this is one project that has to start with a total demolition of the old tile and a rebuild from the framed walls out.

The one exception here is mirrored tile, which can be removed in a few careful steps. To prevent dangerous breakage and shattering, start by covering the surface with contact paper to hold the tile together. Then use a piece of piano wire (wrapped around dowels on each end for an easy grip) to access the space between the mirrored tile and the wall, moving it like a saw to cut through the glue holding the tiles to the surface. In most cases, you'll still wind up with some damage to the wall surface behind those groovy mirrors, but that can be remedied with an application of drywall or other surfacing. Mirrors can break during the process, so be sure to protect yourself with safety goggles, gloves, and clothing that covers as much of your skin as possible.

The Wall as Your Palette: Selecting Paint

Paint is one of the most affordable means of transforming a room, but it can end up costing you cash and future aggravation if you don't prepare well for the job. Trust us on this: every time you sit down in your family room, the first thing you're going to notice is where you ran the chocolate wall paint up into the white ceiling area. Save yourself from that OCD[14] moment, and just get it right the first time, taping off your chocolate from your vanilla.

Choosing the perfect paint color is easier now thanks to retailers and manufacturers who offer online visualizers, pre-coordinated color palettes, and, best of all, trial-size paint samples that allow you to audition your transforming tone before you buy and apply. Paint samples are available as either poster-size color swatches or two- to eight-ounce containers of actual paint that can be applied

13.) Plastic is forever. 14.) OCD stands for Obsessive Compulsive Disorder. If we had to define it for you, you are probably safe.

either to a piece of scrap board or directly on the wall to literally be seen in a different light.

When making paint color decisions, consider the color across an entire day's light spectrum. Different times of day reveal various combinations of direct sunlight, indirect sunlight, and artificial light that can transform your perception of a color. Painting on large-scale swatches is the best way to ensure that you'll enjoy living with your selection around the clock.

Along with color selection comes the choice of paint product that'll work best for the room you're redoing. Paint comes in latex and oil-based formulations and finishes ranging from flat to high gloss (see table on page 9). The combination you choose depends on use and traffic in the space you're painting.

For long-lasting results with any selection, you should plan on applying two coats, preceded by a primer of the same formulation. Once you've tallied the resulting quantities, add a bit more paint than you think you'll need. Many stores are actually willing to accept returns on unused paint, even if it's in a custom color, and having extra means you'll avoid color-matching problems if you run short. Store any extra paint in an airtight container. Leftover take-out food containers (pints or gallons) are a perfect storage item because you can easily see the color you are looking for and they are also very portable for those inevitable touch-ups. Store the leftover paint where it will not freeze, and mark the container with the name of the room in which it has been applied so you always know which paint goes where.

Finally, remember that the cost of painting is mostly labor,[15] so buy the best-quality paint you possibly can from trusted brands with good track records. It doesn't cost that much more to buy better in this category. If you try to do painting on the cheap, you won't get the coverage you need or the typically five to seven years of wear that you want.

Tom's Tip: Those Pesky Popping Drywall Nails

Nail pops are pesky problems that frequently come up in the first few years after a home is built. As the framing lumber dries out, it expands and contracts and sort of "spits" the nail back out of the hole it was originally driven into. As I've explained to many a panicky caller over the years, nail pops are normal and don't indicate a structural problem. To fix them, drive another nail next to the loose nail, being sure to overlap the heads. If the nail is really loose, remove it and replace it with a drywall screw, and respackle the wall.

Shop for Supplies

Along with paint and primer, shop for the tools that'll make the job a success. Brushes are a good starting point, and are available with either synthetic or natural bristles, also known as "china" bristles. For the best results, use synthetics with latex paint and natural bristles with oil-based paint. Rollers make quick work of large surfaces, except when you've chosen a roller cover with the wrong pile height and nap for the finish, so follow the paint manufacturer's guidelines. Take care to remove any loose fibers from the cover that could mix with the paint and wind up on your wall.

Other items to add to your shopping list for painting and surface preparation should include:

- Roller pans and liners
- Drop cloths (use plastic types on the floor and cloth types on top to prevent slipping)
- Spackle
- Spackle knives in a variety of widths
- Fiberglass wall tape (for cracks)

15.) Not real hard labor, mind you. Kitchen remodeling is in the next chapter.

- Nail filler
- Sandpaper
- Drywall nails
- Painter's tape

> **Leslie Likes: Sharp Stripes**
>
> *If stripes or patterns are what you're creating with tape, here's one of Leslie's tricks-of-the-trade to make sure it comes out great. First, paint your base color. Then, after that coat has dried, apply the tape to outline your desired effect. Next, paint over the tape again using the first color. This allows the first color of paint to bleed under the tape and seal the edge. Lastly, and only after the first color is thoroughly dry, apply the accent color or sheen into the masked areas. Follow these steps, and you'll have sharp, crisp lines when you remove the tape!*

Preparation Equals Perfection

One of the biggest mistakes with painting is skipping to the color coat without doing the surface preparation that makes for a beautiful, durable finish. We know it's not as much fun, but take the time to clean, patch, and prepare your walls. You'll be making the most of the paint you've purchased and increasing your satisfaction with the finished product.

Start out by scrubbing away accumulations of smoke, oil, and grime that can keep your new finish from adhering. Use Liquid Sandpaper to remove buildup from trim, and wash down walls with a TSP (trisodium phosphate) solution, available at most home centers and hardware stores. You can add efficiency to this chore and remove the risk of a ladder-and-liquid mishap by employing a sponge-head floor mop for application. Leave about two hours for surfaces to dry completely, more if humidity is high.

Once cleaned surfaces are dry, smooth them out. Take time to fill all holes and cracks with spackle, following with a thorough all-over sanding and removal of the resulting dust. Fix nail pops by either removing the popping drywall nail or driving a new nail in on top of the existing one, driving it just it below the surface. Repair cracks by applying fiberglass wall tape followed by a few topcoats of spackle applied and smoothed with progressively wider spackle knives.

Once you think you're done, grab a really strong flashlight and hold it against and parallel to the wall you've just repaired. As the light bounces over the repaired area, you'll be able to see exactly how the surface will look when the sunshine hits it in that typically unflattering direction. If this test reveals unsightly details, go back and smooth them before packing up the sander.

Marvelous Masking

One more detail round to go: protecting everything you don't want painted and creating a clean edge for every coat. Take your time and plenty of care with this step as well, because whatever you leave to chance will only be defined by the new paint. Apply painter's tape along trim and glass edges, and use it in combination with plastic sheeting or masking paper to cover fixtures that can't be moved and large surface areas to be left out of the equation. Also take the time to remove switch and socket plates (followed by a bit of tape over remaining switches and plugs) and all possible hardware.

Primer Makes Perfect

Before starting in with the paint, check your thermometer—paint won't adhere if it's below 55 degrees and won't go on smoothly if it's above 90 degrees. All clear? Then get started with a coat of primer that helps paint stick and provides a smooth topcoat that'll show fewer brush or roller marks. If your walls have any tough stains like water marks or smoke damage, we recommend using oil-based primer rather than water-based, as it does a better job of sealing in stain-damaged surfaces.

When you're ready to swing that paintbrush into action, do the edges first, then fill in with a roller using a "W" motion, always maintaining a wet edge, so that the next roller-ful of paint can blend into the one that came before it. If you need to take a break, stop at a corner and not midway across a wall. After the primer has thoroughly dried, apply your new paint shade in two rounds using the same technique for a durable, beautiful finish.

Perfect paint technique: Start with a "w," then go back over the same area until the wall is covered completely.

Select Your Sheen

Sheen Style	What It Looks Like	Where it is Used	How it Holds Up
Flat	Matte appearance with no sheen.	Great coverage for surfaces with imperfections and texture changes.	Not for use in high-traffic, high-touch areas as it shows dirt and fingerprints and is not easily cleaned.
Eggshell	So named for its resemblance to the surface of an actual eggshell, which is mostly flat with a hint of sheen.	Smoother finish reflects more light as it hides imperfections.	Somewhat washable, but not as durable as satin or semigloss.
Satin	Has a silky sheen that reflects just enough light when applied to walls.	Works well in kitchens, bathrooms, children's rooms, and hallways, and can be applied to woodwork and trim.	Stands up to grime and cleans well.
Semigloss	A shinier appearance than satin, reflecting between 35 percent and 50 percent of the light that hits it.	Best for fingerprint-prone elements such as trim, moldings, doors, and cabinets; also works in kitchens and bathrooms.	Durable and highly washable.
High-gloss	The highest shine of all.	Use for utility or playrooms where washability is a must.	Very easy to clean, but shows every surface imperfection.

Leslie Likes: Fantastic Faux Finishes

If faux finishes are your style, then look no further than a trip to the paint store for everything you might need to get the job done. Regardless of your skill level, there are several different styles of faux techniques that are easily achievable for your home:

- ***Sponging:*** *A simple technique that is done with a natural sea sponge and can be used to incorporate several colors onto your walls. Just paint your walls a base color, wait for them to dry, then dip a natural sea sponge into an accent color and apply the paint to the wall by pressing the sponge delicately to the surface. Twist the direction of your hand to create different patterns with the sponge.*
- ***Ragging on:*** *A technique similar to the sponge effect, except the faux technique is applied using natural cloth rags or inexpensive painter's rags. If the accent color paint is too thick for this technique, mix one quart faux glaze to one gallon of paint to help thin the color and extend your working time.*
- ***Ragging off:*** *This technique is a bit different from ragging on. After your base coat is dry, mix your accent color with faux glaze and apply to the wall using a roller in sections, to ensure uniformity. Then, approach each section with a clean, dry rag gathered in your hand and stamp the wall, thus removing paint from the surface and "ragging off."*
- ***Wet blends:*** *A nice way to create color and movement on a wall's surface. This technique can be done easily with several 4-inch paintbrushes and two paint colors. Simply choose two tones of the same color, dip a brush in your first paint color, then slightly dip the brush in water. Apply the first color to the wall using an "X" technique. Once a small area is covered, go in with your second brush and color and paint around all sides of the first color section. The water and wet paint will help to blend the areas together and create a smooth transition between each color, giving the surface the color and the movement you are looking for.*

Ask Tom & Leslie: Paint Preservation

Q: How long can I keep opened cans of paint, and how do I get rid of them?

A: That's tough to say. The truth is that if paint is kept sealed and in a cool area that won't freeze, it can really last indefinitely. The best way to preserve your paint is to make sure you do a good job wiping the lip of the can before resealing it. One way to keep paint from building up in this area is to add drain holes when you first open the can. You can easily create these using a sharp screwdriver and hammer to pierce the inside of the lip of the can.

As far as disposal goes, regulations for disposal of paint in liquid form vary from town to town. However, one option is to just leave the cans open until the paint gets hard. Adding kitty litter into the leftover paint will help it to dry more quickly and allow you to dispose of it much more quickly, too. Unless local government regulations tell you otherwise, toss the cans out with your regular trash.

New Life for Old Furnishings

As long as we're talking finishes, think about giving fresh ones to beloved furnishings that still have plenty of wear and could have a place in your new room. Furniture refinishing and upholstery are definitely DIY projects, and can create statement pieces out of items that previously blended into the background.

Just as you did with an entire room, determine your approach and choice of materials by assessing the furniture piece you'll be updating. Construction will play a role, as will the material. Laminate will require different preparation and treatment than solid wood. "Great bones" mean that reupholstery will be worth the time and trouble, and yield great results. Also take a look at the existing surface. Unless it's chipped or loaded with layers of old finish, there's no need to strip the piece; a good sanding will do.

If the piece does require stripping, that's something you may want to outsource. Tom farmed out the stripping of two beautiful old rockers he wanted to update, and then brought them home for repairs and refinishing. In the upholstery zone, there are some larger, more complex projects that a shop should handle, but Leslie has literally written the book on several fabric fix-ups that are well within your reach: *Fear Not, You Can Reupholster Anything.*

Trim a Room with Molding

Molding is a beautiful finishing touch for a room, adding depth and distinction. A range of profiles are available to tie into any style from Victorian to contemporary, and can be applied as crown molding, chair rails, detailed baseboards, and even as on-the-wall frames to set off a collection of art or photos. Basic carpentry skills are needed to properly cut, fit, and install most molding, although product innovations in the synthetic realm are making it possible to literally snap on a new look without complicated cuts.

Molding is available in the following configurations, at varying price points:

- **Clear.** This is the most expensive variety, as it has no visible joints and is designed to be stained and finished with a clear polyurethane or varnish.
- **Finger-joint.** This wood trim is less expensive than clear, and is designed to be painted. It's made up of several smaller pieces of molding attached to each other with wood joints.
- **Primed.** Typically this is finger-joint wood trim that is already primed. It's very handy to start with this, as it is easier than having to prime it yourself.
- **Synthetic.** Various types of synthetic molding are available, including urethane, PVC, and even composite mixtures of wood, and can be painted, stained, or left in their manufactured colors. Unlike wood, synthetic will have no defects that could cause it to twist or turn.

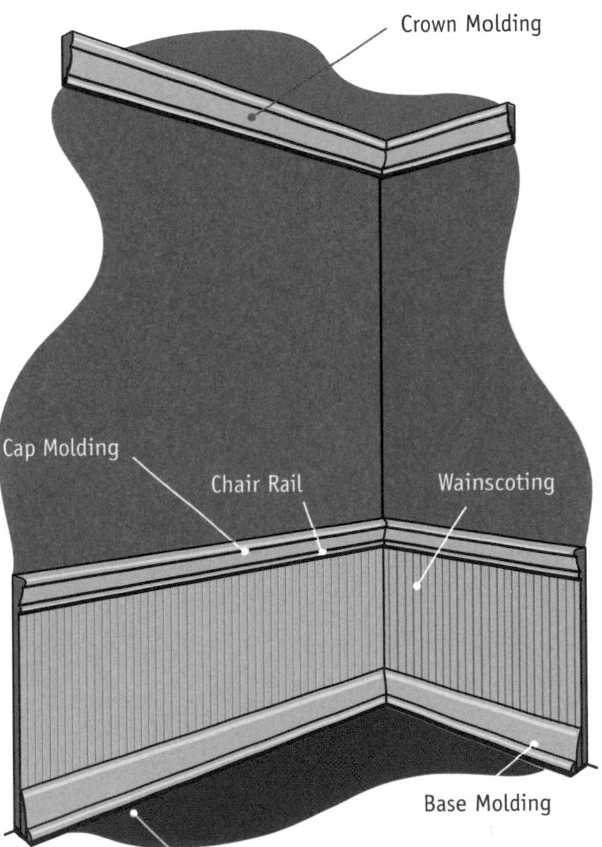

Cover It with Wainscoting

Another great surface accessory is wainscoting, which lends texture, definition, and variety to walls. Wood paneling and built-from-scratch systems are probably the most traditional means of achieving wainscoting effects, but a number of synthetic solutions made of cellular PVC and other maintenance-free materials are available to instantly create a classic look that can stand up to moisture, offer easy care, and be customized with paint and stain. Cap it all off with a decorative trim molding or a combination of a few, and finish the base edge with quarter-round molding for a craftsman's touch.

Give New Wallpaper a Bath

If you're installing new wallpaper, make application easier and amp up the tack with a quick dip in warm water. You can use your bathtub or any other basin that is wide enough for the sheet. After dampening the entire back surface of a section of wallpaper, touch the two edges of the glued side together for a moment, and then pull them apart. The newly tacky edges are now perfectly prepared for smooth application to the wall. This process is called bookmaking.

Finding Your Way to Fabulous Flooring

Never underestimate the power of a floor—it helps set the tone for the character of your entire room. And, not surprisingly, no topic generates more questions to *The Money Pit* than flooring, the decorative element always underfoot, often audibly, with the squeak that drives you crazy.[16]

This category also happens to be one where there is fast-changing product technology combined with so many styles, colors, and materials that it's easy to get, well, floored.

If you're thinking of putting in a new floor today, there's a wide array of floor choices with inspiring looks that range from genuine materials such as hardwood and ceramic to such great pretenders as laminate and vinyl.

Before you decide which floor is right for you, think about the lifestyle and performance needs of the areas in your home it will serve. First, consider the warranty. Different floor types are warranted for different physical attributes, such as wear-and-tear, delamination, or color fading, and for different lengths of time. Consider the floor's life expectancy when making a decision about materials. Some floors, such as hardwood and ceramic, may last a lifetime if properly maintained; others such as laminate may last for 15 to 30 years, while still others, such as peel-and-stick vinyl tile, may only last for a few years.

Do you have an active household? Some floor types are better than others at standing up to traffic, pet claws, and liquid spills. Vinyl sheet and vinyl tile are excellent choices for homes with kids and critters.

And finally, consider the care and maintenance of the flooring type. Most of today's floors offer easy maintenance to keep them looking good over time. Some are easy to care for with nothing more than simple vacuuming and mopping, while others require periodic refinishing. Laminate and vinyl sheet are two of the easiest-care floors.

Following is our at-a-glance guide to flooring. Stroll through and review your options before we move on to refinishing and repairs.

16.) Yet also functions as a handy alert system for curfew violators.

Flooring Material	Pros	Cons
Hardwood	Beautiful, natural looks with durability that can often extend beyond a century.	Difficult to install, and susceptible to rot and other ravages of moisture.
Engineered Hardwood	Designed to withstand moisture, it can be installed below-grade (in basements, for example) without the warping and buckling common to solid hardwood flooring	Can't be easily refinished, although pre-finished floors generally last a long time.
Laminate	One of the most durable and versatile flooring products around, available in looks resembling wood, stone, and more. Easy to install and maintain, and highly moisture-resistant.	Insufficient underlayment or faulty installation can result in a hollow sound underfoot; also, some finishes scratch and ding easily.
Vinyl Sheet	Wide variety of patterns and colors, offering easy care and durable finish.	Must be installed by a professional; seams or cracks can trap dirt and lead to premature wear. Almost impossible to repair tears.
Vinyl Tile	Easy-to-install material available in a range of patterns and colors, and can be placed atop most existing flooring materials.	Though tiles are individually replaceable, can be difficult to match replacement tiles to the older patina of the existing tiles.
Carpet	Adds warmth and instant comfort to a space; available in various piles and weaves.	Susceptible to water damage, mold, and mildew (not for use below grade); dust and dirt can break down fibers in the absence of regular cleaning. Carpets also provide safe harbor for allergens like dust mites and mold.
Ceramic Tile	Water-resistant, easy-clean materials offer a variety of design looks, from rustic natural to high-concept patterns and palettes. Proper abrasion resistance (PEI rating) prevents slips and slides.	Can be hard and cold underfoot. Cracked and otherwise damaged tiles are difficult to replace; surface may require occasional sealing and regrouting.
Bamboo	Resilient, renewable flooring material offers the warmth of wood with a contemporary twist. Available in various finishes and cuts.	Some finishes scratch and ding easily.
Cork	Another durable, renewable flooring option available in several tints and patterns.	Requires sealing for moisture resistance.

Spruce Up Hardwood with a New Finish

If you're fortunate enough to have beautiful, salvageable hardwood floors, refinishing them on your own is a definite DIY possibility. The materials are readily available, the tools are inexpensive or can be easily rented, and the results are always worth the effort. Here are the steps to take toward new life for your floor.

1. **Get ready.** Refinishing your floors will take a room out of service for some time, quite possibly for longer than you've originally planned. Use this opportunity to remove, store, or toss anything that you don't need on your way to creating the blank canvas of a floor you'll need to work on.

2. **Vacuum the old floor.** Remove as much dirt as possible so that it doesn't mix in during the sanding process and grind into the floors.

Ask Tom & Leslie: Can This Flooring Be Saved?

Q: Can I save my existing vinyl flooring?

A: We don't recommend trying to repair sheet vinyl, but vinyl tiles can be replaced individually. . . . The only trick is that the new tiles rarely match those that have been underfoot for years. Replacing individual ceramic tiles is possible, but it's largely hammer-and-chisel work, and color-matching the grout can be a challenge.

Q: How about resurfacing an existing floor?

A: Wood floors can be refinished, stained with one of the latest color washes, and even embellished with stenciled or hand-painted details before sealing. Natural stone floors can get new life and sheen with a professional polishing.

3. **Sand the floor.** Sanding the floor is an important step. If it isn't badly damaged, a light sanding will do, but if it is damaged or you're changing the color of the wood and need to remove all the old stain, then a heavier sanding should be done. For light sanding, rent a floor buffer with a sanding screen or use a machine called a U-Sand. However, if the floor is badly damaged, a floor belt sander is needed. This is a difficult tool to use, so unless you have lots of experience, hire a pro to handle this step.

4. **Remove the dust.** After sanding, you'll need to do a good job of removing as much dust as possible. Vacuum the floor thoroughly, use a tack cloth, or damp-mop it. If you don't remove the dust, it will get trapped in the new finish, float to the surface, and make it rough.

5. **Apply the finish.** Use an angled brush to "cut in" the new finish along the walls. Then, using a lamb's wool applicator (this looks like a sponge mop and is available at most home improvement centers), apply oil-based polyurethane, working your way out of the room as you go. Apply two to three thin coats, allowing plenty of drying time[17] in between. Although water-based polyurethane is available, we don't recommend it for floors. It simply doesn't wear nearly as well and with the work it takes to refinish a floor, it's not a project you'll want to repeat anytime soon.

After the last coat of polyurethane, you'll need to plan to stay off the floors for several hours of anticipated drying time. In fact, it's best to avoid heavy traffic on a floor for several days after the last coat is applied to give the finish time to really set in. However, if practical detours aren't available, use drop cloths for a few days over the areas you need to walk on. This'll protect them while allow-

17.) No matter what the can says, "quick dry" polyurethane is a big fat lie. Don't ask how we know that.

ing enough air to get to the floor so that the drying process can continue.

6. **Move your furniture back in,** plop down on the couch, and say a little prayer that you didn't just scratch the new floor.

Silencing a Squeaky Floor

It can happen with any floor, old or new, and it's the number one question to *The Money Pit*. How do you stop a squeaky floor?

The squeaks come from loose flooring moving as you walk over it. Seldom does it mean a structural problem; rather, the sound stems either from two loose boards rubbing together or from nails that hold down the flooring moving in and out of their holes.

The solution in either case is simple. Surprised? Here's the deal: you need to resecure the floor to the floor joists (a.k.a. the beams underfoot that floors are nailed to). If the squeaks are coming from under a carpeted surface, it's best to remove the carpet and drive hardened drywall screws next to every nail in the floor. Screws never pull out, so they're a great solution against future squeaks.

If removing wall-to-wall carpet is too much for you to tackle, you can leave it in place and use a stud finder to locate the floor joist beneath the carpet in the area of the squeak. Once you've done so, drive a 10d or 12d galvanized finish nail through the carpet and subfloor and into the floor joist. Make sure to drive the nail in at an angle to prevent future loosening, and drive in nails in two or three positions at the source of the squeak. Finish by grabbing the carpet by the nap or pile and pulling it up until the head of the finish nail passes through it.

If you've got a squeaky hardwood floor, the same procedure applies—it's just a little trickier because you'll have to blend repairs into the existing surface. Once again, use a stud finder to locate the joists in the neighborhood of the squeak (they'll be sitting 1 to 1½ inches under a hardwood floor, so a "deep scan" stud finder will work best). Either screw down or renail the area as suggested above for carpeted flooring, predrilling the holes. If you're going to use screws, a bit that includes a counterbore is ideal because it'll leave a hole that's exactly ⅜ inch in diameter and perfectly sized for filling with an oak plug, a small disk or cylinder of wood designed for filling such holes. And if you'll be nailing the floor, be sure to use a drill bit that's slightly smaller in diameter than that of your finish nails.

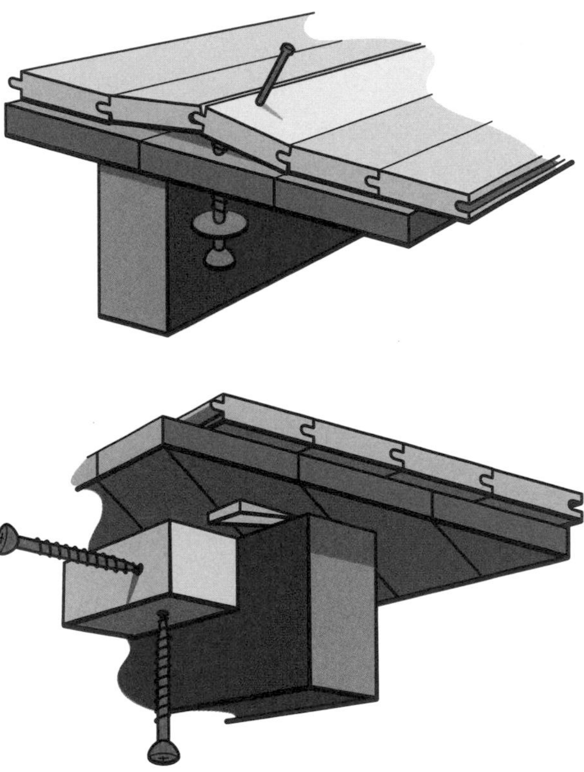

Solutions for Squeaks: Floor squeaks can be fixed from the top down or bottom up.

Other Flooring Repair Challenges

Knowing what's literally behind the damage of an existing floor helps in making the call on whether to repair or replace. Cracked tile, for instance, is the result of a weak underlayment. Sure, you can replace a tile here and there, but when you have weak underlayment, the problem isn't going away. Loose carpet is another big deal to fix, requiring re-stretching by a pro with the tools to do it correctly.

Vinyl seams and tears that collect grime are also nuisances, but offer the possibility of being repaired with remnants of the same flooring (as a last resort, you can always remove a bit from a pantry or other hidden area and use it as a patch). This fix isn't necessarily permanent, but can get you through until you're ready to install new flooring.

Access Everyone: **Not Slip-Sliding Away**

When you're selecting new flooring for your home, think ahead to the number of years and life stages during which you plan to enjoy it. Smooth, stable, slip-resistant surfaces, such as laminate, hardwood, tile, or vinyl with no-trip thresholds, are a better choice than wall-to-wall carpets and will offer both easy care and easy access for family members with varied mobility.

Trim Tip

Hardwood floors naturally tend to expand and contract, a phenomenon you can easily detect around the edges. Cover the gap and give your room a decorative edge by adding a shoe molding slightly above your flooring and around its perimeter.

Leslie Likes: **Underground Lessons in Flooring**

When we bought our house, there was carpeting in the basement. And I kept thinking, "Oh, how cozy and nice. It'll be so comfy for my home office down there!" Tom kept telling me I was going to be really sorry that I had carpeting underground. And I was like, "What do you mean? We keep the basement dry . . . there's no water . . . I'm running a dehumidifier . . . I'm on top of it." But he insisted. "One day, mark my words, you'll be sorry."

And sure enough, that day came. The gentleman we bought the house from had made a point of telling us how hard he'd worked to keep the basement dry, and we'd pledged to do the same. But at one point I was on the road for about a week and a half, and getting constant reports on the rainy weather back at home from my husband. Well, when I got back from my trip at around midnight one night and padded down to the basement to stow my laptop, I heard a horrible squishing sound. That's right, the entire carpet in my office zone was saturated, thanks to a misdirected, overflowing gutter outside. So immediately not even going to bed I put my laptop on a shelf well above the waterline, moved the furniture, cut out the wet piece of carpet, and took it directly to the street. And the next day, I ordered laminate flooring for the basement.

Worse, I had to tell Tom he was right!

Tom: *There are other reasons why carpet is a bad idea below grade. No matter how good a housekeeper you think you are, carpet holds dust, dust mites, and moisture, a recipe for a potentially unhealthy flooring surface. Keep the carpet for above-grade spaces only.*

Looking Up: Ceiling Solutions

When planning a room redesign, it's easy to get preoccupied with dressing the walls and floors, but don't forget to look up. Remember, your guests will, just as soon as you step out to get the drinks and hors d'oeuvres.[18] Ceilings need attention, too, and there are a lot of beautiful options for freshening them up or converting what you've already got in place.

Repairing and repainting is one way to go. Decorative embossed metal tiles are another. Dropped ceilings are seeing a stylish renaissance with innovative new grid and tile materials, available in profiles ranging from richly coffered ceilings to subtle textures. You can also use these new products to update an existing suspended-ceiling system, allowing you to both maintain access to wiring and other utility elements while keeping update costs under control.

Probably the biggest challenge up in the ceiling zone are those lovely "popcorn" finishes found in homes from the paneling-and-disco era.[19] At the time, they were an acoustic solution and a handy way for builders to cover up construction mistakes (with the added distraction of those little sparkle bits that were scattered across the ceilingscape), but today, they can be an inconvenient eyesore.

Removal is possible, but it takes some pretty intense work to accomplish: you'll have to soak the popcorn surface with water (we recommend using a pump garden sprayer for this) and then scrape it all away with a 6-inch drywall knife. You'll then be left with a lot of material that should be disposed of properly, not to mention some significant ceiling repair, before applying an oil-based primer and a flat finish.

There are maybe a million better ways to spend a Saturday, starting with your annual dental cleaning. If you can live with the texture, you can always use a high-pile, slitted roller to apply a new coat of color that coordinates with the rest of the room.

While you may be feeling like that ugly kitchen can't wait another day, take a break between adventures. Put your feet up, look around, and take a moment to appreciate the beauty and accomplishment every time you conquer a new summit in your home improvement adventure.

Okay, that's enough. Next up, into the heart of the home we go with the kitchen.

18.) You know who you are. Well, yeah, and us. But then again, we check out which brands of toilets, refrigerators, and air conditioning our friends have, too. We can't help it. 19.) What's up with the 1970s?

Cooking Up the Kitchen of Your Dreams Without Getting Burned

You go in and out of your kitchen every day. You see the same old cabinets, the same old dishwasher, the same old faded linoleum floor, every single day. One day, whether it's because you got your tax refund—or a call from the Board of Health—you decide that it's time to fix that kitchen.

The kitchen is one of the more heart-pounding home improvement adventures. Take the heart of the home out of commission for a few weeks, and you'll feel some stress. The outcome can be a huge adrenaline rush, however. The kitchen is where you entertain, it's where your family gathers, and it's where your kids' memories are being made right now. Everything functions better when you have a good heart.

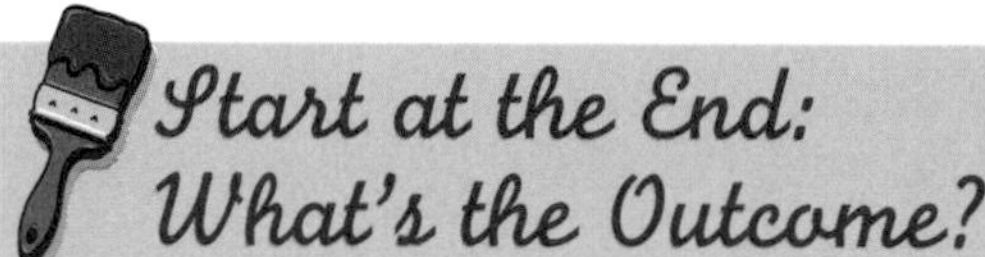

Start at the End: What's the Outcome?

For most people, the first answer is: "The kitchen I just loved in *Country Home*" (or insert your favorite magazine/TV show kitchen here). But that's just style. While obviously an important consideration, you also need to consider how your kitchen fits your lifestyle. How do you need your kitchen to function? Do you have enough space? Enough storage? Does your kitchen work as hard as you do?[20]

Beyond clippings, ask your friends what they like and dislike about their kitchens. Look for home tours in your area to get a sense of local solutions for things like recycling. Ask questions at the local home improvement store. Heck, call our radio show 24/7 at 1-888-MONEYPIT and ask us! Keep notes on things you learn about, and then google them online to learn more. Just as you have a file of design ideas, start racking up ideas that'll help solve the problems of your everyday life.

> **Where Do We Spend More Time: Bedrooms or Kitchens?**
>
> *The answer is the bedroom, but the catch is that (regrettably), most of that time is devoted to sleeping. When it comes to waking hours, the winner is the kitchen,[21] according to an international survey conducted by Gallup.*

Then play a fun family game that Tom calls Chopper 5: Post a sheet of paper on the fridge, and ask family members to record kitchen traffic jams and accidents as they happen—or within 48 hours of conflict resolution arising from the sibling crashes that don't require hospitalization. Everyone who uses the kitchen should participate, with someone elected to interpret for the pets.[22] Eventually, you'll have something like this:

Monday, 5:30 P.M.: "Billy keeps poking me with his elbow when it's our turn to make dinner."

- For parents, this is usually the cue to push both kids aside and whip up a margarita. To us it means that you need a solution that increases your workspace so there is enough room for everyone to work and still a place to mix margaritas.

Thursday, 6:00 A.M.: "You know, I actually wouldn't mind dancing with you like this some night when we can get a sitter. But right now, you and your stupid smoothie machine are in the way of my morning coffee!"

20.) We personally refuse to work any harder than our kitchens. 21.) Except when there are dirty dishes in the sink. 22.) We're serious. Fido is totally tired of having to walk around the table to get to his dish.

CHAPTER 2

Songs to Work By:

Tunes to help you get through your projects.

- *Breakfast in America*—Supertramp
- *Come and Get It*—Paul McCartney
- *Bread and Butter*—Newbeats
- *Refrigerator Car*—Spin Doctors
- *Stoned Soul Picnic*—Laura Nyro
- *Soul Kitchen*—The Doors
- *Scarborough Fair (Parsley, Sage, Rosemary, and Thyme)*—Simon & Garfunkel
- *A Taste of Honey*—Herb Alpert and the Tijuana Brass
- *Cocktails for Two*—Spike Jones
- *Feed Me*—*Little Shop of Horrors*
- Anything by Meat Loaf

- This tells us two things: (1) You need to organize your kitchen more effectively for how you use it and when, and (2) You need to call a sitter for this weekend.

Saturday, 7:30 P.M.: "Wow, I can't tell you how great it is to have all of you in here when I'm really stressing about this roast and you're everywhere I want to be."

- Don't fight it, accept it. No matter what's happening in the living room, everybody will end up congregating in the kitchen. Snapping at your sister just before Thanksgiving dinner won't change that. Affordable options to expand your existing space just might.

One more note on those clippings: In the last chapter, we said you should pick styles and colors that make you happy and that there is no "right" answer. That's still true in the kitchen with one caveat: a major chunk of a buyer's perceived value of your home is stationed in its kitchen. If you plan to stay in your home a long time, by all means, go for that ultramodern industrial design aesthetic in your otherwise traditional center-hall Colonial. Just understand that the financial stakes are steeper in kitchen remodeling decisions than in other areas inside your home. Choosing styles and materials that match style and value of the house may make your home an easier choice for a prospective home buyer. Some home sales happen faster than others, and oddball design elements can make people pass on an otherwise perfect property.

How Much Can You Do on the Kitchen of Your Dreams?

So now you know you need more workspace, better traffic patterns, and an apology to your sister.

You can handle the latter, but for a major kitchen remodel, you will likely have pros involved for at least part of it. A kitchen remodel like that can involve just about every type of home construction material, and hitting the wall is literally where it almost always makes sense to get help. If you're planning to move plumbing or redo your lighting scheme, it's even more likely you should budget for a pro.

What about design services: are they worth it? We like to say that there is no unusable space in the kitchen, but that doesn't mean everyone has the skills to make the most of that space. Kitchen designing takes a special expertise that might very well help open up your kitchen to easier chores for kids and less-claustrophobic entertaining.[23]

Plans from an architect or trained kitchen designer can run anywhere from several hundred

23.) Can you put a price tag on keeping the kids out of each other's way when they do chores? Can you?

dollars to more than $1,000, but this can be money very well spent in a complex space like the kitchen. Professionals have more experience and training in devising less-expensive solutions to complex problems. They will also know the newest products and technologies that could best fit your budget and design situation.

The National Kitchen & Bath Association (www.nkba.org) certifies designers with rigorous criteria, including testing and ongoing professional development. Professionals like these have the know-how to suggest solutions before you can even finish describing the problems. While all Certified Kitchen Designers (CKD) provide design services, some also act as general contractors and will supervise the entire project. For more tips on hiring pros for your projects, see Chapter 15, Hiring Help.

Another reason to budget for a pro: getting this remodel done and over with. Yes, we know the joke about contractors taking forever to finish a kitchen. But there are no jokes about the crash-and-burn scenario of dual-career, two-child, three-pet households running into those inevitable delays that plague the average complex construction project. That's because it's not funny.

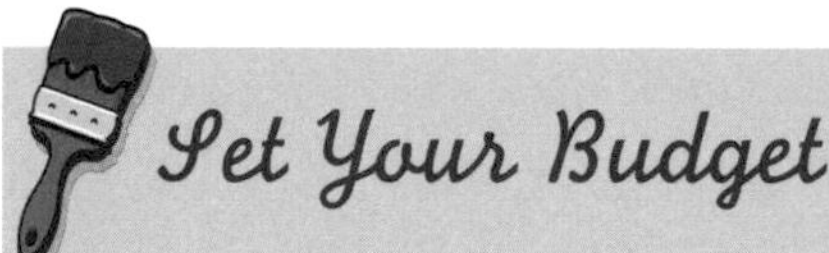

Now it's time to put it all together. What will it cost?

Kitchen remodels can cost anywhere from a few hundred dollars for a cosmetic facelift to well over $100,000 for a subfloor-to-rafters redo. The "average" kitchen remodel is usually around $8,000 to $10,000 and typically includes changing the countertops and décor elements, such as flooring and lighting. More comprehensive remodels with new appliances and cabinetry start at $20,000, an estimate that will need to be increased if you plan to move walls or utilities.

If your dreams are bigger than your pocketbook, there are several places where you might be able to save money.

Good Bones

You've always known it's great to have good bones, and that's true with kitchens, as well. New cabinets and appliances form a major part of the expense, and these are areas where your inventory will really help you plan your budget. If your stove can still handle Thanksgiving, then give thanks and keep it for another year. Same for cabinets and built-in components like moldings and woodwork. Basically, if your kitchen has "good bones," you may not need the big budget you thought you did. Or you can get more for your money than you'd originally planned.

Don't change the plumbing, and don't go behind the walls. Budgets get sucked down the drain in a hurry when you start fantasizing about moving that sink over there. It means going behind the walls. Don't go there if the budget is tight.

Write It Down!

Jot down the condition, age, usable (or, perhaps at this point, unusable) features of every major appliance, and note any possible new features that would help to clear up traffic for the family, such as an icemaker in the fridge or a warming drawer for entertaining.

Using your file of magazine clippings and your field research, think about new ways you'd like to use your kitchen. Maybe you can expand the phone zone into a mini office center and homework perch. If you give up that set of cabinets, can you open up easy-to-access pantry space where you can actually reach your party trays, backup china, and chafing dishes?

A kitchen is one of the projects where we really, really mean it when we say that you should devote 20 percent of your budget to contingencies. As a result of the complexity of the project, this particular remodeling adventure has more unexpected and expensive hazards than average, not to mention the increased cost of eating out for weeks on end while your project is underway.

Link Up: Renovation Recipes

The Money Pit *audience has submitted cooking ideas using only portable appliances. We now have tons of tasty dishes that can be made with just a toaster, an electric skillet, hot pot, or gas grill. If you get creative, you can feed your family more than pizza during your kitchen's downtime. Check out some samples online at www.moneypit.com.*

Mental Toughness

Accept that kitchen remodels are stressful. Going into it with that mindset is half the battle. It's fairly typical to encounter unanticipated problems behind the wall, delivery delays, and weather delays. It's also possible that you'll experience the heartbreak of mismeasurement —particularly unfortunate in the case of nonreturnable products.

Like air travel, a minor delay in one part of the project can have massive ripple effects. The tradespeople—plumbers, electricians, and carpenters—all work in sequence, requiring coordination of their schedules. All it takes is one guy or product delivery getting stuck when the highway shuts down for five hours, and all the steps and professionals that follow have to be rescheduled. Try as you (or your contractor) may to keep the project on-track, the point here is that there are lots of specialists and hard-to-find products involved in a kitchen remodeling project. Delays are inevitable, so set your expectations accordingly and save yourself some stress along the way.

What Are Kitchens Good For, Anyway?

You thought that kitchens were exclusively used for cooking and eating, eh? Think again. A recent Gallup poll discovered that only 24 percent of the 14,000 people surveyed used the kitchen strictly for eating and cooking. How else do people commonly utilize their kitchens?

- *35 percent family discussions*
- *35 percent socializing and entertaining*
- *16 percent hobbies*
- *15 percent playing with children*

Yes, we know this adds up to 101 percent (if you include the 24 percent, it makes 125 percent). People were not limited to selecting just one use for the kitchen, because no one uses the kitchen for just one thing!

Kitchens remain somewhat usable until the sink and stove get yanked, so before your remodeling pro grabs the first crowbar out of his toolbox, establish a family dining plan that includes a temporary camp kitchen. Outdoor grills, crockpots, microwaves, and electric skillets can all help you establish your camp kitchen, but remember not to overload electric circuits. Pizza delivery on speed-dial is always an option.

Plan temporary housing for your kitchen items that keeps your most-used items handy. Since wildly swinging hammers and saws don't mix well with breakables, get those tucked safely away along with any valuables before the construction crews arrive.

The Basics of Kitchen Space Planning

Just as architectural styles date houses, kitchen layouts can also date a home, often in an unflattering way. Kitchens used to be a place where one person[24] cooked and washed dishes, and that's how a lot of kitchens still are in the older homes of the Northeast and Midwest.

Today, more than one person had better be stepping up to cook and clean.

Our audience frequently asks us about the importance of the "work triangle" when planning for a new kitchen. This commonly used term simply refers to the triangle shape created by the traditional placement of the stove, refrigerator, and sink. It was designed to reduce the number of steps needed to accomplish common kitchen tasks.

A well-designed work triangle is still a highly recommended goal for your kitchen remodel. But now the layout has to incorporate all the steps and tasks of all the people who use the kitchen, which can include all ages and life stages doing everything from gourmet meal prep to Web surfing. This is way more geometry than we ever learned in high school.

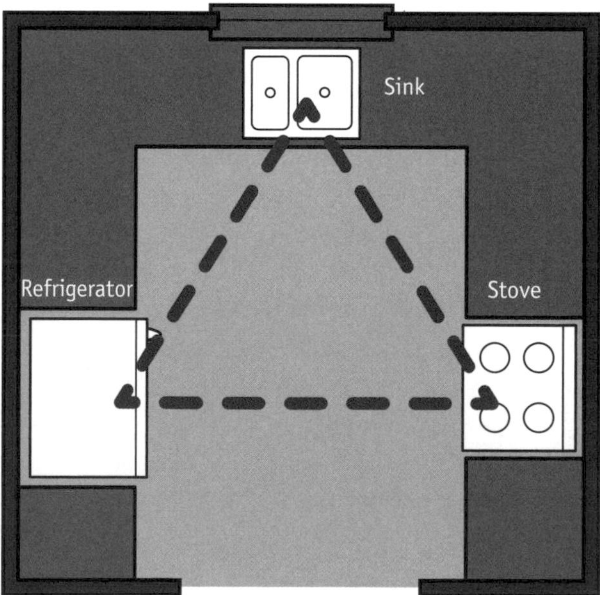

Kitchen Working Triangle: In a kitchen, this is the distance between the sink, stove, and refrigerator.

It includes thinking about workspace height, as well as workspace area. Consider who will be using the kitchen's work zones; you can easily vary the heights of surfaces to accommodate a range of ages, as well as accommodate present and potential future physical challenges.

Smart Storage Solutions

No matter what the size of the space you're dealing with, you can make it more roomy and convenient with a little smart storage planning. The recent wave of home organization solutions has inspired many manufacturers to design creative, compact cabinetry solutions, and you can amp up the convenience factor with space-expanding inserts for everything from spice collections to recycling bins.

All in all, there's no space in a kitchen that's unusable—every nook and cranny is fair game. An unused cove, for example, can be cleverly converted into a mini office or mail center. Add utility by planning storage for cookware and tools in the zones where you'll use those most. Rolling carts and other free-wheeling furnishings can help make for better work flow. We love magnetized backsplashes or magnetized strips that can hold spice racks, knives, and utensils. Such cool solutions make use of space in a clever, modern way that works with any kitchen décor.

In plotting your storage master plan, think about what you use every day versus what you use only occasionally. If you entertain often,

24.) Her name was June Cleaver.

Access Everyone: **Kitchens for All Ages**

If you're planning to be in your home for many years to come, work universal design principles into your kitchen plan so that the space's convenience and access work for all ages and abilities. Sensible design changes now can make your kitchen far more usable for everyone—things like adding countertops at varying heights, installing pull-down shelves in upper cabinets, using draw-style microwave ovens (mounted under the counter) and dishwashers, and even adding a contrasting color on the edge of the counter for easy visibility.

AARP has great information on this smart, family-friendly approach to kitchen design. Check out their Kitchen Checklist, product selection tips, and more at www.aarp.org/homedesign. AARP, along with the National Association of Home Builders also offers a contractor certification program in coordination called CAPS, which stands for Certified Aging in Place Specialists. CAPS contractors are specially trained in accessible design issues and can help make sure your kitchen works for family members of all ages. For more tips, see Chapter 15, Hiring Help.

you can work in a contemporary spin on those old-fashioned hidden service areas by designating a pantry or in-between space as a just-back-from-the-store unloading zone. Add a small prep sink, warming drawer, or even microwave nearby, and you'll create a sense of behind-the-scenes serving magic and efficiency.

Making the Right Connections: Basic Utilities and General Safety

There's almost nothing as frustrating—or expensive—as attempting to reconfigure the power and water connections in a kitchen. So think carefully and creatively about the placement of your new appliances and plumbing, with your present connections in mind. Going back to the work triangle, we recommend identifying which point is going to be the easiest and most cost-effective to move, and moving forward from there.

It's also wise to understand the limits of your kitchen's electrical and gas load before you follow your dream of installing that professional-grade range. Specialized appliances call for specialized power and fuel supplies, and ignoring these needs can have dangerous consequences. Proper venting is also part of the utilities scene. Make sure your vent is functional, has a quality motor to power away exhaust, and is sized to the demands of your appliances.

Leslie Likes: **An Office in Your Kitchen? Absolutely!**

One kitchen redesign I worked on for Trading Spaces *involved some very unique curved cabinetry that flowed around the refrigerator and diagonally into the living area. With a little shelving and space for a small computer, this tail-end of the cabinet system was a natural spot for the kids' homework and Mom's budgeting chores. Well, natural to everyone except Mom, that is—she was actually furious to find a desk in her kitchen when the remodel was unveiled. Fast-forward to a few weeks later, however, and the joy of family togetherness had taken over. Mom now felt that the mini-office was the best feature in the kitchen because it created the opportunity for her to be with the kids while doing tasks that would usually take either her or them to other, more isolated workstations in the home. Our little design addition literally brought everyone together!*

Kitchen Flooring: Begin at the Bottom, and Everything Starts Looking Up

Kitchen floors are special, because they get more day-to-day wear and tear than floors in any other room. You want to think about durability, maintenance, and ease of cleanup when you shop.

Kitchen Flooring Materials

- Linoleum
- Sheet vinyl
- Vinyl tile
- Ceramic tile
- Natural stone tile
- Natural slate
- Terra-cotta tile
- Laminate strip/plank
- Solid hardwood strip/plank
- Prefinished hardwood
- Engineered hardwood
- Cork

Available in sheet or tile form, vinyl is the easiest and least expensive material to replace. Vinyl tiles are a project that handy homeowners can install themselves, while sheet product is better left to the pros since it requires exact shaping and can often be so large that it's just unwieldy.

Laminate flooring is one of the most durable and versatile flooring materials for kitchens, available in realistic wood, tile, stone, or even vinyl-like patterns. Most laminates are highly water resistant and won't warp or twist even if you pour water directly onto their surfaces. They're also easier than ever to install with lock-together, glue-free designs that can "float" over a variety of older floor coverings.

Ceramic, stone, and terra-cotta tile are each a treat style-wise, especially when it comes to the overall effect provided by large-format tiles. For the kitchen, you need to look at slip resistance, stain resistance, sealing options, including—or especially!—the grout, since gravity and tomato sauce can work against you. Tile floors can be hard underfoot and a challenge to keep clean—something for serious cooks to consider—but once they're installed, they'll outlast both you and your Money Pit.

Tom's Tip: The Laws of Physics

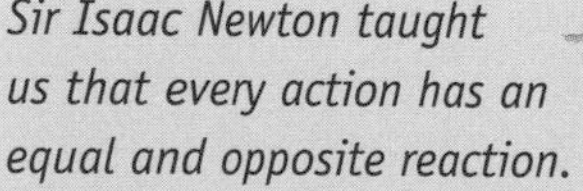

Sir Isaac Newton taught us that every action has an equal and opposite reaction.

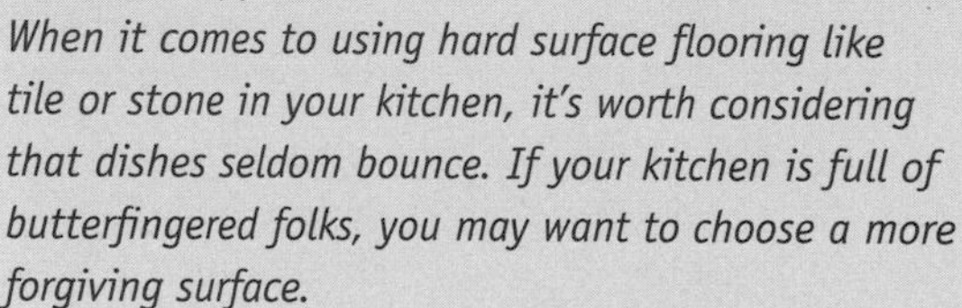

When it comes to using hard surface flooring like tile or stone in your kitchen, it's worth considering that dishes seldom bounce. If your kitchen is full of butterfingered folks, you may want to choose a more forgiving surface.

Avoid Dishwasher Disasters

If you are replacing the kitchen floor, there's one appliance in particular you need to keep in mind: the dishwasher. Built-in dishwashers are set between cabinets and under a countertop. If you add a new layer of floor in front of your dishwasher, you may never get it out when it breaks down and needs to be replaced, which will most likely happen as you're gluing the last floorboard in place! Instead, disconnect and remove the dishwasher before installing the new flooring. Then you can adjust the height of the legs and slide it back into place.

Counters: High-tech Tops for Beauty, Convenience, and Safety

Once upon a time, countertops were simply wooden tables. If you had to knead dough, you lugged a slab of marble onto the table, and then took it off again. This was the kitchen routine until someone left the marble slab on the wooden table one night instead of putting it away,[25] creating the world's first countertop.

Today, countertops are made from many types

Countertop Material	Pros	Cons
Tile	A range of colors, sizes, textures, materials and styles available, and the surrounding grout has many color options.	Can chip or crack, necessitating complicated replacement. Grout can attract and hold mold and fungi unless treated with an antimicrobial additive.
Stainless Steel	Sleek look and easy cleanup.	Easily dented and dinged, shows fingerprints and requires professional preparation and installation.
Natural Stone	Durable and heat-resistant, and provides a high-end, one-of-a-kind look.	A pricey option that requires professional installation and careful area calculation and slab selection for a coordinated look. Can also be scratched and stained fairly easily. Occasionally needs to be resealed.
Engineered Stone	Durable and heat-resistant, with a nonporous surface that resists stains. A range of colors available.	Another pricey option requiring professional installation.
Laminate	Wide range of colors and patterns at comparatively low prices. Easy to keep clean.	Requires design and installation by a manufacturer-certified fabricator. Higher-end pricing depends on size and shape requirements of kitchen.
Concrete	Durable, unique-looking surface available in a range of colors.	Installation is best left to a pro. Occasional cracking can occur.
Wood	Traditional, natural look.	Home to E. coli and other dangerous bacteria. Must be thoroughly cleaned with each use as well as properly oiled and maintained annually to keep those dangers at bay.

25.) We're pretty sure it was a teenager.

of material, including ceramic tile, laminate, solid surfacing like DuPont Corian, natural stone such as granite or slate, reconstituted natural quartz, and even concrete. Mixing and matching materials is also allowed and encouraged to create specialized task areas, such as using that old-fashioned marble slab for modern-day baking projects.

Being the most visible horizontal space in your kitchen, the countertop material you choose will be a major style statement. When selecting countertop material, consider your housekeeping resources as much as your budget. For instance, if your family cuisine involves a lot of berries, soy sauce, and red wine, then stain-resistant, easy-clean countertops can literally change your life.

Granite is the most popular choice for kitchens: it can handle a hot pan, is very durable, and just looks gorgeous, although it's essential it be resealed every year. If you want the dimensional stability that natural stone provides with easier care, then ***engineered stone*** such as Silestone might be for you. Silestone is made from quartz, comes in a wide variety of colors, and is a nonporous surface that resists stains and scratches for easy maintenance.

Ceramic tile is a true classic among building materials (the Egyptians used it to decorate their own abodes as far back as the fourth century B.C.). To avoid the hassles of cleaning grout, choose darker colors and seal the grout right after applying (when the Egyptians had to keep unsealed grout clean, they invented cursing). Use grout with an antimicrobial additive to resist mold and fungus. Continue your tile right up over the backsplash for a whole new look.

Laminate is another popular option thanks to its durability, wide range of stylish colors and patterns, relatively low price, and wide availability. It can't be painted, but you can add a fresh layer of laminate on top of the existing surface. So if you currently have laminate counters that are worn but you like the basic configuration, think about a new layer. It's available in many colors and patterns, including stone looks and even wood veneer options, from several manufacturers.

Leslie Likes: **Tile Style**

When you're redoing a sink-and-counter workspace with a tile backsplash,consider this quick, custom makeover.

Remove a few tiles or a whole row, and replace them with tiles featuring an image, color, or texture that creates a point of interest and visual depth. Even on a limited budget, you can capture the look of those amazing, high-design kitchens by choosing tile in your price range and applying it in such a way that it stands out.

Whether your backsplash sits just above the counter or takes up the entire space between the counter and the upper cabinets, tiles can add a stylish focal point to your kitchen. Think diagonal applications, creative color combos, and mixing various tile sizes, or incorporate border tiles around the backsplash space.

If your budget permits, ***solid surfacing*** is a great way to go. The investment in money up front pays dividends in maintenance hours spent over the lifetime of its installation. No crying ever again over spilt grape juice—just buff it out.[26] Solid surface also enables design highlights like custom shapes, specialized edge patterns, and under-mounted sinks. Fabricators should be able to provide a portfolio of their artistry with your desired material. Luxore, a nonporous heat- and chip-resistant stone, and Swanstone, a reinforced, moisture-resistant surface with seamless joints and no need for fabricated edges, are becoming increasingly popular.

When working with any of these surfaces, hire the manufacturer's certified installers to do the work. They've received training in the material's properties. Same goes for all the cool countertop materials you see on TV, like slate, stainless steel, and concrete.

26.) You'll always cry over spilt wine, even though it can also be buffed out.

Now, a note about ***butcher-block countertops***: They were once pretty common and, admittedly, provide a look that still works well with traditional kitchens. We get a lot of questions on the show about updating them. Unfortunately, it's not a great idea. We now know that *E. coli* and other nasty bacteria are hard to clean from wood, where they move in and raise a family that threatens yours. While regular treatments with bleach solutions can help keep bacteria at bay, a better option is to transform classic butcher block into a storage solution or conversation piece, and leave food prep areas to modern, easy-to-maintain surface materials that approximate a classic look.

Finally, we aren't big fans of prefabricated countertops, unless you have a high skill level. Houses are never perfectly square, and neither are kitchens. You either have to cut the wall to make it fit, or you have to cut the countertop or the cabinet to make it fit.

Access Everyone: **Counter Intelligence**

As you shop countertop materials for that perfect kitchen look, also consider building-in a range of comfortable working heights. The standard height is about 36 inches, but including a surface that's 28 to 32 inches high will provide a work area suited to young chefs and a more comfortable chopping and prepping height for you. A sit-down workstation is another addition that you'll appreciate over the life of your kitchen. Make it 30 inches wide and 27 inches high for comfortable access from a kitchen chair or wheelchair. Multiple countertop levels also give the kitchen a very unique look and extra depth because there's not just one continuous flat surface. You may also save money by being able to use scraps of counter material.

Cabinets: Put It Away

Cabinets are the place where you stash your spices, cache your cereals, guard your glassware, and put your pots and pans. If your workspace is crowded with lots of gadgets that don't have a home, cabinets and today's smart shelving systems can put everything into its place.

Cabinets can also be the single biggest expense in a kitchen remodel. We hear lots of questions and concerns on *The Money Pit* about kitchen cabinets—how to repair, reinforce, or refinish them, and how to plan a new room layout around them.

When our listeners ask if we recommend refinishing cabinets, our answer is usually, "Absolutely!" Most old cabinetry was built well, so preserving it is usually worthwhile. Sometimes, sprucing up cabinets can be accomplished with a thorough cleaning. And today's range of finish and painting techniques provide a multitude of makeover options.

Just be sure to do a careful assessment of your cabinets' construction before diving into a DIY facelift. If they were installed in the disco era or later, they are likely constructed with solid fronts and paper-thin veneers on the rest of the box. Veneers can't be sanded or stained, so painting will be the only option if they're involved.

Refacing the cabinets is another story. Wood, laminate, or other veneer is glued to the cabinet surfaces, and door and drawer fronts are usually replaced. We generally don't recommend this, because the cost can be as much as half that of replacing the cabinets. Plus, with refacing cabinets, you're pretty much stuck with the layout you currently have.

Ask Tom & Leslie: Can Kitchen Cabinets Be Painted?

Q: I have vintage-1965 solid wood kitchen cabinets. I've been there and done that as far as trying to refinish in their original wood tones goes, and now want to paint them. Can this be done with long-term durability?

A: Sure, painting is a great option for old solid-wood cabinets. First, clean them out and pull off the doors and drawers, and remove all the hardware. Then sand them by hand, or with a product like Liquid Sandpaper that leaves the surface clean and ready for the paint coat. Next, prime them using an oil-based primer, which does a more durable job of getting the surface ready for the finish coat. Then paint away! We also recommend using an oil-based glossy paint for the finished coat. These surfaces tend to be harder and offer better wear protection than water-based acrylics.

Adding cabinets gets expensive as they have to be built from scratch and then refaced to match the rest of the kitchen.

If you're going to replace the cabinets, there are three levels of cabinet customization:

Stock cabinets. The least-expensive, stock cabinetry is produced en masse and available through your local home improvement center and cabinet dealers. What you see is what you get, with few chances for modifications or specialized specs. Manufacturers offer such wide variety, however, that stock cabinetry can be a perfect solution that saves considerable cost. One source we love for such systems is IKEA. Instead of messing around with leveling and shimming to install straight cabinets, IKEA provides a bar that's mounted on the wall and you actually hang the cabinets from it. What's more, their floor cabinets have adjustable legs that are hidden behind a kickplate.

Semi-custom cabinets. The middle ground between stock and custom, this variety allows for slight modifications (usually height, width, and depth) at the time of production. There's a wider array of associated moldings, trims, and finishes available, and of course, the price goes up accordingly.

Leslie's Cabinets

Our kitchen cabinets are solid wood, so we knew they were going to be keepers when we moved in. But there was an open soffit area above them that wasn't useful for storage or big enough to open up the space visually. So, using red oak to match the existing cabinets, I built a new piece that connected the cabinetry to the ceiling, trimmed it all out with oak molding, and had it stained the same sort of warm reddish-brown. I was able to cover all the seams with a different trim, and now it looks like an original, completely custom built-in system—almost like furniture.

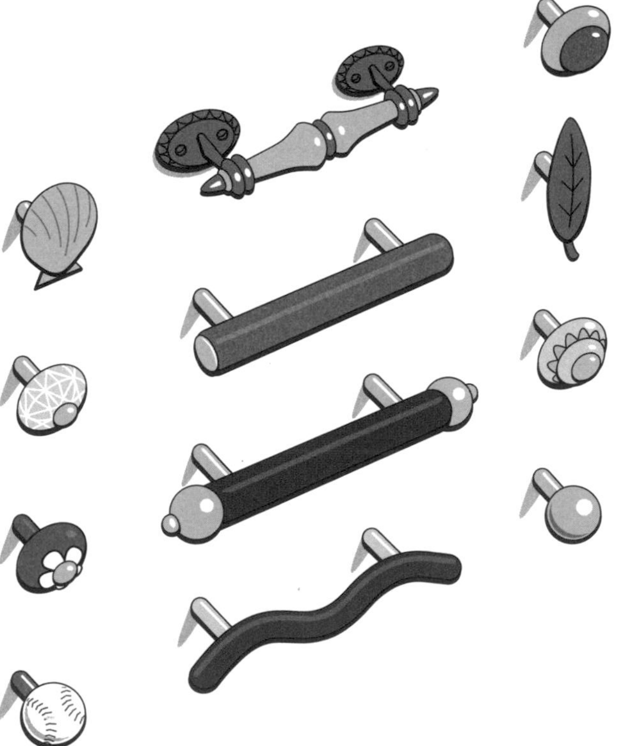

Jewelry for your kitchen: Add some "bling" to your kitchen with a selection of new door and drawer knobs and pulls. Small changes like these can create big visual impacts.

Custom cabinets. Created especially for you and your kitchen by a cabinetmaking professional whose experience and skill will be evident in the pricing. Cost is determined by complexity of design and materials used. Aficionados of fine wood craftsmanship find it hard to consider any other option.

Style-wise, there's been a big resurgence of high-gloss glass cabinetry with traditional coloring that can work in any sort of environment. And you aren't limited to tall and narrow, either—look at a mix of horizontal and vertical units to create visual interest, as well as a wider variety of storage options. Light-colored cabinets with a mix of open shelves and glass-fronted doors provide the visual depth that opens up a kitchen.

Tom's Cabinets

Our cabinetry was classic, so we kept it. We also created a desk space in the kitchen because we didn't have one before and knew that we wanted the computer to be in a central, parentally supervised area. To accomplish this, I decided to replicate the wainscoting that went around the kitchen and bought one 18-inch IKEA cabinet base, which became the left side of the desk, connected to an existing Corian countertop. That cabinet base tied in perfectly with the existing wainscoting, and it was a very easy, inexpensive way to plug a desk into the kitchen.

And don't forget the jewelry. Small changes in hardware, like new door handles and drawer pulls, can make a huge difference in the overall look of a kitchen. The rule of thumb is to choose one or two standout pieces of hardware, balancing more neutral looks with your flights of whimsy.

Are Our Kitchens Making Us Fat?

Kitchen designs have changed over the years. In the 1950s, American kitchens averaged about 80 square feet and were walled on all four sides. Dinner was served in the dining room and the kitchen was closed after supper.

Today, kitchens are larger, spanning about 225 square feet, and are a gathering place for the whole clan. According to an American Institute of Architects survey, kitchen islands are one of the most requested new kitchen features and with them, the tendency to serve dinner buffet-style—and that's "a disaster waiting to happen," says Dawn Jackson Blatner, a registered dietitian and spokeswoman for the American Dietetic Association, as quoted in the Washington Post. *"I see about a hundred patients a month for weight-management issues. One of the first things we suggest is that people stop eating 'family style,' where they keep the food out on the island and tell people to help themselves. Rather, we really want people to put one serving on a plate, take it out of the kitchen, and eat it in a dining room. If food is in our sight, it will most likely end up in our mouth."*

Plumbing: Solutions for Sinks

Your kitchen sink and faucet have to work at least as hard as your kids do in the kitchen, or you'll definitely hear about it. Most of today's kitchens have more than one sink, along with different faucets, fittings, and accessories that make food prep and cleanup fast and easy.

Most people aren't aware of the fact that lots of sinks are offered in several bowl configurations and installation alternatives, including undercounter, self-rimming or drop-in, apron-front, and tile-edge (flush with tile countertops and sealed in with grout), just to name a few. Custom accessories like integral drainboards add functionality to the prep zone, and pantry and bar sinks can be installed in other areas of the kitchen to minimize traffic congestion at the main sink.

For a kitchen sink, deep is good. Determine the maximum cutout size permitted by the cabinets and countertop where the sink is to be installed, and then get the deepest bowl possible.

The most common material for kitchen sinks is stainless steel, which comes in a range of thicknesses or gauges. Lower is better here, and 18-gauge stainless is an optimal thickness in that it provides strength and rigidity for large bowls while allowing tight-radius corners that maximize the flat work area in the bottom of the bowl.

Other popular materials are cast iron and fine fire clay. Durable and dependable, cast-iron sinks are heavy-duty structures which sometimes require extra cabinet support. Cast-iron sinks are available in a wide variety of colors and are typically porcelain-coated. Fine fire clay is a ceramic fired at a lower temperature than the ceramics used for tiles and toilets. The technique permits sharper design details and more angular profiles than possible with vitreous china or cast iron. All surfaces exposed to water are coated with a colored ceramic glaze that is fused to the sink body when fired.

Solid-surface or "integral" sinks are created using the same material as countertops for a sleek, seamless, one-piece appearance where spills can be wiped right into the sink. Solid-surface sinks are stain-, chip- and crack-resistant, and the nonporous surface makes it impossible for mold or bacteria to take up residence and grow.

Convenience on Tap

Today's faucet styles literally reach new heights with spouts that are positioned to handle large pots and pans, just as in a restaurant kitchen. Convenient integrated sprayers are also the norm, allowing you to control water patterns and even put the spray on pause with the touch of a button. What's more, you can select a faucet equipped with a water filtration system to instantly reduce exposure to harmful bacteria, metals, and chemicals while minimizing odors and improving the taste of the water.

There's a big difference between a $79 faucet purchased at a home center and a professional-style, drip-free model that makes food prep and cleanup much easier. Features like sprayers that pull out of the faucet with multiple spray patterns are both cool and convenient. Plus an extra-long hose on your faucet sprayer just might allow you to fill that heavy pot on the stove top. Yes, part of that difference is also the price—especially the decimal point—but consider the fact that the faucet is the most prominent feature on your countertop besides the countertop itself. Look for an easy-care finish that can disguise everyday wear and tear; we prefer brushed finishes over polished ones for the way they stylishly hide fingerprints.

One caveat about filtration systems is that you must commit to changing the filter regularly or have a system smart enough to alert you to do so. Otherwise, you'll be creating a haven for bacteria.

Waste Away

Add efficiency to your new sink with a high-tech food waste disposer. Yes, we know that you have been calling that thing that grinds potato peels and eats apple cores a "disposal" for years, but that's only the case if it was made by the fine folks at GE, who trademarked that name back in 1938 as a "machine for cutting or grinding garbage or the like." For the rest of the world, it's officially known as a "food waste disposer." But, enough of the history lesson.[27]

Today's high-tech disposers have the smarts to amp up the power to pulverize tough food waste, handle higher volumes, and do their job much more quietly than their predecessors did. Their virtual liquefication of waste is also safer for and easier on your septic or sewage system.

27.) And trademark defense.

Disposers aren't expensive, and we consider them to be the kind of appliance you never knew you needed, until you learn you can't live without them. Besides preventing many a stinking garage pail, feeding easily grindable stuff to a disposer will reduce your number of trips to the garbage can, easily saving you many steps over the life of the appliance.

Lighting for Task and Effect

When it comes to illuminating your kitchen, think "lightscape." Just as landscaping can beautify your exterior space and highlight activity zones, lightscaping can beautify your kitchen's interior while defining and improving the functionality of work areas.

Kitchens require three types of lighting: ambient, task, and accent. Ambient lighting is the overall light in the room, generally provided by larger fixtures and natural light from windows. Task lighting is focused and calibrated to specific work areas, such as counters. And accent lighting does just that—accents and highlights architectural details or objects within your redesigned space, such as lighting that points up from the top of your cabinets or rope lighting lining the undersides, which, incidentally, is a really easy do-it-yourself project.

When designing your light plan, realize that more light in the kitchen is not necessarily better. Smart lighting is. Make sure to match the amount and quality of light to the function in each area of the room. Compact fluorescent lamps, for example, use 25 to 35 percent less energy than incandescent lamps, provide the same amount of illumination, and last 10 times longer.

There's no shortage of fixture styles and sizes to choose from for each of these lighting types. And it's definitely okay to mix and match fixture styles. Put chandeliers over the dining area and install interesting pendants for task lighting. And to shed additional light on the subject, we love sticking little halogen puck lights under cabinets.

Pendant lights are an attractive task lighting solution.

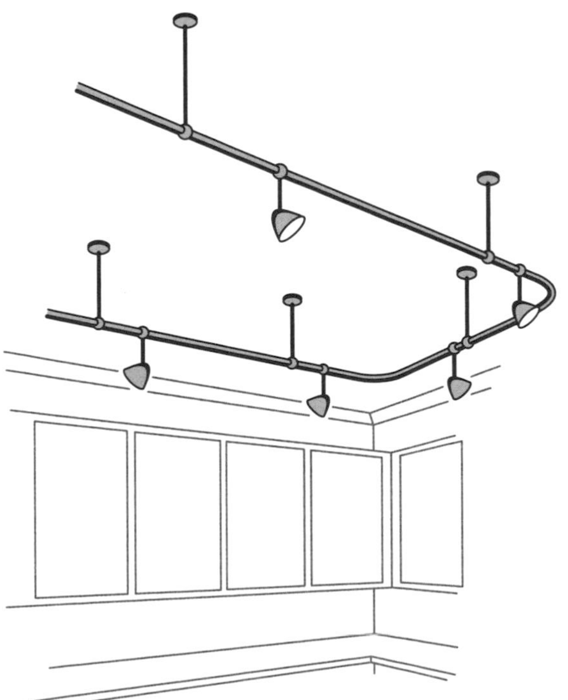

Track lights, strategically arranged, can create dramatic effects in your kitchen.

Chandeliers can create a wonderful dining experience especially when combined with a dimmer.

Set the Mood with Dimmers

In addition to better windows and designated light fixtures, consider incorporating dimmers into your lighting plan. Easy to install, dimmers work well to deliver just the right amount of light, depending on your mood. With dimmers, you can keep the lights at full brightness while preparing your meal, and then dial them down when it comes time to serve and entertain.

Get Naked

We mean your windows, not you, although what you do on your own time is not our business. Kitchens are a great place to forgo window treatments and create the "naked" window for maximum light. Since windows contribute to the ambient light in the room, leaving window coverings off can boost the brightness level significantly. Installing a bay or bow window or skylight can help to maximize the flow of sunlight while creating an expansive, open feeling in the space. Placing mirrors across from the windows amplifies the effect.

Leslie Likes: The Light Box Window

If a window won't fit in your kitchen, try a little stagecraft. Buy a light box or create your own with fluorescent tubes and decorative wood. Insert a transparent photo of your favorite vista, or create a piece of stained glass artwork to be illuminated from behind when placed over the plastic top of the box.

Tom's Tip: Let the Sunshine In

Velux Sun Tunnel skylights are tubes that run from the roof to an interior ceiling on any level. Sun Tunnels are mirror-coated on the inside so that they can bring in a lot of natural light without the expense of building a traditional skylight. I've installed these in kitchens, and when track lighting was added above the cabinets, it created some interesting colors in combination with the skylight.

Green Scene: Natural Light

Make use of natural light for a warm, welcoming kitchen with the following:

- *Minimize window treatments to allow more light in and create a transition to the great outdoors.*
- *Add a bay, bow, or greenhouse window to capture the light and create new space for seating, storage, or decorative displays.*
- *Bring in sunshine from above with traditional skylights or light "tubes" that shed natural light into dark spaces via their reflective linings.*

Appliances: Where Most Kitchen Remodels Begin

Fun factoid: Most kitchen remodels are born when an appliance breaks down, part of that "might as well" home improvement adventure thinking we discussed in the warm-up.

Kitchen appliances have an average life span of anywhere from 10 to 20 years. By the time one of these needs to be replaced, the kitchen décor is typically also outdated, so before you know it, the appliance replacement budget is quickly creeping skyward as new home improvement projects get added to the list.

Should you repair or replace a broken appliance? Several factors must be considered, including the age, cost of repair, and the chance that the appliance will break down again.

Use the chart below to help you decide. Here's how it works: Say, for example, you have a side-by-side refrigerator that is seven years old, and the compressor breaks. A new appliance would cost $1,200 but the compressor repair alone would be $350. Should you repair the compressor or replace the whole unit? Using the chart, you would note that a seven-year-old refrigerator still has low risk of a repetitive failure. Therefore, it's okay to spend up to 40 percent of the replacement cost on repair. Since the $350 repair cost is less than 40 percent of the $1,200 replacement value, you should go forward with the repair.

Repair or Replace? *That* Is the Question[28]

APPLIANCE	ESTIMATED COST		AGE RANGE	
RISK OF FAILURE		LOW RISK	MEDIUM RISK	HIGH RISK
Refrigerator	$500–$2,700	up to 8 years 40%	8 to 15 years 30%	16 years & up 20%
Range	$400–$1,900	up to 15 years 30%	15 to 25 years 20%	26 years & up 10%
Dishwasher	$450–$1,400	up to 10 years 40%	10 to 15 years 30%	16 years & up 20%
Built-in Microwave	$300–$1,200	up to 4 years 20%	4 to 10 years 15%	11 years & up 10%
Food Waste Disposer	$100–$350	up to 1 year see note	1 year and up Always Replace	Note: Food waste disposers are disposable. Repair only if under warranty. Otherwise replace.

28.) And about as close to Shakespeare as Tom ever gets.

If the decision is a close one, use the Energy Star ratings as a tie-breaker. In fact, replacing appliances even before they wear out can actually be cost-effective in the long run. A 10-year old refrigerator, for example, uses twice the electricity of a newer Energy Star–rated model. Today's refrigerators run on the same electricity as a 75-watt lightbulb, and there are new dishwashers and laundry appliances that clean more effectively with less water.

Be critical in assessing special features and their associated costs (will you really use that in-door icemaker enough to justify the price and the freezer space it takes up?). Be practical about the applications of appliances' overall design and their impact on your home's existing systems. A double oven may look stunning, but may also stun your home's power load, so a single-oven model with professional styling may be the better recipe for success. Double-door refrigerators with freezers on the bottom always have room for frozen pizzas. Newer smart designs for dishwashers and refrigerators replace single units with a series of drawers, but that convenience comes with a price.

Prerinsing Dishes: Do or Don't?

Let's settle that argument with your mother once and for all. Newer dishwashers include something called a turbidity sensor. When the dishwasher first comes on, it splashes a lot of water around and the turbidity sensor actually tells the dishwasher how dirty that water is and then adjusts the cycle time and the amount of soap to clean that level of dirtiness, so to speak. So if you prerinse the dishes and you remove all that easy-to-get-off stuff so that only the really hard gunk remains, the dishwasher's not going to properly detect the gunk level, and won't run as long as is needed to clean it away.

Access Everyone: Make Stoves Kid Safe

Stoves are a real danger zone. To prevent accidental burns and fires, turn all pot and pan handles away from the front of your stove and use the back burners whenever possible. Pull the lighter knobs off the stove when not in use and keep them nearby in a drawer. (Most knobs come off very easily for cleaning.) Teach kids to stay away from Mommy or Daddy when you're cooking. Also, when installing a new oven range, make sure you install the anti-tip brackets which prevent tip-over if kids ever climb up on an open oven door.

Ask Tom & Leslie: It's Good to Vent

Q. We have a vent fan over the stove that doesn't seem to have an outlet. Is this any good? Doesn't the stale air just keep circulating around the kitchen?

A. Well, yes . . . It would be more accurate to call what you and millions of others have a "non-venting" hood. These exhaust fans simply take your greasy, smoky cooking fumes and run them through a wimpy filter before sending the gaseous cloud right back atcha. In the best-case scenario, a vent fan should really vent—preferably outside your house. If your range happens to be on an inside, rather than exterior, wall, you can accomplish this by running a metal duct through the ceiling and out of the nearest exterior wall. If you choose not to run the vent to the exterior, make sure you clean or replace the filters regularly depending on the type your vent hood requires.

There are different types of fans, priced according to the how powerful the fan is and how much air is moved, measured in cubic feet per minute. If you cook a lot, and cook often with oils and grease, go for a more powerful vent. Prices also vary according to style, and vent hoods can be quite a design statement. Pay for function first and dedicate what's left to style.

Green Scene: Appliance Ratings

Although appliances may look the same from the outside, there are many differences under the hood. When replacing yours, choose ENERGY STAR–rated appliances. This designation means the appliance exceeds Department of Energy guidelines for efficiency by at least 10 percent. In addition to saving money on your energy bills, you may also be eligible for rebates offered by your local energy supplier.

The final wild card in the keep-or-dump-your-appliance game is an appliance's warranty. If you're one of the rare but fortunate folks who have the breakdown during the warranty period, go ahead and get the appliance fixed. However, we never, ever recommend you purchase extended warranties unless you are feeling extremely unlucky and, even then, you'd probably get a better return on investment working the slots in Las Vegas. Extended warranties are expensive for the coverage they provide. If you just can't stand an occasional unplanned expense, you'd be better off starting your own appliance repair fund.

Stainless steel is the look of the moment, yet most people are surprised when they try to put magnets on the refrigerator and they fall right off. If your fridge is your kids' art gallery, but you really want stainless steel, think about a bulletin board as an alternative.

Pulling It All Together: Kitchen Remodels

Yes, we've been there. It's worth it, we promise!

Leslie: From Pepto Pink to Perfect

When we bought our home, the kitchen countertops and backsplash were this horrible pink laminate. In fact, everything in the room was pink, including terra-cotta floors and cabinetry in this sort of warmish red-brown color. It was like a Pepto-Bismol nightmare in there, albeit a tiny nightmare, at just 130 square feet.

We pulled out all the countertops and, because we had such limited counter space, I was able to replace them with really high-end, fancy granite. I completely rebuilt the original breakfast nook, using an exterior newel post that's all turned and curved and pretty for the support leg. Next I painted the apron, the piece of wood that faces you below the countertop, as well as the new support leg, a beautiful, bright white and added a granite counter. Just adding that bit of white really helped tie everything together and made the warm brown cabinets stand out.

For the backsplash, instead of just putting up a new laminate or continuing the granite, I splurged on a crackle-finish tile, choosing the least-expensive detailed style, and made it look really grand and gorgeous by turning it on its side to create a diamond pattern. Then I closed

Leslie Likes: Appliance Makeovers

If your appliances are still in good working order but you can't stand the color, the best tip you'll ever learn is that appliances are often shipped with multiple color panels hidden behind the one you see. Changing your décor can be as easy as removing a few screws and pulling out a black or white panel for an instant update. Some appliances can also be repainted with help from a pro experienced in working with the appropriate finishes and techniques, and easy-to-use products like Liquid Stainless Steel allow you to brush on a new look quickly and affordably.

off the top where it blended into the upper cabinetry using a coordinating border tile.

By the way, I hired a pro to do the tiling so I could get that special diamond-pattern effect done efficiently instead of going through a box of tiles and a ton of trial-and-error cutting mistakes on my own.

In summary, we replaced the counter, added a different backsplash, built the cabinetry up to the ceiling, added crown molding through the entire space—some got painted, some got stained to match the cabinetry—and changed the sink and the faucet. The grand total for the project was about $7,000.

Tom: Kitchens Bright and Dark

My 300-square-foot kitchen was built in the 1880s, redone in the 1980s, and was horribly dark—dark tan walls, brown floor, dark stained-wood beams crisscrossing the ceiling, dark wood wainscoting halfway up the walls, and dark cherry cabinets.[29] We repainted all the walls and the ceilings the whitest white we could find, and added a skylight and a planter window to brighten the room. The brown flooring was replaced with a slate gray laminate floor, the countertop with stone-patterned Corian, and all the antique hardware on the cabinets was replaced with polished, era-appropriate knobs and pulls.

In our case, we hired a professional for the Corian. Even though I had the skills to build the Corian tops, I knew pros who worked with it every day were bound to be able to do the job better than I could.

For the countertops, flooring, and paint, we spent about $7,500.

Now that we have a great kitchen,
don't you think the bathroom could use some work?

29.) Did I mention the kitchen was dark?

CHAPTER 3

Bathrooms

When we were growing up, the role of the bathroom[30] was pit stop, plain and simple. A place for the necessaries, which at the time wasn't defined as different hair products for each family member. There are still many homes boasting those pinched spaces from another era, often accompanied by some decidedly ugly tile and fixture colors. We know. We've been there.

Today, people want a full scope of emotions and services from their bathrooms.[31] It's still where you bathe, but now it's more likely to be upright in a shower that might have multiple showerheads and sprays. It's still where you groom, but now it may be in a separate area complete with a lush custom-built vanity. It's still where you answer nature's call, but now that might be in a separate water closet or WC. It's where you need super high amounts of light and super low amounts of light, adequate hot water delivered as efficiently as possible, and a strong (ideally silent) venting system.

Considerations for bathroom remodeling include plumbing, electrical, structural issues, ventilation, and safety, all before you even start thinking about the vast array of cool products and styles. To keep your sanity in planning, as always, start at the end for best results in creating a safe, comfortable, and personalized bathroom space.

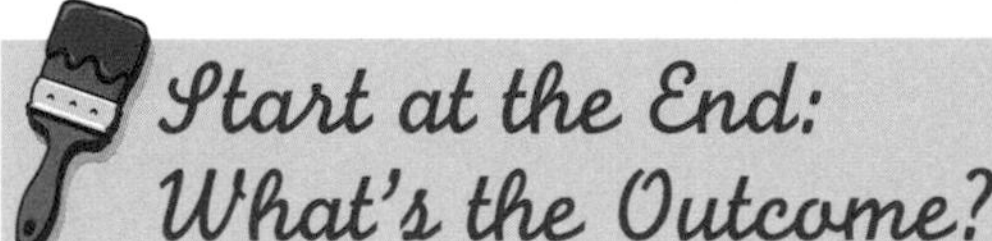

A lot of bathroom remodels start with a case of the uglies, so it's pretty easy to determine a goal to update outdated colors and styles. So the first thing to define is how your new bathroom will be used. Is this a high-traffic daily-use bathroom by you or your kids? Small children or teenagers? What kinds of guests will use the space? All ages, shapes, and sizes? For bathroom remodels, it's worth considering additional goals such as accessibility, safety, and comfort. Planning to add a stylish grab bar[32] near the toilet, for example, is a simple way to achieve just that.

If your bathroom is crowded and busting at the seams, you may need a more complex remodel to achieve the goal of more space. Ditto if your goal is to create the whole sanctuary experience with an in-home spa. A master bath should be fitted to its masters. Large baths can be great at resale, but prepare yourself for a major undertaking. Big bath remodels are time consuming and costly

Songs to Work By:

Tunes to help you get through your projects.

- *Born to Run*—Bruce Springsteen
- *Takin' Care of Business*—BTO
- *She Came in Through the Bathroom Window* —Joe Cocker or the Beatles
- *Splish Splash*—Bobby Darin
- *Take Me to the River*—Talking Heads
- *Rubber Ducky*—Ernie on *Sesame Street*
- *Cool Water*—Marty Robbins
- *All Things Must Pass*—George Harrison
- *Bath Water*—No Doubt
- *Never Miss the Water*—Chaka Khan
- *Standing in the Shower . . . Thinking* —Jane's Addiction
- Anything by Creedence Clearwater Revival

30.) Singular. Most homes built through the 1960s had one or one-and-a-half baths. If you don't believe us, watch *The Brady Bunch* on TV Land. Mike the architect didn't foresee the need for six teenagers to have more than one bathroom. 31.) Plural. The National Association of Home Builders reported that a quarter of all homes built in 2005 had three or more bathrooms. 32.) Yes, there is such a thing as a "stylish" grab bar. Several manufacturers make grab bars that match faucet finishes and other bath hardware to deliver a very non-hospital look for your space.

projects that can involve several professionals and take parts of your home out of service for some time while the work is being done.

Another consideration is ventilation. Peeling paint and constant mildew battles in the bathroom are a wake-up call to consider improving ventilation. Noncontrolled humidity can cause allergy problems, as well as damage windows, walls, and ceilings by encouraging the growth of molds, mildew, bacteria, dust mites, rot, and insects.

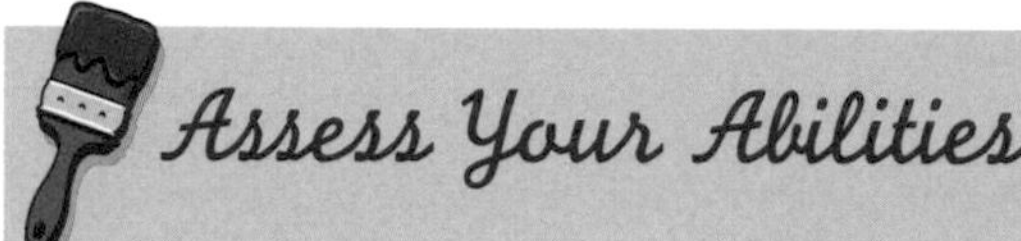

Assess Your Abilities

Bathroom facelifts—even those that include replacing the toilet and faucet—can often be done by do-it-yourselfers, thanks again to manufacturers making products that are easy to install.

As with the kitchen, you want to consider calling in a pro before you hit the wall. Your overall system must be calibrated to the needs of new fixtures—adequate hot water, adequate venting, adequate floor support. Filling up a cast-iron tub on a second floor could cause a real letdown, for instance . . . right onto the first floor.

If poor ventilation is turning your bathroom into a Petri dish, you'll want to call in an HVAC pro for a consultation. While most baths can be adequately vented with a ceiling fan, an option that's more powerful and quieter might be a remote fan. This professionally installed system uses ducts to draw air from the bath ceiling to an exhaust fan located somewhere else in the house, like the attic, where both steam and stink can be swiftly carried outside.

As with kitchens, the trickier the space, the more likely it is that a designer or architect will add value to your bathroom remodel.[34] Design services make sense at two ends of the bathroom remodeling spectrum: remodeling a very large bathroom or trying to fit everything into a small one. Designers with specialized expertise can also be invaluable in creating a bathroom remodel to accommodate someone with special needs.

Building Bigger Baths

We know you have your eye on the kids' rooms for taking over and expanding the bath when they spread their wings and fly from the nest.[33] Is it a good investment? We would say yes because it means your child can't boomerang back after college . . . and also because larger bathrooms and multiple bathrooms are major selling features in today's new homes. The easiest place to put in a second bathroom is above, below, or next to the existing bathroom.

One situation where we'd think twice, however, is knocking out a closet to accomplish a larger bath: adequate storage trumps just about everything else in a resale situation. A good compromise might be adding a half bath with an adequate grooming area to accommodate guests, without encouraging long-term settling-in of the boomerang kid.

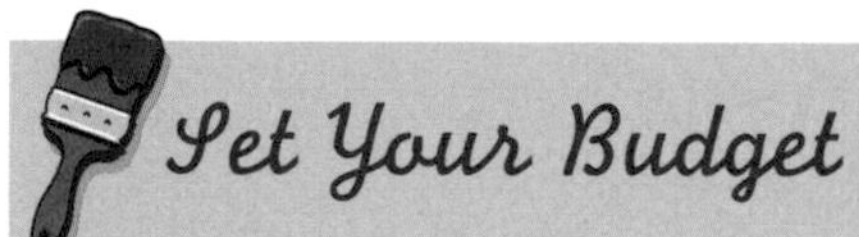

Set Your Budget

The "average" bathroom facelift remodel can run from less than $1,000 to $5,000, depending on your replacement plans for flooring, faucets, and fixtures. Complex bathroom remodels, such as replacing a tub

Link Up: Comfort and Safety Checklist

Build safety and comfort into your bathroom remodel with the help of AARP's Bathroom Checklist, and browse product shopping tips at www.aarp.org/homedesign.

33.) If not sooner. 34.) Unless he's Mike Brady.

with a shower system or expanding the footprint, start north of $10,000, most often in the $15,000 to $20,000 range.

A design plan can run anywhere from several hundred to more than $1,000, but may be money very well spent. Pro designers can help you avoid hiccups in your plan and keep your Port-a-Potty time to a minimum while the project is being done.

Facelifts: The Lighter Side of Bathroom Remodeling

If you're planning a facelift for the typical small bathroom, remember that light colors always open up a small space visually. Beyond wall color and linens, you can bring in lightness through a vanity with lighter woods or, even better, vanities that incorporate glass. Small spaces can benefit from selection of clever storage options like étagères, "totems," and apothecary cabinets that are tall and narrow. Furniture and a pedestal sink with expansive surface area can make it look like you bulldozed the wall on your old 5-by-7-foot bathroom.

Painting in the Bathroom

A new coat of paint is a super-affordable start to a facelift, especially with all of the moisture-resistant formulations and colors now available. In some new bathrooms, we see tonal minimalism: fewer colors—often shades of beige and white—with a layering of textures.

Bathroom Flooring

Presumably, it goes without saying that bathroom flooring needs to be waterproof. It should also be slip-resistant. Good materials for bathroom floors include tile and stone. Proper abrasion resistance (PEI) ratings are an indication of the tile's hardness and can help you choose styles that are manufactured for the amount of traffic an area will see. Ratings run from PEI 1 to PEI 5, and the lower the number, the softer the finish will be.

Slip resistance is also a critical consideration. Floor tiles can be used for walls, but wall tiles should never be used for floors, as they are too slippery. Most tile manufacturers will list the "COF" rating of their tiles on the packaging or in the literature. This stands for the "coefficient of friction" and is a measure of how slippery the surface is when wet or dry. A COF of "Class 0" means that the tile should only be used on a wall, while a COF of "Class III" or better is best for most residential floor applications. Basically, the lower the number, the more slippery the tile.

A less common but equally appropriate flooring choice is laminate. Highly moisture-resistant, and easy for DIYers to install, laminate can look like tile, stone, or even wood.

Tom's Tip: **Caulk as a Style Statement**

Recaulking as a style statement? Actually, it's true: the bathroom can look brighter and newer by simply recaulking your tub and its surround. Want real caulk drama? Red Devil offers a caulk coloring system called Create-A-Color that allows you to mix up almost every color in the rainbow.

Accessories, Faucets, and Hardware

Often considered the "jewelry" of the bath, faucets, accessories, and decorative hardware are similar to jewelry in that trends in finishes are always evolving. Today, it's warmed-up cool tones such as nickel and bronze that are popular. As styles change, these are easy elements to replace in a bathroom.

Ideally, they are only replaced for style reasons, and not for performance. Bathroom sink faucets at moderate price points should last for years, with today's better-protected finishes and drip-free valving.

Low-maintenance faucets can include brass or chrome, as well as old-world-looking finishes like brushed nickel or antique finishes that are applied using PVD (physical vapor disposition) technology. The PVD process provides a durable, scratch-resistant coating from an electrostatic application of extremely thin but extremely dense coatings of exotic metal alloys such as titanium nitride. No matter how protected your new finish, however, be gentle with your faucets if your want them to keep looking great. Matte finishes do a great job of hiding fingerprints.

If you've shopped for faucets and found two that looked almost alike, but had a wide variance in price, they probably have different engineering and valving technology. Seamless, one-piece cast-brass bodies are easier to clean; and it's definitely worthwhile to invest in faucets that have ceramic disc valving, because that's the gold standard in drip-free performance.

Fancy Faucets: Sink faucets can be mounted on the sink itself, on the deck or countertop, or above the sink on the wall.

Bathroom faucets come in all kinds of configurations: deck-mounted (meaning mounted on the countertop), wall-mounted, and sink-mounted. They come in single-control and two-handle styles. Avoid a tiny faucet on a big, bold sink, and vice versa. Remember the jewelry idea: no delicate pearls on bold patterns!

Green Scene: Aerators Slow the Flow of Utility Dollars

Slow the flow of utility dollars by installing a water faucet aerator on your bathroom sink. Some older faucets out there may still be running at a rate of 4 gallons per minute when fully opened, but by simply replacing the existing aerator with a low-flow unit, you can cut the volume back to 2.5 gallons per minute—that's a 40 percent reduction.

Access Everyone: The Most Dangerous Room in the House

The bathroom is actually the most dangerous room in the house, and not just after your father-in-law has been in there with his Wall Street Journal. *Smart bathroom design is accessible design. Think nonslip floors, fixtures with comfortable heights, grab bars in strategic locations, and rocker light switches. Install shower stalls with doors that open outward in the event that you do slip and fall, and need some help getting out. Single-control faucets also offer the convenience of one-handed control over volume and temperature, enabling easy rinsing of the other hand. Some single-control faucets feature a temperature limit stop that allows you to restrict how much hot water is mixed with cold, providing safety from scalding in bathrooms used by small children as well as energy savings.*

Let There Be Light . . . Lots of It!

Bathroom lighting is about stylish design as well as function. It's one of the easiest ways to set a mood in the space, as well as the first defense against walking out the door with way too much blush on. Ideally, your bathroom should feature three kinds of lighting: task or general lighting, accent lighting, and decorative lighting. Natural light is also important as part of the scheme in an up-to-date design.

Let's start with that grooming station. For best results with the shaving and makeup details, task lighting in this zone should illuminate your sink area with 60-watt, 120-volt bulbs. If you have a wide vanity, consider a four-lamp fixture or bar light mounted above the mirror to send light cascading downward. There are lots of beautifully designed, ready-made fixtures out there, and you can also create your own by purchasing a light base at your local home improvement center and mixing and matching shades that complement your bathroom's style, all for around $50.

For a single pedestal sink, use vanity wall sconces as accent lighting on each side of the coordinating mirror to illuminate the space. These typically use 40-watt, 120-volt bulbs and range from simple styles to elaborate bases with hand-blown art glass.

Task lighting in the shower is also cool, although at first blush the idea of mixing water and electricity seems, er, shockingly counterintuitive. A flush ceiling light with a 100-watt, 120-volt halogen lamp provides great light and a brushed stainless steel housing that prevents rust.

Decorative lights showcase the architectural features of the bathroom. If it has tall ceilings and crown molding, consider a small antique chandelier to dress up the room. Or, if there's a stand-alone whirlpool, use decorative pendant lights to provide subtle illumination for the bath. You can also use toe-kick lighting under a sink vanity to deliver a cool glow to a dark space.

Natural light is ideal, if you can swing it in your space. Use windows that incorporate built-in blinds which never need cleaning, or check into the new smart windows with gas-filled panes that electronically darken for privacy at the touch of a button; use glass or plastic blocks to build windows or partition walls; or install skylights that flood the bathroom with sunshine (those Sun Tunnel skylights we talked about back in the Kitchen chapter are a great option for bathrooms as well). Smart use of mirrors can also help you throw some light around, so shop for pieces that'll serve you well in terms of both utility and décor.

Another addition that can dramatically change the existing lighting in your bath is to simply replace your old-fashioned toggle switches with dimmers. We love these easy-to-install solutions for both their utility and mood-setting potential. Separate controls for each end of a two-sink vanity allow each groomer to adjust the lighting level to the task at hand, whether it's creating that sanctuary vibe for a long soak in the tub, shedding light on a close shave, or dimming all the way down until you get some coffee into you.

Best Bath Lighting: For best bath lighting, combine vanity, wall sconce, and ceiling fixtures to illuminate all angles. Hang your mirror no more than 6 inches under the upper light fixture and place sconces at both sides of the mirror approximately 60 and 72 inches off the floor, depending on the height of family members.

Plumbing Fixtures

New sinks, showers, tubs, and toilets are the centerpiece of any bath remodel. Here are solutions that will leave you flush with excitement.[35]

Selections in Sinks

Stepping up to the bathroom sink, there are a few different styles to dip into, depending on the space you have and the level of installation difficulty you're willing to take on. Drop-in sinks are the easiest to install, as their name implies, and are simply set into a cutout in the surface of your bathroom countertop or vanity cabinet. Correct sizing between the two is critical, and you'll also want to make sure that there are no obstructions

35.) Sorry, we find it hard to resist any opportunity for toilet humor.

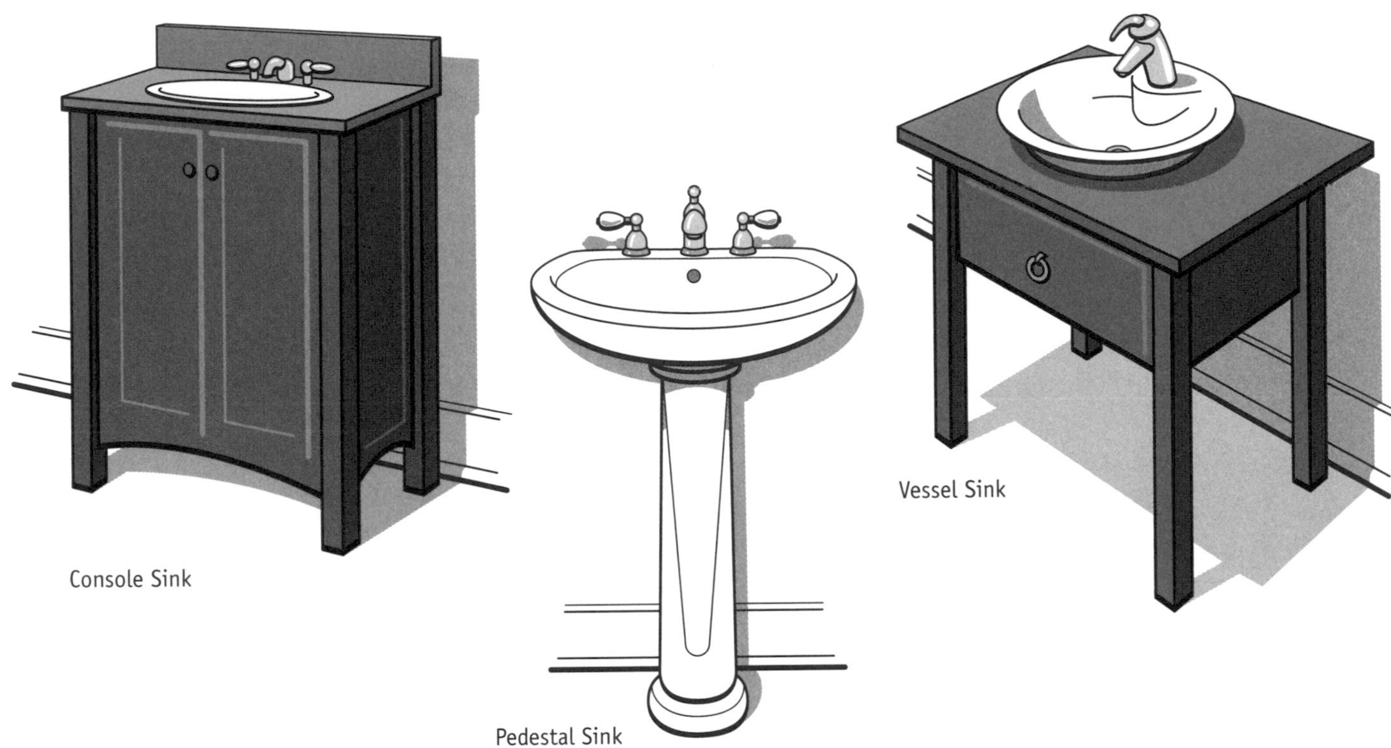

Console Sink

Pedestal Sink

Vessel Sink

underneath to interfere with the plumbing or the bowl itself. Under-counter mounting is another way to go, contributing to a sleek countertop surface and easy cleaning, and focusing attention on the fancy faucet mounted on the countertop above.

Bigger statements can be made with pedestal sinks, console tables, and vessel sinks, which all have a stand-alone, custom-furnishing feel. Pedestal sinks typically offer sophisticated styling, larger-than-standard bowls, and make a small bathroom appear larger. Console sinks with legs achieve the same visual illusion, but often with the added benefit of added storage and more counter space.

Vessel sinks sit atop surfaces like objets d'art, ranging from petite Asian tansu chests to swatches of stone. If you're drawn to the vessel look, shop for a faucet that directs water into the center of the bowl. Faucets can also be mounted on the wall behind the vessel sink or atop the furniture item it is placed upon. Check to make sure the water in your delicate curved vessel sink doesn't shoot back out and indelicately drench the user. We recommend vessel sinks for use in powder rooms, where they get the attention they deserve, versus using them as everyday sinks.[36]

Leslie Likes: **Separate Grooming Spaces**

Even in bathrooms with small spaces, when the budget and plumbing capacity will allow, nothing brings harmony to our bathroom like separate grooming stations. Two sinks, two mirrors, two areas, one for each person to get ready.

We went from apartment living for eight years to a house that has two sinks, and it's the greatest thing we've ever had in our entire life. We get to use the space separately even though we're together, without interfering in each other's routines.[37]

36.) It can be disconcerting to spit toothpaste in an objet d'art every day. 37.) Tom adds: I love my wife, but I'd just as soon not groom with her.

Finally, make sure your new faucet matches the hole drillings in your sink, or, for an undermount sink, that you have room on your countertop to drill through.

Today's bathroom furniture options go well beyond consoles, and are so much smarter than those old vanities with the voluminous wasted space under the sink. It can be awesome to retrofit an old vanity to create a custom piece, but we really like furniture that comes from bathroom experts, like Kohler and American Standard. It's scaled appropriately with storage options built cleverly around the plumbing.

Finally, install sinks and vanities at a comfortable height of around 34 inches that allows for standing or sitting while washing.

Toilet Tricks for Determining House Age

Ever wonder how old your house really is? Here's a trick of the trade that can flush out the answer—literally! If your home has its original toilet, remove the lid and look at the underside. Toilets are almost always date-stamped by the manufacturer as they rolled off the assembly line. The date is typically expressed as a four-digit number like "1954," but it might also be preceded by a letter and have just the last two digits (for example, "M54"). Other plumbing fixtures like sinks also have the dates stamped somewhere in their castings, but those on the toilet are often the easiest to find. Spot a date on your toilet, and you can bet your home was constructed with in a few months or a year of that date.

Potty Talk: Tips for Toilets That Really Work

Running toilets and clogging toilets drive our audience to distraction, generating lots of calls to us and lots of desperate "Honey, where's the plunger?" calls.

By now, you're probably familiar with the Energy Policy and Conservation Act, the law that took effect in 1994 that required all toilets manufactured in the U.S. to use no more than 1.6 gallons (6 liters) of water per flush, rather than the previously allowed 3.5 gallons per flush (GPF).

Pulitzer Prize–winning humorist Dave Barry told MSNBC's *10 Questions* in 2007 that his column about that law and its impact generated one of the biggest responses during his career as a newspaper columnist: "We bought a house and we had new toilets and they didn't work very well, and I thought there was something wrong with our toilets. And the plumber came and I said, 'Can you fix our toilets?' and he said, 'No. That's the law now.'

"I wrote a column about it, and it turns out about nine million Americans had the same experience. That got an incredibly strong reaction that still reverberates. I am known as the guy that 'tore the lid' off that story."

If you've heard of the law, it's probably because you, like Dave Barry, had occasion to experience one of the early 1.6-GPF toilets. Which also means many of you are also fairly close pals with your plunger(s).

The good news is that today's toilets work. It took manufacturers a few years to catch up to the change in the federal law, but many contemporary toilets work better than the originals—some flushing on even less water! If the plunger is still a big part of your life—or if you're still clinging

Link Up: Who Has Higher Test Scores, You or Your Toilet?

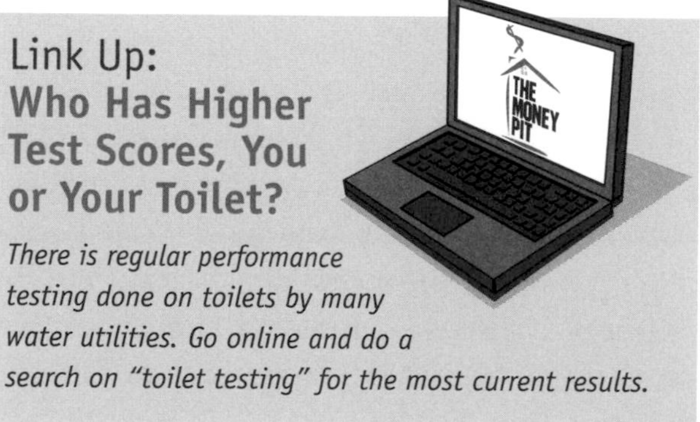

There is regular performance testing done on toilets by many water utilities. Go online and do a search on "toilet testing" for the most current results.

Access Everyone: Pint-sized Toilets

For the younger members of your family, there are actually cute little toilets you can buy from both American Standard and Gerber that are smaller and more accessible for the newly toilet-trained among us. Yes, you'll have to replace the toilet in a few years, but it's not a big deal to do so. American Standard also makes a great vanity called Generations with a convenient pull-out step for kids that doubles as a safe, handy stool when you need to replace lightbulbs over the vanity.

to an old water hog while you and your neighbors are subject to watering bans in drought-stricken areas—you can definitely benefit by overthrowing the old throne.

Toilets have long been made of a durable china called vitreous china, and are available in one-piece and two-piece styles. One-piece versions are sleek in design without the crevice between the tank and bowl that can collect splashes and be difficult to clean. Two-piece toilets are generally less expensive.

There have been some pretty fancy innovations in the tank, so your first peek inside won't look anything like you might remember from watching Dad fix the toilet. These are technologies that have arisen since the days when Dave Barry rallied a nation to reject bad flushers. Things to look for include wide, fully glazed trapways—the part that snakes out the back of the bowl—with the proven power to scour the bowl clean with each flush. By the way, trapway is a bit of a misnomer, since the better toilets have wider traps so they don't, well, trap the you-know-what.

Toilet bowls are offered in elongated and round-front. Elongated bowl rims are about 2 inches longer (front-to-back) than a round-front

Green Scene: What's WaterSense?

The folks who brought ENERGY STAR labeling to the world of electrical appliances have now made it just as easy to shop for water-wise fixtures. The WaterSense label made its debut in 2007, first showing up on qualifying high-efficiency toilets (HETs). HETs cut down on the current standard maximum of 1.6 gallons per flush (GPF) by 20 percent to 1.28 GPF.

If the thought of giving up even more water in your toilet fills you with clog dread, relax. The WaterSense label tells you a product will conserve more water and perform more efficiently than one without the label. To earn the WaterSense mark, products are tested to meet stringent guidelines such as being able to flush away a minimum of 350 grams of soybean paste (you get the idea) and include a flush valve flapper or seal on the flush with the test-proven chemical resistance to ensure that exposure to chlorine and hard water won't lead to leaks over time.

Next up for this program is a WaterSense label for water-efficient bathroom sink faucets, followed by other indoor plumbing products like showerheads that use 1.5 gallons per minute (GPM) or 40 percent less water than current code requirements. Manufacturers are ahead of the curve on this one, with specially engineered showerheads that create a more forceful flow using less water. For the latest on the program, go to www.epa.gov/watersense.

Tom's Tip: Don't Take a Leak

Think your toilet is leaking? Drop some food coloring into the tank, then wait a couple of hours and check the bowl. If any of the food coloring shows up in the bowl, your flush valve is leaking and needs to be replaced. The job takes about 15 minutes and costs just a few bucks but can save thousands of gallons of otherwise wasted water.

Link Up: **Professor Flush**

For toilet repair trouble-shooting, we recommend consulting with Professor Flush at www.fluidmaster.com. Here are a few common problems and their solutions:

- *If the linkage between the flush handle and trip lever or metal tank lever is so corroded that it won't move up and down freely, tighten the set-screw on the handle linkage or replace the flush handle/lever.*
- *Clogged flush passages, the small holes under the bowl's rim, can restrict the flow of water during a flush; reach and clear away any obstructions using a piece of wire.*
- *Got a tank ball or flapper that closes before the tank empties? Adjust the chain length so that it has only the slightest amount of slack, or replace the tank ball or flapper.*

Ask Tom & Leslie: **Busting Ghost Flushing**

Does your toilet flush all by itself?[38] *"Ghost flushing" and leaky toilets generate frequent questions from* The Money Pit *audience.*

The culprits behind both bathroom phenomena are the fill and flush valves, which happen to be the only moving parts inside a toilet. The flush valve sits at the bottom of the tank and opens to drain the water out of the tank to refill the bowl; the fill valve refills the tank once that happens. Both can wear out from cleaning chemicals, sustained exposure to water, and the rigors of regular use, leading to leaks. Once the flush valve starts to leak, the bowl's water level drifts down to the trigger point, and the fill valve jumps into action to make up the loss, leading to that mysterious flushing. You can stop the leaks and the haunting with a few dollars and a quick trip to the hardware store for replacement valves, which are easy to install and pay for themselves over and over again in water savings.

bowl. Most people are more comfortable using an elongated toilet bowl, while round-front bowls can save space in smaller baths.

Toilet seats have a seat of power now in the bathroom, with features like heat (see the section on "Biggest Bathroom Remodels"). If you can swing it, opt for helpful features like seats that snap off for easy cleaning, and slow-close seats that increase the chances of men in your home actually putting down the seat.

Bathroom Décor: The Finishing Touch

You can make a big statement in the bathroom without a lot of time or cost. Repaint and buy new linens, a shower curtain, and rugs, and you might actually elicit a faint smile of approval from your mother-in-law.

We recommend creating a calming retreat by appealing to all five senses in your new bathroom design:

- **Sight.** Clear away any clutter, which only serves to clog the mind and stress the spirit. Use baskets or other containers to keep essentials in place. Choose soothing, nature-inspired colors, especially watery hues like blues, greens, and aquas. Add a dimmer switch to control lighting, and add candles to create a relaxing mood.

38.) And notice how it's never after one of the kids forgets to flush?

- **Touch.** Accessorize with lush, luxurious bath linens, and create a welcoming display by placing rolled towels in a basket with a few special soaps. For more softness, add area rugs instead of bathmats.

- **Smell.** Aromatherapy or scented candles can enhance your bathing experience.

- **Sound.** Add a sound machine, docking station for your MP3 player, or extend your home's built-in audio system to the bathroom.

- **Taste.** Accompany your relaxing bath with a steaming-hot cup of cocoa, coffee, or tea. You might even consider adding a single-serving coffeemaker in your new space.

In recent years, bath décor has been taking cues from high-end hotels that go to great lengths to create an experience that is pleasing to their guests. Elements like a curved shower rod, architecturally interesting towel bars, or a tone-on-tone color scheme can add class and functionality to a small space.

In larger spaces, go for the unexpected. Vintage accent pieces such as a slipper chair can be a lot of fun!

Biggest Bathroom Remodels: Home Spa Sanctuary

If your bath remodel dreams are big, you're probably pining for a gentle bubble-bath experience or maybe a shower spa, stepping out onto a perfectly heated floor, reaching for your toasty heated towel, and easing back onto a prewarmed toilet seat.

Steamy assignations such as these will need a good hot water system and adequate ventilation. But let's start by looking at the fun stuff: shower systems, whirlpools, and radiant heating.

Shower Smarts

In the old days, every bathroom had a bathtub, but the need just isn't there anymore. Most of us prefer showering. And you can get a lot more room in a small space by replacing an old tub with a walk-in shower.

To keep a handle on costs, plan around your existing drain as an alcove, your basic three-wall design, or possibly a larger corner neo-angle. A corner shower typically gives you more elbowroom than an alcove shower.

Shower valves are nearly all single-handle these days, an accessible design feature that gained mainstream acceptance because it's just so much easier to use. At a minimum, you'll want a pressure-balance valve—required by code in many places—to keep water temperatures in a consistent, comfortable zone. Moen's popular Posi-Temp is a pressure-

Access Everyone: **Preventing Door Jams**

If you're doing a major bathroom remodel, take the opportunity to widen the door to at least 32 inches across, have it open outward, and use an easy-grasp lever handle. Another alternative is a pocket door that can increase usable space as well as accessibility to the bath and other rooms. For existing doors, replace standard hinges with "offset" hinges to gain an extra 1 to 2 inches in width when the door is fully open.

balancing cycling valve which maintains water pressure so effectively that when running a dishwasher or flushing a toilet, this valve ensures that the water remains a constant + 3°F to keep the shower temperature consistent, comfortable, and safe.

Another nice-to-have is a thermostatic shower valve. These valves maintain comfortable temperatures through changes to the temperatures of the hot and cold water supplies, not just changes to the pressure. Once you know your favorite shower temperature, it's simply a matter of opening the on/off valve that controls the desired sprays. As a result, less water is wasted waiting for the perfect temperature. In addition, thermostats usually offer greater flow rates for shower systems operating four or more sprays at once.

If we just lost you with that last line, we're not surprised. Planning a luxury shower with multiple sprays is best done in consultation with your plumber and/or designer. A successful outcome to a luxury shower adventure includes:

- Available water pressure
- Household hot water capacity
- Locating control valves for safety and convenience
- Supply and drain pipe sizing and conditions
- Local plumbing codes

Access Everyone: **Walk-in Bathing**

Make your walk-in shower comfortable and usable for all generations. A hand-held shower is a much better option than a wall-mounted showerhead because it can be adjusted up to reach your tall brother and down and out to reach Rover. Add a seat to make it easier to bathe when you're sick, injured, or otherwise limited in mobility, such as when you're out of coffee.

What about those bathtubs with the doors? In theory, not a bad idea, but for the money, we strongly recommend going the shower/shower seat route. When your bathing is done, you step out and dry off, rather than sitting waiting for the tub to drain.

Types of showerheads include rain showerheads, body sprays, overhead tiles, and shower towers that combine all of the above. The shower system folks at Hansgrohe call these "vertical whirlpools"—a pretty accurate assessment and far more lyrical than "human car wash." These elaborate systems with multiple sprays require specialized valving to control the flow of water to the various outlets. That includes on/off volume controls to direct the flow of water to a showerhead or other sprays and diverters to distribute water among the showerheads and other sprays.

Code requires each showerhead to deliver no more than 2.5 gallons of water per minute (GPM). That's per showerhead, which means a shower with multiple showerheads can use a lot of water in a very short time. So most folks don't actually use all the showerheads at once, but instead use diverters to create a series of experiences using different combinations of the showerheads and body sprays.

Less-expensive alternatives are so-called shower towers that can be installed without going behind the wall. American Standard's VertiSpa is one such product we love. It installs in 30 minutes without the need to replumb your bathroom.

Tom's Tip: **Flush Your Faucets**

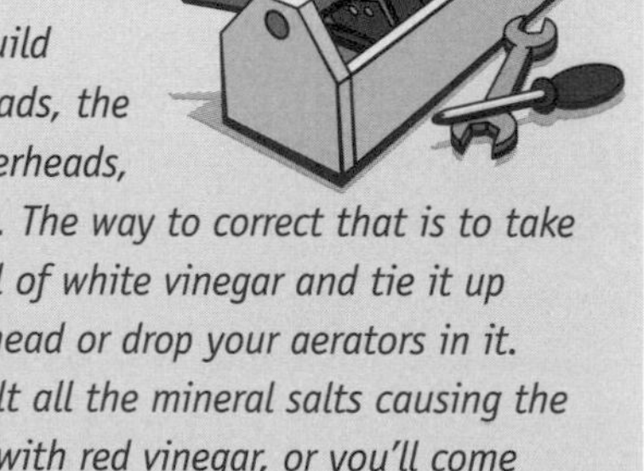

Mineral salts can build up in the faucet heads, the aerators, and showerheads, clogging water flow. The way to correct that is to take a plastic baggie full of white vinegar and tie it up around the showerhead or drop your aerators in it. The vinegar will melt all the mineral salts causing the clog. Don't try this with red vinegar, or you'll come out of the shower smelling like a salad. Don't ask how we know. We just do.

Blown Away: Whirlpools, Air Baths, and Bathtubs to Soothe Sore Home Improvement Muscles

Few moments are more relaxing in life than dropping into a bubbling tub after a hard day of hammer swinging. But taking that dip into the bathtub replacement scene requires ticking off a checklist of sizing and water supply factors. Work with a plumber to understand limiting factors such as access points for pumps, drains, and water supplies.

Sit in the tub before you purchase it. We're serious. You wouldn't buy a car without sitting behind the wheel, and a bath should be no different, although we do recommend staying fully clothed or risking an incident. Some tubs that look smashing in photographs aren't all that comfortable. Keep these questions in mind: Does it fit your body type comfortably? Are the controls conveniently located? Do the jets aim at the right spots or dig right into where you want to sit? Check lumbar and neck supports, as well as armrests and grab bars. Most manufacturers offer a wide range of choices, from contemporary to traditional, in an array of different colors. Find your comfort, and then pick your color.

Types of Installation

Bathtub installation is tricky business. Choosing the right one for your space can mean the difference between a successful soaking and having to bathe using the garden hose. Here are the options:

- **Recessed.** If you have a small bathroom, you probably have a recessed tub with three sides of the tub directly attached to walls. You can actually get nice, deep soaking tubs and whirlpools to fit into this space.
- **Corner.** Similar to recessed, but only two sides are attached directly to walls. You need some space to consider a corner tub.
- **Drop-in/undermount.** These can be dramatic designs, the type you see in magazines. The tub is surrounded by a platform, which is often finished with breathtaking natural stone. Safety is key—don't use stone for "steps." And no one does sunken tubs anymore, because it's just too easy to step back to check your makeup and fall backwards into the tub.
- **Freestanding.** The look is amazing: old-fashioned claw-footed tubs and other sculptural bathtubs. Elaborate trim such as shower walls, overhead showers, and even body sprays are offered on these high-end luxury baths. For master bath and high-use locations, check the comfort of free-standing tubs to make sure you can live with the style over time. The combined weight of cast iron and water should be considered for second-story installations, not to mention the weight of getting the tub up there in the first place.

Whirlpools/Air Tubs

After a hard day of taming your Money Pit, there's nothing quite so nice as dropping into a relaxing whirlpool bath. To put you in the lap of luxury, today you can choose your massage therapy: hydro, air, or both.

- **Hydro massage.** This is the more common type, in which a water pump recirculates bathwater out several jets. Most offer user control to mix air into the water coming out of the jets, which reduces the force of the water as well as adding an invigorating feeling from the air bubbles. For regular users, a heater is a nice option to consider. Ask about the noise level of the motor to make sure your planned relaxation doesn't sound like you've just been permanently seated next to the jet engine in row 36.

- **Air massage.** Tiny bubbles, better than the song. Air pumps engulf the user with thousands of tiny bubbles coming from small holes in the bottom and sides of the tub. People tell us they like them better than whirlpools, because they are quieter and more relaxing, but we couldn't tell you because we still have tiny bathrooms. Better systems heat the air before it enters the tub, as cool air can quickly lower the temperature of the water.

If you can't decide, and whirlpool bathing is a big part of your life, look for tubs that have the best of both options. If money is absolutely no object, tubs that have chromatherapy (colored light) and sound systems sound like a dream to us.

Leslie Likes: Deep Thoughts

I stayed at a hotel in Austin, Texas, that had the deepest, biggest bathtub I've ever experienced in my entire life. I could literally sit up in it with my legs straight and the water up to my neck. It was the most miraculous thing. I took a bath every day. If you can get a nice deep bath—even a deeper one that fits in an existing space or recessed area, go for it!

Smarter Hot Water

The grander the bathroom, the more hot water delivery becomes an issue. One of the things we get asked about most is, "Why does it take so long for me to get hot water in my bathroom?"

Think about the physical distance between your water heater, wherever that is, and the bathroom itself. Until the hot water that's being generated at the water heater has a chance to travel that full distance, you're not going to feel it at the tap.

The next question is usually, "If I add a tankless water heater, will I get hot water more quickly?" And the answer, of course, is "no" if that tankless water heater is going to be in the same place as the existing one. Since tankless water heaters are smaller than traditional tank-type heaters, you can add one to your existing system and effectively zone your domestic hot water system by having two complete supply loops (one upstairs and one downstairs, for instance). That way, you're not pulling water all the way from the basement up to a second-floor master bath every morning, waiting and wasting a lot of water in the process. For more tips on water heating options, see Chapter 8.

If you're thinking of adding or upgrading fixtures, be clear on whether or not your existing plumbing system will be able to provide the water supply, pressure, and temperatures required. The age of your home is the first clue, because that'll tell you what kind of piping you have to work with. For instance, if you have a pre-1930s classic of a home, you've probably got steel or iron pipes. These cut down on water pressure and supply over time thanks to interior rusting that actually closes down the flow, kind of like a clogged artery.

Pipe replacement with a more modern, dependable material (such as strong, flexible PEX) is definitely an option if you fall into the clogged-pipe zone, although it's also definitely expensive and complicated. A three-step approach can help control costs and isolate the problem areas, and we recommend starting by replacing the main water line from the well to your house. Second, replace all accessible, horizontal steel pipes, such as those in the basement. Then finish by replacing any inaccessible pipes, such as those that feed the upstairs baths, on a case-by-case basis.

Heated Tootsies and Tushies

Winter mornings in New York and New Jersey aren't as bad as in some parts of our country, but come January, we love the idea of stepping out of the shower onto a nice warm floor.

Adding radiant heat to the bath can actually be a do-it-yourself project, assuming experience with electricity. Radiant heat panels—like mini electric blankets—can be placed under wood, laminate, or tile. A thin electric mat installed in thin-set cement and controlled by a timer-thermostat will cost about $500 to $700 to install in an average-size bathroom, and will operate on less than 10 cents a day in electricity.

For the ultimate creature comfort, consider one of the most advanced toilet seats we've ever seen. It's made by TOTO and is called a Washlet. Designed to fit on select TOTO toilets, it features a built-in bidet and warmed seat that automatically opens when you approach and closes when you leave. The manufacturer lists other benefits including "front and rear washing," "automatic air purifier," and our favorite, a "wireless remote control."[39] Seems like they've thought of everything!

Vent Your Steam

Bathroom fans are essential when remodeling to prevent peeling wallpaper and mildew, and to keep the air clean. Look for fans that are powerful enough for the room's size and make sure the noise level is to your satisfaction. Utility exhaust fans are great for reducing odors and moisture, such as in the kitchen, while fan-forced heat models are most common in colder rooms such as the bathroom.

We recommend installing the bathroom fan on a timer circuit. You might want to have it hooked up to what's called an occupancy sensor so it comes on when people enter the bathroom and stays on for a few minutes after there's no motion detected in the room.

There are two kinds of fans that can do the job: bath fans and remote fans, also known as multi-port ventilators. Bath fans are installed directly in the bathroom, usually on the ceiling, and discharge moisture to the exterior via a duct.

Multi-port ventilators are mounted elsewhere in the building, such as the attic, and use ducts to exhaust air from one or more baths at the same time. In addition to being able to handle larger baths, one popular advantage of a multi-port ventilator is that it's extremely quiet. Since the fan is mounted in a remote location, very little sound is transmitted to the bath.

With either type of fan, you can also add efficiency by installing a timer circuit and occupancy sensor to ensure that the vent works when it should and for the right amount of time to properly vent your space (after a hot bath or shower has concluded, the vent should be running an extra 15 or 20 minutes; with the help of a timer, the job is done and you don't have to worry about going back to flip a switch yourself).

Besides choice of fan, the other major factor here is making sure that the fan is vented correctly and free of obstructions such as insulation. A lot of homes were built with the bathroom venting into the attic or back into the house, which only transfers the moisture and mold problem to another spot in the home. Efficient bathroom ventilators must vent to the outdoors, sending moisture back into the environment.

For bathrooms up to 100 square feet in area, the Home Ventilation Institute (HVI) recommends that an exhaust fan operate at a rate of 1 cubic foot per minute (CFM) per square foot (approximately eight air changes per hour) to properly ventilate the

39.) A remote you really don't want to misplace.

It Happened to Tom: **The Vent to Nowhere**

In the years that I spent as a home inspector, I'd find vents installed and that was it—they wouldn't be ducted out. Or the vent was installed and was just pointing up into the attic. I've also found insulation covering vents. In these cases, you're just moving your problems from one room to the next, because when you dump humidity and moisture into an attic space, a couple of things happen.

First of all, insulation becomes very ineffective. If you add just 2 percent moisture to insulation, it loses its effectiveness (R-value) by a third. So in other words, if you have R19 and you put moisture into that, now you've got, like, an R13 or less. So you're wasting insulation. If you want to know if it vents out, look for the vent flapper (a.k.a. the damper) on the outside of the wall and see if it opens when you turn the vent on. Sometimes I've found that a builder has put in the bath fans and installed exhaust ports on the exterior, but never connected the two.

bathroom. For example, if the bathroom is 8 feet by 5 feet (with 8-foot ceilings), your bathroom area is 40 square feet. At 1 CFM per square foot, the minimum recommendation is a fan rated at 40 CFM.

For bathrooms above 100 square feet in area, HVI recommends a ventilation rate based on the number and type of fixtures present. In this calculation, figure 50 CFM each for the toilet, shower, and bathtub, and 100 CFM for a jetted tub. To accommodate the total CFM demand in a bathroom of this size, you have two options:

- Install a 50-CFM fan over the tub, one in the shower, and one in the water closet. This method is very effective, providing targeted ventilation when and where you need it.
- Install one 150-CFM fan. The air will then be pulled through the entire room and exhausted at a central location.

For more information on bathroom ventilation, visit www.hvi.org.

Pulling It All Together: Bathroom Remodel

To conclude our time together in the bathroom, Leslie shares her experience balancing big dreams with small spaces.

Leslie: Affordable Transformation

If I could have taken everything out of our home's bathroom, I would've, but we had to work around a few things. I started by changing out the damaged drywall for a moisture-resistant variety, and removed the hideously pink border tile. Then, with a tone-on-tone hotel aesthetic in mind, I installed a more subtle border tile and changed the light fixtures, adding a third one between the two vanity mirrors. Next I changed out the faucets, installed matching-finish double towel bars, and added a critical and previously absent vent fan.

So, for a very limited amount of money, I was able to completely transform our bathroom without getting to the guts of it. It looks completely different and functions more efficiently. Plus, doing the work on the bath ourselves made us reorganize our existing mess of a closet and streamline our belongings. To keep the closet organized we added bins and baskets to keep related items together to help restore the storage that we love. I still hate our bathtub, which feels like it's all of 8 inches deep. But what are we going to do? We don't know our neighbors well enough for them to allow us to bathe at their place for two weeks while we install a replacement.

Bathrooms can be cool places to recharge and reconnect. To give your kids something to do while you steal away for a little Mommy and Daddy time, let's consider conquering their spaces next.

CHAPTER 4

Kids' Spaces

Whether you're creating a room for a new arrival or updating a space for kids who insist they're not little anymore, working on a child's room can be a fun, creative adventure. Just as home layouts have changed over the years, so have the options and possibilities for the rooms belonging to the youngest members of your clan.

Architecturally speaking, it used to be that all family bedrooms were huddled together in one end of the home. Rooms were tiny, and kids' rooms had space for only a few decorating options. But today, every family member gets their own "zone," ready to be designed to reflect their style, favorite pastimes, and busy schedules.

The trick is to go in knowing the parameters of what you can spend, the smarts of materials selection, and how to make the space safe, healthy, and adaptable as the junior designer grows. Believe it or not, it's possible to combine coolness and practicality, safety and organization for a room both you and your child will love. Here's where to begin.

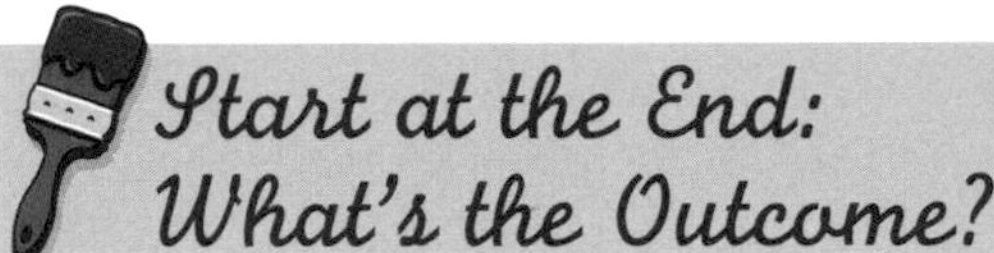

Start at the End: What's the Outcome?

Before jumping into the fun and somewhat overwhelming world of color selection and beginning an online shopping rampage, think through how many kids are using this space now, and how many will be in the near future (the next two to five years). What are the kids' present ages, and what age landmarks will they be hitting in the next few years (think baby-to-preschooler, gradeschooler-to-tween, tween-to-teen)?

What activities need to be accommodated? Sleeping and homework are two obvious, though hated necessities. Play, arts and crafts, and sporting goods storage need to be considered, as well as what you feel comfortable allowing in the kid zone versus the family zone.

And the million-dollar question: How much say are you willing to give your child when it comes to the room's design? Designing spaces with your kids is like a competitive sport: you'll have what you want,[40] and they'll have what they want.[41]

Sometimes Father really does know best, and it's because Mom said so, that's why. Just make sure to decide what that point is before you embark on a project with any offspring who have learned to talk.

Assess Your Abilities

Most of the adventures in kids' rooms are basic-to-novice-level projects. In fact, that's how you want it, unless money is no object and you can hire painters and contractors every time your child declares herself to be "too old for this room!"

In other words, if you don't mind repainting over what will become a too-young color or stenciled motif a few years from now, great. We just always want our audience to think before stenciling.

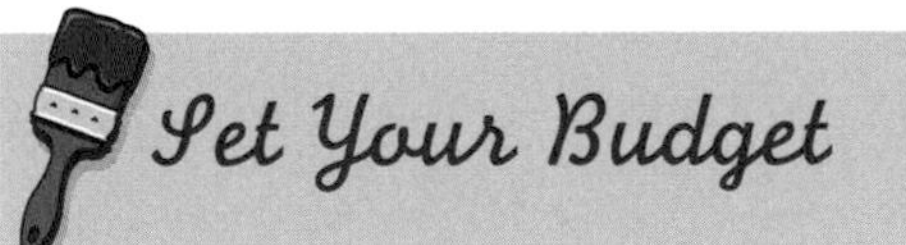

Set Your Budget

Pay the most for what you hope to use the longest, things like neutral styles of shelves and bookcases, even an upholstered chair or a well-designed desk. You can change the look of

40.) The colors you saw in last month's *Country Home,* with the TV and computer relegated to family places for sharp parental oversight. 41.) Colors they saw on someone's *MySpace* page, a home theater, fully-stocked mini fridge, maid service...

your kids' rooms through well-chosen colors or patterns without painting or repapering, and it doesn't have to cost a lot to get a good return on your investment in the form of safe, happy kids.

Spaces That Grow

For the best return on your time, money, and sweat equity, create a space that's easily convertible as your child grows. That includes everything from choosing a color palette that can serve as a long-term backdrop for ever-changing tastes and interests, investment furniture pieces, and storage solutions that will be useful over the long haul.

Storage has perhaps the biggest impact on design of a kids' space, as it not only gives you the room you need to hide all their stuff, but also frees up floor space for activity zones in the room design. Typically, when kids are small, their stuff is big, and as they grow, personal belongings tend to get smaller but multiply. Storage needs to be flexible for changing needs. Closets can be refitted and expanded with smart organizers and bi-level clothing rods, and there are great opportunities in the realm of two-for-one solutions: adding a window seat, for example, will create a story-time zone as well as handy storage for playthings kids need to create their own stories.

Also consider how your organization plan can create valuable housekeeping behaviors in the room's pint-sized occupants. Yes, home improvement can actually lead to getting chores done. It's like anything else: do what you can to make it easier. Putting storage within kids' reach and laying it out in easy—and even fun-to-use—ways helps to get them to act on the tried-and-true mantra of "a place for everything and everything in its place."[42] They'll take ownership and pride in their space as a result, and you'll enjoy reasonably stress-free visits to their room, at least until they become teenagers.

When choosing furnishings, look for durable, classically styled pieces that work for a range of ages. Tom's kids, for instance, are still making use of a cool IKEA dresser that began life in the family 14 years before as a changing table (thanks to a foam diaper pad Tom snapped on back then). Leslie's cousin did some smart shopping for her new baby's room, selecting a crib that'll convert to a small starter bed in a few years. Such options are more and more prevalent out there in the children's furnishings market, but even if you just shop for finishes that'll coordinate well with later additions (whitewash,

Songs to Work By:

Tunes to help you get through your projects.

- *Teach Your Children*—Crosby, Stills, Nash & Young
- *Sweet Child o' Mine*—Guns N' Roses
- *Little Children*—Billy J. Kramer
- *Take Good Care of My Baby*—Bobby Vee
- *Baby Baby Don't Get Hooked on Me*—Mac Davis
- *New Kid in Town*—Eagles
- *The Kids Are Alright*—The Who
- *Sugar Shack*—Jimmy Gilmer
- *One for My Baby*—Frank Sinatra
- *Mary Had a Little Lamb*—Stevie Ray Vaughn
- Anything by Kid Rock

42.) Same idea actually works for adults. Don't you love the Container Store?

colored paint, and classic wood finishes are easy to find) and fairly classic, doodad-free designs, you'll be in good shape. Just because the furniture is for a child's room doesn't mean it has to be juvenile. Choose pieces that reflect the same style as is found throughout your home.

Finally, colors. Consider the level and frequency of investment you're willing to put into the room's backdrop. If you don't mind repainting over the current color a few years from now, great. Just remember that there's a lot you can do to update the look of well-chosen colors or patterns without painting or repapering if they've been selected with future change and a fair amount of neutrality in mind.

If You Go Vintage, Shop Carefully

One perennially popular decorating strategy is bringing the fun of vintage graphics and styling to a room through cool furnishings and accessories found in antique shows, tag sales, and online treasure troves. This approach works for kids' spaces, too, with a few precautions: steer clear of anything with a chippy, possibly lead-based finish. Furniture is even trickier: avoid cribs and other furnishings with out-of-date latches, hardware, and constructions; and make sure any railings or openwork trims won't allow inquiring hands and heads to get stuck. Also search the Consumer Product Safety Commission website (www.cpsc.org) for recalls to make sure any vintage finds won't create an unsafe situation in your house.

Easy Care and Cleaning

Plan for finishes that allow you to quickly contain and clean the messes that are natural hazards of kid territory. Easy-clean paints are ideal for walls and trim (see our paint sheen guide in Chapter 1 for formulations that'll fit your requirements). Low-pile carpeting, laminate, and durably finished natural wood all work great for floors.

Cleanliness for a kid's room should also extend

Green Scene: Kid-Safe Cleaners

It's easy to be green as well as clean with our favorite natural alternatives to household cleaners.

- ***Glass cleaner:*** *Fill a spray bottle with one quart water and add one tablespoon of white vinegar. For larger jobs, like floor and tiles, add a quarter of a cup of white vinegar to one gallon of hot water.*
- ***Disinfectant:*** *Mix half a cup of borax in one gallon of hot water to clean counters, floors, cabinets, and tiles.*
- ***Mildew remover:*** *Use equal parts white vinegar and salt, or use strong thyme tea.*
- ***Sink and toilet cleaner:*** *Mix a paste of either baking soda or borax with water and add a squeeze of lemon juice. Borax or baking soda can also be used solo to replace abrasive cleaners. For toilets, drop either a few vitamin C capsules or denture cleaning tablets into the bowl and let them sit overnight.*
- ***Carpet freshener/cleaner:*** *For odors, sprinkle dry cornstarch or baking soda onto the carpet and vacuum. Or leave two parts cornstarch and one part borax on the carpet for an hour and then vacuum. For stains, rub borax into the dampened area, let dry, and then vacuum; or repeatedly blot with vinegar and soapy water.*
- ***Furniture polish:*** *Add half a cup of lemon juice to one cup of vegetable or olive oil.*
- ***Brass cleaner:*** *Mix equal parts flour and salt into a small amount of vinegar.*

to air quality. Not just the two-week-old gym clothes under the bed—we'll let you deal with that one. Our concern is the presence of allergens and toxins that can impact health and general comfort. Thanks to the increased awareness of both childhood allergies and green living, it's very easy to find VOC-free finishes, fabrics, and furnishings that'll help keep the air clear and head off harmful reactions. You can also cut down on potential off-gassing by allowing carpeting and furnishings to air outside, in the garage, or another well-ventilated space before they enter your child's new room.

Safety Considerations

When it comes to safety in the kid zone, it's all about perspective. To identify possible dangers, you literally have to get down on a child's level and check out the view of room elements and furnishings that you might otherwise take for granted from yours. Nothing short of a rubber room can be made completely child safe, but using an eagle eye and common sense, you'll be able to design safety and comfort into the new space. Here are some things to watch out for on your safety tour.

Risky blinds. Babies love to play with window blinds, but can get tangled in and strangled by long cords. Shorten all long cords and tie them up and away from the reach of little hands. A free blind tassel shortening kit is available by calling the Window Covering Safety Council at 800-506-4636.

Crash courses. Glass doors, like outside sliders or storm doors, are an invitation for trouble. Kids often forget the door is there and walk or run right into it. If the glass breaks, serious injury can result. Apply decorative decals at the child's eye level as a constant reminder of closed doors. Also make sure your glass is "safety glass," which is designed not to shatter when it breaks. This is usually stamped on the glass near a corner. If it's not, have the glass replaced immediately.

Window warnings. Houses with windows low to the ground dare a child to climb out. Even if your windows are higher, kids can climb off the back of a couch or up on a bed to reach one. Invest in screening as well as safety bars or latches and install them on any window your child might reach.

Bumps and lumps. Look for sharp corners on walls and cabinets. Install soft corner guards on coffee tables, cabinet edges, nightstands, and any other sharp edge you find. Use baby gates at both the top *and* bottom of stairs to deter the youngest mountaineers in your family!

Prevent trips and falls. Arrange chairs, tables, shelving, and other furniture so that they're not easily toppled. Secure area rugs to prevent tripping by adding anti-slip pads underneath, and add tread mats or carpet to steps along with handrails that kids can reach.

Risky railings. Be sure any railing in your home is at least 36 inches tall and has no more than 6-inch spaces between any of the spindles. While legal under most building codes, this 6-inch space is still too wide for a really small child who could squeeze through the railing and fall. If you have a small toddler, pick up some childproof netting and install it temporarily on the inside of the balcony to prevent little bodies from slipping through. The netting can be removed when the child gets bigger, and it won't damage the railing.

Prevent poisoning. Buy inexpensive, easy-to-install locks for all your cabinets that contain any household chemicals, including normal cleaning solutions, paint supplies, nail polish remover, and other such poisons. With medicine cabinets, install the latch high up on the door since kids can climb up on the vanity in an attempt to reach it. Also make sure that all finishes are lead-free, and remove any items that are chipped.

Try leaving one "safe" cabinet open for kids, just so they don't get too frustrated. Let them play with your Tupperware without any danger!

Always store cleaning solutions and other household poisons in the original packaging. There have been cases of child poisoning when one parent used a juice bottle for cleaning fluid and the other parent unknowingly fed the "juice" to their child.

Air warnings. In addition to smoke detectors, install carbon monoxide detectors outside of all bedrooms and in main living areas for immediate warning of CO's presence and prevention of poisoning. (Combination smoke/CO detectors are also available as a two-for-one solution.)

Sure shockers. For children, outlets are one of the most dangerous electrical devices in the home. They are at perfect kid-height, and children love to try to stick just about anything in them. The solution is simple: install plug protectors on every outlet. There are many different types of outlet covers, and most will do the trick. But avoid those that only cover a single plug, since they are small enough to be swallowed by a child; use at least the double-plug size. Also make sure that any electrical cords are up and out of the way.

No climbing. Make sure children understand which are the safe and unsafe areas for climbing and exploring (counters and shelves fit into the latter category).

Play safely. To prevent choking and suffocation, ensure that mesh-sided playpens have holes no larger than a quarter of an inch. Replace latches on toy chests with slow-closing hinges, or remove their lids altogether; add ventilation holes as

Create a crib safe zone by making sure anything near the crib is well outside the reach of the children.

well, in case your little one ends up in the toy chest. Remove hanging crib toys when babies are able to pull themselves up.

Don't get locked in. Ensure that all doors to rooms and closets can be unlocked from both sides.

Crib zone. Look carefully around your child's crib. This ought to be the safest area in the house. Kid-proof anything that could cause trouble including blinds, outlets, shelves, and furniture that can be pulled down, and remove all plastic bags and coverings (even the plastic wrap on a crib mattress can cause suffocation). Also make sure that the movable sides of cribs and playpens are always in their raised, locked position, and that crib mattresses fit tightly, with no more than two finger-widths of space between the mattress and crib frame.

Keeping out the Bogeyman

In addition to planning comfort and safety into your child's room, listen in for things that may go bump in the night and bring on a fright. Clanking pipes, whistling windows, and creaky floors can all fire up a child's imagination in a negative way, so take time to remove or at least minimize the sources of these seemingly strange sound-offs, or look forward to lots of midnight wake-ups. Better yet, take your child to the source of a scary sound in broad daylight, which will help to alleviate fears as well as inspire their curiosity and interest for future smart management of their own Money Pit.

Lighting can also go beyond utility to offer comfort and security. Supplement overhead, general, and task lighting with a small, easy-to-switch lamp within reach of your child's bed, and shop together for cute, convenient night-lights.

Giving Your Kids a Say

Now that we're through the basics of kid spaces, it's time to loop back to décor choices and all the ups and downs that come with them. There are so many theme ideas, furnishing styles, and accessories out there that we couldn't even begin to make suggestions, but we can offer a few tips to help you and your child on your way to a happy, affordable result.

As with any other situation in parenting, you should start by setting boundaries and sticking to them. For this kind of project, we recommend maximum control when the child is youngest or when the investment is largest. From there, start a dialogue with your child to help set the theme, figure out favorite colors, and decide what additions need to be made and projects need to be done to get to their dream room on your budget.

Here are some questions to help you and your young ones choose the right overall plan and feel for their space:

1. **What are their favorite colors?** Allow them to choose several, then pick up paint swatches that best represent their choices and look for ways to incorporate a few of them, whether by painting two colors on wainscoted walls or incorporating an accent wall. Remember that colors can be brought in with decorative accessories, too, so let them help in color choice. Creating stripes or patterns on the wall is easily achievable with some clever taping. Geometric shapes and color blocking can be done in the same paint color using different sheen levels to draw attention to their

design. For younger children, a free-form wainscoting of green can create a grassy base for a garden or jungle display on the wall.

2. **What is their favorite hobby, activity, or sport?** This can help you decide if you would like to incorporate a theme into the design. If your child loves skateboarding, you can create shelves using skateboards and brackets. Skiing or snowboarding? Make a headboard out of used skis or snowboards. Beach bum? Have a fun family beach photo turned into a mural for an accent wall. If kids love arts and crafts, create a work area within the room so they can do their favorite activity there. Camping? Create a tent with fabric over the bed for a permanent campout.

3. **Is there someplace in the world that fascinates them?** What about a time in history or a modern-day role model? If they dream of Far Eastern places, add fabric and colors that suggest those locales, or try Hawaiian tiki and beach prints to deliver a tropical vibe. Bring in aspects of their favorite locale, like using coconut shells for storing hair ties or jewelry. You can also achieve a totally global vibe by using clever accessories with details that reflect the theme.

4. **What are the activities they do in their room?** And, most importantly, what do you want them to do in their rooms?

5. **What furnishings can you keep? What do you need?** Can you repurpose or refinish current pieces to make them work with the new design plan and theme?

6. **Just as you ask yourself before every home improvement adventure: What do they love and hate about their room now?** You're actually training the next generation of home improvement enthusiasts!

Transport your teen to far off places by creating a room inspired by their dream destination.

Create a room any sports fan will love with the right accessories.

Depending on the age of your child, this planning period can also be a learning experience, building confidence in their ability to make decisions and revealing the consequences, even if mistakes or changes-of-mind occur. It's all in how you position it. When Leslie was a kid and wanted to rearrange her bedroom, her architect father would have her and her sisters create a scale drawing of the new plan on graph paper. Smart dad: Leslie learned a lifelong and lucrative skill, and her dad wasn't moving furniture back and forth until his back ached.

It's easiest to be flexible, especially where creative decisions are concerned. We talked earlier about selecting a color palette with longevity, but if you're designing with a teenager who's set on a raging fuchsia that all her friends adore, you can bargain with her to keep her room clean in order to get the color she wants.[43]

Working together to make a repair, apply a color or design, or build something new teaches lifelong skills while also giving a child a sense of accomplishment and renewed pride in the home you share. They'll also feel that much more at ease in the new space that results from both of your efforts—a place where they can feel like their best selves, and really aspire and dream.

Pulling It All Together: Kids' Room Remodels

When it comes down to it, kid room remodels are very likely to be the first "home improvement" project your kids participate in. Make it an engaging and happy experience, and you are likely to sow the seeds of a lifetime of successful remodeling projects. Here are some ways we've let kids help.

43.) Which will last all of two days.

Leslie: A Room That Both a Mother and Daughter Could Love

One of my first experiences in designing kids' spaces was a bedroom for a two-year-old girl. It got off to a bizarre start because the mother kept insisting that the girl wanted a shabby chic bedroom. And I kept saying, "She's two. How do you know she wants this? Does she like it? Does she talk about it? Or is this what you want in the space?" Her response? "My daughter is *very* girly . . . very princessy. She likes things ruffly and flowery and in rich pink tones. And we both really like that shabby chic aesthetic."

Stranded in a nebulous pink zone, I wanted to understand what it was that her daughter liked to do activity-wise, and what things mother and daughter liked to do together. At this point, the mother said, "You know, I really love to read to my daughter. And I'd love to have a window seat with an adorable chandelier." Thanks to this response, I was able to determine a few other needs for the space, namely, storage and organization.

So, in this window seat I designed for them, there was storage underneath the cushioned bench, which of course included a safety latch so that if it were to close it wouldn't slam shut. And on both ends of the window seat, which was L-shaped, I built in recessed bookcases so that there was a place to put all of the stories they'd be sharing.

To make the daughter's first "big girl" bed special, I created a custom headboard from wall art purchased at a craft store, fabric, and some lumber. And I took all of her toys and pieces of furniture and created a little vanity/dressing area that would grow and adapt from her current love of playing dress-up to a spot that'd work for grooming and getting ready for school in her tween and teen years.

Throughout the room, I made sure that the furnishings were all very classic but feminine. I also added a lot of fun things like hooks at easily reachable heights and butterfly wings to wear for dress-up. All of it was done with accessibility and usefulness built in for all members of the family, but centered on the little girl, her personality, and how I thought her design tastes might develop when she really gets up in age, like five.

> **Leslie Likes:**
> **Being a Kid Again**
>
> *Check out these fun, easy ideas for snapping up your child's new space:*
>
> - *Set up show-off storage for action figures and other toys by adhering iron-on pockets to an existing curtain.*
> - *Create a scheduling center on a closet door with chalkboard paint.*
> - *Place a map of a vacation destination between a tabletop and a layer of plastic glass, accompanied by erasable markers for planning and plotting.*
> - *Apply Blik wall decals, which are very cool stickers made specifically to change a plain wall into a hip, well-designed piece of art. Large and colorful graphics like robots, geometric shapes, pirate ships, fun scroll-like patterns, and even letters to create messaging are all available. Blik even makes a version that is removable so that wall decals can be changed to keep up with changing kid styles.*

Tom: Your Child's First Day at the Home Center

It's a big day in the life of a parent—the day your child takes his or her first steps into the local home center. Preparing kids' spaces is a great chance to introduce kids to their future realities as Money Pit owners, so bring them along while you're shopping. Help them get acquainted with the aisles of supplies. Read signage and product labels. If an in-store recommendation is needed, your courteous exchanges with store staff are great examples of problem-solving and reminders that we all need a little help from our friends.

After you're back from the store, enlist your child's help to prepare the project zone, teaching the skills of good preparation for a safe and satisfactory outcome. Make sure you're both properly suited up and accessorized for the task at hand. Your child's age and the complexity level of the project will determine what they can safely handle, but there's always a way to get them involved, even if they keep busy with a few simple items or kid-sized tools while you work with the more complicated stuff nearby.

Now everything's perfect in your kids' rooms! Well, except that they still leave their dirty clothes on the floor. For that, we think perhaps some smart redesign in the laundry room will make it easier for the kids[44] to sort clothes and maybe even do laundry. Okay, we exaggerated that last point. But you can make it easier, following our guide to better laundry rooms and mudrooms in our next adventure.

44.) Read: husband.

CHAPTER 5

Laundry Rooms and Mudrooms

Ah, the laundry room . . . where women sort and men make pink underwear! Or at least that's the way it's typically been until now. Today, (almost) idiot-proof machines and clever space planning can make laundry day just a few folds away from being completely effortless. The laundry room has become a functional, often used, and well-designed and outfitted space. Some might even say it's their favorite room in the house, although we wouldn't go that far.

Mudrooms are a gathering place for more than the mud that gets dragged in the door. These utility spaces become an indispensible crossroad of family life, proving storage solutions for sporting goods and clothing alike. Some laundry rooms also double as mudrooms, so we're going to tackle those together in this chapter.

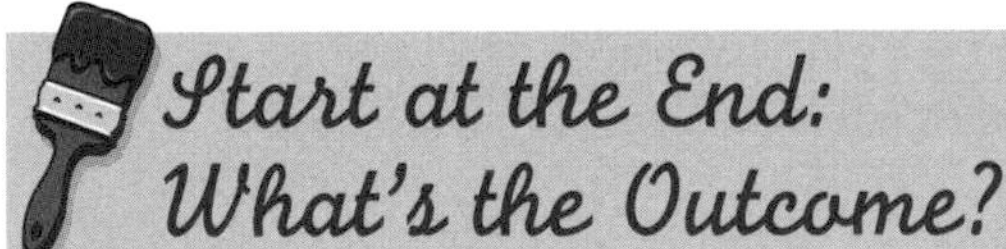

Start at the End: What's the Outcome?

To make sure everything you wish for in a laundry solution comes out in the wash, the first thing to consider is if you have the most efficient appliances for your family's needs. Thanks to greatly improved energy efficient washers that use less water, are easier on your clothes, and lead to greatly shortened drying cycles, it is almost always a good bet to replace an older appliance with one that meets modern ENERGY STAR standards.

Besides the energy your appliances need, your own personal "energy efficiency" should be considered. Does the space work with you, or does it work against you?[45]

The storage gods have smiled upon laundry rooms and mudrooms, so you will want to research options like special shelving, pull-out bins, paper holders on a cabinet edge for gift wrap, built-in ironing boards, etc. Locker-style storage can prevent constant letdowns.[46] Think through the year-round roster of activities the space needs to accommodate.

Songs to Work By:

Tunes to help you get through your projects.

- *Dirty Laundry*—Don Henley
- *Waiting on the World to Change*—John Mayer
- *Dirty Water*—Standells
- *Shake It Up*—The Cars
- *Mud Slide Slim*—James Taylor
- *Mississippi Mud*—Hank Williams III or Bix Beiderbecke/Paul Whiteman & His Orchestra
- *Basin Street Blues*—Louis Armstrong
- *Wet Laundry Blues*—Steve James
- *Whole Lotta Shakin' Going On*—Jerry Lee Lewis
- *Thirsty Boots*—John Denver
- Anything by Muddy Waters

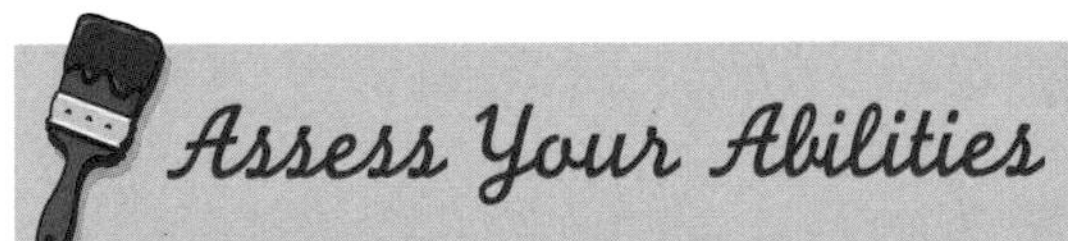

Assess Your Abilities

These rooms are DIY-friendly, assuming you don't plan to move around electrical and water supplies. Super-smart, energy-saving appliances are becoming the norm, but they can't work their laundry day magic without the proper connections and venting. If you're not sure, learn about safe hookups below.

45.) Like your teenagers. 46.) Letdowns of a book bag or five, a briefcase or two, and a pile of mail that won't get read until the day before the bills are due.

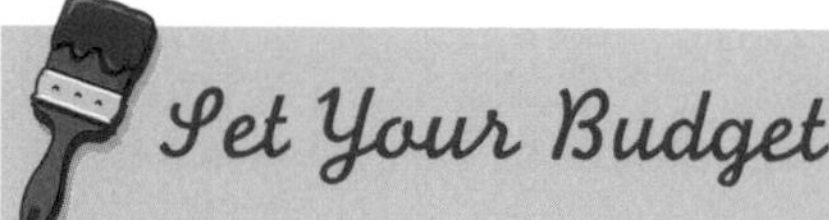

Set Your Budget

As with kitchens, the decision to replace laundry appliances is usually the factor that drives laundry room and mudroom remodels. So a good start for budget planning is the appliance costs, and we've outlined things to consider below.

Your next biggest expense will come in storage and organizing solutions, which can be as simple or as grand as your desire to reduce clutter. Manage budget priorities by staying true to what you want from the outcome: is it more important to make laundry easy or to get the "letdowns" under control?

Laundry Rooms: Spaces to Keep You and Your Clothes Happy

The idea here is to create a space that both you and your clothes will be happy to hang out in. If your plans include new appliances, you'll need to know about safe hookups.

For starters, check your washer supply hoses. Typical rubber-based water supply lines are susceptible to dangerous, room-flooding breakdowns thanks to their habit of swelling and bursting. Make sure they don't burst your bubble by replacing them with the braided steel water supply type made to withstand daily stresses. Another smart installation is an automatic shutoff valve for the water lines. Such smart shutoff valves can detect an out-of-the-ordinary water flow,[47] before it leaks down to the floor below.

Speaking of valves, it is a good idea to make sure your washer valves are accessible and functional. It's a good practice to turn off the valves between loads and add a single-lever turn-off valve, which turns both hot and cold water supplies off at the same time.

Also scope out your dryer venting situation, and plan to stay on top of maintaining it by cleaning it at least once every six months. Every year an average of 14,500 dryers catch fire and are responsible for up to 10 deaths due not to wiring problems but the lint that collects in the dryer's exhaust ducts.

Leslie (Doesn't) Like: **The Lint Balls of Autumn**

We moved into our house in autumn, a time of beautiful and somewhat blustery days. And just about every time I'd pull into the driveway during those first few weeks, there'd be the weirdest tumbleweed of lint rolling across in front of me and my car. At first I was thinking, "Whoa, pretty unusual weather we're having!" Then I was wondering where in the heck it had come from, and called Tom to commiserate. "My house is coughing up lint balls—it's the only answer I can imagine." And he said, "Well, then we need to clean out your entire dryer vent." We did, and now I do a follow-up cleaning every six months . . . no more roving lint balls, and it's actually one of my favorite home maintenance activities!

Laundry Appliances

If you're reading this chapter, you're probably planning to replace a laundry appliance, but let's still consider the trade-offs in repairing versus replacing a broken appliance.

If your laundry appliances are more than 10

47.) Think water spilling down through your ceiling light fixtures.

years old, you'll probably be better off in many ways if you update to better performance at improved energy savings. That change can actually put money back into the very pockets you're washing.

Energy Star labeling is the thing to look for when shopping for a new clothes washer, as it's your guarantee that a product meets the strict energy efficiency guidelines established by the EPA and U.S. Department of Energy. Qualified clothes washers, for example, use 50 percent less energy than standard washers, and slosh through 18 to 25 gallons of water per load versus the traditional 40.

Interesting factoid: Energy Star doesn't evaluate and label dryers. Why? Because all dryers use about the same amount of energy. Rack up some savings by making use of the dryer's moisture sensor option for shorter, more efficient drying cycles. Choose the high-speed or extended-spin option on your washer, and you'll cut down significantly on the water your laundry carries into the dryer. Which in turn significantly shortens the drying cycle, saving you both energy and wear and tear on your clothes.

Green Scene: High-Tech High Efficiency

For the best energy savings, invest in a high-efficiency washer. These offer lots of high-tech benefits, including:

- ***Energy and water savings.*** *High-efficiency washers use half the energy of a conventional appliance and one-third to one-half less water. The spin cycle is also super fast, which means clothes come out of the washer both drier and cleaner than they would with a standard washer. As a result, the dryer runs less, saving wear and tear on your clothes and your wallet.*
- ***Gentle cycles.*** *With high-efficiency appliances, clothes are tumbled and not spun. This leads to less wear and tear because the friction caused by the process of washing is far less. These machines also handle delicate items with ease.*
- ***Less detergent.*** *High-efficiency washers use specially formulated "HE" laundry detergent and a lot less of it (about two-thirds less) compared to conventional laundry detergent. Fast spin cycles also mean more detergent is flushed out of each load, making clothes that much cleaner.*
- ***Bigger loads.*** *High-efficiency machines can handle large and bulky items like comforters, blankets, and sleeping bags with ease.*

High-efficiency machines do cost more than conventional appliances, but the cost savings can be recouped over the life of the appliance due to the increased efficiency, and all the while you'll be enjoying cleaner clothes that don't wear out nearly as quickly.

Sharp Styling

The ergonomic design of modern machines means they're not only gentler with clothes, they're gentler with you. The best choice will depend on both your lifestyle and your laundry style in particular.

The wide variety of appliance heights, sizes, and configurations available today allows everyone to find the best fit for them and their laundry space. The increasingly popular front-loaders offer easy access and tangle-free retrieval of laundry. Just as important, their waist-height, easy-access doors are a lot easier on your formerly aching back.

Another interesting benefit in front-loaders is the ability to have a full-size and stackable installation. Stackable appliances used to be limited to smaller-capacity machines that had you doing laundry almost every time someone needed a change of clothes. Stackable units are now available in a range of dimensions that allow you to save time as well as valuable floor space. Larger baskets in both washers and dryers help to trim down the number of wash loads, and when you add manufacturer-provided

Washer/Dryer Options: Many of today's full size high-efficency washer/dryer pairs can sit side-by-side, on storage drawer pedestals, or even stacked to save room.

pedestals under units and comfortably placed, ample counter space for folding and stain treating, your days of laundry strain are over.

Appliances That Talk

Actually, they talk and listen, quite possibly one of the healthier relationships you'll experience. Better yet, they listen to you. GE makes a high-efficiency washer/dryer pair called Profile Harmony with a communication system called CleanSpeak. Instead of guessing which cycle won't trash your new delicates, you tell the washer what to do, and it turns around and tells the dryer what to do.[48] From there, all you'll need to do is have the family chat about separating fabrics and colors and not overloading, and your crew will be good to go.

> **Link Up: Fabrics, Appliances, Detergents . . . Oh My!**
>
> *The people who make GE appliances got together with some clothing and clothes-care folks—big names like Cotton Incorporated, Procter & Gamble, Milliken, and Vanity Fair to do scientific testing of clothes-care performance with new fabrics, wash chemistry breakthroughs, and new appliance technologies, including high-efficiency appliances. Learn more at www.fabricology.com.*

Laundry Room Layouts

Creating an organized, easy-to-use laundry room is your other best defense against pink underwear. Outside of moving the room closer to the source of laundry generation, which may be a possibility in some homes (see Tom's laundry remodel and "Bonus Spaces" in the next chapter), arrangement of the workspace and laundry-friendly surfaces can make it easier for the job to get done . . . by anyone. Make an ultra-clean break from laundry hassles with our design checklist below to get the most out of whatever space you have to work with.

Step up to the counter. Station countertops at varying heights to accommodate a range of laundry

48.) They never ask "why" or put it off until after the game. They just do as they're told. It's a beautiful thing.

room chores (a waist-level surface, for example, is great for folding and organizing laundry). Additionally, easy-clean countertop materials such as granite and solid surfacing help you to maintain quality control.

Cabinets and cubbies. Plan your cabinetry for handy, roomy storage of the items you'll use around the areas where you'll use them. You can also get creative with easy-to-scan open storage and display space. Wire baskets on tracks below an upper cabinet are a great spot for dryer sheets and cleaning products. Wall-mounted brackets for irons and specialty items help clear up valuable counter space. Cabinetry can be as simple or as ornate as your design style allows.

Supplemental storage. Thanks to coordinating accessories from appliance manufacturers, it is easy to transform an already-great pair of machines into a storage bonus. Options include appliance-top work surfaces with spill guards, supply trays and backsplashes, laundry storage "towers" that nestle between or to the side of units for quick access to detergents and supplies, and washer and dryer pedestals with built-in storage drawers.

Sort it out. Add those handy industrial-style sorting bins to keep wash loads in order, set apart items headed for the local dry cleaner, and sequester clothing in need of mending. Beautiful baskets with embroidered fabric liners describing their responsibility can become a stylish laundry sorting solution. To prevent any surprises from getting into the mix, keep a small basket or bowl within reach as a catch-all for stray change and other pocket finds.

Organize for safety as well as efficiency. In addition to having a place for everything and everything in its place, make sure you're storing all laundry room chemicals out of children's reach while keeping them handy enough to avoid grownup-sized strains as you reach for them (heavy, bulk-size containers call for extra consideration here). Consider painting a section of the wall near your laundry work area with chalkboard paint to keep a handy list of stain treatments.

See what you're doing. You'll need abundant, reliable lighting for detecting stains and other laundry room quality checks. It doesn't have to be the most attractive lighting ever, just the most effective for the tasks at hand (i.e., fluorescents will serve you well in this space). Track lighting options can also be both decorative and illuminating.

Faultless flooring. Install moisture-resistant flooring such as tile or laminate so that you're

Access Everyone: **Front-Loading Comfort**

Front-loading machines make it easy for everyone to help out with the laundry. Plan for plenty of space in front of your machines for an easy approach and maneuvering, and ensure that each unit's door opens out and away from the other for easy transfer of laundry between machines.

Washing Machine Hygiene

Did you know that your washing machine may not be washing the germs out of your family's clothes? Over the years, washing machines can become contaminated with bacteria, potentially leaving millions of germs behind in your laundry. To correct this problem, run the washer without clothes using just hot water and one-half gallon of bleach. The bleach will sanitize the machine and all its plumbing components, killing any bacteria that have been left behind.

protected if the odd appliance disaster occurs. It's also possible to format a floor into one big drain, although this approach adds expense and can be tricky to accomplish in a room retrofit.

Add amenities. Go beyond basic washing and drying cycles by customizing your laundry zone with foldaway ironing boards and drying racks, under-cabinet hanging rods, and even a steaming closet. Add a utility sink to the mix, and you'll surely wash away all the hassles you used to associate with laundry day!

Accommodate other activities. If your laundry area (or mudroom) is used for other family tasks and pastimes, plan them into the room's storage and work surfaces. Handy additions such as an art paper roll-holder attached to a counter's end can be a boon to young artists planning projects nearby. Add a chalkboard to fuel the imagination of your young artists while you are folding clothes. If crafts are a favorite pastime, add extra outlets or additional lighting to make your hobby that much more enjoyable.

Super-clean design. Decorate your laundry room with colors and patterns that put out a clean, fresh vibe. Choose colors that are bright but not neon to help keep the chore of laundry a happy and peppy one. Blues with periwinkle tones, yellow, crisp greens, even reds can upstage a plain neutral. If painting all four walls in a happy hue are a bit too much "happy" for you, choose just one wall for your colorful accent. Also keep window treatments simple and streamlined, and use easy-care surface treatments for long-lasting beauty. White cabinetry can perfectly play against rich dark-toned granite with any color of paint or wall covering you enjoy. Bring in framed art for the walls to make it feel like your favorite room in the house.

Leslie Likes: Extra-Long Ironing Spaces

Accommodate extra-large ironing projects with a custom ironing pad to fit a handy countertop or table. Visit your local carpet store to pick up a scrap of felt carpet pad, and bring it home for sizing to your new ironing surface. Cover the pad with white muslin or canvas to create a smooth ironing surface, and add straps or other fasteners to help hold it in place while it's being used.

Putting It All Together: Tom's Laundry Remodel

Besides the space inside the four walls that make up your existing laundry room, consider how your laundry experience might be improved by moving your laundry room to a different place in your house.

Tom: Moving Laundry on Up

I'm one of the many homeowners who had laundry equipment on the first floor, meaning we didn't need a StairMaster. We[49] would truck the dirty clothes all the way down from upstairs bedrooms and bathrooms to get loads going, then carry them right back up again after the wash and dry cycles were over.

Now, the trend is to move laundry upstairs altogether, and that's exactly we did. We had a laundry room that was off our kitchen because we had a very old house. When I was renovating my first-floor home office and had the ceiling open, I knew it was a prime time to move the laundry plumbing so we could relocate the room to a small, unused bedroom upstairs. Since this bedroom-to-laundry conversion, we can do our stair-climbing workouts separately from our laundry.

49.) This is Tom's wife Sue. Who's we, Kemosabi?

Mudrooms: The Official Entrance of Your Family

The classic mudroom, a.k.a. utility room, is the most-trafficked entry of your home, but it's special: it's the Official Entrance to Your Family. While generally not a space where you hang out for long, it is where a lot of your gear hangs out—possibly literally.

Start by making a list of all the seasonal stuff that needs to live in your mudroom. Skis and pool noodles? Boots and beach towels?

Layer your everyday needs on top of the seasonal stuff. Come to terms with the fact that book bags, briefcases, shoes, coats, and hats will also be dropped here, so bring on the bins, trays, pegs, and hooks that can catch the incoming. If you have space, a comfortable, sturdy bench increases the ability to contain mud to its own room, as well as gives folks a place to pull off, put on, or lace up shoes and boots.

Locker-style cabinetry is a fun and functional solution for kids' day-to-day school needs and their individual activity items. Metal trays can serve as boot storage areas that won't dirty and scratch a wood floor. Baskets under an entry bench each assigned to a child or activity serve as a store-all and help with transport out to the car.

If you've got the space, a mudroom is also a great spot for recycling bins—easy to add to, and easy to roll out to the sidewalk on collection day.

Consider surface materials that can stand up to both moisture and errant athletic equipment. Drywall typically can't do it on its own. Check into synthetic wainscoting and other durable surfaces that won't show scratches or dings but will clean up easily and nicely.

For your floor, install tough, attractive laminate or glazed ceramic tile. We also like the addition of an all-weather rug, available in small-area sizes or as runners. They'll catch the dirt shed by returning family athletes, and are easily cleaned outside with a good hosing down. These rugs are designed in solid colors, natural-looking fibers, or patterns to work into your design style.

Creative catch-alls and mud-arresting containers can blend easily into an otherwise formal space. Slip a deep, rectangular pan or painted planter base under the entryway bench to catch wet, muddy shoes and boots; position an attractive umbrella stand right next to the door, and add an oversize basket to catch big bags. Such little additions can have a major impact on the comfort and welcome to your Money Pit.

Now that we've covered the basics, in the next two chapters we're going to talk about big additions: the home improvement adventures that give you more space, through existing "bonus" spaces or by adding on new spaces.

Bonus Spaces

Feeling a little cramped, but not ready to take on a home addition? Then look up, down, and around, because your home most likely already contains a space ready for conversion to a comfort zone, storage space, or recreation area.

We call these bonus spaces, the often underutilized real estate in your Money Pit. When you think about it, many basements and attics have the same amount of square footage as the floors above or below them. The least expensive "addition" you can do is to convert these areas into truly functional spaces.

There's more bonus space on the walls, and even on the ceilings in your garage. Better storage might mean you can actually fit your car inside, not to mention create space for a workbench.

Moving a bonus area from its current state to a livable space is akin to taming the wild, and navigating the unfinished takes some smarts to prevent very real discomforts later.[50] *These are adventures in the high-adrenaline category, but the outcomes can be truly exhilarating for both you and your personal worth.*

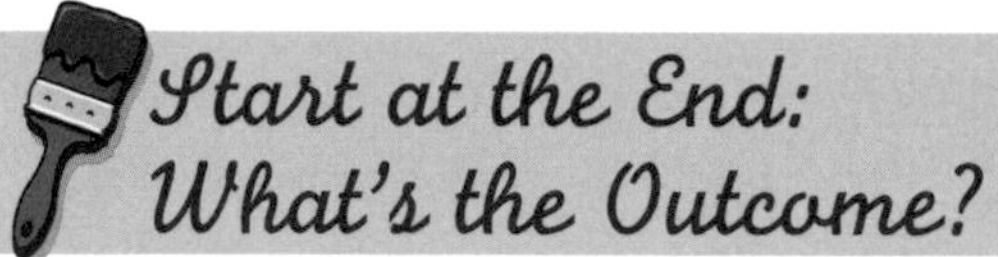

Start at the End: What's the Outcome?

There are so many ways to go in converting a bonus space, and every use will have a different set of requirements for access, finishes, installations, and storage. Here's a short list of possible bonus space uses:

- Extra bathroom
- Home office
- Home theater
- Game room
- Place to seal off teenagers, while keeping them close
- Home gym
- Music or art studio
- Guest bedroom
- Mother-in-law apartment[51]
- Hobby room
- Workshop
- Laundry room
- Wine cellar
- Sauna
- Utility room

As you match up your desired outcome with the existing structural conditions of your bonus room, first be realistic about what can and can't be moved. Lally columns and girders may not be your first choices in room décor, but they're there for a very good reason. You want to bring the house down with your wit and personality, not your home improvements.

What's a lally column? A *Money Pit* radio show listener once called asking what kind of a tool he'd need to cut a plumbing pipe that was in the way of the planned pool table. This didn't sound right to us. We asked him if this "plumbing pipe" went up into a wood beam. He said yes. And did it have a metal plate at the top? Again, he said, yes, it did. Then Tom said, "That's not a plumbing pipe it's a lally column, and it holds up your house!"

Bonus spaces are also famous for more head-banging than your son's favorite garage band, what with the sloped ceilings and exposed pipes. And, they're a common location for functional elements such as boilers, furnaces, water heaters, appliances, and all-important shutoff valves.[52] All will need to be serviced and eventually replaced, so don't enclose them so well that a door or wall has to be torn out when it's time to make the switch.

It's also important to match the style factor with access and environmental conditions. Take it from us you don't want to find out on delivery day

50.) One of which is hearing "I told you so" for a very long time. 51.) Or storage, depending on how you feel about her. 52.) Handy to avoid unplanned basement swimming pool incidents.

that the cushy new home theater couch you've splurged on won't fit through the door or go down the stairs. Or find out after the first rainy day that your fluffy new carpeting has turned into the New Jersey Meadowlands.[53]

We also encourage you to geek out by not only measuring for but mapping out your furnishing plan with to-scale sketches on graph paper and kraft paper cutouts of your furnishings' footprints, just for extra assurance of a happy, predictable result. Not only will this ensure that the furniture layout flows, it will help you plan for important utilities. You need a good cable connection for that big-screen TV. You'll need a place to plug in the sound system. A wet bar is more fun, but you need to plumb the wet part.

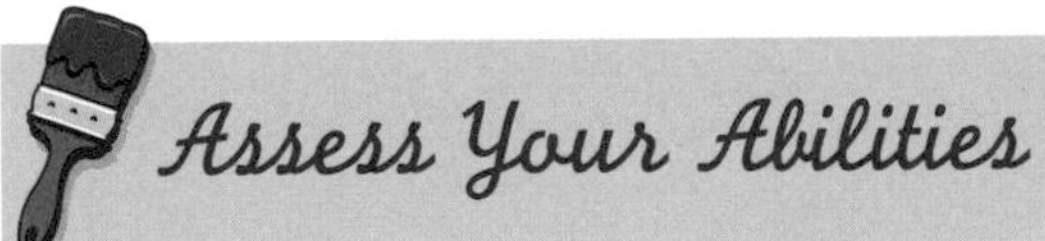

Assess Your Abilities

With the exceptions of any special rewiring or HVAC system adjustments in your bonus space, most finish and furnishing jobs are well within the reach of an experienced do-it-yourselfer. There are a range of easy-to-use products and finishing systems on the market, many of them suited specifically to the challenges and requirements of basements, garages, and attics. So, with proper planning and smart shopping, your job is made easy, and the road to the grand opening of your new space is made dramatically shorter.

There is one service regarding basements that you need to be forewarned about: basement waterproofing companies, a group of notorious fear-mongerers who frequently panic-peddle their way into the homes of unsuspecting consumers who either have or fear having a wet basement and its associated structural and mold problems. As you'll read below, their expensive drainage systems are rarely needed and often ineffective in dealing with these issues. We'll tell you how to correct and maintain any drainage and dampness issues with basic homeowner smarts and seasonal maintenance.

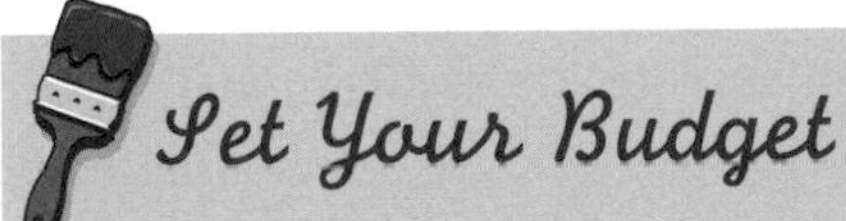

Set Your Budget

Bonus space conversions vary in scale, structural requirements, and style, so again, start with an honest assessment of your existing space and what it'll take to transform it to your liking. Workshop shelving in a garage will have a very different price tag from a tricked-out home theater in the basement. Remember the 20 percent reserve rule—always important when you start opening up walls and scheduling professionals who need to work in succession.

One advantage with these projects is that you can build toward your dream over time, as resources become available. After all, since these are truly the "extra" spaces around your home, everything you do is, well, bonus space you didn't have before!

Songs to Work By:

Tunes to help you get through your projects.

- *Up on the Roof*—Drifters
- *I Don't Want to Go Down to the Basement*—The Ramones
- *In the Basement*—Etta James
- *Shed Some Light*—Shinedown
- *Toys in the Attic*—Aerosmith
- *In My House*—The Mary Jane Girls
- *Drive My Car*—The Beatles
- *Gardening at Night*—R.E.M.
- *Somewhere That's Green*—*Little Shop of Horrors*
- Anything by The Cars

53.) A swamp made famous in *The Sopranos*. You want that in your house?

Basements, Not Wetlands

The basement is a tremendous bonus area, a huge source of extra space in homes fortunate enough to have one, but many homeowners just don't utilize them as they could or should.

Far and away, the biggest problem we hear about concerning basements is water, in all of its manifestations—seepage, leakage, dampness, flooding, you name it. Many people just take it for granted that wet basements are a fact of life. It's a favorite call-in topic on *The Money Pit,* and it keeps a lot of good home inspectors and not-so-good waterproofing contractors busy. Poor ventilation, poor lighting, condensation, odors, and mold are also high on the list of things people hate most about their basements. Even those issues all come back to water intrusion.

Here's what we say: Basements don't have to be dungeons. And if you do get water in your basement, it's usually easier and less costly to fix than you think. Once it's properly dry and watertight, you can turn your basement into any kind of room you want, without worries—make it a family room, office, entertainment center, or even extra bedrooms. If it's done right, you'll probably forget it's a basement altogether. It'll just be another room in your house.

Fix for Flooded Basements

Soil sloping into the basement wall, as well as disconnected downspouts can cause basements to leak.

Dry up leaking basements by extending downspouts away from the foundation wall and regrading the soil to force water to run away from the house, as shown on the right.

Don't Get Soaked by Wet Basements

Let's start by examining how *not* to solve the problem. Ask 10 people how to fix a wet basement, and you're likely to get answers that include use of jackhammers to break up basement floors, backhoes to dig out dirt from foundation walls, sump pumps that have to be wired and plumbed, and other such drastic and expensive measures.

While these solutions may seem to make sense, they all attempt the impossible: to seal a foundation so tightly that it will somehow hold off water like a boat. Unless your Money Pit is a houseboat, we're not trying to get it to float.

A popular myth is that wet basements are caused by a high water table, the natural level of water in the soil under the building site. Not true! Homes are not built below water tables. Builders attempting such a feat would find themselves constructing a foundation in a muddy mess.

Likewise, it's not rising water tables that cause your basement to flood after a storm. A water table moves slowly and seasonally. If leaks show up after a heavy rainfall or snowmelt, you're lucky[54] because it means leaks will be easy to spot and to fix.

The majority of basement leaks can be traced to trouble with the drainage conditions around the outside of the house. If too much water is allowed

54.) Although we guarantee that won't be the first emotion you will feel.

Ask Tom & Leslie: **Beware Basement Waterproofers**

Q: A waterproofing company charged me $14,219 to correct a problem with my basement flooding. Two of that firm's inspectors insisted underground water was being forced up into the cellar via hydrostatic pressure and only a "French" drain would correct it. They installed a long, deep ditch running alongside the interior of the home's foundation walls. That graded ditch was supposed to feed rising water into two underground electric pumps and eventually pump floodwater into the city sewer system.

I always felt the water was coming from the surrounding earth, flowing through a rather thin foundation wall and slowly running down into the cellar doorway. Now it seems that I was correct! The company is stalling, wanting to take photos and "brainstorm" their next move. Have you any suggestions?

A: The last thing you want from these contractors is more brainstorming! Unfortunately, it sounds like you've been taken by a common scam perpetrated by so-called basement waterproofing experts. These snake-oil salesmen use high-pressure sales tactics and scary terms like "hydrostatic pressure" to talk consumers into hiring them for expensive and almost always unnecessary repairs.

Let's examine the claim that forms the basis for the frightening prospect they pose, which is that your home will collapse from the pressure of the water against its basement walls. In order for any water on the outside of your foundation to get to the drains they carve into your basement floor, it has to run against the foundation walls and then leak either through the walls or under the footing below the walls. Hence, your foundation walls are subjected to the very same "hydrostatic pressure," either with or without that $14,000 solution!

A truly honest professional would have examined your exterior drainage conditions. As you correctly pointed out, the condition of the surrounding soil and, more importantly, the functionality of the gutter system on your roof, have far more to do with correcting the basement leakage than any subsurface drainage system.

The type of system they installed is needed only when the problem can be traced to a rising underground water table. This is rarely the case and is easy to spot. If your basement leaks are consistent with rainfall or snowmelt, the problem is not a water table. It's a drainage issue that can be easily corrected without spending a pile of cash.[55]

to collect in the soil around the foundation, it will naturally leak into the basement through the walls, or even up through the center of the floor.

Now for some good news: it's easy and inexpensive to improve your drainage conditions. It all starts up on your roof—the main collection point for water during any rainstorm, big or small. A functional, well-maintained continuous gutter system can carry things in the right direction, especially if it has at least one downspout for every 600 to 800 square feet of roof surface. Downspouts should extend to discharge at least 4 to 6 feet from your home's foundation. Gutters must also be kept clean and clear of the debris that dams up water's flow, sending it right where you don't want it: up against your foundation.

Next to gutter problems, the angle of the soil around a foundation's perimeter is the second major cause of wet basement woes. This soil should slope away from the house on a downward angle of 6 inches over the first 4 feet from the foundation wall. Thereafter, it can be graded more gradually, but should never allow water to flow back toward the house to collect against outer walls.

Know the enemies of good drainage: brick or wood edging placed too closely to a home's foundation can hold water against the building, and can lead to heavily overgrown bushes and trees. If you need to improve your grade, do it with clean fill dirt and add just a small layer of topsoil over

55.) This story had a happy ending, as we learned by e-mail several weeks later: "Much appreciation for the advice on my basement water problem. The waterproofing company scared me enough to purchase a $14,000 system that simply wasn't necessary. You gave me the courage to threaten binding arbitration. Long story short: they offered a return of $9,400, and I'm settling on my attorney's advice. You two were EXTREMELY helpful and I can't thank you enough for your excellent advice."

Tom's Tip: Gutter Talk for Your Basement

I remember inspecting one home where the homeowners complained about basement flooding. When I drove up and saw seedlings growing out of their gutters, I knew that even Inspector Clouseau could crack this case. Gutters must be kept clean and clear of the debris that dams up water's flow and sends it straight toward your foundation. Trees growing out of your gutters is always a sign that you've let things go a little too long!

that to support grass or other plantings. Heavy amounts of topsoil can hold water against a foundation and should be avoided when the job is to improve drainage.

Following these simple guidelines will solve 99 percent of wet basement blues. The improvements are inexpensive and can usually be done yourself or with a little help from your friends.

Exposed: Concrete and Condensation

The exposed concrete in most unfinished basements can experience condensation, which people often mistake for water seepage through the walls. The water comes from introducing warm, moist air to the earth-cooled surface of the concrete. Once that warm air cools, the moisture it holds is released, materializing as the water droplets you see on the wall.

There are two ways to cure this kind of moisture problem: warming the concrete to the point where condensation won't form, and isolating the basement's concrete surfaces from the interior living space.

The former is simply a matter of looping the basement space into your home's overall heating and cooling system, while the latter enhances the comfort of the area by adding visual warmth to the space via freestanding wall systems. These walls may consist of traditional studs and drywall or one of the new, more breathable and moisture-proof technologies like Owens Corning's Basement Finishing System.

Dehumidification is another way to control indoor humidity, but for most people this means using a portable unit that runs day and night, condensing water out of the air which collects in a tub that must be emptied periodically. A better way to solve the problem once and for all is to install a whole-house dehumidifier. Installed in your heating and cooling system, a whole-house dehumidifier works 24/7/365 to take out excess humidity.

When Mold Gets Scary

Your parents lied to you when you were little—there really can be monsters in the basement. Particularly scary varieties include *Aspergillus, Stachybotrys chartarum,* and *Fusarium* molds. Under certain conditions, these microfungi can produce mycotoxins that impact human health, and because their spores are smaller than those of other molds, they can remain airborne for a longer period of time and thus be easier to breathe.

If you run into these dangerous intruders or any of their moldy cousins, don't attempt a cleanup on your own. Call a professional mold expert to inspect the area, identify the variety in residence, and determine what needs to be done to remove it. A pro will have the knowledge and tools to take this last step safely and without contamination of the rest of your home—something you probably wouldn't be successful in accomplishing on your own.

To get advice on how to find one, we turned to our trusted mold expert Jeff May, Principal Environmental Scientist of May Indoor Air Investigations (www.mayindoorair.com). Jeff is author of *My House is Killing Me!, The Mold Survival Guide, My Office Is Killing Me!,* and *Jeff May's Healthy*

Home Tips, all published by the Johns Hopkins University Press, and a major contributor to *The Money Pit's Mold Resource Guide,* available online at www.moneypit.com.

Jeff says the best place to start looking for a mold expert is by asking neighbors and vendors. Look in your local Yellow Pages. Call a local Board of Health, or the office of an allergist or pulmonologist. But that's just the first step. Once you have the names of a few companies, be sure to:

1. **Ask for and call references.**

2. **Request a sample mold-test report.** If you don't understand the report, see if a company representative can explain the results. Be sure the report includes information about the possible location of the mold growth and guidance on how to get rid of the problem.

3. **Require proof of training or certification.** There are a number of organizations that train and/or certify mold and indoor air quality professionals, including:
   - American Conference of Governmental Industrial Hygienists (ACGIH) in OH (513-742-2020; www.acgih.org).
   - American Indoor Air Quality Council (AIAQC) in AZ (800-942-0832; www.iaqcouncil.org).
   - American Industrial Hygiene Association (AIHA) in VA (703-849-8888; www.aiha.org).
   - Association of Energy Engineers (AEE) in GA (770-447-5083; www.aeecenter.org).
   - Indoor Air Quality Association (AIQA) in MD (301-231-8388; www.iaqa.org).

Finally, a note about those do-it-yourself mold-test kits, available in many hardware and home centers. Jeff says these kits may look pretty attractive when you're overgrown with mold, but they actually can be poor indicators of indoor mold problems. DIY kits only test for live spores floating around in the air, most of which may be from the outdoors, particularly in the spring, summer, and fall. Plus most of the mold spores that originate from indoor mold growth are dead, so those that land in the test-kit dish don't grow. Yet such spores are still allergenic and can cause problems.

Bottom line: if you are having symptoms that may be attributed to mold exposure, you should hire an experienced professional to do mold testing.

Do a Radon Test

If you spend any time in your basement, make sure it's tested for exposure to radon gas, which forms naturally in the soil and is known to cause cancer. Testing is a simple, do-it-yourself endeavor involving an adsorption (rather than absorption) canister that is placed in the basement. Expect to pay about $15 for a DIY test kit or $100 or so to have it done by a pro. During the two to seven days of the testing period, the rest of the house should be closed except for standard exits and entries (i.e., don't attempt this test in summer unless your house has central air conditioning). Once that period is over, the canister is sent to a lab for reading and determination of your radon level.

Your results will be reported in picoCuries per liter of air. A reading of either 4 or more pCi/L will necessitate installation of a radon mitigation system. Such professionally installed systems vent the radon present under your home to the outside for safe dissipation. Systems are moderately priced and their presence shouldn't lead to a dip in home value. Radon is a fairly common issue and by installing a mitigation system, you're saving future buyers the expense and dangers that radon's prolonged presence can cause.

By the way, testing your house for radon is a good idea even if you don't have a basement. Go to the Environmental Protection Agency's radon website www.epa.gov/radon to learn more.

Escape Window

dition to the obvious stairway entry from the house above, a room that's completely below ground may require a secondary exit, especially if the basement is used as a bedroom. Typically small basement windows can be replaced with larger ones incorporating "escape" wells, essentially an oversized window well designed specifically to provide an exit in the event of an emergency. These have the additional benefits of reflecting more natural light into the room, as well as adding space for small plantings to enhance an otherwise limited view.

If you're fortunate enough to have a house situated on sloping property, you may already have a door that exits to grade or it may also be possible to excavate and install a walk-out entrance to your basement.

Make Way for Mechanical Systems

Homes that have basements probably have mechanical equipment in them. That's just where you put things like the furnace, water heater, fuel oil tank, or well pump.

These can't be sealed away. At best, it degrades their efficiency and performance. At worst, it can create life-threatening situations, such as carbon monoxide buildup. If you're not sure about something around these vital organs of the home, stop and make a call to consult with a heating and air contractor before finalizing your project plans.

Mechanical systems will also need to be serviced as well as replaced. So it's not only about access, it's about maintaining clear and generously sized access via stairways and doorways to take out the old and bring in the new, whether it's appliances, a big-screen TV, or fitness machines.

Exit Strategy

As you get more comfortable with the idea of living in your basement, you'll also have to consider how you'll get out of it in case of emergency. In ad-

Basement Décor Challenges

Let's start with the aforementioned lally columns.[56] So many of these structural elements stick up in the darnedest places that manufacturers and retailers have responded with attractive column covers made of wood or other materials. If the lally columns run in a straight line below the main girder,[57] you can enclose them in a partition wall.

Exposed hanging air ducts and plumbing pipes may be somewhat easier to move, but design solutions will nearly always be cheaper. Ducts and pipes can be hidden behind drop ceilings, but be careful not to make your new living space too claustrophobic. Finished ceiling heights should be around 7 feet (although if your daughter starts dating the captain of the basketball team, your altitude may vary). Creatively coffered ceilings are another way to go—just make sure easy access to ductwork and pipes remains.

Another way to consider it is to work with it: make your basement a place to create a look of urban chic. We saw a great basement room at a press event Trane hosted in New York that was painted all white, but had structural elements painted in hot pink, a color that was also picked up in the artwork and

56.) Those things that hold up your house. 57.) Those other things that hold up your house.

accessories. This look is great for exercise rooms, family rooms, and even home offices. Match knobs and pulls on furniture in a similar style of brushed chrome. Basement concrete walls also play well into this style, especially when painted in light gray or silver.

Another option is to look at paneling or wallpaper in brushed metal styles that continue the industrial design aesthetic created by exposed pipes.

Design for Living

With your basement dry, warm, and safe, you're now free to transform it into any kind of living space you like. Whether playroom or guest room, workshop or wine cellar, there are plenty of finish materials that can help you achieve the desired effect.

Basement Flooring

Flooring is the starting point, and there are plenty of great options underfoot. Engineered hardwood is one of the more recent additions, designed to withstand moisture as it floats over a plastic-sheeting vapor barrier. Laminate is another great choice for basements: it's durable, cost-efficient, and literally a snap to install, thanks to many tongue-in-groove solutions that don't require gluing or nailing.

Vinyl tile and sheet, ceramic tile, and linoleum are also on the basement flooring roster. As graphically mentioned earlier, carpeting is not recommended, but you can add area rugs, or modular FLOR carpet tiles if you want to give more warmth to the space. More on that below.

Light and Color

Lighting is literally a pivotal element in creating a finished lower level that feels as airy and welcoming as any other place in your home. A combination of natural lighting from sparsely dressed windows and well-placed artificial lighting fixtures is the optimum way to accomplish this. When it comes to the latter, avoid old-fashioned fluorescents and

Paneling? You're Kidding, Right?

Remember paneling from your old rec room growing up? Okay, now you can forget about it. Today's paneling is available in cool styles like surprisingly realistic-looking brushed stainless steel and carbon fiber. Full walls or wainscoting of decorative tongue-and-groove panels can create the feel of custom-built wood paneling and give you the country, modern, or library style you dream of. Check out New England Classic at www.newenglandclassic.com for some beautiful options. Also look for paneling made from hardboard, a naturally green manufacturing process that uses wood's own natural binding agents, with no added formaldehyde. It's also the most durable: none of that warping we remember from the paneling we had growing up. In garages and workshops, pegboard styles in the same metallic looks cost 60 percent less than slot wall, another common storage system. Tom was among a panel of judges that selected DPI's brushed stainless steel wallboard in a product competition for Woman's Day *Home Remodeling. See DPI's website at www.decpanels.com for more options.*

Leslie Likes: Colors in Concrete

If your basement has a concrete floor that's in nice condition, use what you've already got to add style to the space. Acid staining is one process that adds interesting color and texture to concrete, with the chemical application almost etching itself into the upper layers of the material for a permanent treatment that won't flake away. There are also ways you can overlay two different kinds of staining solution to create imagery, designs, and patterns whatever it is that you like for your floor space. Do-it-yourself products are available at crafting stores, home centers, and via online retailers. Also consider painting your concrete floor and adding a resin clear-coat on top for the look of a highly polished, high-end surface boasting saturated color.

Link Up: Starve Mold

For great mold-proofing tips, check out the Mold Resource Guide posted on www.moneypit.com.

instead go for incandescent or compact fluorescent bulbs in a mix of indirect up-lighting to give the low-ceilinged space an expansive feel. Add recessed ceiling fixtures for task and overall illumination, and strategically place floor and table lamps to help illuminate the space. Go a step further with light-shedding structural features, such as half-height interior walls and dividing walls containing windows, and hang mirrors to amplify and reflect light as well as extend the illusion of space.

Another important consideration is the material you use to build walls and ceilings. The wrong wall and ceiling materials can lead to serious mold issues. For example, typical drywall is paper-faced and will feed mold. Instead, use a product like DensArmor Plus from Georgia-Pacific. This wallboard looks, cuts, and paints just like regular drywall, but with one critical difference: it has no paper to feed mold. DensArmor Plus is faced with fiberglass, an inorganic material that won't attract, breed, and feed a mold problem. You can also maintain a mold-free but cozy basement zone by installing specially made foil-encapsulated insulation behind wallboards.

Finally, let's talk color, which helps to define a basement and brighten up this subterranean space. Put some careful thought into the colors you apply to the walls, highlight through furnishings and accessories, and even roll out with area rugs. There is no reason why this room should be any different from all the others in your home. The space should reflect all of your personal style as well as suit the use of your new room.

Since basements are low on natural light, choosing a soft and light color will help keep the room from feeling like a cave. If you must have a deep or saturated color, use this in your accessories or as decorative paint highlights on the walls. For example, you can create an accent wall art piece by layering geometric shapes in different tones of your deeper color choice. This will allow the color in with out being too overwhelming.

Create art panels by covering a sheet of medium-density fiberboard (MDF) with bright or fun wallpaper and lean against a wall for instant style. Cover a wall with a grouping of photos all relating to a theme in one style of frame. Area rugs can be created using FLOR carpet tiles, puzzle-like tile squares that can be mixed and matched and, most importantly, pulled up and replaced when the kids spill something that just won't come out. Adding decorative lamps will also cast a warm and welcoming glow. Little changes like these can make all the difference when it comes to how you feel about your "new" space and how often you and your family put it to use.

Basement Storage Smarts

Whatever the living space you're about to create with your basement, we're betting storage will be part of the scene. Keep the following in mind for easy, moisture-safe access year-round.

- *Go with galvanized metal or fabricated plastic shelving, both of which resist wear and the effects of moisture.*
- *Make sure the lowest shelf is about 6 to 8 inches off the floor to protect stored items.*
- *Always think "up" and use as much available space as you can.*
- *For at-a-glance access, store items in well-labeled clear plastic bins.*
- *If you're dealing with limited storage space, rotate items so that the next season's goods are already at the front of the shelf when it's time to unpack them.*

Budgeting for a Home Bar

If you're planning to step up to your own basement libation creation, consider the following ingredients to create the perfect mix of utility, space-smart features, and style.

- ***Location, location, location.*** *Finding real estate within your real estate is the first step in the mix. Depending on its size and scope, a bar can discreetly furnish the corner of a room, embellish one side of a passageway, or even occupy a converted closet. Put it in your master suite, and your neighbors will think you're way hipper than you really are.*
- ***Features and functions.*** *Also consider the appliances and amenities you'd like to include, and the utilities they'll require. Some will call for the extra electrical juice of a new circuit, and a basement-based wet bar will necessitate a gray-water pump in addition to standard plumbing elements.*
- ***Build for comfort.*** *The optimum height for a sit-down bar is 42 inches, and 46 inches for a standing-room-only, "continental" style. Plan a 1-foot overhang so knees won't get knocked as soon as your customers take their seats, and allow a 2-foot width per stool to provide comfy elbow room.*
- ***Styling the scene.*** *In addition to your personal tastes, the style and décor of your home bar will be determined by its surroundings. Subtlety and coordinated styling are called for when the bar is incorporated into a more formal living area, and you can also choose one of the many portable models to deliver beverage service where and when it's needed, and be stowed away when it's not.*
- ***Customize with bar hardware.*** *All the traditional touches you've admired at old-time pubs and brassy barrooms are available for your own home bar through specialty retailers. Also look into reclaimed bars and backdrops salvaged by demolition pros from original public saloons. Experienced craftspeople can customize these treasures to accommodate modern amenities while preserving their classic charm.*
- ***Stock it up.*** *In addition to popular liquors and mixers, you'll need a brigade of glassware in various shapes and sizes, an ice bucket and tongs, a bottle opener, a blender, bar towels, and a bartending recipe book or two.*

Garages That Kick Butt

If you're like many of us, your garage doesn't kick butt. It's packed so tightly with stuff, you're lucky if you can get your butt in there.

According to www.DesignerDoors.com, the word garage comes from the French "garer" meaning to protect, and, more recently, to park.[58] Now a catch-all for sports equipment, toys, tools, and, the occasional automobile, garages have recently emerged as a new frontier in home improvement. If you can organize it here, you can organize it anywhere.

Just as with basements, you can transform this household dumping ground into a well-organized, functional space that's a safe, comfortable harbor for you, the cars, and all the stuff you need to stow. As more companies offer specialized garage storage systems, the options are endless.

Start by assessing the space and matching it up with the hoped-for end result. On your way to that workshop-and-storage nirvana, safety considerations will be critical to planning and preparing the space, so let's tackle those first.

58.) We assume that the suffix "age" means "your junk."

Garage Safety: Toys and Toxins Don't Mix

Besides being a thoroughfare for daily family traffic, the garage is a place where we tend to mix things together that would never meet anywhere else in the home. Toys and toxins are a dangerous combination, but check any garage, and you're likely to see just that: toys, bikes, and balls stored within inches of insecticides, turpentine, and gasoline. It should be no surprise, then, that these same spaces can be sources of many injuries. If this describes your garage, job number one is to get that sorted out right away.

Keep dangerous chemicals out of the reach of children, or better yet, in a locked cabinet. Also be sure to keep chemicals in their original containers with the labels in good, readable condition. Never purchase chemicals in quantities over the limit of what you'll use in a reasonable period of time. While it might make sense to buy a case of canned veggies at the local grocery warehouse, storing leftovers from a six-pack of ant poison isn't worth the risk or the bargain price.

Storing combustibles like gasoline, propane, and kerosene is also something that requires careful planning. These fuels must be stored in containers designed especially for them. Gasoline cans, for example, have special vents to avoid the dangerous buildup of combustible fumes. Storing gas in anything else is an explosion waiting to happen.

Finally, those common, everyday products like ladders and lawn tools can be unsafe if not stored correctly. Ladders, for example, should always be stored in a horizontal position so that children cannot climb on them and tumble over. Rakes, hedge trimmers, and shovels left on the garage floor or leaning against a wall can easily fall underfoot and cause injuries. To be safe, use wall-mounted storage racks to keep as many of your tools off the floor as possible, or relegate these to exterior garden sheds.

Door Dos and Don'ts

An overhead garage door is most likely the largest and heaviest door in your home. As such, a few safety considerations are needed while admiring all the great styles.

While garage door openers have been required to have automatic reversing mechanisms since 1982, these mechanisms can wear out or otherwise fail if not properly maintained.

To be safe, test your door's ability to reverse by placing a 2x4 under the open door, and activate the closing mechanism. If the door doesn't immediately reverse when it hits the wood, replace it. Newer doors also may have electric eyes across the bottom that can be checked by breaking the beam as the door is coming down to make sure that it immediately will reverse.

Another issue is pinching, since most garage doors are made of four large, horizontal panels on hinges. We like pinch-free garage doors from Wayne-Dalton that are so well done, the doors received the Consumer Product Safety Commission Chairman's Award.

Flying springs can be really scary. Most garage doors are powered by very large, heavy springs that provide the extra strength to lift the door. Eventually, these springs will break. When this happens, they'll fly off the door and across the room, potentially injuring anyone in their path. The solution here is a simple: thread heavy picture-hanging wire inside the extended spring when the door is in the closed position, and secure it to the eyelet at each end. With the wire in place, a broken spring will have nowhere to fly except safely back onto the wire itself.

By the way, if your opener is more than five years old, it's smart to replace that, too. A garage door opener is an important piece of safety equipment, and it's just not worth taking a chance with an old one.

Garage Elements: Fire and Light

Most garages are not well lit. Fluorescent lamps tend to dim in colder weather, and the typical garage simply doesn't have enough fixtures. Let there be light! Be sure garage circuits are protected with a GFCI (ground fault circuit interrupter). While regular circuit breakers are designed to prevent wires from overheating and causing a fire, a GFCI breaker is specifically designed to prevent shocks.

Building codes require that garages be constructed to protect the rest of the home from fire damage should they become engulfed in flame. For the most part, this is accomplished by what is known as the firewall, the original meaning: a wall assembly constructed to keep fire at bay by the use of fire-resistant drywall and other tactics.

Unfortunately, older homes may not have firewalls and many modern homes have had theirs rendered ineffective. For example, installing a fold-away attic stair in the ceiling of the garage creates a "hole" in the firewall and a shortcut for fire to take out your entire home. To be safe, make sure all walls and ceilings between your garage and house are constructed with at least 5/8-inch-thick drywall and that any attic stairs are covered with sheet metal for fire resistance. Equip your garage with a fire extinguisher rated "A-B-C," which means that the extinguisher can handle all types of fires, including those generated from wood and paper, electrical appliances, gasoline, or grease.

Organize It

Now that you know the limits and safety concerns involved in a garage space, it's time to go forth and organize. With that vision of the end result hovering in the back of your mind (storage, workbench, and, wonder of wonders, parking for the car), designate a few consecutive days in good weather for unloading and sorting of the garage's current contents. This is best done as a family effort, and if you're having trouble getting everyone motivated to participate, set a date for and advertise your upcoming garage sale in the local paper.[59]

Once you've winnowed down belongings to keepers, you can go forward with buying and installing the appropriate storage to accommodate your gear. The only thing that should be on the floor is your car or truck; everything else can be stowed on wall-racks: storage cabinets, hooks, and shelving systems. Make sure they're anchored for proper support of heavy items stored inside, and incorporate a flame-proof unit for storage of flammable items such as spray paints, stains, and cleansers.

Before reloading your garage, however, give it a good cleaning. Start with a broom, then wash away old grease stains with a solution of TSP (trisodium phosphate, a powdered detergent available in most home centers and hardware stores). Once

Greasy Rags Must Go!

Old towels and T-shirts may make convenient rags for garage-based projects, but when they become soiled with grease, oil, gasoline, or other flammable substances, they've gotta be tossed. Such rags are nothing more than kindling that, with the right ignition source, can turn into a fireball that destroys your home.

We know it's a challenge in our increasingly "recycle and reuse"–oriented consumer culture, but you should also resist the temptation to wash used rags like these. The petroleum hanging out in them after use will leach into your washing machine and leave your next load of laundry smelling like yesterday's lawn-mowing session. Placing a rag that has contained a flammable substance into a hot clothes dryer is also extremely dangerous.

Rags are cheap. Always safely dispose of the ones you've used, and find new candidates for your next project. Many communities offer a STOP Program (Stop Throwing Out Pollutants) that will accept a variety of hazardous materials and other items that need to be properly disposed of.

59.) Nothing moves faster than a teenager who thinks you're about to sell a box of her favorite childhood toys.

the floor is dry, you can also amp up its looks and stain resistance with an epoxy finish in the color of your choice, or lay down a durable rubber floor or garage floor tiles. If you like, mark the parking zone with colored tape or paint—it'll help keep you, the car, and all your stored stuff in line.

So now, it's time to load up. Group items by season and use, put toxic chemicals far away from toys and sports equipment and the reach of little hands, and station heavy machinery and other items on bottom shelves. Then keep up the good work—maintenance is far easier than the garage overhaul you've just finished, especially when you have a good-looking space to appreciate!

Warm It Up

If you're going to work in your garage, you might want to consider adding a little extra heat and insulation to make project time more comfy. Garages by their very nature are unheated spaces, and typically don't have standard insulation outside of that firewall between the garage and the house. So, finish off the other three walls with insulation and drywall, and then you can think about adding a heater. Portable gas or electric floor models or ceiling-hung units like those in commercial shops are great options. Just be sure to upgrade electrical wiring, gas lines, and gas venting for installation in accordance with the unit manufacturer's recommendations.

Tom's Tip: Should You Live in Your Garage?

In my 20 years as a professional home inspector, I've seen many garages converted to living spaces. I've also seen my share of botched garage conversions.

It's not my favorite use of a bonus space, since converting it can cost nearly as much as an addition. But if you're thinking of going this route, go all the way. Don't keep the telltale garage giveaways like the large door that no longer opens because you've installed a wall behind it, or a driveway that leads right up to the exterior wall. If you want to protect your home's resale value, make this renovation look like a garage was never even a part of the house plan to begin with.

There are plenty of other garage design peculiarities that also must be dealt with. For example, most garage floors are sloped. To level yours out, you may need to build a wood floor on "sleepers"—beams that sit on the floor and are cut at a reverse angle to give the appearance that the floor is flat. You'll probably also need to build up a section of the exterior wall with concrete block where you took out the overhead door in order to match the rest of the foundation.

Perhaps the trickiest part of a garage conversion is adding heating and cooling to the formerly unconditioned space. Be sure to check with an HVAC pro to determine the best way to do this for your particular project. It's important to ensure that your existing heating system has both the capacity to heat more space and that your building has the room to add the needed ductwork or hot water heating pipes.

Lastly, remember that garages are generally only insulated on the wall that connects them to your home (a.k.a. the firewall). You'll need to add insulation to the remaining walls, and if they're already covered with wallboard, consider having some insulation blown in.

Up, Up in the Attic

At the top of most Money Pits is the attic, which can be big enough to accommodate several bedrooms and baths, or just small enough to crawl across when it comes time to pull down holiday decorations.

In general, attics weren't designed as storage

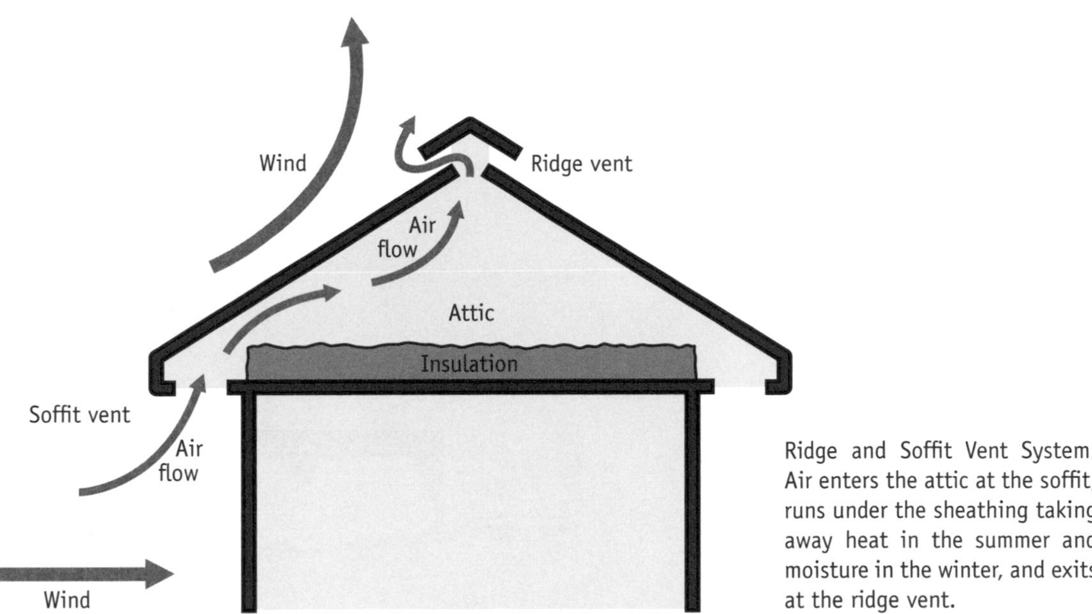

Ridge and Soffit Vent System: Air enters the attic at the soffit, runs under the sheathing taking away heat in the summer and moisture in the winter, and exits at the ridge vent.

spaces; rather, they're a part of the raw underbelly of structure that holds a house together and protects it from the elements. Because of this, installing a floor to accommodate stored items pretty much always involves some level of disturbance.

If the roof structure of your home was designed with prefabricated trusses, adding weight is a big no-no. Roof trusses are specifically designed to take the weight of the roof (and the snow, wind, rain, etc.) and distribute it downward and outward to the load-bearing exterior walls through a series of interconnecting wood framing pieces known as "chords." Adding storage to any other part of this finely tuned structural marvel risks weakening the roof system—creating discord, if you will.

If your home was built with standard conventional lumber, however, the risk of causing structural imbalance isn't nearly as high. But you still need to be sensible. Ceiling joists are designed to hold up the ceiling, not a floor loaded with the *Encyclopedia Britannica* collections you grew up with.

Be aware that your home's energy efficiency almost always suffers when the attic is converted for storage. Since an average attic needs 12 inches or so of insulation, the insulation is always thicker than the ceiling joists or trusses. As such, adding a floor causes the insulation to compress, squeezing out the insulating ability of the fiberglass.

With all of these challenges, you might be starting to think the attic adventures should be avoided. If you don't need a lot of storage, think of flooring just part of the attic, such as a small section around the attic opening. This way you can preserve the maximum amount of energy efficiency in the rest of the home. Since homes tend to be colder the closer you get the exterior walls, keeping this floored area to the inside center of the attic is smart.

To avoid crushing the insulation, raise the height of the joists by attaching 2x3s to their top edge before you attach the floorboards.

The Well-Ventilated Attic

An attic fan is generally a lousy way to cool the attic if your home already has a central air-conditioning system. Attic fans will not only suck away the hot air upstairs but also suck up the

Dormers can create new space from a usable area with the addition of light. Turn your newfound room into a great guest retreat, family entertainment area, or hangout zone for the kids.

cool conditioned air from downstairs through the many small voids in the structure.

Instead, go with a ridge-and-soffit vent system. Air will enter the attic at the soffit, run up under the roof sheathing where it carts away heat in summer and moisture in winter, and exit at the ridge. This 24/7 ventilation solution is far more effective than any other type of mechanical or passive ventilation solution.

Attic Living

Converting the attic to living space is even more ambitious than storage space, for all the reasons mentioned previously, as well as the height of the space. Determine your head-banging potential by measuring from the floor to the height of the highest point. If you've got 7 feet or more and can walk comfortably down the center of the attic, you can probably make a go of it. Adding more usable height beyond the ridgeline can be accomplished with a dormer, an extension of the roof line that delivers more usable space and can be quite charming at the same time.

We strongly advise working with both installers and architects, starting with the architect. These design pros can help you work through the issues and provide a set of specifications to present to competing contractors detailing exactly what needs to be done and how to accomplish it safely and effectively.

Plan on beefing up the floor joists during the conversion by having "sister" joists installed next to their undersized siblings. Properly installed, these can span over load-bearing walls and support normal floor traffic.

If you presently access your attic by pull-down stairs, you'll need room for a proper staircase for permanent access. You'll need 14 feet or so of space to build a straight stair, and as much or less for angular configurations, depending on how many turns the steps need to take on the way up. This is another reason an architect can bring real value to an attic conversion. Stair height and related structural framing are all dictated by building codes and have to be correctly constructed for safety.

You want your finished attic space to look hot, not be hot. It's unlikely that your present HVAC configuration can adequately provide enough comfort, so you may be installing a second zone of heating and cooling just for the upper floors. Insulation needs proper ventilation, so it's not a case of stuffing as much insulation in a rafter as it will hold. To the contrary, if your home has 8-inch-deep rafters, you should only be adding 6 inches of insulation, installed flush with the bottom of the rafter, leaving a 2-inch gap above it to facilitate the flow of air. This will need to be matched with the continuous ridge-and-soffit vent system described above that allows air to enter at the base of the rafters, travel up the roof sheathing, and then exit out a ridge vent at the top.

To create a comfortable living space, some parts of the mechanical systems in your attic can be moved, while others require creative decorating solutions. Rerouting the vent pipe from your bathrooms will be easier than, say, rerouting a brick chimney. Remind whiners that exposed brick walls fetch a high rent in New York City, and don't hesitate to try to collect that premium from whichever child wins the claim to the attic.[60] Use the chimney as a background for a grouping of your latest art endeavors or your starburst mirror collection. Use assorted profiles of lumber and architectural corbels—those intricately carved brackets—to create a decorative mantel to dress up the chimney. Build a wraparound bench to make the chimney a part of your hangout zone. Bottom line: let the structural details become a rustic and charming detail that can meld into a country or modern setting.

Finally, think about lighting. With few wall spaces, most light may come in from skylights or roof windows, which, if properly spaced, can add drama and sophistication to your new lofty nest.

If the attic space isn't a good candidate for conversion, you may need to consider other lofty goals—like an addition. We call those "new spaces," and we embark on those adventures in the next chapter.

60.) "Try" being the operative word

New Spaces: Additions and Repurposing

Sometimes, you just can't squeeze another square inch of usage out of your Money Pit. To move or improve: that becomes the question. Moving we tackle later in the book. Here, we'll look at adding on and making major changes to accommodate growing households and evolving interests.

The construction aspect of these spaces builds in a new set of questions and considerations, starting with the mysterious world of building and zoning codes, which is your first step in determining the final outcome.

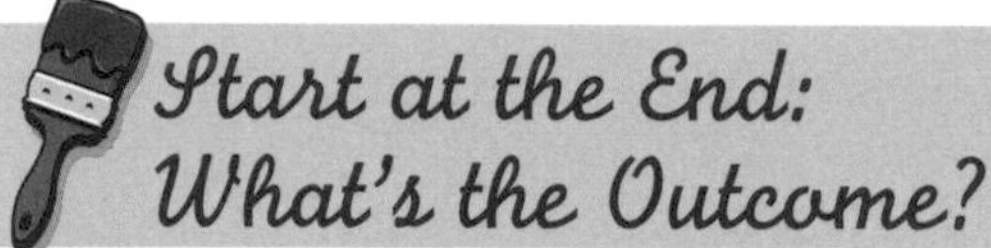

Start at the End: What's the Outcome?

Instead of making an expensive move, you've decided to make an expansion. Think not only about which family members will use it and how, but also what will happen if you decide to move sometime down the road.

Songs to Work By:

Tunes to help you get through your projects.

- *Who Says You Can't Go Home*—Jon Bon Jovi
- *The Times They Are A-Changin'*—Bob Dylan
- *Since You've Been Gone*—Kelly Clarkson
- *Mother in Law*—Ernie K-Doe
- *Space Oddity*—David Bowie
- *Knock Three Times*—Dawn with Tony Orlando
- *Your Mama Don't Dance and Your Daddy Can't Rock 'n' Roll*—Loggins & Messina
- *Mother's Little Helper*—Rolling Stones
- *The House Is Rockin'*—Stevie Ray Vaughan
- *Changes*—David Bowie
- Anything by The Mamas and the Papas

The ability to profit from the investment in a new space depends on a range of factors including the condition of the rest of the home, the value of neighboring homes, and what's going on with property values in the area overall. For best results, strive to have the improvements complement and coordinate with your existing structure and the neighborhood at large. Anything with an outer-limits, over-the-top look and feel will deter buyers, detract from a home's value, and incite present and future neighbors to whisper behind your back.[61]

Start your new-space planning by taking a good look around the neighborhood. Check in with local real estate agents and contractors regarding current remodeling trends and beneficial projects done in homes in your area. That way, you'll be able to create a valuable, livable, comfortable result without falling into the trap of serial renovation and other new-space pitfalls that can end up haunting you later.

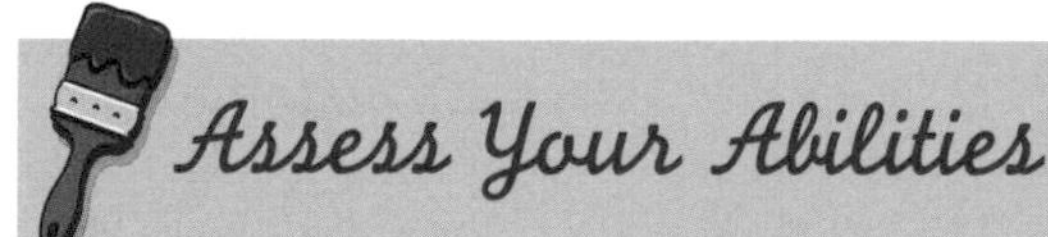

Assess Your Abilities

Additions are generally the provinces of the pros, not places to go boldly into if you haven't been a skilled DIYer for a long time. To put it bluntly, your homeowner's insurance won't cover your incompetence. That being said, also make sure that

61.) More than they do now.

the pros you hire are licensed and insured, because if they cause a collapse, fire, or flood, the same response from your insurance company will apply.

It's also likely that you will want an architect or designer involved to assure the look and functionality of the finished space. Specialized professionals such as heating and air contractors will be able to advise on the best mechanical systems for a comfortable new space. More tips on hiring pros for your project are covered in Chapter 15, Hiring Help.

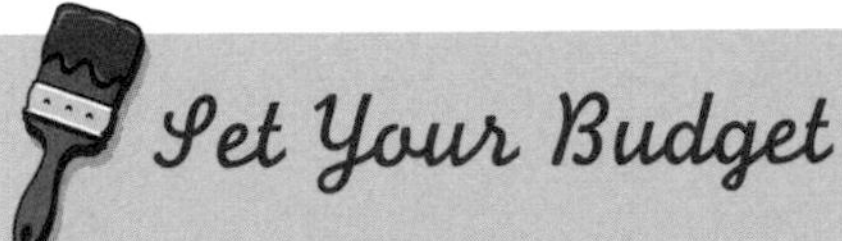

Set Your Budget

Once you get into structural changes, project price tags tend to shoot skyward. New spaces usually start in the five figures, and it's not uncommon to hit six figures.[62] As stated above, we advise prioritizing the investment to make sure the exterior views are in line with the neighborhood, with a second priority being the comfort, efficiencies, and safety of the mechanical systems.

Getting Permissions

There's an old saying that goes, "It's easier to apologize than to ask permission." This may apply in social circles, but when it comes to adding on to your home, failing to secure the right permissions from local, county, or state authorities can cost you dearly. "I know of homes where entire second floors had to be removed," says Gordon Gemma, a noted land use attorney based in New Jersey. "It's always important to understand local requirements before you start your project."

Gemma suggests that a good first step is to contact the local building department to ask about the "entitlement process"—a legal term that refers to the permissions your town requires. "Every jurisdiction is unique," he says.

For example, in Tom's home state of New Jersey, planning boards establish what can be built and where, but zoning boards grant permission for any projects that deviate from those planning laws. In other parts of the nation, county governments dictate what can and cannot be constructed. There are also situations where outside agencies could be needed for the A-okay, such as a project that impacts a protected wetland or other environmentally sensitive area.

So before you get too deep into your project, make sure you do the research necessary to color between the lines. If the project is big enough, consider consulting an attorney specializing in land use. Hiring a pro to guide you through the process is money well spent and can save you loads of time, effort, and aggravation.

Look Out Below

Once you've gotten permission for your project and figured out how to pay for it, you need to determine what lies beneath. A lot of critical utilities run right through your property, and there may even be some old home systems that go waaaay back hiding underground as well (see the "It Happened to Tom" sidebar). Always check in with local utility companies before you dig (or even think of doing any

Move or Improve?

Debating whether to move or improve? Here are some important financial factors to consider. Remodeling can have a big price tag, but can increase your home's current value. Moving takes you somewhere new, but can cost 10 to 15 percent over the value of your present home. Do the math, and make sure you're making the right move. If you ultimately decide to stay and improve, be sure you're not overdoing it for the price range of your neighborhood. Home value estimators like those at AOL Real Estate (www.realestate.aol.com) can help you get a handle on what your home may be worth.

62.) That's before the decimal point, in case you weren't sure.

work) to ensure that you don't cause a dangerous disturbance to water or electrical lines that could make you a pariah in your home or entire neighborhood (especially if you knock out the cable right before the big game). The local phone book should make this step easy, as most have a section of city services phone numbers that'll put you in touch with every party involved in renovation issues.

Live in a condominium, co-op, or covenant community? Then one more major hurdle awaits. Your homeowners' association will likely have its own set of rules and standards to ensure a uniform look across the units' exteriors, as well as guidelines regarding interior renovations and remodels. Also remember that if you share a wall, floor, or ceiling, fixes on your side are impacting someone else's property or a part of a structure owned by the association. So make sure you're up-to-date on who owns what, where the project limits fall, and which items need to be approved by your association board to prevent an un-neighborly outcome.

It Happened to Tom: Finding Buried Treasure? Not!

When my kids were young, we set up a swing set in the backyard, and mysteriously, there was an area underneath it where grass never seemed to grow. I always assumed this was because of the kids playing around on that spot, but one day, after the swing set had been up for a little over a year, I was over in the grassless zone and kind of absentmindedly stomped my foot on the ground. And I noticed for the first time that it sounded hollow. And I was thinking, "That is so unusual. . . . Why would this sound that way?" Then curiosity got the best of me, and I went off to get my shovel and started digging. About 12 inches down I ran into a big hunk of wood, at which point I excitedly thought I'd finally found buried treasure that some thoughtful ancestor had left for his future heirs!

Well, I was partially right. What I'd found was indeed left by my ancestors[64]*: an old abandoned septic tank. Likely a bona fide original from when the house was built in 1886, this tank was so old that it was made of brick, instead of the usual one-piece poured concrete. It was about 8 feet by 10 feet and had a wood door on top, probably preserved by layers upon layers of good old-fashioned lead-based paint!*

At this point, realizing I wouldn't be named Parent of the Year anytime soon, I dismantled the swing set and then excavated enough of the tank to break up the brick so that the tank walls collapsed inward. I loaded it up with fill dirt and gave it a good tamping, after which the swing set was moved back in place for safe play minus my ancestors' buried treasure trove of DNA.

Talking Generations: Special Spaces for Life Stages

As we duly noted in the warm-up chapter, designing for all needs and life stages is smart, even if you personally don't ever expect to be infirm or elderly.[63] New spaces open up opportunities to work these recommendations into your Money Pit:

- Doors should be at least 32 inches wide, with a lever-style handle for easy grasping (incorporating locks where necessary for child safety), and open outward if at all possible. Interior doors can also have their hinges replaced with offset hinges that will allow for an extra 2 inches of width clearance. A pocket door is even better, simple to operate and granting quick access for those with wheelchairs or walkers. Pocket doors require plenty of usable adjacent wall space for installation, but can also be mounted on the wall surface if needed.
- When it comes to the floor, choose a nonslip surface and make sure there's enough space for comfortable navigation by wheelchair.
- Equip all stairways inside and out with secure handrails running along both sides of the

63.) Good luck with that. 64.) Who I'm sure were now gathered together laughing their heads off around some heavenly watering hole.

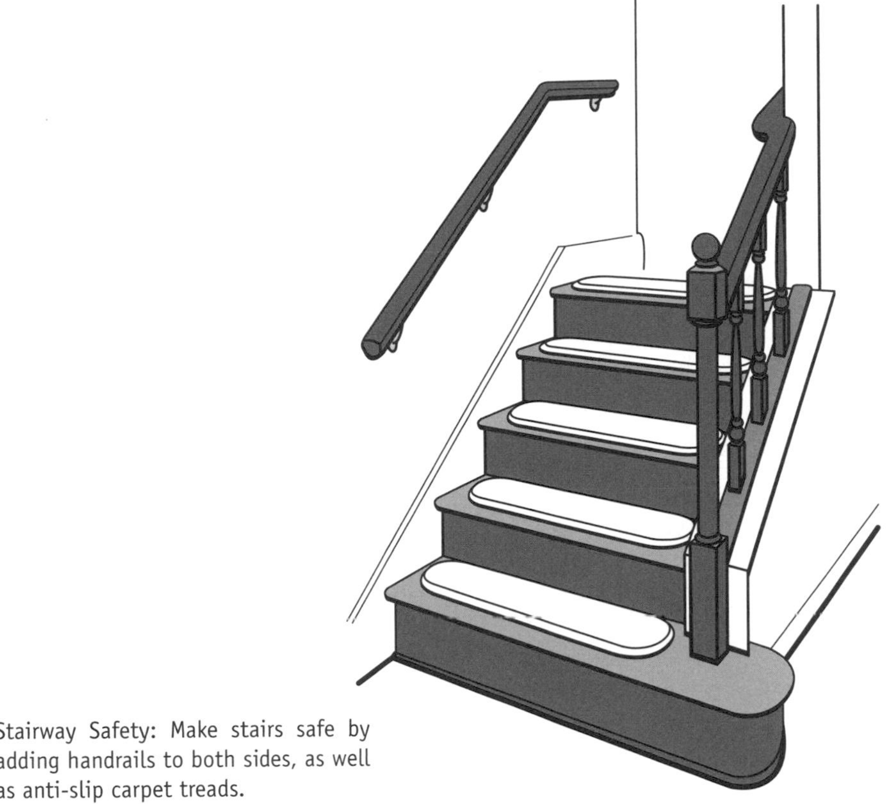

Stairway Safety: Make stairs safe by adding handrails to both sides, as well as anti-slip carpet treads.

steps. Also make sure that stair treads are roomy enough to prevent trips, and edges are marked for easy visibility (use a different color of tile, stain the edge of a wood step with a contrasting tone for a helpful and decorative detail, run a metal edge along a carpeted step, or accentuate with colorful tape).

- Fill the space with plenty of bright lighting, and have a night light on duty at all times. Larger, rocker-type light switches are handy for everyone, and even come in illuminated models.

- At first it may sound like a five-star hotel luxury, but having a phone in the bathroom can actually end up being a lifesaver.[65] Select a wall-mounted, non-portable model with the largest touch-tone keys you can find, and install it at a height that's easy to reach even if you're lying on the floor. Preprogram the phone with important numbers.

- Outfit cabinets with easy-to-grasp hardware.

- Keep closets accessible as well as organized, with easy-to-reach clothing rods stationed between 20 and 44 inches off the floor and full-extension storage drawers located no higher than 30 inches off the floor. Higher drawers should be shallow and lower drawers can be deeper.

- Eliminate excess clutter, seriously. Everyone can be motivated by a life-or-death issue, which means preventing trips and falls, while maintaining safe exit access. Maintain one step-free entrance into the main living area, and repair any holes, cracks, or loose masonry on all pathways and entrances around your home.

Despite the downright smart functionality of improvements like these, they can be accomplished with both safety and style. Thanks to the teaming of

65.) Please, no business calls from in there.

AARP and the National Association of Home Builders, there are now pros in most communities who can easily make your personal design plans Universal. Certified Aging in Place Specialists (CAPS) are contractors trained in the unique needs of aging residents and can assist with design modifications that extend independent living and keep spaces barrier-free as well as attractive and welcoming. They know codes and standards inside and out, and have the project and product knowledge to make your new space a great value for years to come, whatever your age and needs and those of family members residing with you. Learn more at www.aarp.org.

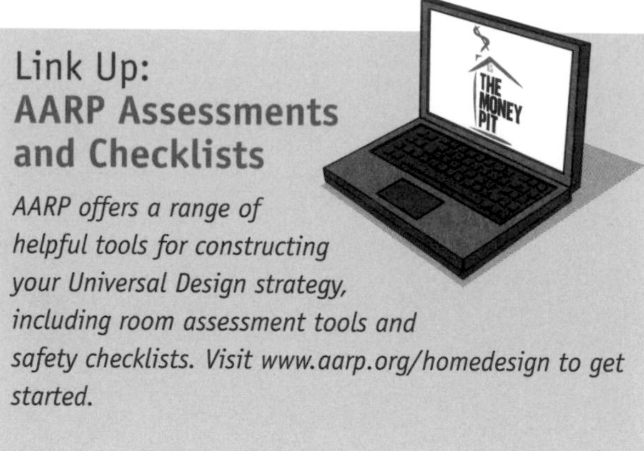

Link Up: AARP Assessments and Checklists

AARP offers a range of helpful tools for constructing your Universal Design strategy, including room assessment tools and safety checklists. Visit www.aarp.org/homedesign to get started.

Can't We All Just Get Along? Designing for the Peaceful Coexistence of All Family Members

Along with the Universal Design considerations that can make a space friendly to all family members, your new space may call for features that help maintain friendliness *among* family members. Whether you're creating an apartment for a "boomerang kid," accommodations for a nanny or other caregiver, or a posh suite for long-term guests,[66] build in access and comfort. A separate, independent entrance may be needed, noise-reducing wall and flooring treatments incorporated to create a relaxing retreat, and supplemental water heating power worked in to prevent shower shortages on busy mornings in a full house.

Masterful Master Suites

One of the most popular new spaces is transforming an old master bedroom into a custom in-home retreat. Pretty much standard in today's newer homes, older homes generally need significant expansion to create your suite of dreams. The latter approach can be either a plus or a minus for your home's value, as the number of bedrooms it has is a major selling point, so do your homework before having plans drawn up.

Building an addition is likely to be the better approach versus taking over existing bedrooms to expand your space. "If you have a three-bedroom home and merge two of those rooms to create your master suite, you may severely limit the marketability and general appeal of the home," says appraisal expert Dr. Donald Moliver, director of the Kislak Real Estate Institute at Monmouth University in West Long Branch, New Jersey. He added that if you have four or five bedrooms and lose one to the improvement, the potential loss of value is less.

Once you've determined the size and the scale of your new space, think about what areas of usage you can create within it to best suit your definition of luxury. Maybe separate closet spaces and dressing areas with custom furnishings appeal to you, or you'd like room for a cushy sitting area for reading and relaxing. Smooth, easy-access transitions to the master bath and other zones of the suite contribute to its flow and

66.) Just remember, the nicer the guest room, the longer they will stay. Make it too nice, and you'll be adding them as dependents on your tax return.

comfort, and maintaining a few flexible spaces for changing needs (such as a mini-nursery that can later become a dressing area) will help it to hold its value over time.

Ultra-custom amenities continue to be part of the master suite scene, and folks will go to great lengths to create an in-home retreat that they never have to leave. Mini bars are expanding into mini-kitchens with refrigerators, microwaves, and gourmet coffeemakers at the ready, although Leslie questions the wisdom of having the lingering smell of microwave popcorn in your bedroom. The warmth and romance of a cozy fire are almost instantly possible thanks to the efficient new vented gas-burning fireplaces and vented gas heaters that look like woodstoves. And you don't even have to stop at having one master suite thanks to new designs that marry two adjoining, mirror-image suites for super-personalized getaways.

Cool Workshops and Creative Hobby Rooms

A space devoted exclusively to favorite projects and hobbies is the dream of many homeowners, and can become an efficient and fun reality by adding new space to your Money Pit.

The first step is to identify the key needs of the space you are planning. Woodworking, metalworking, or scrapbooking, for example, each have a unique set of spatial requirements. Your ability to enjoy your hobby space will depend largely on a clearly laid out and organized plan that functions for the specific hobbies you need space for. Think about actual workspace, storage, power, and adequate ventilation. This is another good time to do the layout on paper before committing to purchasing products for your hobby or workshop. It's a lot cheaper to adjust a plan on paper instead of your foundation.

Remember the work triangle and other geometrics we discussed in the kitchen chapter? Kitchens are designed to keep the physical distance between the range, refrigerator, and sink as short as possible. For your workshop or hobby room, what is your equivalent of the three most important areas? If you're a woodworker, that might be the table saw, radial arm saw, and workbench. But if you enjoy sewing, that might be the space between your sewing machine, fabric cutting table, and ironing board. Identify these key areas and plan your space on paper around them to maximize efficiency.

Power planning is the next consideration, as you may need to literally amp up the available electrical capacity to accommodate and operate your tools and project appliances. For the best results in your new project zone, you'll need to step up the power to a 20-amp circuit to keep the lights on and power all your gear.

Improved ventilation is also a must, especially if your hobby involves fumes, dust, or any tool that releases exhaust. Plan your hobby work triangle with this factor in mind, and build in convenience and safety with smart storage for tools and supplies using pegboard and enclosed storage systems. Repurpose glass jars into storage for craft or office items; use matching boxes and bins for a finished feel.

Entertainment Centers and Home Theaters: The Vacation Home within Your Home

We're right with you on wanting a family entertainment zone like this one. As with the other new spaces we've discussed in this chapter, access, comfort, and power delivery are prime concerns to build around.

- Carefully map out placement of equipment and seating for the best sights and sounds possible. Speakers will need to be strategically stationed around the room for optimum effect, and large-scale screens require specific amounts of clearance between them and the audience for comfortable viewing.
- Plan for a power load much larger than that required by a standard television, stereo, and DVD player setup.
- Install lighting that is both targeted and adjustable depending on the viewing situation, such as track lights.
- Sound-proof the room with proper insulation, carpeting, panels or drapes along walls and ceilings, and fabric-upholstered furnishings.
- Furnish with comforts and conveniences such as adjustable seating, roll-away snack carts and tables, and food and beverage storage.[67]
- Take out a gym membership, so you don't sink totally into couch-potato-hood.

Also remember to have fun with the décor of your in-home movie palace. Classic movie posters, autograph collections, and memorabilia displays can all add star quality to your personal home theater.

Home Offices and Family Computer Centers That Work

Now that technology has become central to family living, the computing zone typically needs to accommodate a range of ages and uses. This is where we return to the traffic report approach, tracking who's using the area and when for an efficient space that provides the access and comfortable coexistence everyone needs to get along with a lone computer in the mix.

Define the Space

The first step to creating a functional home office is to define the space. For both you and your family's sanity, it is important to identify the borders of the area you will be using for your homework. Home offices can be entire rooms or carved out portions of an existing room. But once that space is identified, the goal is to establish border

67.) Do we even need to mention the popcorn machine?

security. Convince family members to give it the respect it deserves so that it doesn't morph from a functional workplace for telecommuting parents to the kid's coloring corner.

When setting up your home office, think not only about the physical needs of the space, but also about environmental impacts, like noise, fresh air, a pleasant view, and distractions. Choosing a location that is fairly exposed inside your home enables you to keep an eye on everything else that's happening in the house, but privacy is degraded. If you plan to conduct serious business, barking dogs or a toddler suddenly succeeding at toilet training can affect your credibility pretty fast.

Functional Flow

Once your space has been identified, setting up an efficient and functional workspace is key, especially since so much work accomplished in the home office happens while you sit. Considerations like whether you are right- or left-handed when choosing the location of the printer or file cabinets can make a major long-term difference in how well the space performs. Harkening back to our discussion of the "working triangle" in the kitchen (see Chapter 2), think about where you are going to sit and how far you'll need to move to have access to the three most important areas of that office (computer, printer, fax machine, office supply storage, shredder, etc.). By keeping the points of the triangle as close together as possible, you'll conserve lots of personal energy on an ongoing basis.

If space is in such short supply that you have to share with the rest of the family, the basic home office setup of desk, component and supply storage, and media connections can become more family-friendly with a little clever customization and new spin on work zones. Build in fun, individualized areas of storage with old-school-style lockers, and bring in a communal work table that can do duty for homework as well as crafting projects. Adjustable, movable seating also helps keep things rolling in the right direction, as do storage carts for project and office supplies.

Finally, working comfortably and efficiently also requires good lighting, ventilation and additional outlets. Think about adding overhead lights to keep the space bright and cheery, as well as possibly having a pro expand your HVAC system as necessary to assure plenty of ventilation. Also consider that whatever electrical outlets your room may have had in its prior life might not be enough to power your new work center. Besides electrical wiring for lights and outlets, you may also need to add or extend your phone lines and internet connection to this area as well. For cost efficiency, bunch all these wiring projects together and have your local electrician do them all at the same time.

Tom's Office Studio? **His Grandmother's Closet!**

In your search for home office space in your house, don't neglect to consider that additional space may only be a few saw cuts away. In Tom's family homestead, he converted a studio apartment his grandmother used to live in when he was a kid to a fully functioning home office and broadcast studio. Needing space for his radio broadcasting gear, he eyed a closet that was constructed beneath the second floor staircase. By removing the closet's walls and adding soundproofing, he was able to build a broadcast studio in the space that once used to serve as his grandmother's closet! Most homes are filled with hidden spaces like this. Whether they are unused closets or voids behind finished walls, spaces like these are buried treasures that once uncovered can deliver functional solutions for your office or storage needs.

Throughout these indoor Money Pit adventures, we've frequently touched on mechanical systems, such as heating, cooling, and ventilating. We wrap up the indoors in the next chapter with the guts of these systems, also known as how to avoid freezing, sneezing, frying, and fizzling . . . and freaking out over utility costs!

CHAPTER 8

Avoid Freezing, Sneezing, Frying, and Fizzling . . . and Freaking Out over Utility Costs

When it comes to our heating and cooling systems, most of us prefer to, in the words of the legendary Ron Popeil, "set it and forget it." They're usually an inherited aspect of the home—you didn't choose them, but they seem to work okay, so you hope they'll continue chugging along. What's more, a lot of homeowners aren't always exactly sure of what their systems' components or power sources actually are, other than big metal things in the basement, attic, and backyard.

In this adventure, we invite you to go gear-head and Meet Your Home Comfort System—whether it's your existing system that needs maintenance or a future system that you're contemplating.

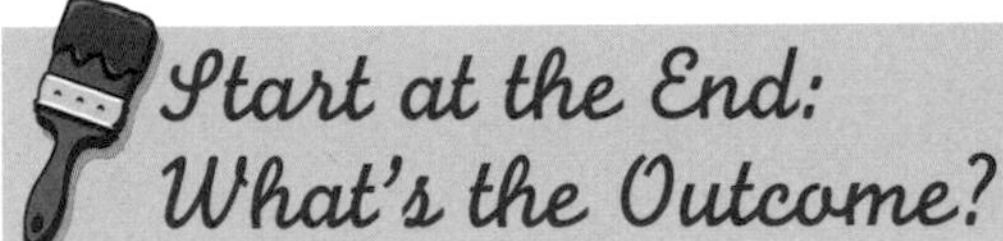

Start at the End: What's the Outcome?

A fully functional, dependable system is important to your home's structure, as well as your family's personal comfort. That means your outcome is well-functioning system components programmed to deliver ideal temperature and humidity levels. Unless your favorite me-time is writing large checks to utility companies, improved efficiency should also be a major objective of your mechanical systems.

Does that mean repair or replace? In some cases, you can improve comfort and efficiency with adjustments to and ongoing maintenance of your current system. In the cases of much older systems, investing in a new system today will definitely cut your comfort costs.

We recommend starting with a home energy audit to determine the weak and strong points of your existing system. Your local utility may offer low-cost to no-cost home energy audits. Or visit the Energy Star website (www.energystar.gov) for more ideas.

Assess Your Abilities

Because heating and cooling systems are typically complicated and can be dangerous to work on,[68] an HVAC pro or two will be coming into your life if replacement is the plan. We also recommend that annual system maintenance be done by a pro, with all the specialized diagnostic equipment they have. By the way, HVAC stands for

Link Up: The Best Energy-Saving Website, Ever!

If you want to know even more about making changes to save energy in your house, check out the Energy Star website at www.energystar.gov. There you'll find the "Energy Star @ home" tool and lots of helpful information to make your home more energy efficient. A few simple changes can make a big difference, and you'll be helping to reduce the effects of global warming.

68.) Natural gas, electricity, and ignorance don't add up to good times

Heating-Ventilation and Air Conditioners and is pronounced "H-Vac."

In between, however, there are plenty of smaller tasks that most DIYers can take on, such as changing the filters, adjusting the vent, and cleaning the components.

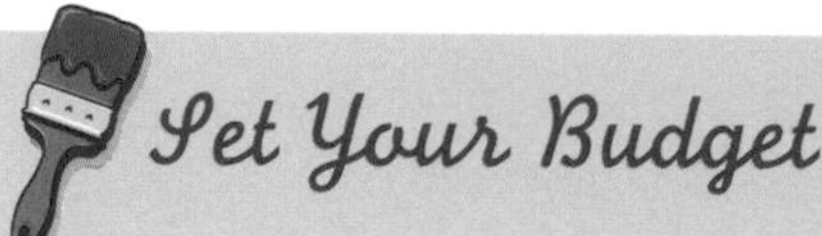

Set Your Budget

Maintaining your home's HVAC system is like taking care of that fuel-burning machinery that resides in your garage. Occasional tune-ups, fluid refills, and cleaning keep it going, and neglect does just the opposite. If you aren't doing so already, it's time to create an HVAC care routine, which starts with knowing what kind of system you have and how best to take care of it. This is one area of home maintenance where an annual service plan is a great investment (it costs pennies compared to replacement of an entire system).

If you're going the replacement route, you want to get the highest efficiency and best comfort you can afford—a calculation that not only includes upfront costs to buy and install, but ongoing operating costs. That includes considering how long you plan to be in your home to reap those rewards. If you're looking at replacing a system, we also recommend upping the investment a bit and adding a whole-house air-cleaning appliance. Whole-house units are a better buy than the room portables advertised endlessly on TV. By the time you buy enough room purifiers to do the job, you'll have outspent the cost of a whole-house system.

The toughest part of replacing an HVAC system is understanding the equipment and tradeoffs. That said, HVAC system components are not hard to understand, and nearly all major manufacturers have informative websites and glossaries to help in training for this adventure.

Link Up: HVAC 101

These links will help you train for system replacements:

www.americanstandardair.com
- *System Recommendation by Zip Code*
- *Replacing or Upgrading?*

www.residential.carrier.com
- *Home Heating and Cooling 101*
- *Efficiency and Cost Savings*

www.lennox.com/residential/
- *About Your Air*
- *Energy Calculator and Tax Credit Information*

www.rheemac.com/home_cooling.shtml
- *How Does It Work?*
- *Choosing a System*

www.trane.com/residential
- *Customize Your System*
- *Your Dealer's Expertise*

Songs to Work By:

Tunes to help you get through your projects.

- *Breathe*—Nickelback
- *The Heat Is On*—Glenn Frey
- *Cold as Ice*—Foreigner
- *Cool Night*—Paul Davis
- *Some Like It Hot*—Robert Palmer
- *Speed of Sound*—Coldplay
- *Catch the Wind*—Donovan
- *The Air That I Breathe*—The Hollies
- *Cool Change*—Little River Band
- *Heat Wave*—Martha & the Vandellas or Linda Ronstadt
- *Hazy Shade of Winter*—Simon & Garfunkel or Bangles
- Anything by Kool and the Gang

Heated Discussions about Heating

There's a tendency to think that homes are heated by one giant blast of hot air, but in reality, most people don't have politicians who visit that regularly. Air is constantly being recirculated, reheated, and redistributed to create the desired comfort level. There are two types.

Products for Forced-Air Systems

Indoor/outdoor system (also split system). *Refers to a comfort system with appliances in two locations. Common examples include an outside unit, such as an air conditioner, and an indoor unit, such as a furnace with a coil.*

All-in-one system (also packaged system). *An air-conditioning and/or heating system in which all components are located in one cabinet. Used in certain localities and for certain building types, the all in one system is installed either beside or on top of your home.*

Air conditioner. *Any device that can change the temperature, humidity, or general quality of the air. In central air systems, the air conditioner is an outdoor unit.*

Air handler. *The indoor component of your air conditioner or heating system that moves air throughout your home.*

Furnace. *That part of a forced-air heating system in which the combustion of fossil fuel and transfer of heat occurs.*

Heat pump. *An outdoor unit that warms your home in winter and cools your home in summer. More common in moderate climates that don't have many extreme days, a heat pump is installed in place of an outdoor air-conditioning unit. Heat pumps can be either electric or geothermal, which uses the constant temperature of the ground to heat and cool the home.* —courtesy of Trane

Forced Air

Forced air is the most common type of heating system, largely because it's the most economical for home builders to install. One ductwork system blows both hot and cold—you know the type.

Forced air is generally pretty effective. It includes supply ducts delivering conditioned air throughout the home, and return ducts which take air back to the heating and cooling appliances, which may include a furnace and air conditioner or some other equipment combination.

Most problems with forced-air systems stem from imbalances, also known as hot and cold spots. You know what we're talking about if you have a room over the garage—exposed to the elements via walls, the roof, and the floor. To make matters worse, the HVAC appliances are almost always located far away from that room. The good news is that hot and cold spots don't have to happen. A good HVAC contractor can compensate for this by putting additional ductwork or additional returns in the room to make sure it gets the right amount of heated and cooled air by season.

Wet Heat

In the old days, we'd call this steam heat. We also called it terrifying when we were kids and knew for absolute certainty that those clanking, clunking old radiators were actually monsters.

Today, the politically correct terms are radiant or hydronic heating, and it's much quieter and far less terrifying. Popular in Europe, these systems are less common than forced air on this side of the pond because they require a separately installed distribution system, which can be a major investment in an existing home. But we love

Invest in an Annual Service Plan

We don't usually recommend purchasing service contracts for home appliances and systems, but HVAC is one of the few exceptions. Arranged through your local utility, this kind of plan ensures that you stay on top of the critical maintenance checks that only a pro can handle, and that you're covered for any surprise service calls. The few hundred dollars you'll invest in a service plan will not only provide peace of mind that your system is always safely in shape, but they'll also seem like a bargain compared to the hundreds if not thousands you'd have to spend to repair or replace a neglected heating or cooling system.

them: they are enjoyed for the comfortable, mostly quiet heat they provide.

Hydronic heating is efficient and comfortable because it uses water to transfer heat throughout the building, and water can hold more heat than air. According to the Hydronic Heat Association, you would need a 10- by 18-inch forced-hot-air heat duct to carry the same amount of heat that can be transported by a 1-inch-diameter hydronic heat pipe.

Hydronic heating systems can also be easily zoned (split to cover different rooms or sections of the house) and are also ideal for improving indoor air quality, since there are no ducts to trap dust or allergens, and no blower spreading those sneeze-makers around.

In a typical hydronic system, water is heated in a boiler, which is typically either gas- or oil-powered. The water is then circulated through pipes as either liquid or steam to radiators and convectors located in the rooms of your home, which distribute the heat as it circulates and returns water back to the boiler to be reheated.

In some cases, boilers also supply hot water for your domestic needs, like cooking and bathing. In this case, the water actually follows a separate path through the boiler and never mixes with the heating water. Boilers that supply domestic water do so by

Ask Tom & Leslie: **Does a Heat Pump Heat?**

Q: I have a heat pump. Last night the temperature dropped to 20 degrees outside. The heat pump usually works pretty well. I put a thermometer on the vent just to check the output temperature, since it didn't seem like the air was hot. The temperature was reading about 78 degrees coming out of the vent. I turned up the thermostat (just to turn on the "Aux," auxiliary heat), and the output temperature rose to 85 degrees. Are these output temperatures normal? I am pretty sure that the output temperature varies depending on how cold it is outside.

A: Yes, what happened to you is totally normal. Here's why. Heat pumps are really two heating systems in one. The primary is the heat pump, actually the same as an air-conditioning system that cools your house, with one main difference: a reversing valve. The reversing valve reverses the flow of refrigerant in the heat pump to deliver warmth in the winter as opposed to coolness in the summer.

A common complaint about heat pumps is that they "blow cold air." Typically, it's not really cold but is also not nearly as warm as what you might get from a gas or oil furnace. A heat pump operating normally will usually deliver heat at around 90 to 100 degrees or so. The fact that yours was blowing 78 probably means that it's short on refrigerant.

Heat pumps are supposed to do most of the work to maintain the heat, but automatically bring up the electric resistant heat if the difference between thermostat setting and the room temperature is more than two degrees. It might also be that there is a problem with the thermostat that prevented this from happening properly.

So what about that big boost when you switched to auxiliary heat? The secondary heating system within a heat pump is a set of very-expensive-to-run electric heating coils. When you turn on the "Aux" switch, you are firing up those coils, giving the heat a big boost, but also more than doubling your electric consumption. Talk about pain at the pump! Call in a pro today.

Products for Hydronic Systems

Boiler. *That part of a hot-water or steam heating system in which the combustion of fossil fuel and transfer of heat occurs. Boilers heat water under pressure, which is then distributed either as heated water or steam to a system of radiators or convectors to heat a home.*

Distribution system. *Typically made from steel, copper, or PEX pipes, the distribution system routes the hot water or steam from the boiler to the radiators or convectors.*

Radiators. *Radiators or convectors are types of heat exchangers that transfer heat from one medium, typically water or steam, to air. In a residential system, radiators are typically made from cast iron or steel and can be found as baseboard or freestanding units. Steam radiators get much hotter than hot-water radiators and are therefore smaller and often need vented covers to protect occupants from burns.*

Radiant heat. *Usually refers to a distribution system that is concealed in a concrete slab or behind a ceiling. In these systems, the distribution piping circulates heat to the material to be heated, such as the concrete, and then that material transfers its heat to the occupants. Radiant heat is considered a very comfortable system since it delivers high-quality heat behind the scenes.*

storing it in a tank next to the boiler where it is fed as needed. The disadvantage of this type of a system is that the boiler has to run all year long and it is usually less efficient compared to a standard water heater.

Just like a furnace, the boiler in a hot water or steam system will need annual servicing to run efficiently and safely. Radiators also should be kept clean inside and out. They should also be free of any obstructions either in front or on top, and furnishings should be kept out of their path so room air can flow freely around them.

Radiant floor heating, mentioned earlier in the bathroom chapter, also falls under this category, and has become much more dependable and rugged with technology and time. Where old systems depended on metal piping that could wear down and break, today's radiant heating systems make use of durable PEX (cross-linked polyethylene) piping. Some manufacturers have made radiant flooring even easier to incorporate into room remodels with efficient, easy-to-install panel and blanket fabrications. Waking up to warmed-up floors warms up your heart all day long, even in a cold world. Radiant systems tend to be more popular in northern climes where heat is valued more than air conditioning. But forced air and wet air can reside happily in the same home, so the radiant systems can be installed anywhere.

Electric Heat

If you're relying mainly on electric heat, we're sorry to hear it. It's the most expensive option, so with all the cash you're likely shelling out during the heating season, you technically should receive a big "thank you" bottle of champagne from your local utility every year.[69]

Made to heat a limited space, electric heaters can serve as helpful supplements to larger HVAC systems, but if they're all you've got, you might want to consider installing a different, more efficient system so you can go back to buying your own champagne again.[70]

Electric heat has some benefits: it's the easiest system to zone and a good choice as auxiliary heat. Since each electric radiator can have its own thermostat, rooms can be turned on or off as needed. It's the least expensive way to add heat to a space, since it only needs power run to it—no gas piping or venting. Therefore, we might recommend adding electric heat for less-demanding situations, as with a basement rec room that generally stays warm but needs heat just one or two months out of the year. For that purpose, it's worth paying the higher cost to run the electric heat for the short period of time it's needed.

69.) Which you would guzzle straight from the bottle when you see how much your electric system guzzles from your utility budget. 70.) We love champagne, but we really prefer drinking it from flutes by the fire rather than straight from the bottle in desperation.

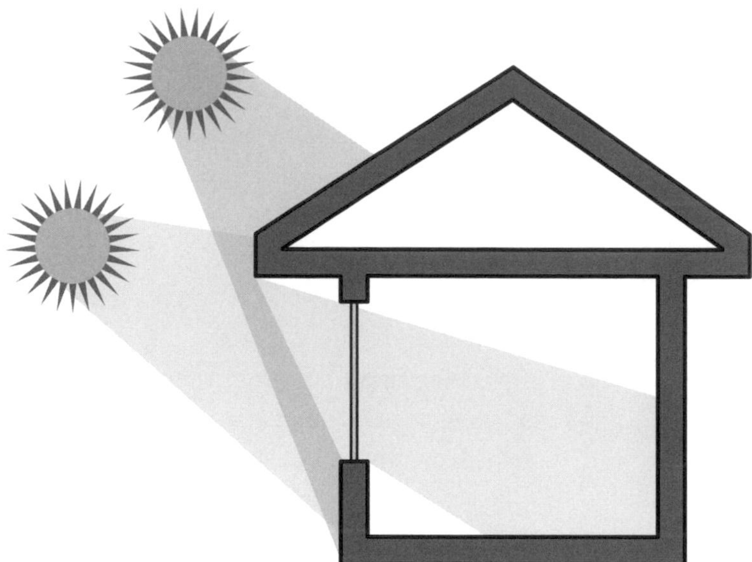

Simple Solar Design Changes Save Energy: Changes in the building's design can reduce energy consumption: For example, a slightly larger overhang blocks the hot summer sun but allows plenty of light in during the winter when the sun is low.

One type of electric heating device that makes sense is an electric radiant floor, also known as a mat system. Typically used in select rooms that need just a little bit more comfort like baths, three-season sun rooms, or mudrooms, electric radiant mats are installed beneath the floor and can be wired to a programmable thermostat so they operate only when needed, like early in the morning in a bath, which beats having cold feet! Modernization of electric radiant mat systems have made them affordable, as well as easier than ever to order and install.

Solar Heat

There are two kinds of solar heat: active and passive. Active solar involves solar panels or shingles mounted on the roof of your home, where they capture the warm rays of the sun and transform them into energy to power home heating and other systems. Active solar can be a great accompaniment to a hot water or electric heating system, and as the technologies are fine-tuned for solar success, many states are offering rebates to consumers who install these earth- and resource-friendly systems.

Passive solar is a great HVAC supplement. It can be easily incorporated into any home comfort scheme just by following the sun. Homes designed to take the best advantage possible of seasonal sunlight travel patterns allow warmth to easily enter during the colder months, with strategic shading from window dressings and outdoor plantings screening out the sun's rays during days when you just want to stay cool.

One example of this is designing a long overhang into the roof where it meets the south-facing side of a home structure: it'll block sunlight in the summer, when the sun sits higher in the sky, and let sunlight in during the winter, when the sun sits lower.

Cool Down: Air-Conditioning Talk

Central air conditioning is probably one of the most appreciated creature comforts available in homes today. Utilizing the ductwork of a forced-air system, an outdoor compressor unit and an indoor unit containing an evaporator coil team up to create and distribute the cool.

The Alphabet Soup of HVAC Systems

What is about home improvement and confusing acronyms? Some may feel this verbal shorthand is only meant to confuse consumers and amuse pros. Here are some definitions to help you figure it all out:

***AFUE** is Annual Fuel Utilization Efficiency. Indicated as a percentage, your furnace's AFUE tells you how much energy is being converted to heat. For example, an AFUE of 90 means that 90 percent of the fuel is being used to warm your home, while the other 10 percent escapes as exhaust with the combustion gases.*

***BTUIS** British Thermal Unit. Used for both heating and cooling, BTU is a measure of the heat given off when fuel is combusted. Or for cooling, it's a measure of heat extracted from your home. (One BTU is approximately equal to the heat given off by a wooden kitchen match.)*

CFM stands for Cubic Feet per Minute, a measurement of airflow that indicates how many cubic feet of air pass by a stationary point in one minute. The higher the number, the more air is being forced through the system.

***EER,** Energy Efficiency Ratings, measure the efficiency with which a product uses energy to function. It is calculated by dividing a product's BTU output by its wattage.*

***EAC** is Electronic Air Cleaner, an electronic device that filters out large particles and contaminants in indoor air. It then electronically pulls out tiny particles that have been magnetized, such as viruses and bacteria, drawing them to a collector plate.*

***HSPF,** the Heating Seasonal Performance Factor, is a measure of the heating efficiency of a heat pump. The higher the HSPF number, the more efficiently the heat pump heats your home.*

***MERV,** or the Minimum Efficiency Reporting Value, is the standard comparison of the efficiency of an air filter. The MERV scale ranges from 1 (least efficient) to 16 (most efficient), and measures a filter's ability to remove particles from 3 to 10 microns in size.*

***SEER,** the Seasonal Energy Efficiency Ratio, is a measure of the cooling efficiency of your air conditioner or heat pump. The higher the SEER number, the more efficient the system is at converting electricity into cooling power.*

—courtesy of Carrier

Tom's Tip: Cool Enough for You?

Not totally cool with the output of your central air conditioner? Then grab a standard room thermometer and use it to measure the temperature of air coming out of the supply ducts and air going into the return ducts. If these temperatures are 12 to 20 degrees apart, your system is probably cooling normally; if the difference is larger or smaller than that range, something's amiss and it's time to call your local HVAC pro.

Ductwork: To Clean or Not to Clean?

With all the air they carry to heat and cool your home year-round, ducts eventually end up holding onto some dust and debris. However, this doesn't mean you should put the system through frequent, rigorous cleanings, as these can end up causing major air quality problems if poorly executed. Instead, make sure to change filters frequently, and have expensive duct cleanings done only around every five years or so or following a major home renovation project that has kicked up an inordinate amount of dust. That'll be more than enough to keep your ducts in a row!

For the best results and most efficient cooling, annual cleaning and maintenance of system components is critical, and filters need to be changed or cleaned frequently (about once a month, unless you have a high-efficiency unit). You might also like to do some rebalancing of duct dampers for better-targeted cool in every room of your home.

Of course, there are always other, smaller air-conditioning units you can incorporate into an HVAC scheme. Window-mounted or through-the-wall units can be helpful, although they can also end up making fall and winter a little extra cool, too, if they're not installed and sealed correctly. We don't recommend through-the-wall units unless they are professionally installed, as they can impact a home's structural integrity.

The better supplemental AC option, in our opinion, is a ductless split system. Tom has a split system in his home office, which works extremely well to augment the central air conditioning that can't quite reach the office space. With a ductless split system, a wall blower hangs on the inside wall of your home. This is connected via a refrigerant line to a small compressor that sits outside, just like a central air system. The compressor supplies chilled refrigerant to the blower inside, which circulates the cooled air.

Another way to spread around the coolness is by installing a whole-house fan. Not to be confused with attic fans, which will actually suck up the precious proceeds of your central air system and send them toward an unappreciative stratosphere, whole-house fans make the most of cooler nighttime temperatures. Usually installed in the ceiling of an upper-level hallway, a whole-house fan will draw cool air indoors through slightly opened windows around the house, and push warm air up and out through the attic for an efficient and fast change in temperature that also serves to give your central air system a well-deserved break. If you have a whole-house fan, install it on a timer so you can set it to run for an hour or two in the evening to keep the house cool while everyone is drifting off to sleep.

Hot Tips for Comfort and Efficiency

A cool, comfortable house is a welcome escape from summer heat, but sometimes you can end up just as uncomfortable inside your home as outside. Whether your indoor cooling system consists of central air or a few well-placed window fans, here are additional ways to keep your cool without spending a fortune:

Efficient windows. Roughly 40 percent of the unwanted heat that builds up in your home comes in through the windows, so installing energy-efficient units can make a clear difference. Since most energy efficient features can't actually be seen, it's important to know what to ask for. For starters, request double-pane windows with low-E glass. The "e" stands for emissivity, and that's what stands between you and lots of heat-producing UV radiation that drives up your cooling bills.

Humidity control. You've probably heard it said a million times: "It's not the heat, it's the humidity." Portable dehumidifiers need constant emptying, but professionally installed whole-home dehumidifiers run 24/7 to keep humidity down throughout your entire home and never need emptying.

Smart shading. Carefully positioned shade trees can save up to 25 percent of a household's energy consumption for heating and cooling. On average, a well-designed landscape provides enough energy savings to return your initial investment in less than eight years. Trees can reduce surrounding air temperatures as much as 9 degrees because cool air settles near the ground, and air temperatures directly under trees can be as much as 25 degrees cooler than air temperatures above nearby blacktop. A well-planned landscape can reduce an unshaded home's summer air-conditioning costs by anywhere from 15 to 50 percent. The type of tree you select will vary depending on the part of the country you live in, so check with a nursery to choose the best one for your yard.

Improve your grading. Homes will stay cooler and drier if the outside grading and drainage conditions are maintained. Poor drainage leads to higher moisture levels inside the home, which are uncomfortable as well as unhealthy. Your yard and roof are the two major drainage zones to watch and correct if needed. In the yard, soil should slope around the house so that it diverts water away from the house. And where the roof's concerned, make sure it's rimmed by clean, operable gutters that carry water well away from the house and its foundation.

Work at night. Run heat-generating appliances like ovens, dishwashers, and clothes dryers only at night when it is cooler, avoiding the need to use your air conditioner to overcome their heat as well as the sun's earlier in the day.

Storm window shutdown. Close storm windows in rooms where you're running window AC units, and in others reached by a central air system. The same air that leaks in during the cold winter months also makes an appearance during the summer and drives up cooling costs.

Reverse spin. If you have ceiling fans, take advantage of their one energy-efficient feature: reversible motors. By controlling the direction of the blades, you can use the fan to pull cold air up in the summer and push warm air down in the winter. You can further upgrade fan efficiency by installing an ENERGY STAR–qualified model, which is up to 50 percent more energy efficient than a conventional fan.

Thermostats

Helping you manage the heat and the cool for both forced air and hydronic systems is your thermostat, the temperature-sensitive mini control panel connected to your home's systems.

Thermostats are getting smarter and smarter all the time, with many models programmable for your ideal comfort every day of the week. Better yet, you can actually program many of them now without the help of a Silicon Valley engineer. Large backlit screens and one-button programming make it easy to maximize your system for comfort on workdays, weekends, vacations, and when guests start to overstay their welcome. For more efficiency and lower heating and cooling bills, we recommend making the most of this feature by setting your thermostat to kick back by a max of 10 degrees overnight, warm the house again about an hour before you wake, and then dial temperatures down while you're away from the house during the day.

Water Heaters

Unlike heating system boilers that primarily distribute water to warm your home's radiators, water heaters[71] deliver hot water for domestic tasks like washing dishes and taking baths. Water heaters are fueled by gas, electricity, or oil.

Traditional water heaters heat water whether you need it or not. Set the temperature to 120 degrees or so, and the water heater maintains that temperature 24/7, even when water is not being used. This built-in inefficiency can be conquered by installing a tankless water heater, but first let's talk about how you can make the tank water heater you have more efficient.

If your water heater is gas-fired, it is important

71.) Notice we did not call these "hot water heaters" because, well, that would be redundant.

that it be serviced. Gas water heaters can develop combustion deposits that make the burner inefficient. Plus, that combustion gas is about 80 percent water vapor and very corrosive, leading to lots of large rust flakes that can form and land on the gas burner, making it potentially dangerous to operate. Just like any fossil-fueled appliance, it needs to be cleaned regularly to operate safely and efficiently.

Electric water heaters exhibit wear and tear a bit differently. These heaters rely on electric coils, usually two of them, with each heating one half of the tank. As the coils age, they burn out. The surest sign of this is when you all of a sudden start running out of hot water quickly. Repair is a matter of draining the tank and replacing the coil, a job best left to an experienced plumber or electrician.

One way to save operating costs with an electric water heater is to have a 240-volt timer installed by an electrician that allows the water heater to come on only when you need it. In a typical day, you'd set the water heater to come on an hour before you wake up to handle the morning showers, then go off during the day only to come back on in the late afternoon and into the evening to handle chores like washing dishes and even baths. Set correctly, you'd only need to heat water 8 to 10 hours a day, rather than 24.

Oil water heaters need the same sort of maintenance that any oil-fired boiler or furnace might, regular cleaning and adjustment of the burner. But oil-fired water heaters have one very distinct advantage over gas or electric heaters: an extremely high recovery rate. A 30-gallon oil-fired water heater can easily serve a family of six. You'd need a 40-gallon gas or 50-gallon electric unit to even come close to that.

Regardless of the type of fuel you have, it makes sense to spill out 2 to 3 gallons of water from the drain valve every six months or so to clear any sediment that may have settled in the tank. Sediment can act as an insulator between the heat and the water and make the unit inefficient. To do this, hook up a garden-type hose to the drain valve at the bottom of the unit. Open the valve, and let the water drain into a sink or to the outside. Then close the valve, remove the hose, and dry the area up, and double-check that it is fully closed and water is no longer leaking out of the drain.

It's also a good idea to add a water heater blanket to gas or electric units to reduce loss through the shell of the water heaters. Water heater blankets cost only a few dollars and are easy to install by following the manufacturer's instructions.

Going Tankless

Tankless water heaters, fueled by natural gas or propane, are the smarter way to deliver cost-effective hot water to your home. We love tankless water heaters. There are many advantages, first and foremost of which is that they never run out of hot water, but they don't sit around heating it all day either. These "on demand" marvels only heat water as it's needed, and are also controllable because the water temperature can be changed instantly. Some models even offer a wireless control that can dial up the temperature of your water heater from anywhere in the house.

So how does a tankless water heater actually heat all that fast-flowing water? It's a pretty simple process, actually. As you turn on the hot water, the tankless heater senses a flow and fires up. The water is run through a very efficient heat exchanger (sort of like a hot-water radiator) where the heat generated by the tankless unit's gas burners transfers to the water as it passes by.

Tankless water heaters burn very clean, and the combustion is usually sealed inside the unit, reducing or eliminating any carbon monoxide risk. They can last twice as long as a tanked unit. Tankless water heaters do cost more than tanked water heaters, but considering the advantages, this adds up to a great value over the life of the unit.

Contemporary units have easy-to-use digital

Ask Tom & Leslie: A Tankless Task

Q: My wife and I live in an L-shaped home. The water heater is in the middle, with a master bath at one end and the kitchen at the other. It takes a long time for hot water to reach the faucets. Would a tankless water heater help, and are they cost-effective? Would we need two units?

A: Tankless water heaters deliver hot water on demand and are far more efficient than their potbellied counterparts. However, in your case, tanked or tankless won't get the water to your bedroom any more quickly. To speed the delivery of hot water to your distant faucets, you'd need to shorten the physical distance the water needs to travel. However, since tankless water heaters are about a quarter of the size of the regular unit, there are many more installation and venting options available. Have a plumber inspect your home to determine whether or not a second unit is practical.

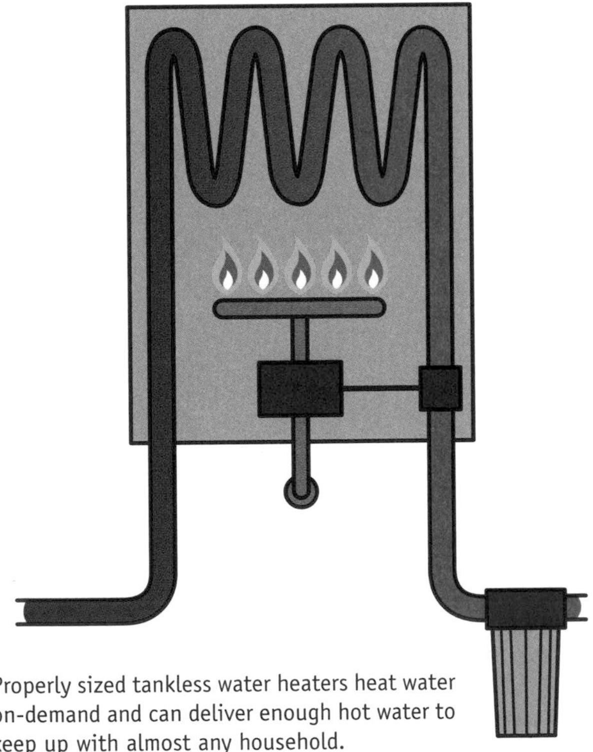

Properly sized tankless water heaters heat water on-demand and can deliver enough hot water to keep up with almost any household.

controls, making it easy to dial warmth up or down as needed—an advantage when the elderly and the young are visiting, with their higher risk of scalding accidents.

Tankless water heaters will not improve the time it takes to get hot water if you install them in the same spot as your previous water heater. There is, however, their size advantage. Tankless units are small—very small—compared to traditional water heaters. As a result, they can be installed practically anywhere, even outside in warmer climates. You can also use multiple tankless units to divide your domestic hot water supply into two zones. One can be fed from the basement or first floor, where it's a short distance to the kitchen and powder room, and another can be fed from the attic or a second-floor closet, where it's just steps away from the bathrooms. As a result, you can have both a cost-effective and convenient source of hot water.

Tankless water heaters are at their most efficient when powered by propane or natural gas, and typically need gas lines larger than their inefficient tanked counterparts. So if you're considering working one or two into your home's plumbing system, start by consulting with a service professional or the appliance manufacturer. Electric tankless units are available, but not efficient enough to warrant replacing your standard electric tank unit.

Even the government has gotten in the act of recommending tankless technology. The Energy Policy Act of 2005 granted tax credits for qualifying energy-efficient improvements, including tankless water heaters, to homes built between January 2006 and December 2007. The government, being, well, the government, has since (as of the time of this writing) chosen not to continue extending tankless tax credits. Regardless of the political winds, we still say the savings, safety, and convenience make going tankless a smart move. For the latest news, go to www.energystar.gov and search "Federal Tax Credits."

Troubleshooting System Snafus

Even with standard maintenance, HVAC systems can be the sources of occasional mysterious knocking, unbalanced output, and other causes for troubleshooting. Here are a few common issues, their sources, and guidance on how to sort them out.

Unbalanced Heating or Cooling

Poor duct design and sealing are often the culprits behind an unbalanced HVAC system. In a perfect world, rooms would be designed with completely balanced temperature distribution.[72] The challenge is a blend of your local climate and construction demands.

Improvements begin by inspecting your ductwork and sealing any leaks. Add insulation to improve comfort for more predictable room-to-room temperatures. Make sure that the air-return portion of a forced-air system is functioning properly, because that can also have an adverse impact on room temperatures. One way to ensure this is by undercutting interior doors so that there's enough space between the door's bottom and the floor—at least an inch. With that, air can escape to the return vent even when the door is closed.

You can check and adjust airflow by doing a "tissue test" at each room's supply and return vents. Here's how: Switch your thermostat to "fan" and then go from duct to duct, holding a tissue in front of the vent to determine airflow. Supply vents should blow the tissue toward you with a good little gust, and return vents should pull the tissue right up against themselves.

No Heat or A/C

If you wake up to having no heat or air conditioning one day, the first thing to check is the power switch to the furnace or air handler. Disguised to sneakily appear as a mild-mannered light switch where it can frequently be turned off by accident, this key component can shut down the entire system in, well, the flick of a switch. The HVAC power switch is usually near the HVAC equipment, or in a basement installation, at the top of the stairs. To save some hassles, find yours and make sure it is clearly marked. A strip of electrical tape over the top can also serve as a reminder when you reach out to hunt for a switch in the dark.

Oilcanning of Ducts

This noisy phenomenon happens when metal ducts rapidly fill with air as your system starts up, expanding with a big bang, just like an old oilcan would—hence the name. Repair is easy, a simple matter of proper reinforcement of the ducts. Just to be sure that oversized airflow or other elements aren't the issue, it's wise to have an HVAC technician check things out and help determine safe solutions that'll keep the air moving, but much more quietly.

Banging Pipes

Banging pipes and radiators are common complaints when it comes to steam systems. The knocking sound is the result of tiny steam explosions that occur when water collects in the radiator rather than heading back toward the boiler to be reheated.

If a little knocking sets your world rocking, there's an easy fix. Literally tip the balance by repitching the unit so it sends the excess water back toward the unit's inlet valve. You can do this by adding a shim—a small piece of wood—under the legs on the end of the radiator opposite the inlet valve.

72.) But then again, in a perfect world, we'd have completely balanced people, too.

Cold Radiator

If too much air gets trapped in a hot water radiator, water won't be able to move smoothly through it, and you'll wind up with the radiator either totally or partially cold, when the heat is on. Occasional "bleeding" of the radiator will help you maintain efficiency. To do this, you'll need a radiator key, a simple wrench designed in the shape of a key to fit the air bleed valve on the top of the radiator. Turn the heat on and once all the radiators are warm, use the key to drain out any air that has become trapped at the top of the radiator. Once hot water starts to "spit" out of the bleed valve, you can shut it off and you'll find that that the entire radiator will heat. Be careful, though, since the hot water can burn you if you're not cautious.

For the most part, HVAC troubles should be addressed by HVAC pros. The best defense against unplanned problems is regular maintenance performed by these experts. This is also a situation where we'd recommend getting an annual maintenance contract through your independent service contractor or utility company. Aside from including needed system maintenance checks, service contracts usually cover the cost of service calls necessary when your system breaks down unexpectedly.

Link Up: HVAC Maintenance Calendar

Just like that valuable piece of machinery in your driveway, a heating and cooling system needs annual maintenance to keep on running efficiently. So plan to have a contractor pay pre-season calls (spring for cooling, fall for heating) to address elements in ENERGY STAR's Maintenance Checklist, which can be found at www.energystar.gov.

Breathing Easy: The Fungus among Us and Other Irritating Irritants

When older homes were constructed, they had lots and lots of natural ventilation, also known as drafts. Older homes provided as many as six to eight air changes every hour, meaning that the home was so drafty that all the air inside was exchanged with outside air that many times in an hour. While this was helpful for breathing easy, it wasn't so great for your carbon footprint.

Today, new homes are built and maintained tighter. Installing new windows, increasing insulation, and sealing with caulk are just a few Money Pit adventures aimed at keeping drafts out. The unintended consequence has been a rise in indoor air quality issues.

Mold: What You Need to Know

People panic over mold. Buyers are frantic about it, sellers are frightened of it, real estate brokers are intimidated by it, and home inspectors are leery of it.[73] People are moving out of their homes, and some are even having their houses demolished because of mold growth.

Mold is today's bogeyman, not without reason, as we've all seen in areas hit by hurricanes in the last few years. Even without natural disasters, mold can build up in a home in very unhealthy ways. Mold spores make their first uninvited appearance in your Money Pit through the tiniest gaps you ever chased with a caulk gun . . . or sometimes just by sashaying right on in the front door or a window.

73.) And your teenager is growing it in his room right now.

Once inside, it's party time, with spores able to grow on clothes, shoes, toys, and even the family pets. The spores are so tiny, that once airborne, they can easily be inhaled deep into your lungs.

Some molds are harmful while others are benign, and how mold affects you depends on your own personal sensitivities. To avoid attracting it altogether, you have to know what makes it tick: moisture, air, and food.[74] The food part can be anything organic, from dust to starch-based wallpaper paste—and when you think about it, scores of similar diners are open 24/7 throughout your home. You can shut them down by running through the following checklist:

Mind the moisture. Keep humidity below 50 percent in basements by improving outside drainage and grading, keeping gutters clean and soil always sloping away from your home; and by using a dehumidifier. Cover dirt crawl-space floors with plastic to reduce moisture. (More on this in Chapter 6.)

Store safely. Keep all storage several inches up off concrete floors and away from foundations where dampness can easily seep in. This is especially important with organic material like cardboard boxes. Avoid using wooden shelves; metal or plastic shelves are preferable.

Heat finished basements. Below-grade spaces like finished basements are more likely to become infested and should always be heated to at least 60 degrees, even when not in use. The warmer the space, the smaller the chance that condensation will form and feed a mold problem.

Build mold resistance. When choosing building materials, use those that won't feed mold. Fiberglass-faced drywall, such as Georgia-Pacific's DensArmor Plus, for instance, is a better bet than paper-faced products.

Ventilate vigorously. Poor or missing ventilation fans in damp spaces like baths and kitchens can leave enough moisture behind to sustain a mold problem. Make sure all baths and kitchens are vented by properly sized fans that take moisture outside rather than into attics. Keep the bathroom door open after bathing to speed drying of surfaces. (Read more in Chapters 2 and 3.)

Avoid basement carpets. More than almost any other material in a house, carpeting can be an incredibly welcoming haven for mold. Even nonorganic carpets can collect the dirt, dust, and moisture that combine to provide mold with fertile ground in which to grow, especially in below-grade spaces where relative humidity tends to be higher. Hard surface products like laminate flooring or engineered hardwoods are always a better choice for basement spaces.

Filter the air. If your home has a forced-air heating and cooling system, using a top-quality air filter is a must. Go for a MERV rating of 6 to 8, or 11 if your family is prone to allergies. MERV stands for Minimum Efficiency Reporting Value and is a rating for filters that describes the size of the holes in the filter that air is allowed to pass through. The smaller the holes in the filter, the higher the MERV rating and the efficiency. Another option is a whole-house air cleaner, which is mounted permanently to the home's HVAC system and uses ionization technology to charge particles and make them stick to filters like a magnet. One of the most effective units is the Aprilaire Model 5000, which can trap virus-sized particles as small as one micron (one millionth of a meter) and needs just yearly filter replacement.

Insulate ducts. Duct systems that carry heated or cooled air throughout your house must be insulated whenever they pass through unheated or uncooled spaces like attics or basements. If not,

74.) Add "football" and you've described the average male.

Link Up: Mold Online

For more mold tips, visit the Mold Resource Guide at www.moneypit.com. We've partnered with leading indoor air quality expert Jeff May, principal scientist of May Indoor Air Investigations LLC and co-author of The Mold Survival Guide: For Your Home and for Your Health *(Johns Hopkins University Press, 2006), to provide the most common mold questions and solutions in one handy resource. Also see www.mayindoorair.com for more information on Jeff's work.*

condensation can form inside the ducts and, when combined with dust in the air, can allow mold to grow in the ducts, and then spores can easily circulate throughout your entire house.

Clean carefully. Use mold-inhibiting cleaners in bathrooms and kitchens. Portable air-conditioning units should be taken apart and cleaned at the start of every season. When painting damp spaces like kitchens and bathrooms, use paint with a mold inhibitor that's EPA-approved for indoor use.

Fix floods fast. If you do have a major leak or flood, quick action can stop mold before it starts. Thoroughly dry soaked carpets and padding, and remove any wet upholstery. Then wash and disinfect all surfaces before the carpet and pad are replaced.

Off-gassing

Another indoor environmental threat to be aware of is off-gassing, which is more than just a term to make your kids giggle. Off-gassing is the release of volatile organic compounds—VOCs, to use industry parlance—contained in finishes, adhesives, and fabrics into the air.

It Happened to Tom: Tales from the Crypt

A few years back, I did a segment for a national television show where I investigated complaints of a sick house. We had gone through the entire house and taken various samples where we thought mold existed, and one of my last stops was the attic, where I really didn't expect to find anything. Still, knowing the house had a bit of a ventilation problem, I wanted to see if that was having an effect on the humidity level.

As I pulled down the attic stair and walked up the steps, I got very out of breath. And I thought to myself, "You are way out of shape, dude." But I slugged through and grabbed some samples of the attic's fiberglass insulation, just because we had tested everything else. Well, that evening, I got a call from the lab asking where the insulation had come from, along with the urgent report that the strands in the sample were completely infested with Aspergillus *mold. Turns out, I wasn't out of shape—I was being poisoned!*

This result got our whole team asking, "How can mold grow in an inorganic material like fiberglass?" Well, it turns out that fiberglass is also a good filter material, and because there were recessed light fixtures cut into the house's ceiling, dust was being sucked up from the house into the fiberglass, where it became the perfect food for mold.

Correcting the problem was pretty dramatic—basically, the roof had to be opened up, all of the fiberglass insulation vacuumed out, the whole attic treated to kill the mold, new insulation installed, and the roof replaced. One interesting thing we found out during the process was that the woman who lived in the bedroom with attic access had been complaining of breathing difficulties for quite some time, and other folks were having a hard time believing her. But she was right, and it was all because of that mold hidden away in the attic, just above her head!

Fortunately, many manufacturers are responding by making products that are free or at least low in VOCs, so look for those options when you shop; also think ahead and prevent later development of air quality issues by choosing such products as paperless drywall (remember how it resists mold?). Whatever the content of furnishings you choose, plan on airing them out for a few days before bringing them inside. If you're planning to upgrade your home's carpeting, ask the dealer to unroll and air out the new carpet for at least one day before it comes home. You can also cut down on dust during removal of the old carpet by vacuuming it well before the installation crew arrives.

Humidity Management

The healthiest, most comfortable homes have moderate humidity levels—not so dry that you buy hand lotion by the drum, but not overly moist, either, which increases your discomfort, along with the potential for very bad things to grow and thrive.

We strongly recommend a humidifier if you live in drier climates or have a forced-air system. Keeping the air at a comfortable level of moisture reduces heating and cooling costs.

There are basically three types of humidifiers: flow-through, drum, and spray. Drum humidifiers have rotating parts that frequently break down, and since water collects in the pan underneath them, they can also breed mold. Spray units aren't much better, as they spray water directly into the air above the furnace where it often drips down and causes rust damage to the furnace itself. The best style is flow-through, in which water trickles over a coil and evaporates into the warm air. Better models even include computerized controls that measure inside and outside temperatures and calculate just the right amount of humidity based on current weather conditions.

On the flip side, too much humidity, like what happens in the summer, can be a bad thing. The solution there is a whole-home dehumidifier. Aprilaire, for example, makes one that can remove 90 pints of water a day from your Money Pit, leaving you cool, dry, and comfortable.

Clearing the Air about Air Cleaners

Regularly changing the filters in your forced-air system is step one in maintaining indoor air quality, and you can go several steps above and beyond by incorporating a whole-house air cleaner. It's a smart upgrade to consider when it's time to replace your current system, and we know homeowners who can tell the difference after having one installed.

Installed by an HVAC pro, whole-house air cleaners are part of forced-air systems, virtually eliminating such airborne contaminants as dust, pollen, pet dander, and bacteria. Today's systems are so good that they can trap virus-size particles. Whole-house air cleaners are also attractive in their low cost and the efficiency they contribute to your heating and cooling setup, and only require annual maintenance.

Carbon Monoxide: Solutions for a Serious Safety Issue

Every year, you read those scary stories about carbon monoxide (CO) killing a family while they sleep. Truth is, we should be scared. Not overhyped in the least, CO is the leading cause of accidental poisoning deaths in the United States, with over 200 people dying annually from exposure to this odorless, colorless killer. The initial symptoms of CO poisoning can be mistaken for many other ailments with headache, fatigue, shortness of breath, nausea, and dizziness.

Annual professional inspection and service of all fuel-burning appliances are a must. Without these preventive measures, CO can leak into the home, so make sure a qualified heating contractor checks your system every year. A thorough examination should include the following:

Heat exchanger. The heat exchanger keeps the air you breathe separate from carbon monoxide–laced exhaust gases. Check the furnace heat exchanger for any signs of rust, combustion deposits, or cracks. If any cracks or holes are found, the furnace should be replaced.

Vent pipe. The vent pipe carries exhaust gases to the outside of your house. If the pipe is rusted, loose, or blocked, dangerous levels of carbon monoxide can back up into the house. Check the pipe for any signs of corrosion. If the pipe is damaged, replace it immediately. The seams of the vent pipe should also be screwed together to prevent the pipe from separating. Moreover, make sure the pipe clears the roof properly. The vent should be at least 2 feet higher than any part of the roof within a 10-foot radius.

Chimney. Like vent pipes, chimneys must be free of blockage and properly designed. If you haven't had your chimney cleaned lately, make sure the job is done well before the next heating season begins. Also consider installing a chimney cap, which is a steel grate that lets gases escape while keeping the chimney off-limits to animals that could build their nests inside.

Blower compartment door. On the furnace, make sure the door, which covers the blower, is secure. If the door is loose, bent, or damaged, the blower could suck carbon monoxide from the burners and distribute it throughout the house.

Flame color. Proper gas combustion will produce a blue flame. Yellow or orange flames often indicate incomplete combustion, which can release higher levels of carbon monoxide. Also make sure the burners are clean and not covered by rust.

Combustion air. All heating appliances, whether gas or oil, need fresh air to burn properly and reduce carbon monoxide levels. If your heating equipment is located in a small room or closet, you may need to add wall, floor, or ceiling vents to make sure enough air reaches the equipment. At a minimum, appliances need 1 square inch of ventilation for every 1,000 BTUs of heating capacity. An average utility room containing a furnace, water heater, and dryer would use about 200,000 BTUs and need at least 200 square inches of vent area.

The Consumer Product Safety Commission recommends professional inspection to confirm that the appliance is operating on the fuel it's designed to use.

Cheap Comfort: Top 10 Tips to Save Costs

Okay, in today's world, energy won't really be "cheap" anytime soon. As energy costs continue to rise, however, you may be surprised to learn there's a lot you can do to ensure that you're comfortable with both your indoor climate and utility bills.

At the beginning of the chapter, we mentioned connecting with your local utility for a home energy audit. Beyond the audit, here are our top 10 favorite low-effort, low-to-no-cost tips.

1. Install a clock thermostat. As mentioned back in the "Thermostats" section of this chapter, programming your thermostat to reduce the household temperature overnight and when you're away can reduce heating costs by as much as 10 percent.

2. Insulate your water heater. Adding an inexpensive water heater jacket can keep heat from escaping. They're easy to install, and can save hundreds of dollars on energy bills over the life of the heater.

3. Reduce water temperature. Turn down your water heater's temperature setting to a safe but efficient 120 degrees instead of the potentially scalding higher settings. If you have an electric water heater, cut the cost of running it in half by installing a timer that allows water to be heated only when necessary, as for a morning shower.

4. Add more insulation. Proper attic insulation—at least 12 inches of the batt or blown types between attic rafters—helps to reduce heating needs by up to 30 percent. Also make sure that the attic is well ventilated, as even slightly damp insulation can lose as much as one-third of its ability to insulate.

5. Keep filters clean. Replace your furnace's filter before the heating season begins and monthly thereafter. A dirty filter will reduce airflow, which makes your system work that much harder to deliver warmth where it's needed. Better yet, invest in a whole-house air cleaner that requires only annual maintenance.

6. Get your ducts in a row. Seal HVAC ducts that can rob you of precious heated air, using either foil-backed tape made for the purpose (rated "UL 181") or duct mastic.

> **President of Energy Efficiency**
>
> *Abe Lincoln was a pioneer in energy efficiency, although he didn't win an award or make a documentary about his involvement because he probably didn't realize it.*[75] *Log homes such as his score big in terms of R-value, a factor used in calculating efficiency. Walls made from logs contain millions of tiny air pockets, which store cool air in the summer and warm air in the winter. Today's log homes offer high-tech modular log assemblies that seal better than Abe's old homestead, but the principle is still the same: those logs make great insulators!*

7. Reduce drafts. Weather-strip or caulk around windows, doors, outlets, and light switches from the *inside* to prevent warm air escapes.

8. Strategic shades. Keep draperies and shades on south-facing windows open during the heating season to allow sunlight to enter your home, and close them at night to reduce the chill you may feel from cold windows. In summer, keep them closed during the day to reduce solar heat gain.

9. Smart lighting. Home lighting can dim your finances, as it accounts for about 10 percent of your electric bill. Move to lower bulb wattages where you can, and select long-lasting compact fluorescent bulbs for further savings.

10. Power down. Completely shut down stereo systems and computers when not in use, as they continue to draw energy even when idle.

A Word on Space Heaters

The fireplace was the original space heater, leading the way in wintertime comfort until cen-

75.) His handlers couldn't believe the missed opportunity.

tralized heating systems became the norm after World War I. Today, mechanical space heaters can be used to supplement systems and warm up out-of-reach cool spots in a home.

We hesitate to recommend using them because they can be very dangerous, especially the ones fueled by kerosene. The mere fact that you have to refill them with a flammable fuel makes them potentially unsafe to handle. Plus, because they're not permanent and can be moved around, they can wind up in spots where they shouldn't be and come in contact with objects that add to the hazard. With all of this in mind, if you absolutely must use a space heater, make sure it's only operated for short, well-supervised periods of time. *This is seriously one time when everyone should read the instruction manual!*

There is one type of space heat that we think bears a positive recommendation. It is called the Reiker Room Conditioner, a ceiling fan that not only cools in the summer but heats in the winter. In the heat setting, an internal heater kicks on to deliver the heat and fan blades reverse to push that warm air down. The Reiker folks call it a room conditioner because when the room heats up to your desired temperature you will have the same temperature on the ceiling, floor, walls, furniture, and bedspread. It costs very little to operate and is a good solution for a room that needs a little extra heat, like a three-season patio room. In Tom's case, he used one of these technological marvels to add heat to his kitchen, an addition that never had quite enough radiators to do the job. And because it's permanently mounted, you can steer clear of floor-based fire hazards. See www.buyreiker.com for more details.

And Now, Let's Talk about Fireplaces

Like a lot of things in life, the idea of a fireplace can be warmer than the reality, but hey, we're suckers for crackling logs when the whole family is huddled under blankets during the holidays watching the umpteenth airing of *It's a Wonderful Life.*

Just know that we're not talking about a particularly efficient heat source. Usually, a traditional fireplace lets as much warm air escape from a home as it delivers into it.

We're also not talking about a low-maintenance relationship. With any fireplace or wood-burning stove, you will get a buildup of creosote that results from combustion deposits combining with steam. This will gunk up the inside of your chimney at a pretty rapid rate, necessitating a good chimney sweeping for every cord of wood you burn (that would be a stack of wood that's 4 feet tall, 4 feet deep, and 8 feet wide). Regular sweeping is important too, as that same gunk can lead to a chimney fire with devastating results.

When it comes to cozying up with your loved ones in front of the fire, we're all for using vented gas fireplaces or gas woodstoves. First of all, they are far more environmentally friendly. They burn cleaner and are more efficient to use, as they are sealed combustion systems drawing air from the outside and exhausting it back to the outside, then running indoor air through a heat exchanger.

Secondly, they take less time to maintain. If the whole point is to spend time with your family, we say make it easy to do so!

Two types of gas fireplaces we don't recommend are unvented gas fireplaces, because they exhaust back into the home, and gas fireplace logs. Gas logs are typically installed into masonry fireplaces designed for wood burning. While more convenient than tending to a wood fire, they use an extraordinary about of gas and are extremely inefficient.

Woodstoves are another popular option. Determining their true efficiency depends a lot on what you'll pay for the stove along with what you pay for wood, or how much you value the back-breaking labor it takes to play lumberjack on your own. Regardless, if you love the stove experience, there are a few things you can do to make sure it is as efficient as possible:

- **Burn Dry**—Burning green (wet) wood wastes energy and contributes to the creosote buildup quickly. Purchase dry wood and store it in a dry place until use.

- **Pay for Efficiency**—Always invest in the most efficient woodstove you can find. Look for the Environmental Protection Agency's (EPA) Certification as well as a UL Certification as your best indication that the stove operates safely and efficiently.

- **Size Matters**—Woodstoves can be sized for the space they need to heat. Buying one that is too small or too big is a waste of money and energy.

- **Burn the Best**—Generally the harder, heavier, and denser the wood, the more heat you'll get out of it. Be selective when purchasing firewood and always burn the best.

For more information on woodstoves, see www.epa.gov/woodstoves.

Finally, pellet stoves are another option to consider if you love having your heating appliance side-by-side with your home's furniture. Pellet stoves burn a mixture of ground waste wood or other renewable fuel. They are very efficient but need electricity to be able to continuously feed the pellets through.

Most importantly, if you want to have a wood stove or pellet stove installed, be sure it is done safely and in accordance with the stove manufacturers' recommendation. Installing stoves is a precise business. Put one too close to a combustible wall or run a vent pipe too close to a wood ceiling beam and disaster can strike quickly. For best results, always hire an experienced pro to do this job.

Charged Up: You and Your Electrical System

Will your home improvement project add electrical wiring to your existing system? Then to quote Meat Loaf, "Stop right there!" One out of every four homes needs an electrical service upgrade before new or additional wiring is installed—more if you're looking at a wired house with "smart" appliances, as we saw in the last chapter. To assess your needs and to do the work, always rely on a licensed professional electrician. While we never recommend you attempt to work with electrical systems on your own,[76] here's a little top-line planning advice on the areas we are most often asked about, including lighting systems, power outage protection, and home security systems.

Home wiring systems have expanded from the early days of home design, when a 120-volt/30-amp load capacity wasn't an uncommon limit. Today, a capacity of 240 volts/150 amps is about the smallest you'd find, but even at that rate, you can run into problems. If running the vacuum cleaner, microwave, and hair dryer overloads a particular circuit in the system, the solution isn't to improve the service capacity, but rather to add more circuits. Think of electric panels as a controlled interchange highway. Like the one on your daily commute, they can hold a lot of traffic, but if you don't have enough off-ramps, your load capacity is going to run into congestion.[77]

One old wiring system we recommend removing is the knob-and-tube type that was common from the turn of the last century through the 1930s. With this style, ceramic insulators are strung throughout the house with the wires hanging between the insulators. Besides being an un-

76.) Electrical do-it-yourselfers are at risk of becoming do-it-to-yourselfers. 77.) Causing load rage.

Link Up: **Repair Aluminum Wiring?**

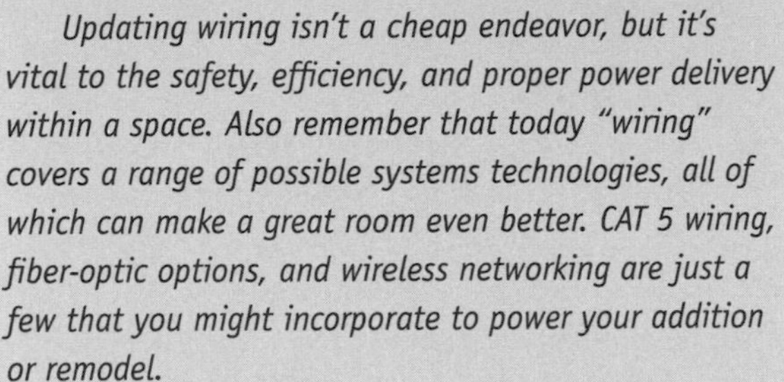

For the latest information on aluminum wiring repair, see www.inspect-ny.com/aluminum/aluminum.htm.

Updating wiring isn't a cheap endeavor, but it's vital to the safety, efficiency, and proper power delivery within a space. Also remember that today "wiring" covers a range of possible systems technologies, all of which can make a great room even better. CAT 5 wiring, fiber-optic options, and wireless networking are just a few that you might incorporate to power your addition or remodel.

Access Everyone: **A Higher Calling for Outlets**

As you design your space, work convenience into the power plan by positioning several outlets higher up on the walls. They'll make occasional use of appliances such as vacuums less of a chore, and can also accommodate such high-tech amenities as wall-mounted, flat-screen televisions.

grounded system, the wire's rubber insulation very frequently deteriorates and falls off, leaving live wiring exposed—not, as they say, a good thing.

Another major danger in the wiring world is aluminum. Used between 1965 and 1972, aluminum wiring has a very high expansion and contraction rate which allows it to loosen at its connection points to light switches, outlets, and other junctions. When this happens, those connection points build up oxidation and overheat, leading to devastating fires. Repair is possible but costly. Options include disconnecting the aluminum circuits and running new copper wiring, or using a repair-in-place method called Copalum, which utilizes a specially designed tool to mechanically crimp Cooper wires to the ends of aluminum wires for connection to the circuits.

Matching Fuses to Wires

For safety's sake, make sure you have the right match between wire and fuse sizes. Fuses are just as safe as more modern circuit breakers, provided they are properly matched to the wire size used in the circuit. Here's a key to proper pairings for standard home wiring:

- *A No. 14 wire gets a 15-amp fuse*
- *A No. 12 wire gets a 20-amp fuse*
- *A No. 10 wire gets a 30-amp fuse*

To make sure your fuses match, have an electrician write the proper fuse size for each spot on your fuse panel. And never, ever, install a fuse bigger than what is noted. If that fuse blows, it's doing its job protecting your home's wiring from overheating and causing a fire. The solution isn't to install a larger fuse, but to reduce the load by turning off whatever it was that you were using which caused the circuit to blow in the first place.

Home Lighting Control Systems

Home lighting control systems are hot and very "cool" because they add convenience, luxury, and security while increasing a home's value. Today's smartest systems are integrating lighting and HVAC controls. In the near future, we'll be programming our Money Pits as well, so if you never mastered setting the clock on the VCR, this will be a brave new world for you.

Lighting control systems let you create the exact mood wanted in every room, at any time. Convenient features include one-button "vacation/alert," "all on/all off," and "soft on/soft off" modes. Security can be enhanced by setting indoor and outdoor lights to go on and off automatically after you leave or before you come home, or when

Green Scene: Not All Lightbulbs Are Created Equal

Picking the right kind of lightbulb is as important as selecting the right light. There's a myriad of choices on the market today, so you need to know what kind of lightbulb your fixture requires before you go shopping.

- ***Halogen.*** *With bright, white light, halogen bulbs offer 50 percent energy savings over conventional bulbs, are more compact, and provide direct light.*
- ***Compact fluorescent (CFL).*** *These bulbs offer long life—up to eight years—and energy savings of up to 75 percent over standard incandescent bulbs. Available in a wide variety of formats, they also work for three-way switches.*
- ***Fluorescent.*** *For soft, diffused general lighting, fluorescent bulbs are ideal, requiring less energy, lasting longer than incandescent bulbs, and coming in a flattering range of colors.*
- ***Incandescent.*** *The least expensive bulb available, incandescent bulbs have long life, color-enhancing options, are ideal for dimmers, and come in a variety of shapes and wattages.*

Ask Tom & Leslie: Dimmers and CFLs

Q: I'd like to change the lighting in my home over from incandescent to the newer energy-efficient compact fluorescent lightbulbs (CFLs). Is there a reasonably priced dimmer that can be used?

A: Good question. Lutron Electronic, whose founder invented the dimmer, does not recommend using their dimmers with CFLs, including those CFLs that are marketed as "dimmable," because the quality of the dimming does not meet Lutron's standards. Though there are no safety concerns, a CFL will flicker noticeably when dimmed and will not dim to as low a level as an incandescent bulb, shutting off instead.

However, you might want to consider that dimmers used on incandescent bulbs do save energy. An incandescent bulb dimmed by 10 percent consumes 10 percent less energy than one on "full" light, and the bulb will last twice as long. Similarly, a bulb dimmed by 25 percent uses 20 percent less energy, and the bulb will last four times longer. Finally, a bulb dimmed by 50 percent uses 40 percent less electricity, and the bulb will last 20 times longer. Dimmers are a great option for saving energy in rooms where homeowners also want to be able to create scenes and moods for different activities.

For the perfect energy-saving combination for your lighting needs, we recommend a combination of both CFLs and dimmers on incandescent bulbs.

you are out of town. Money is saved with dimming and overload detection that extend bulb life and conserve energy. Fashionable switches with attractive LED on/off indicators add a stylish bit of décor and can even be custom engraved.

Wireless lighting control products are designed for homes in the $200,000 to $1 million price range, including more than 18 million existing or "retrofit" homes and 350,000 new homes every year. Using RF technology, wireless systems are installed using existing 110-volt home wiring. Regular switches are replaced with ones that can be programmed to go on and off when desired, and can be set to hundreds of dimming levels. "Scenes" and options also can be operated by the control unit or by remote control, even from your car. Look for an open system design that allows integration with many other home automation solutions, including security systems, electronic blinds, thermostats, and much more.

Outage Protection

Protecting your home from power problems has become the mission-critical Money Pit maintenance must-do in the new millennium. Outages of days and even weeks have followed natural and manmade disasters, such as Katrina and Enron. Have a plan to protect your family's reliance on electricity, starting with the products below:

Whole-house generators. These can run on natural gas or gasoline, and some can repower most of the home's critical systems within a short time of an outage. Whole-house generators are permanently installed and wired into a transfer switch that automatically routes selected circuits to run off the generator within seconds of the power going out and prevents power from being routed back into the power grid where it could endanger linemen's lives.

Surge suppression. We're not talking about those power strips you have all over the house. Surges can occur from outside or inside the home. To protect yourself, you'll need several types of devices:

- **Lightning rods.** Good to protect against blasts of lightning hitting at or near your home. Lightning rods provide a "ground" path to divert this runaway power so it doesn't harm your home's electrical systems. Lightning rods are installed on your roof and connected by a heavy-duty cable to a ground rod set deep into the soil next to your house. See Chapter 17 for more tips on stormproofing your home.

- **Surge arrestors.** Surge arrestors are mounted inside your electrical panel and provide another protection against voltage spikes, which occur from the outside.

- **Surge suppressors.** Surge suppressors provide the second stage of an interior defense system. Most suppressors resemble power strips with outlets, and protect equipment that's particularly sensitive to moderate surges such as computers, TVs, phones, and audio/video systems.

When shopping for surge suppressors, keep in mind that major qualitative differences exist. Generally speaking, you get what you pay for, and finding out your suppressor didn't work can be a very expensive lesson to learn.

Battery backups. Probably the single most effective equipment to protect computers from damage is a battery backup. Known as an "uninterruptible power supply" or "UPS," these small devices will not only protect your sensitive data from surges or spikes, they can also instantly restore power to your computer long enough to allow you to safely save your work and shut down the system.

Arresting Lightning Damage

Each year, the cost of lightning strikes adds up to millions of dollars of damage to electrical systems in homes throughout the country. To prevent this from happening to you, install a surge arrestor. This investment is the initial step for whole-house protection because it safeguards hard-wired equipment like air-conditioning systems or appliances that can't be protected by plug-in surge devices. An electrician can install an arrestor for between $100 and $200, but it could save you thousands if you needed all-new equipment.

As you're probably beginning to realize, home improvement projects are a never-ending adventure. One project begins another, as a brand-new kitchen cries out for new paint in the dining room, which in turn demands a more sophisticated powder room. Tom calls this the "creep" factor.[78] So, now that we've covered the basics, it's time to step it up with some sizzling decorating ideas that won't set you back a lot of dough. Up next, 50 great decorating tips for under $50.

78.) Home centers call it their business model.

50 Design Ideas under $50

We all know that good design is important. Regardless of if you want a room that is energetic, relaxing, or anything in between—you can do it with décor. And the best news is, it doesn't have to be expensive. To help fuel your creativity, here are 50 easy design ideas that you can do for less than $50 each.

1. New Day, New Color: We started out this section of the book with the same advice: changing the color of your room is one of the simplest changes to yield big impact. Go for a linen technique using a mixture of glaze and your color choice. Roll the paint on the wall in sections, and pull a wallpaper brush through the paint vertically and horizontally to create a woven look. Be sure to clean the wallpaper brush frequently to keep your detail crisp.

2. Vintage Backsplash: Use logo sections of wooden wine crates cut to a uniform size to create an imaginative backsplash. If you love the experience of cooking and eating, and you enjoy wine, then this is the backsplash for you! The wood sections can easily be installed over an existing backsplash by attaching them to pieces of lauan plywood cut to the size of your backsplash and then placing the new detail over the old one.

3. Soffit Detail: If your soffit continues up to the ceiling but has absolutely no detail above your kitchen cabinets, dress it up using molding and wood appliqués. You can stain or paint the new detail to match the existing finish of your cabinets and extend the design upward.

4. Soffit Light Box: For a bright, colorful detail that can capture everything from modern to traditional style, create an illuminated design detail using the blank space from above your kitchen cabinets to the ceiling line. Using single or double fluorescent light fixtures, mount them onto pieces of plywood cut to fit into the blank area. Wire the lights so they can be plugged into a nearby outlet, or have a pro hard-wire them for you. Once the new lights are attached, mount glass mosaic tiles onto clear Plexiglas and place the tile about 8 inches in front of the light fixtures.

5. Dressed-up Shelf: Dress up a wall-mounted shelf using beautiful corbel-styled brackets instead of simple brackets. For even more architectural art, attach a painted paneled wood door below the shelf and in between the corbels.

CHAPTER 9

6. Collection Showcase: Whether hanging family photos or a collection of plates and platters, give them more dimension by "framing" them with an ornate frame. Hang a backless and glass-free ornate frame that is larger than the item you are displaying around each piece of your collection. This will give your collection some extra visual oomph![79]

7. Vintage Hankie Collection: Turn a great collection of brightly colored and patterned vintage hand towels or handkerchiefs into art by placing them in simple frames and hanging them together in tight group. You can also attach your collection to artist canvases by using an iron-heated fusing tape.

8. Gussied-up Lampshade: Create instant interest to a plain lampshade by attaching decorative ribbon or trimming to the bottom edge of your lampshade using fabric or hot glue. Multiple layers of trimming can also add depth and texture.

9. Instant Organization: Paint the side of freestanding bookcases, cabinets, or even a dresser with a layer of magnetic paint. Didn't know about that one? It's just like paint, except when you apply it, you'll want to mix frequently to ensure even areas of magnetism. Once the magnetic base layer is dry, add a color coat to match your imagination. Then you can attach your important notices, invitations, assignments, family photos, or even just showcase your prized magnet collection.

10. Homasote Homework Organizer: Homasote is a compressed gray paper board that makes for a terrific push-pin holding organizer for you and your family. It is sold in 4-by-8-foot sheets at lumberyards and home centers. Cut a piece to fit your wall space, then cover with fabric stapling right into the back side of each panel. You can use the fabric as-is, or you can add ribbon to create a fun and useful decorative grid pattern detail to a few pieces. Hang your new organizer on the wall by attaching a picture hanger to the back side. By painting column and row titles, you can keep classes and assignments properly sorted. All you need now are thumbtacks!

11. Unique Side Tables: Use this trick-of-the-trade to turn unusual items into functional side tables. For example, glazed ceramic garden stools make an unexpected and beautiful side table or bath stool. Rain drums, vintage wire baskets, or even stands for musical instruments work just as well. A custom-cut piece of glass is all it takes to complete that item's miraculous transformation.

79.) Leslie's technical term.

12. Roman Shade Rejuvenation: Personalize simple and inexpensive Roman shades by adding wide grosgrain ribbon or rickrack with a fusing tape that uses a hot iron to create the bond. You can use the trim to create a border, striped pattern, or any other personal embellishment you desire.

13. Easiest Desk Ever: Find a pair of old wood or metal sawhorses, the more vintage-looking the better; and use them as supports to create a truly simple and unique desk. For the desktop, purchase a very inexpensive hollow-core door, which can be painted and topped off with a thin piece of Lucite. Or skip the door and use a thick piece of Lucite or an old vintage sign mounted to plywood.

Songs to Work By:

Tunes to help you get through your projects.

- *Money for Nothing*—Dire Straits
- *52nd Street*—Billy Joel
- *Chicken, Beer & Fifty Dollars*—Swingadelic
- *Fifty Ways to Leave Your Lover*—Paul Simon
- *100 Years*—Five for Fighting
- *A Fifth of Beethoven*—Walter Murphy
- *Forty or Fifty*—Spin Doctors
- *Attack of the Fifty-Foot Woman*—The Tubes
- *Fifty Bucks*—Harmonica Bob
- *Fifty Miles of Elbow Room*—Norman Blake
- Anything by Eddie Money

14. Painted-on Wallpaper: If you like the look of wallpaper but the thought of applying it is more than you can stand, create similar patterns using paint and stencils. With many stencil patterns available, finding one that works for you is very simple. Apply the stencil pattern using latex paint over a painted wall or even over plain or textural wallpaper. Then use a stipple brush to apply your paint by stamping it over the stencil. Be sure to clean the stencil between uses to avoid mistakes. If you are going to apply the stencil to existing wallpaper, be sure to test out the end results on a scrap piece first.

15.Wall Detailing: Add visual interest to plain walls by creating paneling using decorative molding. Add a chair rail, crown or base molding, wainscoting, or even use flat molding to add a frame to the wall. Use the frames to add detail to a formerly plain space by highlighting artwork or pieces of patterned wallpaper.

16. Wall Paneling: If you love the look of wood paneled wainscoting but hate the work and the expense, create that same richly paneled look using paneled doors made of either wood or composite. Turn the door sideways and attach to the lower portion of your wall to create instant wood wainscoting. You will have to extend any outlets or connections, which can be done easily by adding an extension box to the existing junction box itself to allow for the door thickness. Then finish off the project by adding baseboard and a length of 1x4 to the top edge of the door for a finished look and an instant ledge.

17. Furniture Redux: Whether you have an existing piece of furniture or a great salvage-store find, this trick can help you instantly give it new life. Choose a table, desk, or sideboard that has very classical styling and paint it an unexpected color, like bright pink, turquoise, or deep purple. You'll find that the mix of color and shape will play together in a fun and surprising way.

18. Book Display: Not case, display. Give your book collection an interesting look by covering the books in a solid-color paper, like white.[80] You can dress up the starkness by adding ribbon in a solid or stripe to create a fun detail. If book covers are not your thing, remove each book's paper jacket for a clean and classic look.

19. Travel to Light and Space: Hang a mirror in your room to make it instantly seem larger. By hanging your mirror opposite a window, the reflection will not only help to make the room feel bigger, it is also going to add lots of extra light to the space.

20. Accessorizing to the Season: Give any room in your home a fresh and seasonal vibe by changing the accessories. Items like throw pillows, candle votives, and other decorative items can set the tone for the warmer and cooler times of the year. Also choose colors and fabrics that evoke the feeling of the season. Light and airy fabrics work great for the summer, while luxurious fabrics in rich and deep tones are perfect for the winter.

21. Texturize Your Windows: Add depth and texture to your room with inexpensive natural bamboo matchstick blinds. When paired with luscious draperies, they help to add an earthy balance to create a nicely dressed-up window.

22. Privatize the French: If your French doors are long on style but short on privacy, hide the view stylishly, as befits their ancestry. Cut pieces of decorative paper, rice paper, and other textural natural papers to the size of your panes of glass and attach the paper with double-sided tape. The soft texture of the paper separates your personal space but allows a soft filtered light into the room.

23. Flower Power: Breathe instant life to any room with fresh flowers. Yes, we know they don't last forever, but they last longer than treating yourself to an ice cream.[81] Group together flowers of assorted sizes in various tones of the same color. Choose a vase that works well with the scale of your flowers, and add florist's tape in a grid at the top to help keep an arrangement in place. For a new twist, you can even group together several small arrangements in one setting.

80.) We recommend keeping this book's cover visible no matter what. 81.) Which, by the way, we also recommend, it just doesn't have anything to do with this chapter.

24. Bling for Doors and Drawers: Instantly update the look of your kitchen cabinets or any piece of furniture by changing out the hardware. With many styles and options of door and drawer knobs and pulls, you will no doubt find the perfect decorative enhancement to suit your style. Yes, a complete kitchen do-over will run higher than $50, but a few whimsical pieces well coordinated to your hardware can be surprisingly effective.

25. Faux Mercury Glass: Turn any inexpensive glass vase into an ultra-stylish piece of mercury glass—the style that looks metallic. Get the look using Krylon Looking Glass mirror spray paint. Groupings of painted glass vases can add instant drama and design to any room.

26. Cabinet Makeover: Turn any glass-front cabinet into a real show-stopper by hanging beautiful patterned wallpaper or craft paper on the interior back side of the cabinet. It is the unexpected details like this that really add a well-designed look.

27. Flat-Panel Disguise: Cleverly hide your flat-panel television behind some beautiful and functional drapery by adding curtain rods along the length of the wall that showcases your television. Hang flat-panel drapes in the same fabric as your window treatments to put that TV out of sight when not in use, and then open them back up for an instant and stylish home theater.

28. Upholstered Headboard: A new or vintage upholstered folding screen can make a unique and beautiful headboard. Fully open the screen so it lies flat against the wall, or pull the bed away from the wall a bit and use the screen in an accordion fashion. If you have a secondhand screen in need of new style, the fabric is easily changeable with a trusty staple gun. Brushed gold or shiny chrome upholstery tacks applied in simple lines or bold patterns can make this project amazingly chic.

29. Paneled Door Headboard: Create your ideal headboard by grouping two or three paneled wood doors together attached across their backs. A queen-size bed is 60 inches wide and works perfectly with two 34- or 36-inch-wide wood doors for just the right amount of overhang on either side of the bed itself. Paint or stain the doors any way you please to work with your décor and deliver a perfect night's rest!

30. Create a Painted Floor: Add visual appeal to an otherwise blank slate by painting a wood floor anywhere in your home. Diamond patterns or decorative rugs can easily be achieved in a few steps and with the right colors can look absolutely charming. Be sure to prime the surface first and then apply your artistic flair. Colors like warm aubergine and chocolate brown instantly make a rich and charming statement. Latex paint will work great on the floor, and when the time comes to finish off your work of art, be sure to add two coats of clear topcoat to help it last a long time.

31. Romantic Outdoor Dining: When the warm evening beckons dining al fresco, add some romantic light to set the mood. A candle chandelier hung above your dining table will help create the perfect setting.

32. Accessorize an Outdoor Room: Bring your indoor décor outside with accessories made for the great outdoors. Once you start looking, you'll find everything from rugs to table and floor lamps, even fabrics and wall décor made especially to withstand everything Mother Nature can dish out.

33. Shade a Pergola: If your outdoor retreat contains a pergola, you can creatively block the sun and the heat. Here's how: Cut and sew panels of outdoor fabric the same size as the openings overhead. Next, grommet the fabric along the length edges, placing two grommets spaced 3 inches apart every 18 inches. Use eyehooks, turnbuckles, and vinyl-coated cable to create a line that will span the length of the upper openings. Before you secure the second side of the cable, thread it through the grommets and then attach the cable to the opposite side. For instant shade or sun, just slide the fabric open or closed along the cable.

34. Screened-in Privacy: For a restful time on your screened-in porch or patio, add operable curtain panels. Run curtain rods the full length of your screened walls along each exposed side of your patio. Then make or buy curtains made of outdoor fabric and attach the drapes with easy-to-operate rings.

35. Summer Fireplaces: Instead of burning a full fire, replace the logs with a stacked and stylish candleholder or group of candles. The dancing light of the flames will have you feeling relaxed and cozy no matter what the temperature.

36. Bathroom Glamor: The bathroom is the last place you would expect to see the high glamor of a gorgeous chandelier. But whether simple iron or ornate crystal, this overhead fixture, when combined with a dimmer, can set the mood for a relaxing bath or early-morning shave.

37. Jazz Up Your Drawers[82]: Go from plain Jane to jazzy drawer fronts on dressers or nightstands. Remove the drawer front and attach assorted styles of molding along the full width of the face. Each piece of molding can be stained or painted in complementary tones to work with the piece's original finish. The end result is fun and fabulous.

82.) We're still talking decorating, remember.

38. Pillow Panache: Simple single-color pillows are an inexpensive addition to any sofa or chair. But cheap doesn't mean it can't be chic. Let your inner designer go free and dress up plain pillows by attaching buttons, ribbons, or cording in scrolled patterns using fabric glue.

39. Nontraditional Coffee Table: Who said a coffee table has to be one large piece centered in your favorite gathering place? For an interesting alternative, group small ottomans or Moroccan-inspired tables side-by-side to work in harmony as a new take on an old idea.

40. Faux Detail: If your room is short on architectural detail and you're short on skills with moldings and miter saws, you can paint on detailing, using a deep tone, a mid-tone of the same color, and a pure white to create the perception of depth. Choose colors that can act as a neutral within your room, whether it is chocolate brown or bright blue, and build from there. It will take a little practice to re-create egg and dart molding or a Moorish archway, but the simplicity and surprise of this painted touch instantly finishes any space.

41. Settee Dining Room Seating: For a new twist on traditional dining room seating, skip the chairs and use two matched settees upholstered in a gorgeous fabric. Work in matching armchairs at the heads of the dining table to create nice balance. This is a great trick in a space-starved room, as one settee can play against a wall to make the room feel larger.

42. Room Transition Tricks: A pass-through between rooms can provide the perfect location for a surprising detail. Draw the eye to a formerly unnoticed architectural detail by adding a transom with glass or a wood spandrel to fill some of the space in the upper area of the pass-through and create an amazing attention to design.

43. Quick Coffee Table Organizer: A decorative tray can make clutter look planned,[83] the perfect catch-all for everyday necessities in your living or family room. Select a tray with deep sides to contain all of those remotes for the many electronic components that make up your entertainment system.

44. Tile Tricks: If you are low on budget but high on design dreams, choose a simple and inexpensive tile to cover the main-field portion of your kitchen's backsplash or bathroom walls. Mix in a few beautiful decorative tiles that are rich in color and style to create visual interest. Since you are using this decorative detail in small quantities, you can really splurge for something that is really special.

83.) Which, let's be honest, it is. You know you're not going to put that mail away right now.

45. Side Table Lighting: Traditional table lamps are not a side table's only option. Have electricity moved to the ceiling above the table and hang a pendant lamp, oversized shade light, or chandelier at lampshade height for an illuminating effect. If hiring an electrician breaks the budget, go for a similar look using a corded light fixture and either dress the cord with a fabric cover and swag detail, or cleverly and tightly attach the cord to the ceiling and wall until it reaches the nearest outlet.

46. Knobby Jewelry Storage: Accessory storage can be tricky, especially when it comes to all of those trends in stylish neckwear. Solve this problem by attaching several decorative knobs directly to your wall or to a piece of painted MDF. The knobs are easily secured using a double-threaded screw. First screw the post into the knob, predrill a starting point on your wall or back plate, and then twist the knob into place. Look for knobs that stand away from the back a bit to allow for necklaces to have room to hang. Stagger them in a pattern so long necklaces don't get all twisted up.

47. Kitchen Storage Found: There is valuable kitchen real estate under those upper cabinets. Add pull-out natural woven and metal bins on easy-to-operate tracks to pick up some storage space where there was none before. This is the perfect place for onions, potatoes, dishtowels, or craft supplies.

48. Shower Curtain Cover-up: Got a weird space in your home where one wall juts out from another, creating an odd space? Quickly cover up those potential areas of storage between two walls by using a spring-loaded shower rod, and finish off with a cloth shower curtain. For another look, use roll-up bamboo curtains attached with shower hooks.

49. Old and New: Simple and inexpensive tables can be converted to rich fine furniture by adding a new top. Buy a small parson's table at a place like Ikea and then add a fabulous stone top. Your local stone supplier can cut it to fit. For best results, let the stone edge overhang the original top by an inch or so on all sides. Large synthetic tree-sized flowerpots also make great table bases. Combine two with a large piece of glass for a gorgeous wall table to display your finery.

50. (phew!) Fabulous Furniture Photo Mural: Create a very personal family photo mural by arranging your photos on any flat coffee or end table and cover with a piece of glass or clear Lucite. Hold the glass in place with a dab of clear caulk placed in each corner. This can also work to show off your mementos from a favorite vacation including photos, museum entrance tickets, foreign currency, or even a preserved flower you picked on your trip.

It doesn't stop at your four walls. The value and joy from your Money Pit comes from outside, too, which is where we're headed next.

CHAPTER 10

Bringing the Inside Outside with Decks, Patios, and Porches

Creating a living space beyond the four walls of your home is gaining ground as one of the most popular home improvement projects of all. Whether that outdoor room is a deck, porch, or patio, creating one can be the least expensive way to extend your living space.

Or the most expensive, if your backyard daydreams include kitchens, fireplaces, and entertainment stations. According to a recent Better Homes & Gardens *magazine survey, such outdoor enhancements form the second most popular category of home improvement projects.*

Not only does building one of these structures create a new space for recreation and relaxation, but it can also be a definite bonus for your home's value. All it takes to install your own deck or patio is evaluation of the space you have, proper selection of materials, and, in the case of most projects we'll talk about here, basic construction knowledge. Oh, and more than a little muscle and time, but by now you've figured out that the mantra of your Money Pit adventure is "No pain, no gain."

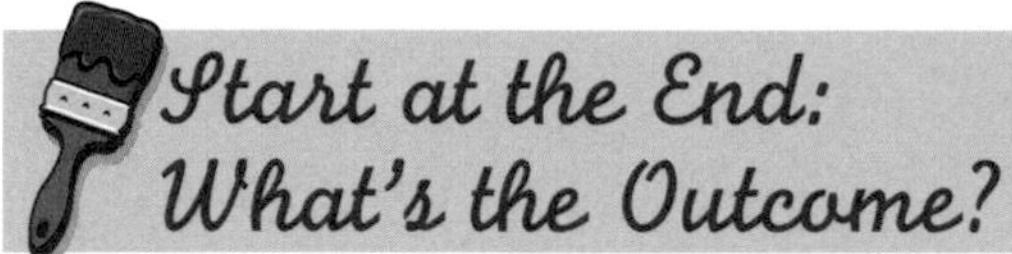

Start at the End: What's the Outcome?

Outdoor living will likely prove to be a brave new world in your Money Pit adventure. Unless you're simply replacing an existing deck or patio, new ways of looking at your backyard open up a myriad of considerations for what you'll do back there, what foliage will surround you as you do it, and what appliances and amenities will make it wonderful.

Deciding whether a deck or patio makes the most sense is part structural and part personal choice. The structural considerations include the size and shape of your lot, along with the height of the exterior door. If your back door is close to the ground (within a foot or two), we would definitely recommend going with a patio. Decks require more vertical space for the posts, beams, and joists to be built, and it makes no sense whatsoever to build those below grade. On the other hand, if you have more vertical height off the back door or if your yard slopes so much that a patio wouldn't be practical, building a deck is a terrific idea.

Consider your landscape design when laying out your deck or patio plan. Done well, outdoor rooms morph into the landscape of the home, creating the appearance of a natural transition space between your home and the great outdoors. Done poorly, we've seen many look like they were slapped onto the side of a building, contributing as much to the value of your home as an old car up on blocks parked in your yard

To begin your outdoor transformation, find your home's most recent plot plan. The plot plan is a document you would likely have received when you bought your home. It's done by a land surveyor and lays out the location of the property lines and structures on your land. Make a bunch of copies and start sketching out shapes for both the physical structure of the deck or patio, as well as the landscaping that will surround it.

A space with multiple levels can add dramatic dimension to the design, as well as construction cost. While admittedly cool to enjoy a view from, multiple levels can reduce the amount of truly usable space your have to work with since furniture can't be placed near stepped-down areas.

Before you run out and buy furniture, fire pits, and water features, think about who's going to use the space and how. In addition to an outdoor dining area, maybe you want a quiet reading nook while the kids need a roomy spot for games and activities. If space is tight, you may also need to plan for movable or convertible furnishings that can accommodate whatever's going on outdoors. As you send all of these considerations outside, don't forget to design in privacy, maintenance, accessibility, and safety for children and pets.

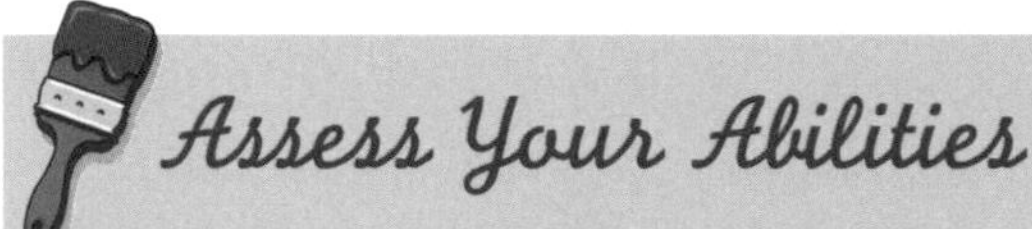

Assess Your Abilities

Decks, patios, and porches all have the potential to be successful DIY endeavors, potential being the operative word. They can also be disasters if not done carefully, properly, and fully to code. Remember, you and your family are going to be relaxing, playing, dining, and sometimes partying on this new surface, so shortcuts and sheer cluelessness could literally end up hurting someone.

We'd also like to remind you about a little thing called gravity[84] when it comes to assessing your abilities: the closer the project is to the ground, the more likely your DIY success. Higher builds involving heavier, bigger structural elements can pose dangers to even the experienced pro while construction is in progress. We'd also get a pro involved for any special wiring or plumbing additions, and definitely when it comes to delivering cooking gas.

Getting a permit is a must. There may be zoning laws that dictate how close you can build your deck or patio to your property line, as well as how high it can be, etc. You may not care for that much government interference in your life, but you wouldn't want your deck to be positioned just on the property line with a bird's-eye view into your neighbor's hot tub, unless you live next to Brad Pitt and Angelina Jolie.

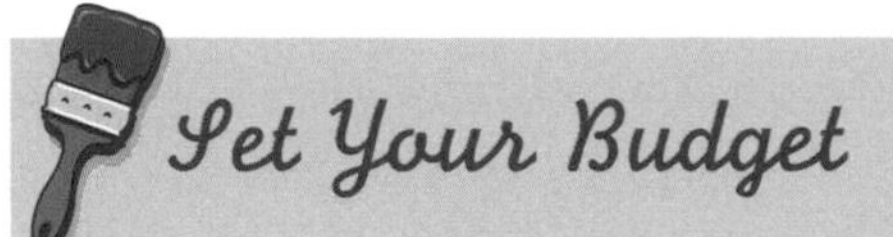

Set Your Budget

Simple decks and patios start at just a few dollars a square foot to construct. Add multiple levels, higher-end materials, and a railing system, and the price goes up from there. Considering all of the elements above and after checking out the materials choices that are coming up next, you'll know what budget bracket you fall into.

A deck, porch, or patio doesn't have to cost a fortune, but structural quality needs to be sound. Don't shortchange the investment in the construction. More than any other space in the house, outdoor rooms lend themselves to being built in stages, so don't be reluctant to start small and build toward your ultimate outdoor space.

Tom's Tip: **Building for the Swelling Masses**

Most folks build a deck for small family gatherings, but decks really get put to the test when everyone you ever knew heads over to your house for a big summer blowout. In my part of the country, we see deck collapses every summer, and they almost always happen when a big crew has been invited over for a party. Before you hang out the "open house" sign on yours, make certain you've followed the building code to the letter so that everyone stays safe.

84.) It's the law.

Getting All Decked Out

The costs and looks of decks can vary widely due to the many choices of materials available. In all cases, we recommend that pressure-treated lumber be used to build a very safe structure that won't rot. Beyond that, here are the three main categories we recommend for your shopping pleasure.

Repair, Restore, or Replace?

The question of repair or replace depends on the deck's condition both above and below the floorboards.

Extreme, pervasive rot and/or a structural design that literally doesn't hold up means it's time for a reconstruction. Starting from scratch means you can revisit the design and determine if it's been working for you or time for a change.

It's also a good time to consider building the deck as a freestanding structure, a construction method that is gaining in popularity. It is safer to double the main beams so that you have one beam close to the house and one at the opposite end. The deck doesn't "hang" off the house, structurally speaking, which can cause it to be prone to failure and even collapse if it's not properly built and maintained.

If rot damage and wear are limited to the surfaces you see and touch, a deck "makeover" may work. Most decks built within the last 20 years have structures built from pressure-treated wood. If that's the case for you and you're confident the connection points to the home are structurally sound, you can leave that portion of the deck in place and simply replace the deck boards, stair treads, and railings with new material. Those options could include not only new pressure-treated wood, but also one of the long-lasting, great-looking composite products.

Refinishing a natural wood deck can also extend its life and good looks if it's otherwise

Songs to Work by:

Tunes to help you get through your projects.

- *Sunny Afternoon*—The Kinks
- *Secret Garden*—Madonna
- *Wide Open Spaces*—Dixie Chicks
- *In the Summertime*—Mungo Jerry
- *Summer Breeze*—Seals & Croft
- *Where Have All the Flowers Gone*—Peter, Paul & Mary
- *I'm on the Outside Looking In*—Little Anthony and The Imperials
- *Garden Party*—Ricky Nelson
- *Lookin' Out My Back Door*—Creedence Clearwater Revival
- *Home on the Range*—Dr. Brewster Higley
- Anything by Green Day

Tom's Tip: A Very Uncool Idea

You know those outdoor air-conditioning compressors that blow air upward? Don't build your deck over one. A compressor actually needs 4 feet of clearance above the fan and at least 1 foot on all sides to do its job of cooling your home's interior. If it doesn't have the right amount of room, you're impeding its ability to do so, costing yourself energy dollars and possibly even voiding the unit's warranty.

Selecting Decking Materials			
Decking Material	**What It Is**	**Pros**	**Cons**
Pressure-Treated Wood	Lumber saturated with chemicals that form a shield against rot, pests, and fungi.	Standard for structural elements in decks of all sorts, as well as a hardy option for boards and railings.	Be careful not to install it where it can come into direct contact with food or drinking water. Give any new installations an entire summer in the sun to air before sealing or finishing.
Natural Wood	Natural wood choices include cedar, redwood, and ipe, a beautiful and resilient exotic hardwood.	Natural beauty.	All are pest-resistant, but require periodic finishing and sealing to retain their beauty and fend off rot. Natural wood will require the most ongoing maintenance.
Composite	Composites are easy-care blends of wood and recycled plastic, available in a range of colors and styles that imitate favorite wood varieties and grains.	Dimensionally stable, this material will stand up to the elements for years.	Needs periodic cleaning to prevent the formation of mildew that can be attracted by the wood that's in the mix. Decking boards are not as stiff as conventional lumber and therefore can look wavy. Special care should be exercised to make sure floor joists are not excessively sagging or crowned.

structurally sound. Clear, semi-transparent, and opaque are the three types of deck stains available, and depending on the condition and features of the wood, you can step up the opacity from the existing finish (i.e., a well-worn but serviceable deck that's been under clear cover could look much snappier with a semi-transparent finish that plays up its best features).

Once you've made your choice in decking materials, deciding how to fasten the deck boards to the frame involves a few trade-offs, and if you're working with wood, you should think through your options. Nailing may be easy, but even galvanized nails can leave stains and rust bleeds on the wood. Plus, as the wood expands and contracts, nails pull out, resulting in loose boards that can be unsightly and even dangerous.

For a more permanent solution, select stainless steel screws. Using a power drill with the right tip, these can be driven to just below the deck's surface where they're difficult to spot. And since the screws are stainless, they can't rust and stain the finished surface of the wood.

Another critical area of materials selection in deck building is flashing. Pressure-treated lumber can be very corrosive and cause fasteners and key deck hardware to fail. For a safe structure, use a high-tech flashing product such as Grace Construc-

Ask Tom & Leslie: **Spring Deck Cleaning**

Q: Outdoor entertaining season is almost here. What do I need to do for a spring deck spruce-up?

A: Take a good look at your deck's surface and check for any splintering, blistering, or cracking. If you see those signs of wear, strip the existing finish so you can start from scratch. If you try to apply a stain over an existing finish that's in bad shape, you're not going to get proper adhesion and will find yourself in the exact same situation next year. Use a good stripper to remove the existing acrylic or oil-based semi-transparent and solid stains, which gets you back to the raw surface where you can apply the finish of your choice.

Next, assess the current condition of the deck. If it's in good condition, you can go for a natural look or a semi-transparent stain that adds color and highlights the grain. If the lumber doesn't look so hot, give it full coverage with a solid stain. If your deck is in good condition but looks weathered, just give it a good cleaning with a cleanser to restore and freshen up its look to bright and vibrant. Now you can give that outdoor furniture a good washing and set up a backyard that inspires relaxation, family fun, or whatever mood strikes you at that moment.

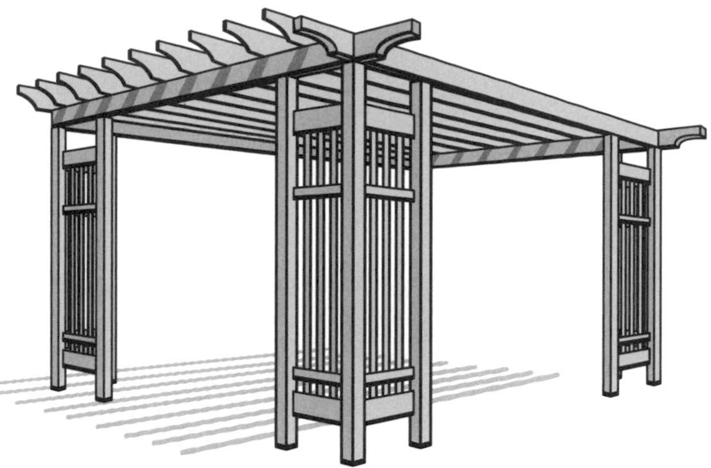

Pergolas, also known as shade structures, are a beautiful addition to any yard. They can be freestanding or attached to your home. Allow a plant to weave its way onto the pergola for a gorgeous effect.

tion Products' Vycor Deck Protector. This critical addition will prevent corrosion and joist rot caused by water accumulation under deck boards.

Leslie Likes: **Perfection with a Pergola**

If you're doing a deck makeover, consider expanding your enjoyment of this outdoor room with the addition of a pergola, an arbor-like structure with an open roof. It can be a single structure or fully span an area, depending on shape and style. You'll not only get a beautiful design feature that serves as a room within a room, but precious natural shade on sunny days. Orient your pergola's rafters north-to-south to cast the widest possible shadow over the deck in summer and let warm sunlight into your home during winter. Encourage the growth of vines for more coverage and more character.

Keep It Clean

Annual cleaning of an otherwise tired-looking wood deck can do a lot to freshen it up. Start with a good sweeping, being careful to remove any debris that has collected between deck boards and around the bottoms of railing posts. Then mix a simple, effective cleaning solution in a 5-gallon bucket by combining 3 quarts of water, 1 quart of bleach, and a half cup of detergent (make sure the detergent is ammonia-free, as mixing ammonia and bleach can form a dangerous gas). Apply the mixture to the deck using a stiff floor brush and let it sit for a few minutes, then rinse thoroughly with a hose. When planning this cleaning project, schedule your work for the cooler hours of the early morning or late afternoon, as the cleaning solution may dry before it has a chance to work when applied to a hot deck.

For an even more effective cleaning, you can bring a power washer into the loop. Just be sure you're educated on and comfortable with its application, because too much power can definitely be a bad thing here, causing damage to your decking and leaving behind a fuzzy, slightly splintered surface that's difficult to smooth over. The basic light-duty pressure washer (1,300–2,000 PSI) is 30 times as powerful as a garden hose, so proceed with care.

Perfect Patios

A patio is a very low-maintenance option for your outdoor space, and also pretty DIY-friendly. Ground preparation varies according to the patio material you choose. But make no mistake: proper preparation is key, as you'd find out the hard way when yours buckles, cracks, shifts, and grows weeds from every nook and cranny.

Here are the main materials to consider:

- **Concrete.** Good techniques and artistic approaches mean you don't have to settle for the traditional gray slab. Patterns can be stamped into it, cast shapes can be formed, custom designs etched in, and color added for a completely custom look and bold statement.

  The sheer heft and specialized labor involved with any style of concrete installation are good reasons to have a pro handle the job. Improper site preparation as well as clumsy mixing and pouring of the material will leave you with a cracked, unevenly settling surface that is costly and difficult to correct.

- **Pavers.** In the realm of DIY patio possibilities, brick and concrete pavers are great choices. Standard rectangular pavers are very specially proportioned when compared to building bricks. Bricks used to build walls need space for mortar and are therefore not quite twice as long as they are wide. Pavers don't need mortar and are exactly twice as long as they are wide. In addition to rectangular formats, paver bricks come in lots of other shapes, such as squares and octagons. Also, because the color is dyed into the bricks, they won't fade.

The most common paver patio mistakes come from not properly prepping the base. We know, it's like prepping the walls before painting. Not the most satisfying part of the adventure, but if you rush through, the bricks will loosen and weeds will form just as quickly!

Start a paver project by carefully assessing the space slated for placement and planning for necessary drainage. For example, downspouts dumping on a paver patio can quickly lead to an area that sags and sprouts weeds. Likewise, a patio that slopes toward a house instead of away from it can lead to flooded basements and crawl spaces.

Once you have identified the area, it has to be excavated down about 8 inches. From there, you'd add about 5 inches of crushed gravel that must be mechanically tamped in place with a power tamper, which could be rented for the job. A sand base comes next, which is also then tamped down, and pavers are set on top of that. Installing a paver patio the right way takes time and careful attention to detail, but the result can be a low-maintenance recreational space that will last a lifetime.

Perfect Porches

There's nothing nicer than kicking back on your front porch with a warm breeze and a cool[85] drink as you watch the world go by. The front porch is back in vogue as families look to reconnect with each other as well as their neighbors. Maintenance, however, is anything but relaxing, thanks to the constant painting and repairs required to keep porches looking good in their front-and-center role.

By their very design, porches peek out from the main structure of a home, exposing themselves to the elements. Whether sun, rain, snow, or ice is in the forecast, there's no doubt that porches are one part of the house that takes Mother Nature's biggest beating.

Besides the weather, porch construction practices invite problems of their own. Old porches are usually supported by brick or block piers and are not connected to the main house foundation. As a result, they settle more quickly over the years, causing everything from floorboards to support columns to pull away from the house, potentially leading to a collapse. Built close to the ground, porches are also targets for wood-munching bugs like termites and carpenter ants.

Fortunately, building material manufacturers now offer a treasure trove of durable, high-tech, and affordable materials that can transform your porch from pitfall to paradise. Here are a few of the most troubling porch parts and new solutions that will have you spending your porch time on relaxation.

Framing

The wood beams that hold up a porch are usually the first to go when age, moisture, and insects attack. Typically, beams rot out where they rest on brick piers. To check yours, slip on some old clothes, grab a flashlight and a screwdriver, and climb under your porch. Probe the framing with the screwdriver to check for rot or insect damage, and use the flashlight to check over each beam for cracks. If you find damage, repair or replace framing using pressure-treated lumber, which will resist termites and decay. And if termites have already set in, your first move should be to call an exterminator—fast.

Floors

In the cooler months, wood porch boards stay damp for long periods of time, allowing decay organisms to attack and leaving you with a spongy mess. In the summer, the sun's ultraviolet radiation causes boards to crack. Get off the year-round damage patrol by installing a composite product that will resist pests and elements alike, and keep maintenance to a minimum (see details under "Selecting Decking Materials").

Columns, Posts, and Railings

Wooden columns and railing systems provide an ornate and stately entrance to your home, but since most are wood, maintenance is a constant chore. The next time you're picking up a paintbrush, think about doing a makeover with synthetic structural components, like a reinforced urethane system. These can include a collection of coordinating elements; they're strengthened with steel to support such heavy loads as a porch roof, and they never need painting. Another great option is decorative columns that would wrap around your existing support post (they provide an architectural detail but not a structural one).

Doors

Fiberglass doors are so popular, so versatile, and

85.) Or room temperature, if it's red wine.

so competitively priced, they're turning wood and steel doors into dinosaurs. They don't crack, dent, warp, swell, or splinter like wood, or dent, ding, scratch, rust, or corrode like steel. And with handcrafted glass doorlights, sidelights, and transoms and a variety of grains and styles, a new fiberglass entryway can add a lot of flair to a façade. Once they're stained or painted, they're virtually maintenance-free for years, and also provide many times the insulation value of wood.

Trim

No porch-building component says "finishing touch" more than trim. Whether it's the corner boards of siding, the facia, soffits, or ceilings, trim is like the frame on a piece of art. It can, however, be one of the more difficult elements to maintain; facia boards, for example, can be impossible to properly paint without removing the entire gutter.

A better option is an extruded cellular PVC product, which doesn't need paint, can't rot, and is cut or drilled just like real wood. It can be used for all non-stress-bearing areas of the home, and is available in large-format sheets as well as regular lumber profiles.

Roofs

Porch roofs often wear out more quickly than a home's main upper roof because they get double exposure to the sun's deteriorating ultraviolet radiation. Here's how: As the sun beats down on your home, porch roofs get both direct radiation and the indirect radiation that's reflected off the exterior wall above the roof. As a result, porch roofing is exposed to more UV rays than other areas of the roof and requires quicker replacement.

If your porch roof is past its peak, many shingle solutions await. We like the new lightweight laminate varieties that have the look of a wood shake while being fire-resistant and pest-proof.

Lights and Wiring

While you're updating the exterior surfaces of your porch, don't forget to look into the lights and wiring. Exterior wiring and light fixtures take a beating from the elements and can wear out much faster than those sections of the electrical system more protected on the inside. Watch out for cracked wiring and rusted fixtures, take the time to make replacements, and have an electrician add ground fault circuit interrupters (GFCIs) to all outside circuits. GFCIs are designed to detect a short circuit, which is what happens when someone gets shocked, and will turn off the circuit before harm is done.

Now that you've literally built a firm foundation for outdoor living, it's time to fill the space with comforts and conveniences that make it a home-outside-of-home.

Bringing the Inside Outside with Outdoor Rooms

Most outdoor spaces include a food preparation area of some sort, and if you'd like yours to go beyond the side shelf on your current grill, systems planning will be involved. Outdoor kitchens require utilities just like indoor kitchens do, but with an extra layer of consideration involved that only the pros will know how to handle. An outdoor sink, for example, calls for not only hot and cold water supply pipes, but those pipes must be set up so that they can be

Tom's Tip: Watch What You Grill

Gas grills can cook beef, chicken, fish, and vinyl siding[86] if placed too close to your house!

Buying a New Grill

If you're ready to invest in a new grill, you're in luck. Today's offerings are better than ever and have lots of cool features to make for a carefree cooking experience. Things to look for include:

- ***Solid hardware.*** *Select stainless steel hardware and a solid aluminum body. These grills are most durable and can take the heat very well.*
- ***Burners.*** *Look for an "H"-style burner. This design provides an even distribution of heat. Make sure the burner is made from stainless steel. If it's not, expect to have to replace it in a couple of years.*
- ***Warranties.*** *Shop for a warranty that covers all parts of the grill, including the burner and valves. Some so-called "lifetime" warranties only cover the grill body, which has no moving parts and almost never breaks down.*

easily turned off and drained in the winter. Likewise, the increased risk of shock associated with outdoor electrical wiring will require the installation of ground fault circuit interrupters (GFCIs) to protect any users from potential hazards.

Beyond wiring and plumbing, the placement and maintenance of your cooking station will have everything to do with safety and convenience. For starters, make sure your cooking appliances are placed well away from the exterior of your home, as they can put structures in danger in the event of a flare-up and do damage to surfaces through routine use. And whether the cooking zone is portable or permanent, cabinetry and other surrounds may be needed to offer weatherproof protection as well as convenient storage. The goal here is to make the food prep and service happen in a way that still lets you enjoy your company. The last thing you want is to be stuck inside on a beautiful day while everyone else has a great time without you.

Setting the Scene: Décor and More

As we mentioned above, renewed interest in outdoor entertaining and living in general has opened up a whole new range of possibilities where al fresco decorating is concerned. Anything goes, really, and it isn't difficult to find the furnishings, accessories, and plantings that will make the space a true extension of your style. Consider the following as you shop for fitting and long-lasting additions for your outdoor room.

Fun furnishings. If you love interior creature comforts such as plush cushions and upholstered pieces, you'll find many pieces to love among contemporary outdoor furnishing collections. Weather-resistant high-density foam and fabrics are turning up in an array of styles, patterns, and sheens on just as many accessories and furnishings, and remove the hassle of dragging upholstered pieces inside when a downpour suddenly strikes. You'll also find synthetic wickers and weather-resistant wood and metal finishes that'll keep looking great for years with little maintenance. Wood furnishings are also a great option but require some maintenance to keep their good looks, just like you and I do.

Smart storage. Easy-access cabinetry and built-in furnishings are musts for stowing everything from entertainment accessories to athletic gear. Materials could be weather-resistant teak or synthetic materials, both of which are totally functional.

86.) Doesn't taste like chicken.

Fire pits can become the centerpiece of an attractive outdoor room. They are available as portables or built-in, and can be fueled by wood or gas.

Also plan off-season storage for furnishings, and purchase weatherproof covers for the items that can take the cold.

Table settings. A growing preference for casual outdoor entertaining is also inspiring a range of affordable and versatile tabletop items to suit every occasion. Look for coordinating pitchers, platters, place settings, glassware, and flatware in materials that stand up to outdoor revels and repeated use.

Artful accessories. Decorative, weather-resistant pillows and rugs, artwork, and statuary add personal touches and contribute to a homey sense of welcome in an outdoor room. Check into architectural salvage resources for unique fencing and window box options. Wrought-iron designs can also be added to areas requiring a little extra architectural interest.

Colorful container gardening. These space-saving displays have always been favorite outdoor elements, and now the trend is going a step further with planters in a range of eye-catching shapes and colors. Such classy containers become artful accessories in themselves, adding interest when planted and arranged in clusters, placed in flowerbeds, created in window boxes, or built up as vertical gardens.

Front-yard landscaping. Where backyards are smaller, water features, fences, courtyards, and patios are moving out front, adding impact and individuality.

Exterior lightscapes. Hardwired lighting illuminates the garden, trees, and house, both to shed light on nighttime activities and enhance security. Placing a light high up in a tree can cast a moonlit glow regardless of the moon's phase.

Water features. Fountains and other water elements enhance sight and sound, while landscaped ponds, streams, and lighted waterfalls offer peace and relaxation.

Outdoor fireplaces. No longer limited to the living room, den, or master bedroom, the fireplace

Ask Tom & Leslie: Entertaining Outside Dreams

Q: We just bought our first house and it has a small yard, but hooray, it's our own! We love to entertain and need some tips on how to most effectively furnish our small outdoor space.

A: Welcome to your Money Pit adventure! A party in the backyard is just the ticket to celebrate![87]! Before you run out and buy furniture, think about how you're going to use the yard. Is it is going to be for outdoor dining, hanging out with friends, relaxing, or all of the above? Since your space is small, you need to prioritize based on how your family will use it. For example, decide if a table for dining is important or if you might prefer a seating area with a smaller table for gathering and having less formal meals.

Next, it's really important to distinguish this area in your yard. Do you want to be in the shade, or can you get by with a sunnier spot masked by an umbrella? You can set up shop on the grass or create an area with beautiful natural stone as your flooring. If you decide to go with stone, remove the grass and level the area with sand. Then add a weed barrier under the stone so weeds don't grow. If a country path is more your idea, loosely space slate tiles and plant moss or other step-able plants in the "grout" lines to give it that aged look.

As for furniture, weather resistance is key. When choosing cushions for seating, remember that the fabric as well as the stuffing should be weatherproof to avoid mildew growth.

Painted Rugs

Want the look of a carpet outside without the damp-then-dry maintenance routine? Then paint one of your own right on the floor of your new outdoor room! Exterior-grade paints and stains made for wood and concrete surfaces can transform a space, add a swath of color and pattern, and create the illusion of a three-dimensional decorative element. Use painter's tape to create borders and patterns, and shop for stencils that replicate intricate details such as tassels and trims. Finish with a clear sealer to protect your work of art, then kick back on your new upholstered chaise lounge and enjoy!

is now becoming the centerpiece of the outdoor living center. Whether a simple portable fire pit or a custom-built structure, a fireplace lends ambiance and creates a focal point for gatherings.

Garden pavilions and gazebos. Outdoor refuges create a destination within a yard and emphasize the comforting, traditional notion of a garden.

Truly green accessories. Shrubs, trees, and flowers can be used as accents, room dividers, carpets, and even curtains.

Smart irrigation systems. Customized to outdoor spaces and supporting the green theme of water conservation, irrigation systems can now think for you thanks to lawn sensors that measure soil moisture and automatically operate sprinklers

Access options. The door to your outdoor room is apt to get a lot of use, so make sure it's a quality product that's easy to operate. Sliders are the first choice and when properly installed and adjusted, can provide almost effortless operation.

87.) What can we bring?

Hinged patio doors, sometimes called "French doors," are a great way to transition from inside to outside.

French doors, also known as hinged patio doors, compete with sliders as the doorway of choice to the backyard, opening into the room like a traditional door. Although they take up a lot of room because of the "swing," these are super-attractive and can deliver that outside-in look during even those harsh winter days.

The thing with exteriors and your Money Pit: it's not just about you. The public side of your Money Pit impacts everyone who drives by, from the neighbor with the perfect lawn who raises an eyebrow at yours, to the prospective buyer driving up. In the next chapter we take on the curb-appeal view.

CHAPTER 11

Curb Appeal and Other Strategies to Keep Your Neighbors and Homeowner's Association Happy

Just as with the clothes and accessories we wear, our homes' exteriors have everything to do with first impressions, something we call curb appeal. And just as we take care of ourselves, most of us want to make our homes look as attractive as possible, not only for our own pride and enjoyment, but also to create a generous welcome for visitors and to keep the peace among our neighbors.

Curb appeal is also an important part of maintaining the value of your Money Pit. When it comes time to sell, potential buyers will conduct an instant assessment of the condition of your home based on their very first impression.[88]

A home's façade and yard cover a lot of square footage, and a tidying makeover can take time and expense. While everything from new siding to a lush lawn has an impact, it's the little things you do that can really make a difference. A stylish new porch light fixture, a fresh coat of paint, the addition of shutters and window boxes, or a few strategically placed containers bursting with colorful blooms can add that sparkle that reads as high home value to passersby.

Whatever level of curb appeal you plan, select products, finishes, and installation techniques that'll stand up to the wear and tear your home's exterior receives from seasonal extremes. Long-lasting good looks mean less expense and maintenance for you and extended admiration from everyone else.

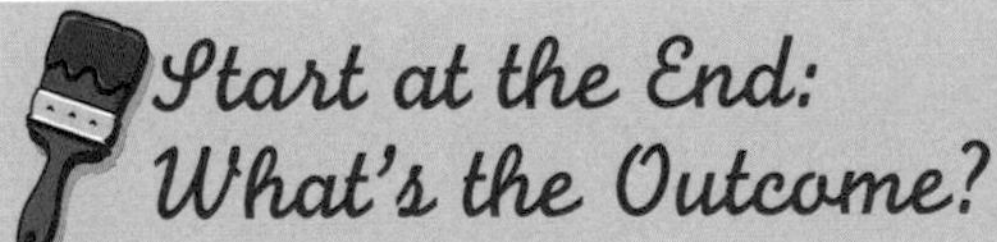

As you consider your curb-appeal goals, keep things in a scale and style appropriate to your home, and tone down the temptation to express yourself a little too personally up front with an overload of accessories (we're thinking overabundant garden gnomes, maidens showing their bloomers, team logos,[89] and political sentiments). If your abode is under the jurisdiction of a homeowner's association, make sure you're aware of any restrictions that impact colors, accessories, and even plantings before investing in items that don't meet standards and aren't returnable.

Songs to Work By:

Tunes to help you get through your projects.

- *Bed of Roses*—Jon Bon Jovi
- *Mansion on the Hill*—Bruce Springsteen
- *Landslide*—Stevie Nicks
- *Let's Lock the Door*—Jay & the Americans
- *The Green, Green Grass of Home*—Johnny Cash
- *Down on the Corner*—Creedence Clearwater Revival
- *Sugar Magnolia*—Grateful Dead
- *Love Shack*—B52s
- *Two-Story House*—George Jones and Tammy Wynette
- *Psychedelic Shack*—The Temptations
- Anything by The Doors

88.) Like you don't do the same thing. 89.) Except the New York Yankees—some things enhance property value, in our opinion.

Assess Your Abilities

There's a lot of great exercise awaiting you outside, where most curb-appeal projects are completely DIY-able. Green lawns, tasteful landscaping, and container plantings, decorative additions, painting touch-ups, and some lighting installations fall into the zone. Professional help is a good idea when you get into mechanics like hardwired lighting systems, sprinkler systems, siding overhauls, and structural updates.

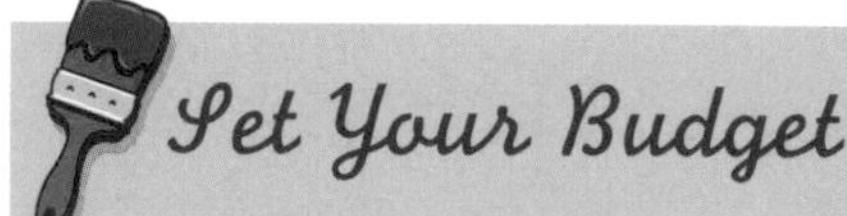

Set Your Budget

Budget depends on how much you need to do and how far you want to go with the makeover project at hand. Remember, though, that you can actually accomplish a lot with a critical eye and very few dollars. There may already be several features in your front yard that will be shown off to best advantage with a little hedge trimming, weeding, painting, and general cleanup—absolutely free and easy fixes.

Points of Arrival: Driveways and Walkways

The condition of any paths leading toward your home, whether they're for foot traffic or arrivals of the drive-up variety, will certainly smooth the way toward a good impression.

We get a lot of calls on *The Money Pit* about the driveway, and in almost every instance the problem is the car, not the surface it's parked on. Persistent oil leaks keep a lot of driveways from looking their best, so do all you can to solve the problem at the automotive level before investing time and money in a comprehensive cleanup. The same goes for other kinds of staining and surface damage: take time to investigate the sources of these and make corrections beyond the parking zone in order to avoid a repeat performance. An improperly directed sprinkler system, for instance, can be the source of driveway rust stains and other mineral deposits.

From there, if you have an asphalt driveway, plan to clean and reseal it—an inexpensive touch-up that you'll only have to repeat every few years. On a clear, dry day, start by soaking up any oil stains with kitty litter and cleaning away other marks with a TSP (trisodium phosphate) washdown. (TSP is available as a powder at home centers and hardware stores and can be mixed with water by following the label directions.) Then use asphalt-compatible products to fill cracks, gaps, and holes, and use a disposable squeegee to apply an airport-grade latex sealer over the entire surface. Make sure that the forecast is clear for the applying and drying time since rain will cause the sealer to run onto sidewalks and streets, leaving unremovable stains. Follow with a generous drying period (up to a couple of days if you can help it), and you'll have an attractive automotive entrance.

Go for the Green

This green idea is about the money. Spending just $500 on entryway landscaping can improve curb appeal and deliver a $5,000 increase in purchase price when it comes time to sell your home. Try getting your stockbroker to commit to those rates of return!

Concrete driveways don't need much maintenance outside of the occasional washing and oil-stain soak-up. If a kitty litter application doesn't do the job or you have a stain that's been sitting for quite a while, take out the TSP and mix it to a paste-like consistency and apply it to the stubborn stain. After letting the mixture sit for a bit, you'll be able to rinse any signs of grease and oil away right along with it.

If you seek the path to an enlightened view of your home, an attractive, well-maintained walkway will get you there. Great-looking, hard-wearing materials abound for this design and utility feature, including prefab pavers, stamped concrete, and natural stone, and you can literally take your entryway in a whole new direction by creating a meandering pathway or adding steps and stops along the way. Just as with patios, meticulous preparation of the surface underneath a walkway is critical to its safety, longevity, and good looks.

Accessibility should also be considered in its design, allowing for a generous width and gradual slope toward at least one household entrance so that those with limited mobility can enter your home with ease.

Days on the Green: Lawns and Landscaping

Lush landscaping has long been one of your home's best exterior assets, almost as long as old guys have been yelling at kids to stay off it. According to the Professional Landcare Network, good landscaping can add as much as 15 percent to property value.

Well-planned plantings have several practical purposes, too: they're an integral part of the exterior water management plan and prevent puddles and pests from gathering. Foliage helps steer roof runoff away from your home's foundation where it can lead to damaging basement leaks, and helps reduce energy use by shading the home in summer and letting sunlight in during winter. Thorny plantings can even help to deter burglars.[90]

Beyond a steady maintenance routine that includes conservation-smart watering (see sidebar on next page), mowing, seasonal fertilizer applications, weeding, and learning how to yell "Git off my lawn," it doesn't take much to create a beautiful, welcoming front yard.

First, take a good look at what the space already has going for it. Maybe all you need is to clean out an abandoned flowerbed, trim back overgrown plants and trees, or repair a border that otherwise adds stylish definition to current plantings. If replacement plants are in order, make future maintenance a breeze by selecting hardy perennials appropriate for your climate zone and the sun and shade patterns in the yard itself. Save a few spots for colorful annuals and maybe a few decorative herbs or veggies for seasonal flair. Seek out climate-specific gardening guides to help you plan and plant, and you can also get great advice by chatting with the folks at the local plant nursery when you're ready to shop. Mulch is also a great seasonal investment because it helps to keep moisture where the plants need it most, slows the growth of weeds, and protects young plants during colder months.

We also love how container gardening dresses up landscapes, whether large or small. Multilevel groupings of potted plantings, window boxes bursting with blooms, and formal

90.) Or visiting relatives.

topiaries are just a few of the possible accents for a grand entry. Small spaces or entries overseen by your homeowner's association can also be personalized with one or two colorful planters showcasing a tidy bit of green. Go with matching containers for a formal, symmetrical look or choose coordinating planters based on color, style, or finish for an unexpected and fun grouping.

Green Scene: Xeriscaping for Less Water, Less Mowing

Outdoor water use can add up to nearly half of your total water bill once summer rolls around. Applying the following xeriscaping principles saves water, as well as the time you have to spend mowing the lawn:

- *Reduce turf area in non-recreational spaces in favor of a wider swath of indigenous plantings and ornamental, low-water grasses. Even a 20-percent reduction in lawn space can have a big impact, and the less you're running your mower, the less exhaust and noise pollution you're sending into your surroundings.*
- *Get into hydrozoning—that is, group plants according to their water needs and their appropriateness for the different environments within your yard.*
- *Get acquainted with the cool array of native plants and other colorful, low-water species available at your local nursery; water-wise definitely doesn't equal boring!*
- *Remember that creative, natural planting schemes draw birds, butterflies, and other welcome creatures to the scene.*
- *Amend soil with moisture-holding additives so that plants' roots can more easily drink in the water you provide, as well as to keep it within their reach for a longer period of time (critical in either normal or drought conditions).*
- *Use mulch to help planted areas hold moisture (use grass clippings for the ultimate in backyard recycling).*
- *Weed and prune regularly, because the resulting healthy, hearty plantings will require less water and fertilizer.*

Water System Smarts

When an automatic sprinkler system doesn't hit its lawn and garden targets, the only thing that'll grow is your water bill. Keep an eye on current systems for sprinkler heads that need to be adjusted for accuracy. Also add a rain-detection device so that the system doesn't repeat the watering when Mother Nature has already taken care of it.

Also, keep an eye out for the EPA's new WaterSense labeled irrigation products and certification programs for landscape irrigation designers, auditors, and installation and maintenance professionals that emphasize water-efficient techniques. Professionals that successfully complete one of these certification programs are eligible to become WaterSense irrigation partners. Hiring one of these professionals helps ensure a healthy landscape that doesn't waste water.

Making an Entrance: Door "Belles"

After beautiful landscaping, a home's exterior is what draws the eye and creates an entrée to curb-appeal compliments. There are few building elements that make a more dramatic visual impact, add to perceived home value, and enhance home security like a beautiful, elegant well-made door. It's a deceptively tricky element to install and adjust thanks to its six surfaces (top, bottom, two edges, two sides), but with a perfect fit, doors are watertight, wind-tight, and energy efficient, as well as eye-catching.

For style as well as strength, a fiberglass door is really the best choice going today. Fiberglass manufacturing technology has made such strides in recent years that it's easy to replicate the look of natural wood without the warping, cracking, swelling, splitting, and rotting that usually follow. Aluminum and steel varieties are also outclassed by fiberglass's resistance to rust, dings, and dents. Add a coordinating door surround system with sidelights and other architectural detailing to enhance the effect, or make the most of this paintable material with a coat of bright color for a more spirited, individualistic welcome.

The strength and stability of today's door constructions also remove the need for the storm doors of old. High air, water, and structural ratings enable them to stand up to the most extreme weather conditions, and multipoint locking mechanisms contribute to security and peace of mind.

Front Door Fashion: Thanks to many affordable customization options available from entry door manufacturers, it is easier than ever to make a fashion statement with a high-performance entry door to your home. Options include door style, hardware, glazing and security, storm resistance, and more. With so many customizable options you can truly create a door that will work with your home design.

Leslie Likes: Doors of Envy

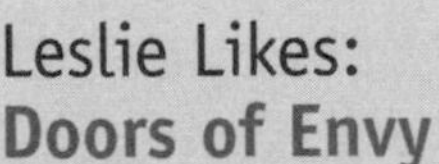

A few years back, my husband and I redid our entire front door and entryway system. As far as energy efficiency goes, we're noticing a great improvement over the former door, which was so leaky all the way around. All the new materials and tightly interlocking elements on the inside and outside maintain a firm seal, and the whole entry looks beautiful, too. People in the neighborhood keep telling us how much they like it, and even the FedEx lady is constantly saying, "I love that door!" And this is three years after we installed it!

First Impressions Pay Off

In a study by fiberglass door manufacturer Therma-Tru, two groups of consumers were shown photos of the same set of homes and asked to estimate the value of each home pictured. One group was shown photos of homes with their original door, and the other group was shown photos of the very same homes with new front doors digitally inserted into the photos.

The result? Consumers estimated that the homes with the enhanced entryways were worth up to $24,000 more than the very same homes with the original front doors.

Fabulous Fences

Beautiful fencing is a great asset when it comes to curb appeal, home value, and stylish definition of your yard and garden. But you aren't the only one who has to live with the fence after it's built—the rest of the neighborhood, particularly the folks next door to you, will likewise experience the benefits and negatives of your choice. Keep the peace by mixing neighborly considerations with style and durability via the following planning pickets.

Plan carefully. There's nothing worse than sparking an ongoing neighborhood feud with a fence built on the wrong side of a property line, so know exactly where yours are drawn. Check plot plans to identify the corners of your lot so that you work within them, and diffuse any suspected ill intent by talking to your neighbors about your fence-building plans before you begin construction.

Make it legal. Not all fencing endeavors require permits, but it's worth checking with local officials to confirm any building parameters. Local ordinances may have strict guidelines for fence height, material selection, picket spacing, post hole footings, and minimum setback distance from the sidewalk or street.

Material maintenance. Fencing is available in a range of materials, including natural and pressure-treated woods, composites, vinyl, and metal. In addition to the look you like, consider the upkeep required by your fencing selection. Natural wood comes with the biggest ongoing demands, requiring repainting or refinishing every few years.

Good side out. In addition to coordinating with and enhancing your home, the style of fencing you choose should look great from both sides. Match the uses of your outdoor space (e.g., help to keep kids, pets, and playthings within bounds), and make the most of your lot lines (open fencing patterns make a yard seem larger). Fencing like board-on-board is designed to look equally great on both sides, but if you choose a one-sided variety like stockade fencing, local building codes will require you to face the good side toward the neighbors. Another great option is to set the fence a bit back from your property lines and then use landscaping to hide the exterior perimeter, adding a decorative natural element that you and your neighbors can both enjoy.

Finish first. For optimum coverage and protection as well as ease, make sure to apply finish to fencing elements before they're assembled. This step should also be taken if you're working with a professional installer: just have them drop off the fencing a few days ahead of the scheduled installation so that you have time to take care of the finish. And speaking of finish, avoid applying a clear topcoat such as shellac or polyurethane finish. It won't stand a chance against the elements, eventually blistering to the point that you'll have to sand all surfaces down and start over with a whole new finish.

Reinforce gates. Gates take the most wear and tear along the fence system, so make sure that yours is securely built and reinforced with diagonal cross-bracing to prevent sagging. And to help make sure that your gate stays shut even when kids leave it open, add a spring hinge that'll help it swing back into place, especially important if you have a pool.

Don't drag. One common installation mistake is to allow the bottom rail of a fence to hover too close to the ground.[91] This encourages rapid deterioration due to rot and insect infestations. Make sure your railing sits 4 to 6 inches above ground level to provide more-than-adequate clearance for nearby grass and proper airflow. The fence will settle a bit after installation, so keeping it up from the start is the best way to ensure it doesn't become bait for bugs.

Set posts properly. Many folks assume that setting posts is the best and strongest way to go, but that method can lead to improper settling, damage, and drainage issues. Most fences will get a better footing if post holes are lined with well-tamped gray gravel: the pressure of the gravel against the dirt is much stronger than a concrete pour, and keeps posts straight as the natural drainage works its magic.

Cap it off. Top off all post heads with a slant, rounded surface, or metal cap to promote water runoff and prevent rot. The neighbors will also compliment you on this fabulous fence finishing point, and, if you're lucky, bring over baked goods to say thanks.[92]

Outdoor Lighting for Safety and Impact

After investing time, money, and creativity in your home's exterior detailing and landscaping, don't forget to turn on the lights. A well-designed exterior "lightscape" enhances a home's best assets, adds drama, and keeps your home safe and secure. Every shimmering result depends on a carefully constructed plan, and here's how to create yours.

Budget for impact. Exterior lighting costs can range from minimal to maximal depending on the investment you want to make. Illuminating a home where you plan to be for only a few years will merit a different level of investment than a longer-term abode where you'll be making ongoing outdoor improvements and additions.

In either case, be honest with yourself and your lighting designer about what's most important to accomplish; from there, system elements and installation plans can be prioritized. You may choose to execute a grand scheme over the course of a few years, or make a smaller, one-time investment.

Style meets function. In the most successful outdoor lighting schemes, function and aesthetics go hand in hand. Consider safety, traffic patterns, and how you'll use outdoor "rooms." Intimate spaces for informal gatherings with family and friends will call for different utility and effects than major entertainment centers.

Long-lasting effects. Whether you're working with a pro or shopping for do-it-yourself systems, go for quality fixtures and components, because you'll definitely get what you pay for. Low-voltage is the way to go, but you really need to work with good materials. Look for durable natural materials like copper and brass, and choose fixtures with glass enclosures. Lifetime warranties are also available on many of the better products. It's also important to invest in a trustworthy transformer for your system; otherwise, you could wind up with a lighting scheme that fades around the edges, or, worse, a complete blackout.

91.) Unscrupulous fence installers do this to guarantee a fence replacement job every six years. Works like clockwork. 92.) Because they'd just as well not see your yard, either.

Up-lighting is a term used to describe objects that are lit from below. Care should be used to make sure the lights don't point toward observers and cause a glare.

Moonlighting is the opposite of up-lighting. Lights placed in trees can cast a dramatic and attractive glow to the ground below and mimic the moon glow. They can also provide security to otherwise darkened areas.

Creating mood and focus. A range of fixtures make it possible to illuminate your home's exterior as well as any Hollywood lighting designer could. But focus, focus, focus is the mantra to have in mind before you go lighting crazy—too much is too much. In the front and back yards, carefully choose focal points to receive the brightest and most dramatic spotlight (whether an unusual tree, water feature, or architectural ornament), and build the rest of the scheme around them. Overall, shoot for a natural look that replicates moonlight streaming softly from above, as opposed to heavy doses of up-lighting.

Safety and security. Harking back to the utility portion of the planning, illuminating for safety and security should be central considerations. Make sure to shed light on all walkways, stair treads, and risers, low-to-the-ground water features, and grade changes. In addition to careful placement, the light's qualities should expose potential intruder hideaways as well as regularly used thoroughfares.

Advanced lighting control systems also protect your home whether you're in or away. Timers, light-sensitive photo cells, remote controls, and computerized systems can all help you manage your new lighting scheme. We suggest a combination of controls, with front yards on automatic timer systems and backyards on more flexible, homeowner-managed networks.

Enlightenment for Those Shopping for Decorative Lighting Fixtures

If your lighting plan incorporates post lights or a lantern or two, don't be fooled by scale when you're shopping—fixtures usually appear to be about 25 percent larger in the store than they will when installed in the yard or at the entry. Also, go for fixtures with frosted or semi-opaque glass, because clear and beveled treatments will draw attention to the bulb inside rather than the attractive fixture surrounding it.

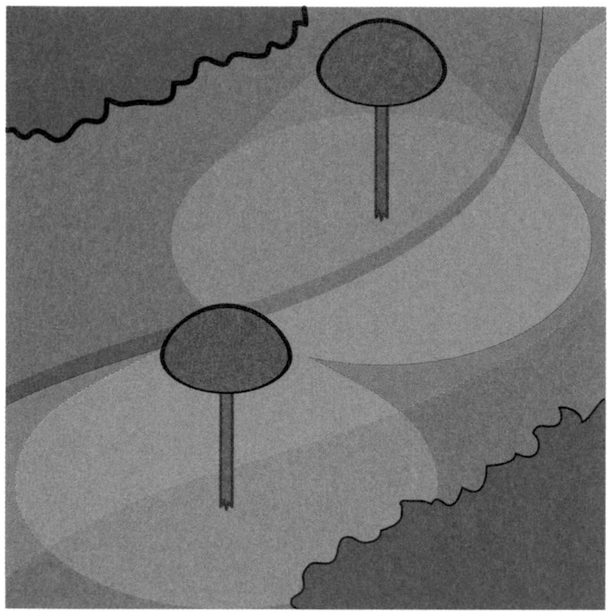

Pathlighting: Low placed path lights are the best for walkways and steps. The globe shields the light from above and focuses it on the pathway. Path lights are available in many low-voltage styles, as well as solar powered.

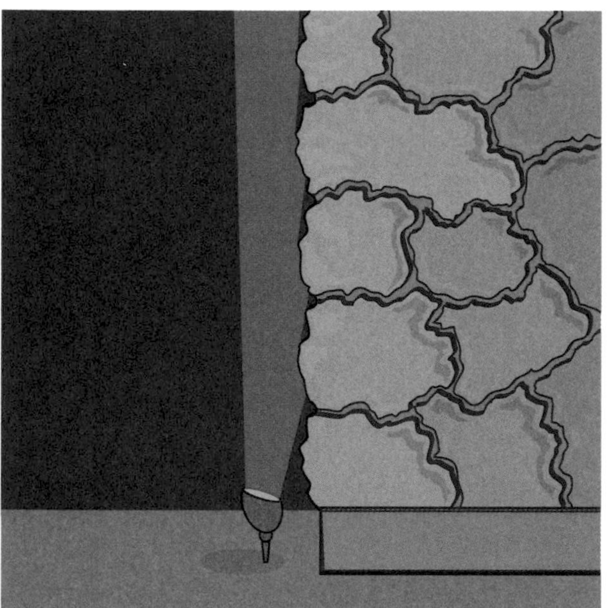

Grazing is a dramatic technique that can be used to cast a glow across the surface of a building or wall surface.

Shadowing: Remember the shadow puppets you enjoyed as a kid? You can use the same technique to light smaller shrubs and cast a big glow on your home. The shadow effect will move as the wind breezes over your landscape, making this technique even more interesting. This also works great for an architectural feature, like an arbor.

Artful installation. And when should you actually start digging in and implementing your lighting scheme? You can install anytime, but it's best to get the designer involved as early as possible in the home renovation or building process. It's not mandatory, but it works to your advantage. In the ideal conditions, lighting pros can usually do installation work in two phases: wiring and system controls are installed before paving and plantings arrive, and after they're in place, the team returns to mount and fine-tune fixtures. Such an approach creates the opportunity to integrate controls with the rest of a home's systems for convenience and a dazzling result.

After your yard and doors, the biggest impact on curb appeal is your siding, roofing, and windows, otherwise known as the "envelope" of your Money Pit. Ready to push it?

The Building Envelope: Siding, Roofing, and Windows

Just like an SPF-50-rated sunblock or a warm winter coat, the exterior of your Money Pit is designed for one thing and one thing only: to protect you from the environment. Be it UV radiation, acid rain, lightning, or (insert your favorite local weather worry here), the skin on your Money Pit must be primed and ready to stop the weather from getting through. In this chapter, we tell you how to do just that.

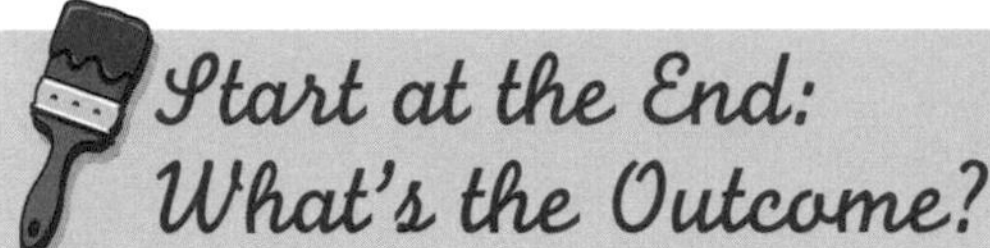

Start at the End: What's the Outcome?

Evaluating products for these adventures comes down to a combination of maintenance, energy efficiencies, and aesthetics. For some, these are personal choices, but in communities with architectural requirements, building envelope adventures with your Money Pit will be subject to higher authorities.

Functional considerations include protection from wind, rain, and stronger forces of nature. These are project categories where new technologies and formulations are arriving on the scene all the time, with rugged good looks to go along with strength and energy smarts.

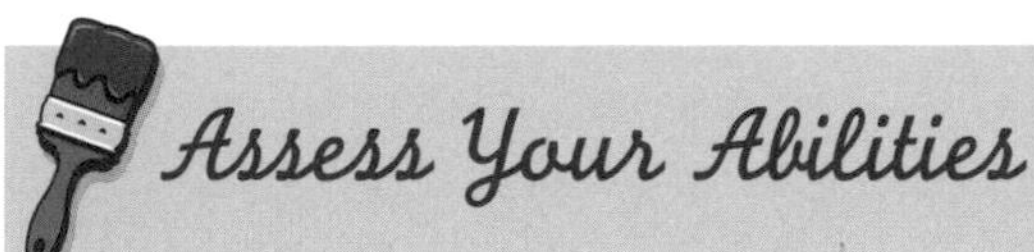

Assess Your Abilities

Siding, windows, and roof work are most often contracted out—well, except if you're Tom, who spent most of his 18th year of life ripping three layers of siding off his parents' two-story house and replacing it with cedar shingles.[93] Painting the exterior is probably one area that an average do-it-yourselfer can attempt, but even doing this chore can be dangerous, with emergency room bills running higher than most painters these days. The fact is that most of these large exterior projects require a good understanding of the forces of gravity, as well as the impact that a stiff wind can have on things like the brand-new window you're trying to wrestle into place. Bottom line, this is one area where do-it-yourselfers can easily become do-it-to-yourselfers, so approach these projects with a dose of caution.

Songs to Work By:

Tunes to help you get through your projects.

- *Who'll Stop the Rain*—Creedence Clearwater Revival
- *Another Brick in the Wall*—Pink Floyd
- *Little Pink Houses*—John Mellencamp
- *Thick as a Brick*—Jethro Tull
- *Up on the Roof*—The Drifters
- *Look Through Any Window*—The Hollies
- *Silhouettes (on the Shade)*—Herman's Hermits
- *Free Fallin'*—Tom Petty
- *Brick House*—The Commodores
- *Window*—Missing Persons
- Anything by The Rooftop Singers

93.) Having learned his lesson at an early age, Tom now contracts that sort of work out.

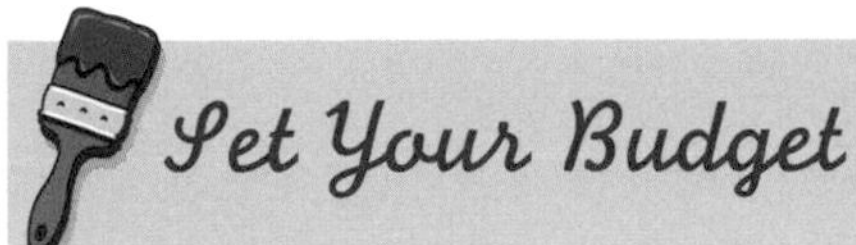

CHAPTER 12

Set Your Budget

Siding, roofing, and windows are not small budget items, so it's important to get a handle on price and what you can spend from the get-go. Do you want siding that has more character and is easier to change as time goes on? Then wood siding, which may run a little more up front, is a good choice. If cost is important, then you might want to look at a vinyl siding product. Likewise, three-tab asphalt composition shingles are probably the most budget-conscious roofing choice and can last 20 or more years. If price is no object, a beautiful metal roof is a great investment that will still be performing well after 100 years, which is more than we can say for us. Clay, stone, and tile have similar longevity, but also a higher up-front cost. There are any number of options that run the gamut in price in each of these three categories, but when it comes to investing in your building envelope, carefully weigh the energy efficiency, durability, storm-resistance, and ongoing maintenance requirements of the product you're purchasing. What looks like a low-cost item now may end up costing you much more over the long term.

Siding Selections

More than any other exterior element, siding delivers your home's biggest visual impact and therefore has an equally large impact on your curb appeal and resale value. While the durability of siding is among the best of any building material, most homeowners will replace siding for wear and tear or simply cosmetic reasons every 20 to 30 years. With the many choices out there, it's easy to get overwhelmed. The best siding selection will balance cost, care, and plain old good looks.

Here's an overview of new siding choices, and a bit of background on what you may have on the house already.

Vinyl siding is the most popular siding in the nation. It is inexpensive compared to other forms of siding, easy to install, and largely maintenance-free. This type of siding does not dent or even show much wear and tear. Vinyl siding is sold with or without an insulating backer, which can add substantial cost to the siding without adding much in the way of energy efficiency.

The most common vinyl siding complaint is wavy siding, which tends to occur more frequently on the warmer south and west sides of a house.

Green Scene: Shopping for Earth-Friendly Siding Options

Just as products for home interiors have been getting greener, there's a growing variety of exterior treatments for creating an ecologically sound home shell. Roofing and siding are both tall orders for new formulations, as they require durability, good looks, and reasonable maintenance. However, there are already some smart offerings joining the traditional materials that have been green all along.

Sustainability in siding means not only green ingredients, but a product that will stand the test of time as both it and your home age. When considering whether or not a siding is truly green, also consider the inclusion of resins and adhesives that may have an off-gassing effect.

Siding Material	Pros	Cons
Solid Wood Clapboards to Shingles	Renewable resource. Can be painted or stained virtually any color.	Needs frequent maintenance.
Fiber Cement	Looks great. Virtually indestructible. Available plain or prefinished.	Can be expensive.
Brick & Stone	Can last forever. Needs very little maintenance.	Expensive. Excessive moisture can freeze and loosen mortar joints, which may need occasional repointing.
Traditional Stucco	Like brick and stone, it has a long life cycle.	May require occasional cleaning, which must be done carefully to avoid damage. Cracks must be sealed regularly to avoid moisture buildup behind the stucco.
Exterior Insulated Finish System	Looks like traditional stucco. Many ornate patterns and looks are possible.	EIFS has a long history of leak problems. Difficult to install. We don't recommend it for wood-framed buildings.
Vinyl Siding	Inexpensive, comes in a range of colors and is virtually maintenance-free.	Is susceptible to heat and artillery fungus. Will appear wavy if installed too tightly.
Cultured Stone Veneers	Come in a variety of colors and styles that mimic the look of real stones that are considerably heavier and more expensive.	Steep learning curve. Should be installed by a pro.
Plywood Siding, T111	Lasts. Looks like planking. Inexpensive.	Needs to be painted or stained regularly.
Hardboard or Composite Siding	Looks like wood.	Not recommended for damp or humid climates. Prone to rotting. Requires regular maintenance. May need to be replaced before other siding options.

How to Choose a Pressure Washer

According to the folks at www.pressurewashersdirect.com, there are three "Ps" to consider when choosing a pressure washer: Pressure, gallons Per minute, and Price.

- ***Water pressure.*** *How much pressure you need depends on the type of job you're going to be doing. The basic light-duty pressure washer (1,300–2,000 PSI) is 30 times as powerful as a garden hose but a good choice for cleaning boats, cars, and siding. Medium-duty (2,000–2,600 PSI) is recommended for cleaning grease and grime, and heavy-duty (2,700–4,000 PSI) for stripping surfaces for repainting.*
- ***Gallons per minute (GPM).*** *The larger the gpm, the more surface area a pressure washer can clean. A higher-GPM flow rate can clean a larger area faster.*
- ***Price.*** *Pressure washers range in price from a low of $100 to more than $2,000.*

The price for pressure washers has really come down, but if you don't want to buy one for your project, you can also rent one to do the job.

Wavy siding results when siding is nailed too tight and expands and buckles. Vinyl siding is made with nail slots (rather than nail holes) punched into it and is not supposed to be nailed tight. If the siding is perfectly installed, you should actually be able take the siding panel in your hand and move it back and forth.

Our pick is ***fiber cement,*** one of the more modern and most durable products around. Some versions look a lot like the asbestos shingles of yesteryear, but this product actually has a completely different formulation. Fiber cement siding is comprised of cement and wood fibers for a durable and affordable solution which mimics the look of natural wood. Although fiber cement siding can be a bit pricey, this stuff is absolutely indestructible and it looks great, too.

Classic ***masonry stucco*** is durable and low-maintenance. Earth- and lime-plaster varieties are among the green choices making a comeback around the U.S. If properly installed, stucco can last forever with very minimal maintenance. Cracks will occasionally form and can be repaired with silicone or epoxy repair compounds. If your stucco was installed over a wood frame, there'll have been masonry lath (steel screening) nailed to the home first. In this case, keep your eyes peeled for areas that bulge. That could indicate that the fasteners holding the lath in place may have rusted out and a repair is due. Otherwise, an occasional light pressure-washing will keep your masonry stucco looking as good as the day it was first installed.

Exterior Insulated Finish System (EIFS) is a type of siding system that became popular in the 1980s when high energy prices made insulated siding a wise choice. When done well, EIFS is beautiful, like real masonry stucco. However, the system has been plagued in the residential market by reports of leakage and the resulting lawsuits. While manufacturers have been working diligently to resolve the problems and the EIFS systems have changed over the years to include

Tom's Tip: Siding Over Siding Is Not Good

As a home inspector, I would often check under the bottom edge of newly installed vinyl siding only to find that the contractor had installed the new siding on top of the old asbestos shingles. This is a really bad practice, as the process of nailing on the new siding would break up the asbestos underneath and cause a real environmental headache for someone down the line. Asbestos or not, it's always a better practice to remove the old siding before installing the next layer.

It Happened to Tom: The Summer of Siding

When I was a kid, our cedar-shingle-sided family homestead, originally red, had faded to become more of a pink house. The siding was worn and cracked, so being at a tender young age where my dad would say I had more courage that ability,[94] I convinced him that the two of us could reside the entire house ourselves.

We set about pulling the old siding off, only to discover that there were two more layers of siding under that. That's about the time when we noticed what it didn't have: insulation. And, because it was an old home, it also had no sheathing and, hence, nothing to nail the new siding onto.

So the simple siding job I had so successfully convinced my dad to tackle ended up to be a project that required removal of three layers of old siding, insulation, and sheathing of all of the exterior walls before we could even think about nailing up the first new shingle.[95]

ways for it to drain moisture that gets past the surface, we are still reluctant to recommend it.

Renewable ***solid wood*** is popular, but high-maintenance, with the added drawback that the most durable varieties come from old-growth trees. You can avoid the latter by selecting only FSC-certified or repurposed wood products. FSC stands for the Forest Stewardship Council, an organization that sets standards for sustainable forest management. More info is available at www.fscus.org.

Wood siding must be regularly maintained with staining or painting. It takes good prep work, repairing or replacing sections of wood rot, caulking holes and gaps to improve energy efficiency.

Cedar is a great siding material as it is naturally insect-resistant. It has been used as siding for well over 100 years and suits many different styles of architecture, from Georgian to Colonial to Dutch Colonial, and can be used to create ornate designs, like scallops, around a gable.

Plywood siding, called T111[96] (and pronounced tee-one-eleven), looks like rough-sawn vertical planking. Plywood siding is good option that delivers structural stability along with protection from the elements.

Composite siding or engineered wood has a well-documented history of failure and a relatively short life expectancy. If you have composite siding, it's not a question of *if* you're going to have to replace your siding but *when*. If an overly anxious contractor drove the nails in a bit too far during installation, they pierce the outside surface of the siding and that lets water seep in. As a result, the siding tends to swell up and rot. While composites might do well in a dry climate, we wouldn't recommend them for anyplace else.

If you choose to use a composite product, stay green by looking for FSC-certified and urea-formaldehyde-free engineered wood to get strength and resilience without harmful off-gassing.

Brick and stone last forever and need very little maintenance. The walls may shift somewhat and cracks over windows and doors are common, but rarely serious. These should be sealed to avoid moisture penetration. Keep an eye on adverse drainage conditions that can cause mortar joints to become excessively wet, such as roof runoff from an overflowing gutter splashing on the ground and up against the brickwork. Brick and stone walls

Shotgun Fungus

There's one fungus among us that looks at lot like someone had blasted the side of your house with a shotgun. Technically known as artillery fungus, it forms when spores are released into the air and stick to the siding. Artillery fungus is very difficult to remove. If you spot it, clean it with bleach-based siding wash as soon as possible. To prevent it from getting worse, remove and replace your shredded bark mulch, a common hideout for fungus spores, with wood chips.

94.) Actually, we think Tom's dad's exact words were closer to "more balls than brains." 95.) Tom's dad was right. See above. 96.) Don't ask us why they call it T111, they just do.

Repairing Loose Siding

Vinyl siding is low maintenance, but occasionally, pieces become loose in a storm. To repair them, pick up a handy little siding tool called a zipper. The tool works by locking the pieces back together as you slide the tool along, just like a zipper, making it easy to snap a loose piece of siding back in place.

can be cleaned periodically, and a pressure washer works well for this. But be careful with that handy tool, because too much pressure will erode the brick and there's no repair for that!

Occasionally, someone in our audience will ask if it's possible to paint a brick house. The answer is yes, but we always caution that after paint comes *re*-paint. If you don't want to commit to a house painting project every five to ten years, learn to live with that original brick color!

Cultured stones are synthetic veneer products that look like stone but are lighter, less expensive, and easier to install than natural stone. They can be used on everything from siding to chimneys and fireplaces. The combination of affordability, availability, and consistency of color of manufactured stone veneers makes the possibilities endless for luxury-loving consumers.

Another benefit: Manufactured stone enables you to roll out backyard improvements as your budget allows. Say you want to create an outdoor living space. Using cultured stone veneer, you can start by building a retaining wall this year, add a built-in barbecue and more trim later, and the tones will match perfectly with what you've already started.

Some old-style siding is still out there, notably cement asbestos shingles and aluminum. If your Money Pit was built during the 1950s and 1960s, you might have cement asbestos shingles. In this application, asbestos is held in a cement binder and therefore cannot be easily released to the air, so you don't have to change it. If you do want to remove it, remember that in some parts of the country disposing of asbestos can be a chore, so be sure to check in with your local waste management folks to understand what's involved before you begin.

There is also no need to remove aluminum siding that is in good condition. If it is faded and worn, you should know that the siding can be painted. For best results, the siding has to be cleaned, primed, and spray-painted. Use an oil-based primer, because latex primer contains ammonia which creates a gas when it comes into contact with the aluminum siding, which can lead to poor adhesion.

Picture-Perfect Exterior Painting

Exterior paint is different than interior paint, and many homeowners often make the mistake of not choosing the correct paint for the job. Exterior paint is formulated for color retention, flexibility to withstand expansion and contraction due to weather, resistance to tannin bleed, and resistance to mildew. Exterior flat acrylic latex paint is the easiest for do-it-yourselfers to work with. For trim, consider a durable alkyd/oil paint that offers high gloss with good adhesion and stain resistance.

For real savings, always invest in premium paint and always buy a bit more paint than you think you'll need. Before you start your paint job, check the temperatures. Paint won't adhere if it's below 55 degrees and won't go on smoothly if it's above 90[97] degrees.

97.) Impacting both paint *and* painters.

Tom's Tip: No Bad Paint—Just Bad Painters

Blaming the paint for an unacceptable result is quite common. Some years ago, a friend mentioned to me that he must have had some "bad paint" because the top gable section of wood siding we were repairing had blistered very badly. My buddy had installed the siding and painted the entire home himself about four years earlier. Upon closer examination, the real culprit became obvious. The "painter" had neglected to back-prime the siding in the gable. Back-priming refers to the technique of priming all surfaces of exterior siding before it is assembled, including the back of the board. Priming controls the amount of moisture absorbed by the board, preventing early paint failure. When I mentioned this to my friend, he recalled that he had completed siding the entire home but ran short of material for the section that failed. When the remaining material finally arrived, he was in a rush to get it completed and took a shortcut that he was now paying for.

Cheap Paint Is No Bargain

When it comes to buying paint, beware of discount brands. You definitely get what you pay for, and the lower the cost, the shorter life the paint will have. Considering that painting is 90 percent labor and 10 percent material, shorter-life paint means your cost per year for the project can be double, as shown below.

Leslie Likes: The Changing Face of Wood

As wood ages, you can enjoy each stage by progressing through the opacities of wood stains from a clear finish to semi-transparent to full opaque. This allows you to change the overall appearance of your home, while maintaining the integrity of the building material, but it also gives you some fresh options. You shouldn't put a solid stain onto brand-new wood siding unless that's the look you want. Consider a natural finish or semi-transparent stain to really enjoy the natural benefits of the wood.

Actual Cost to Paint a House

Thinking about picking up some bargain paint for your next big house painting project? Don't! Cheap paint is never a bargain. Here's why. The true cost of painting your home must be measured on an annual basis and includes both the cost of the paint and the cost of the labor. The longer the paint lasts, the lower that annual cost becomes. For example:

Premium Paint		***Standard Paint***	
Labor	*$7,500*	*Labor*	*$7,500*
Materials (20 gal @ $25)	*500*	*Materials (20 gal @ $15)*	*300*
Total	*$8,000*	*Total*	*$7,800*
Estimated life: 10 years		*Estimated life: 5 years*	
Cost per year	***$800***	***Cost per year***	***$1,560***

Priming is mandatory to create a firm bond between the substrate and finish coat, unless painting your house is something you like to do on a frequent basis. Think of it as the glue that makes the paint stick. Before you prime the house, be sure to give the entire home a good cleaning with a hose or pressure washer to remove any surface dirt and debris, and allow the home to dry thoroughly. Next, remove any flaking or chipping paint you might have and sand to create a smooth transition. Then caulk around windows and doors (using paintable caulk) to create a weathertight and energy-efficient seal.

Now, you are really ready to prime your entire home, including the trim detail pieces. Once the primer dries, you are ready for your topcoat.

Roofing Review

Strength, durability, and a great look should seal your home's envelope at the roof level. Even a spectacular roof won't last forever, though, so we'll take a look at the best options for repairing or replacing that structural lid when the time comes.

Asphalt shingle roofs are the most common type of roof, technically known as composition shingle. Originally, they were made on a cotton mat that was sprayed with asphalt. The older shingles, and there are still a lot of them out there, are very thick and tend to shrink up, curl, and crack. They also tend to show their age, often becoming so brittle that you can literally snap them between your fingers.[98]

Newer asphalt composition shingles, made within the last 15 years or so, use a fiberglass mat which is proving to be much more durable. Not all asphalt shingles are created equal, either, as asphalt marketers are quick to note. They're available in the common three-tab style or varying patterns in what's known as an architectural or dimensional shingle that replicates the great look of a wood shake or slate. Compare warranties too, as some shingles are guaranteed to last longer than others.

Wear and tear on these newer fiberglass-based shingles is a bit more difficult to detect. While they don't curl up and crack like older asphalt shingles, they do tend to split and tear. If you spot these narrow fractures occurring in the shingles, these could be sources for leaks and the shingles should be replaced.

Asphalt ***roll roofing*** is a common roofing material applied either in single coverage or double coverage. It's usually produced in 36-inch-wide sheets on a roll, which are overlapped about 4 inches for single coverage or 18 inches for double coverage. Roll roofing is an inexpensive, short-term roofing solution that's not terrifically attractive, but might be perfectly acceptable for

Cleaning Asphalt Shingles

Moss, mold, mildew, and algae grow on virtually all roofing materials. If you have a roof that's heavily shaded by overhanging trees, you may be especially at risk of having a green scene on your roof.

Trim back those trees so that the sunlight can shine through and effectively dry up any mold or mildew that previously languished in their shade. Wash the roof with a simple bleach-and-water solution or commercially available mildewcide made for this purpose. After applying the cleaner with a pump-type garden sprayer, let it sit and then rinse it off to reveal a bright, clean rooftop.

Keep it clean by using copper or nickel ridge vents along the peak of the roof. As rainwater hits these ridges, some of the copper or nickel will leach out and act as a mildewcide, keeping the roof clean.

98.) Or under your feet as you plummet off the roof. Brittle roofs are dangerous to walk on.

Roofing Material	Pros	Cons
Asphalt, Composition Shingle	Long-lasting (typically 20–25 years). Relatively inexpensive. Available in dimensional shingles that resemble clay tiles or shake shingles.	Must be cleaned occasionally.
Metal	Lightweight. Can be installed over an old asphalt shingle roof. Saves energy. Can last 50–100 years.	Expensive.
Roll Roofing	Extremely durable when properly installed. Can last 20 years or more.	Short-term roofing solution—usually lasts around 5–7 years. Not very attractive.
Built-up Roofs, Rubber, or Modified Bitumen	One of the only roof systems designed for flat or low-slope applications.	Difficult to repair when leaks occur. Some need to be painted with an aluminum oxide paint to reflect deteriorating UV radiation.
Clay	Green option. Goes well with many home styles. Extremely durable, lasting 50 years or more.	Clay tiles are heavy. Roof must be specially framed to support them.

such utility buildings as sheds or pole barns.

Metal roofing is our fave, capable of lasting as long as a traditional slate roof and a smart green choice, too. The paints applied to them today reflect sunlight, so the roof itself doesn't get nearly as hot as it would have in the days of yore, cutting down on the heat transmitted to the inside of your home for energy savings of up to 40 percent. Weather conditions can affect a metal roof's life span, but it still has significant potential for impressive longevity of 50 to 100 years. Metal roofs have one downside, though: they're pricier than other options, by a significant amount.

Natural roofing materials like ***tile, slate, and clay*** offer longevity, literally millennia as you History Channel fans know. Slate is the trickiest: it may need to be replaced if it starts exfoliating, developing a pink and powdery-looking ve-

Green Scene: Apply Metal over Asphalt

Because metal roofing is lightweight, you can apply it over asphalt shingles. You'll save on the cost of stripping away the old roof and help the earth by reducing the amount of asphalt shingles that end up in landfills.

neer. Not your problem if you're installing a slate roof—it'll last anywhere from 75 to 100 years.

The environmental cost in terms of transport fuel is a consideration, a non-green aspect to slate. You can offset this by ordering from a local quarry or working with a supplier dealing in just-as-strong salvaged slate. Slate tiles can loosen and slip out, usually because the nails have loosened. Repair requires the skills of a slater, a slate roof specialist who can be hard to find.

Clay is one of the oldest and greenest roofing materials available, offering good looks that mellow beautifully with exposure to the elements. It works well with both contemporary and traditional home styles, and can be made to replicate vintage fabrications for renovations of classic homes.

In lieu of a slate or tile roof, there are a lot of composite shingles available that mimic the look of tile and slate for less expense and a longer life span. Rubber tiles made from recycled tires resemble slate roofing, offer ease of installation, strength with lighter weight, and, presumably, superb traction.

Wood roofing is available either as smoothly hewn shingles cut to specific, regular sizes or irregularly shaped traditional shakes with rough, rustic texture. As with siding, the trade-off is wood's natural, classic look versus the rigorous upkeep. Local ordinances may also restrict its use due to typically low fire resistance.

Built-up roofing consists of multiple layers of tar and paper. These layers are usually coated with some sort of lightweight stone. In coastal states such as Florida, you'll see seashells used in place of stone.[99] This top layer helps reflect the sun's rays, contributing to the longevity of a built-up roof.

Ask Tom & Leslie: This Is Not Your Grandfather's Metal Roof

Q: Our roof is about 15 years old, and we have asphalt shingles. We are noticing deterioration on a lot of the shingles, and it seems like it might be time to replace it. What are some new roofing options that we might not be aware of?

A: Since asphalt roofs generally last 15 to 20 years, it sounds like you are right on target for a new one! That being the case, we'd recommend you take a look at the fabulous new options in metal roofing. Metal roofs are no longer just the corrugated sheets of steel you might have seen in the past. They have now gone "high-tech" with a variety of energy-efficient and affordable styles that can look like slate, cedar shake, terra-cotta, or just about any custom look imaginable. Metal roofs are also resistant to shrinking or cracking and are virtually maintenance-free. By adding a metal roof to your home you can also save up to 40 percent in annual energy costs and increase the value of your home by about $1.45 per square foot. Plus, metal roofs are made from 30–60 percent recycled materials, so you can sleep well under your new roof knowing that you have helped our very valuable environment. For more information on metal roofs, visit the website for the Metal Roofing Association at www.metalroofing.com.

Why It's Important to Vent Your Roof

Ventilation helps you keep cool in the house and also makes your house last longer, with attic ventilation in particular helping to prolong the life of your roof. Without good roof ventilation, excessive heat builds up in the attic and causes the asphalt roof shingles to overheat and crack. In his years as a professional home inspector, Tom repeatedly saw roofs that had basically cooked away their usual product life expectancy because they were missing that critical element of ventilation.

In our opinion, the best ventilation is a system of continuous ridge and soffit vents. Many homes not built recently have gable vents (located at the peak of the roof), roof vents, or those turbine vents that make a show of spinning

99.) Even if you can't say that last sentence out loud—5 times fast.

Solar Shingles: High tech photovoltaic roof shingles can deliver electric power to your house without the need for bulky solar panels.

Green Scene: Solar Shingles

The next step up from installing large solar panels over existing roofing, solar shingles contribute to both energy generation and savings for a home. Solar shingles can be integrated with existing roofing or cover an entire roof, and though current options tend to be on the pricey side, demand is bringing those numbers down for a great value in combination with the tax breaks you can receive.

around but actually contribute very little in the ventilation department.

A ridge-and-soffit system combines a ridge vent that runs along the whole peak of the roof, opening up the top peak end-to-end, with a soffit vent at the underside of the overhang. This works well because as wind blows against your house, the soffit vents are positively pressurized and they let air in. The ridge, which becomes negatively pressurized, lets air out. As the air rides up under the roof sheathing, it takes moisture out in the winter (reducing condensation and making

Synthetic Slate and Shake Shingles versus the Real Deal

Q: I'm shopping for a new roof and learning that there are a lot more choices for shingles these days. I've decided against using composite asphalt shingles. Natural slate and shake are out of the question for cost and safety reasons. I'm seriously considering synthetic slate or shake and like the colors and textures I've seen, but I'd sure appreciate your opinion.

A: Synthetic slate and shake shingle—made from engineered polymers—have evolved dramatically. The newer generation looks so good that homeowners, architects, and contractors need to squint to tell they're not the real thing. The shingles are high-tech and offer homeowners significant cost and maintenance savings. They look just like real quarried slate or cedar shake and come in a wide variety of colors, thicknesses, blends, and widths.

Besides looks and longevity, their real advantage is cost savings. Compared to natural slate, synthetic is at least half the installed cost. Compared to good composite asphalt, the installation costs are two to three times more, but they're warranted to last two or three times longer. Some manufacturers that specialize in synthetics are so confident of the durability that they offer 50-year warranties.

When shopping synthetics, look for a thickness of at least half an inch. This will deepen shadow lines and convey the look of premium shake or natural stone. Also check for multiple shingle widths, to create a non-repeating, distinctive, and varied pattern. The best synthetic shingles also provide advanced home safety and protection, including the highest fire rating (Class A), the highest impact rating (Class 4), and the highest ratings for wind resistance (110 MPH). Actually, these can save homeowners money, too, when it comes to insurance premiums.

Make sure the shingle has been tested by independent organizations like Underwriters Laboratories (UL) or the ICC Evaluation Service. Verify that products meet certain standards like the International Building Code (IBC), International Residential Code (IRC), and the Uniform Building Code (UBC). UL can confirm the fire rating, impact rating, and wind resistance.

The bottom line: Don't be afraid to consider synthetic slate and shake shingles. Only your roofer knows for sure if this will be the right choice for your home.

Leslie Likes: Asphalt or Clay?

There are a lot of houses that have asphalt shingles where I live, and as I bike-ride by, they look an awful lot like slate roofs. You can see shadowing and depth just like the natural roofing material, but is it? If you have a dimensional roof that appears to be made of clay tile but has a weave valley in it, it's asphalt.

Today's manufacturing processes are so sophisticated that you have to pretty much have to be right on top of them to see that they aren't clay. Here's a great tip for these roofs: to complete the illusion, add traditional copper standing seam valleys.

Attic Fans versus Whole-House Fans

Attic fans should not be confused with whole-house fans. A whole-house fan is designed to cool the house rather than the attic. It's usually mounted in the center hall or the second floor hallway. It discharges air into the attic where an expanded gable vent directs it outside. Open up a few windows and turn the fan on at bedtime or when you want to get some air moving through the house, and it's very effective at pulling a nice breeze in. Having a whole-house fan allows you to cut down on air conditioner use and trim your cooling bills.

insulation more effective) and heat out in the summer. In a cycle that repeats 24/7/365, it's a very efficient way of cooling your roof.

Attic fans can be helpful, but only if you don't have central AC. Otherwise, it's counterproductive, as the fan will suck the cold conditioned air through voids in the walls, potentially raising cooling costs.

Roof Repair 101: What to Look For to Get the Job Done Right

With the generally silent, steady job it does protecting you and your home, it's easy to take your roof for granted—easy, that is, until a leak sprouts or a shingle slips. Proceeding with repair is a big-ticket project loaded with choices impacting the structural integrity of your home, so carefully consider your options before hitting the roof.

Remove or Install a New Layer?

Earlier, we talked about installing a metal roof over asphalt. Can you do that with other materials? In our experience, second and certainly third layers of roof shingles don't last nearly as long as the first layer. The original roofing material acts as a heat sink so the new roof stays hotter. The hotter the roof, the more quickly the oils evaporate from the asphalt, causing the shingles to break down and reducing expected life by as much as a third.

Stripping the existing roof first will increase your budget. Before you go that direction, ask yourself how long you're going to live in your house. If you're going to be there for most of the life of the roof and you want it to last as long as possible, it's probably worth the investment to take it down to one layer. On the other hand, if you may be moving in the next five or ten years, we recommend skipping the stripping to get the best return on your investment.

Product Selection for Weather Protection

An important part of your roof redo is the weather protection incorporated underneath the shingles you see. Accumulated moisture is the ultimate enemy of every kind of roofing material and can cut down on its life span in a hurry, so an underlayment like Grace Ice & Water Shield is a worthwhile investment. This self-adhered material is applied under the shingles and directly to the roof's decking, creating a watertight bond that not only protects your roof from pools of water caused by ice dams, but also from wind-driven rains and snow, preventing most leaks.

Roof Check

Roofs take lots of wear and tear, as they are constantly exposed to all of the elements. Keep a close eye on them, a really close eye, as in using high-powered binoculars (which have the added benefit of alarming the neighbors when they see you own them). Look for any loose, cracked, torn, missing, or warped shingles that are on the surface of the roof. Check carefully around every penetration where flashing can potentially loosen, including plumbing vents, roof vents, skylights, and chimneys. Also check out areas where you have two different roof lines joining one another, different planes of roofing meeting, and any place that roofing touches siding, as at dormers.

Finally, get up on a ladder and look into your gutters. If you have excessive granular loss (little pebbles or bits of shedded shingle), that indicates roof wear.

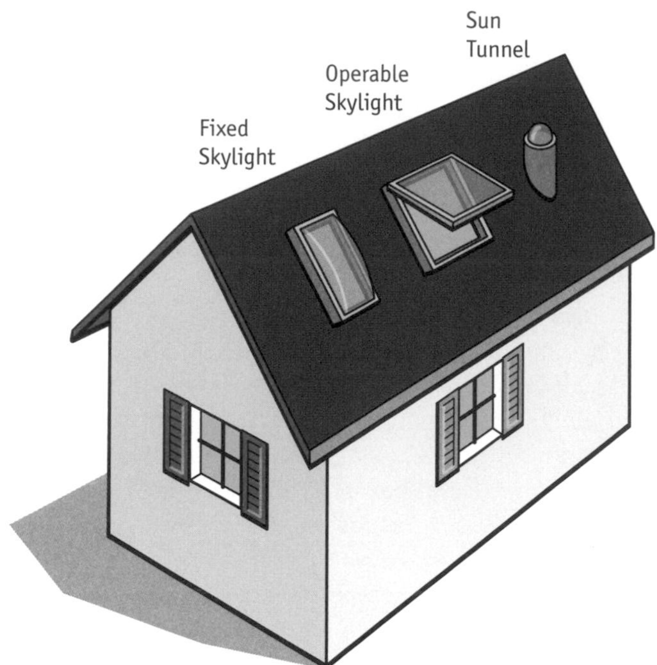

Skylight Options: Bring in the sunshine with either fixed, operable, or Sun Tunnel type skylights.

If you live in hurricane target zones, there are various asphalt shingles designed to stand up to 100-mile-per-hour winds. If this describes potential weather conditions where you live, make sure you use a shingle that's designed to withstand high winds and rain.

Chimneys, skylights, and dormers also benefit from protection, and that's where a material called flashing comes in. Placed where these features meet the roof, flashing creates a water and air-resistant seal for strength outside and comfort and energy savings indoors. Flashing used to be made of metal, but now there are also many high-quality synthetic flashing materials that are even more effective in sealing these difficult spots.

Skylights

When is putting a hole in a roof a good thing? When you fill it with a skylight! When properly installed, a skylight can deliver years of care-free light to your home.

There are several types of skylights. The least expensive and least durable are plastic "bubble" skylights that are installed flush with the roof. These don't last very long, crack easily, and need frequent replacement.

The most common type of skylight is the curbed skylight, which simply means it sits up

Tom's Tip: Roof Ripoff

Years ago when I was inspecting homes in a retirement village, a woman told me she had a brand-new roof, which looked good from the street but still not quite right. When I got up on the roof and noticed that the shadow lines—the slots between the shingles—were just as bright as the shingles themselves, I figured it out: The "roofer" had simply painted the roof with house paint, which, believe me, does not make a roof last longer.

Never let anyone paint an asphalt shingle roof. The only type of roofs that needs to be painted are metal roofs or some flat roofs, which require a special reflective paint called fibrous aluminum that helps shed the sun's ultraviolet radiation.

on the roof like a box. These units rely on a sealant applied between the curb and the roof surface that will break down over time, causing leaks.

The best type of skylight is one that incorporates a built-in flashing system like those from Andersen or VELUX. These have a plain wood frame that is mounted to the roof opening with brackets to hold it in place and a customized flashing kit to complete the leak-free installation. Skylights can be fixed or operable, and even come with built-in or automatic shades. They can be operated manually with a crank or a long rod that reaches up to them for access, or you can operate them via remote control. There is also an easy-to-install version called a Sun Tunnel, which is a tube with a mirrored interior that transmits light from the roof into virtually any interior room or hallway that you want to brighten.

If you're going to install a skylight, absolutely choose low-E glass, especially on the south side of your roof, because there's nothing that brings more heat into your house[100] than a skylight that's not treated with this energy-efficient shield.

Window Shopping

Leaking, sticking, loose glass, drafts, and scary insect invasions all mean your windows need attention. If you're not sure about drafts,[101] hold an incense stick or piece of tissue in front of your windows on a breezy day. If the tissue flutters or the smoke coming off the incense stick streams sideways, you're the proud owner of a drafty Money Pit.

Repair or replace? You can replace loose or damaged weather stripping fairly easily and inexpensively, and you can caulk any drafts around the window frame. Loose glass and deteriorating frames are much more serious problems, however. The cost to repair them might be less in the short-term, but replacing the windows with energy-efficient models is a smarter decision in the long run.

According to research conducted by window manufacturer JELD-WEN, consumers demand, in order of importance, reliability, energy efficiency, and price. We pretty much agree with that—especially the part about price being third on the list. You can either pay for high-quality windows once, or pay for lower-quality windows every month for the life of your home in terms of energy costs. Inefficiency not only delivers higher energy bills, it also creates an uncomfortable home year-round.[102]

A replacement window is different than a new-construction window because a replacement window is designed to fit within the existing opening. The typical replacement window is a double-hung, vinyl window, which typically is taking over for one made of wood. See the next page for a list of options.

Pick a Window Frame

A good window frame improves energy efficiency and reduces maintenance. Vinyl windows are great because the vinyl is through and through. They're energy-efficient, durable, rot-proof and insect-proof, and virtually maintenance-free. Vinyl-clad windows have vinyl on the outside and wood on the inside and are easy windows to maintain.

Wood windows are still common, but not installed as much anymore because homeowners view them as being too high in maintenance. Yet they can be equally efficient and are frequently used in high-end homes because wood windows can be fabricated into beautiful, ornate pieces of art in in-

100.) Except the conversations you'll be having with your spouse if you don't choose the right glass. 101.) You'll have no doubt about insects.
102.) In terms of both temperature and subsequent whining.

Windows	Pros	Cons
Wood	Can be milled into any shape for an infinite number of custom designs. Works well with most home décor. Offers good insulation value.	Requires regular maintenance. Susceptible to rot.
Aluminum	Inexpensive, lightweight. Initially, a low-maintenance product.	Doesn't wear well over time. Many were installed in the 1980s and 1990s due to low cost and now need replacement.
Vinyl	Looks great, virtually maintenance-free. Offers good insulation value.	Choosing a reliable manufacturer is key as glass seals can break down and hardware-like springs may need replacement. If the manufacturer is not around to support these needs, you'll need to buy new windows instead of repairing the ones you have.
Vinyl Clad	Vinyl frame faces the outdoors and is able to withstand the elements, while inside, the frame is wood, which complements most home décor. Personalization options with grills makes it possible to complement any architectural style.	Limited choices of color available for the vinyl exterior.

teresting shapes. If you've considered wood before, give it a second thought, because today's wood windows are much better than they used to be.

Aluminum-frame windows were the first type of double-hung, inexpensive windows that were popular after wood starting losing favor. Today, they're probably the lowest-quality window out there, and don't wear very well.

Choose Window Glass

In the single- versus double-pane debate, we declare ourselves to be double-panes. Double-pane windows save money in the long run by reducing your utility bills. To save even more, look for windows with the Energy Star label. They meet strict energy-efficiency guidelines set by the U.S. government and can reduce your energy costs. Also check out the National Fenestration Ratings Council (NFRC) label, which helps buyers do an apples-to-apples comparison of window products.

If your home already has single-pane windows and you live in a cold climate, consider storm windows. They're almost as efficient as double-pane windows, but one less pain in your wallet. Cut down on drafts and improve the efficiency of single-pane windows by weather-stripping and caulking windows to keep out cold air. Also, remember windows leak just as much in the summer as they do in the winter. If you have central air conditioning, keep those storm windows down in summer too.

Ask Tom & Leslie: **Window, Window on the Wall which Is the Fairest One of All?**

Q: Last winter the energy bills really hurt, so this year we are thinking about installing new windows. Any tips or advice?

A: (Leslie) Changing your windows is a great way to create a more energy-efficient environment inside your home. Faulty windows, whether by installation or just old age, can account for a huge energy loss and higher energy bills. It is also a year-round problem because while cold drafts are obvious in the colder months, "warm" drafts also drain energy bills in the summer air-conditioning season.

(Tom) If the framing around your windows seems to be in good shape, then replacement windows are your best option. Replacement windows allow you to remove just the operable parts of the old window (like the sashes that slide up and down) but keep the original wood window frame. The new window simply slips inside the old window frame, and with a little bit of trim and caulk, you're done. A big advantage of replacement windows is that you can install them quickly and with no disturbance to the siding. The newest-model windows offer low-E as well as double- or triple-pane glass, all excellent options for energy efficiency. It's also a great time to make this energy-saving switch, as the government is offering tax credits for energy-efficient improvements made through 2008. For more information, log on to the Department of Energy's website at www.doe.gov.

Leslie Likes: **Window Dressing**

There are so many different ways you can use windows to decorate, whether you're doing a renovation, adding on, or building a home from scratch. Depending on the location of the window, you have the opportunity to showcase the architectural style of the home through a shape or style of window that suits it (for example, Tudors look great with leaded glass windows). You can order different kinds of glass to replicate those from the era in which your home was built, from seeded to stained specialty glass.

What about triple-pane windows? They are more energy-efficient, and also offer better acoustics and less loss of visibility. The downsides are that they cost more and weigh more. If you're located in the northern part of the country, you're probably going to get a better return on investment for spending more money on better windows than if you live in the central part of the country. If you live in a warmer climate, it doesn't make as much sense to invest in triple-pane windows.

U-Factor: The Solar Heat Gain Coefficient and Low-E

Pardon the science lesson, but this is important: The lower the U-factor, the better the window insulates. The Solar Heat Gain Coefficient (SHGC) describes the solar heat gain, meaning a low SHGC rating helps reduce air-conditioning bills in warmer climates, while a higher SHGC keeps homes more comfy up north.

Low-E (or low-emissivity) windows reflect the ultraviolet rays of the sun back out dur-

Review Rot Resistance

When shopping for windows, consider decay resistance. Several manufacturers incorporate specialized treatments to preserve wood window components. AuraLast, for example, is a dip treatment technology from JELD-WEN that prevents rot in windows, even if cut or sawn. It's a vacuum treatment solution that reduces VOCs by 90 percent and goes all the way to the center of the wood.

Look for the NFRC Label

NFRC (National Fenestration Ratings Council) labels are on most every window product, allowing you to easily compare energy-efficient values for windows, just like home appliances. The NFRC is an independent, nonprofit organization that provides uniform testing, rating, and certification. The rating program takes several variables into account, including energy transfer at the center of the glass, edge effect, the insulating value of the frame material, unit size, inside/outside temperatures, wind velocity, and solar heat transmittance.

Tom's Tip: The Very First Central "Air Conditioner"

Double-hung windows were actually the very first "built-in" cooling system for your home. By opening both the top and the bottom windows halfway, a natural convective loop is created that lets warm exhaust out the top window while cool air flows in the bottom.

ing the summer. We heartily recommend letting your windows help pay your air-conditioning costs. For example, the Woodwright double-hung window from Andersen Windows features high-performance low-E glass that is 35 percent more energy efficient than double-pane glass in winter and 41 percent more efficient in summer. Coatings are used and applied differently depending on whether you live in a warm or cold climate.

Combining the low-E coatings with gas fillings such as argon or krypton increases the energy efficiency even more. Other characteristics to look for include multiple layers of glazing, thickness of air space, low-conductivity gas fill, and tinted glass coatings.

Standard low-E glass has two layers of low-E treatment. It blocks ultraviolet (UV) rays and reduces fade. Low-E 366 (similar to Andersen's low-E glass) has three layers of low-E, a better U-factor, and better SHGC rating.

If You Don't Do Windows . . .

Several window manufacturers offer windows with coated glass that makes them virtually self-cleaning, letting rain run off your windows just like it runs off your car after a fresh wax job.

If you have to do windows,[103] newspaper (black-and-white pages only) and a solution of white vinegar and water are a great natural cleaner.

Impact-Resistant Glass

Impact-resistant glass contains a membrane much like automobile glass does, and though it'll crack on impact, it won't shatter. Windows made with this material are very heavy and about twice the cost of standard windows, but if you live in a hurricane zone,[104], they could be a worthwhile investment.

Pick Your Style

The major varieties include:

- **Double-hung.** With a double-hung window, you push the bottom window upward to open the unit. The top window also slides down vertically. Screens are located on the outside of this style.

- **Casement.** Casement windows are hinged at the sides and are opened by turning a crank. The cranks are available in a stationary position or in a style that folds down and tucks neatly out of the way when not in use. Screens are placed on the inside of the window.

103.) We all do. 104.) Or on a golf course.

Window Types

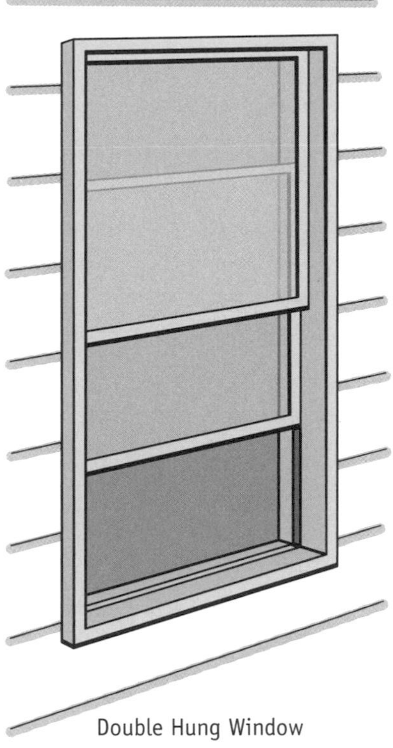

Double Hung Window

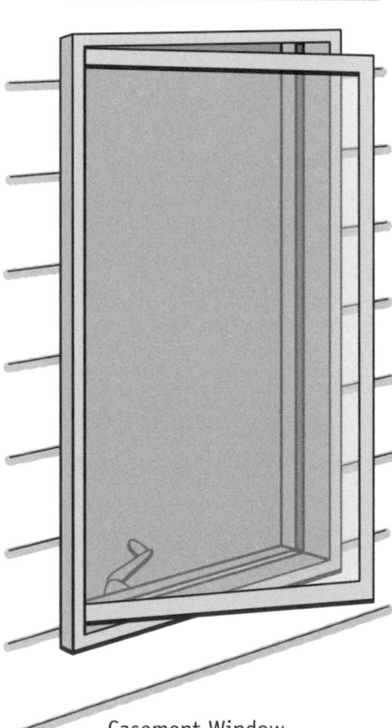

Casement Window

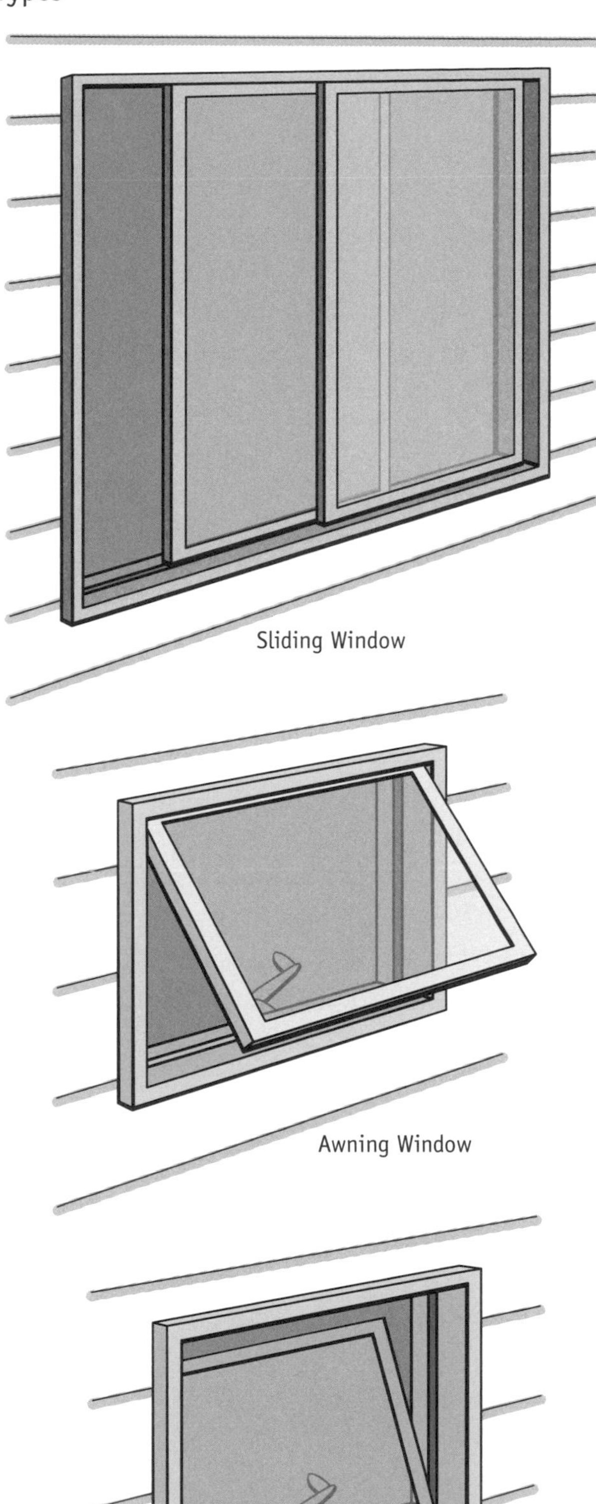

Sliding Window

Awning Window

Hopper Window

Ask Tom & Leslie: Windows That Are All Wet

Q: Why does condensation form on the inside of windows?

A: Condensation forms on the inside of windows for one of two reasons: (1) the thermal pane has failed or (2) the window never had thermal-pane glass. In the first case, condensation can occur with a double-pane, energy-efficient window when the gas within the two panels has failed or wasn't sealed correctly. Consequently, as temperature changes from the interior to the exterior, condensation will form on the glass. You can't repair the gas problem; the only solution is to replace the window sash. If you have single-pane windows, the condensation occurs because they are terribly inefficient.

- **Sliding.** Popular as openings to patios and decks, a sliding window (also known as gliders) can be virtually any size, but only opens about half of its total width (only one side slides horizontally in a single-sliding window). Double-sliding windows are also available, and screens, if desired, are located on the outside of the side that opens.

- **Awning.** Awning windows are hinged at the top and open outward. Screens are placed on the inside of the window.

- **Hopper.** Hopper windows are hinged at the bottom and open inward. Screens are placed on the outside of the window.

- **Fixed/Picture.** Fixed or picture windows can't be opened but do serve to let in light.

In practice, several of these window types can be combined to create multiple window panels. For example, it would not be unusual to see a combination of two casement windows on opposite sides of a fixed center window. Bay and bow windows are another example of this, with multiple window designs combined into a single unit.

Tips for Replacement Window Shopping

- *Work with trained window experts who will answer questions about energy efficiency, give good advice for your project, and help you understand different window types and how each performs.*
- *Choose quality windows with a reliable warranty, because windows are only as good as the warranty that comes with them. Make sure the fine print matches what the salesperson is promising.*
- *Only purchase energy-efficient windows. In addition to the Energy Star label, look for the National Fenestration Rating Council (NFRC) label and use those stats for an apples-to-apples comparison of windows you are considering.*
- *Choose windows with low-E glass. These windows have metallic coatings that reduce heating and cooling costs year-round.*
- *Bring in lots of light and add curb appeal. Studies show that exposure to natural light has positive health effects, both physically and emotionally. Use a combination of windows and skylights to let in natural light and brighten your space.*
- *Get ordering help. Ordering replacement windows (or doors, for that matter) can be complicated. To make sure the job gets done right, have the window salesperson come to your house to do the measuring. Even if you plan to install them yourself, getting the measurements right is critical to the success of your project.*

Window Screens, Child Safety Bars, and Security Bars

One of the window components that is probably more dangerous today than it was in yesteryear is the window screen. That's because years ago

NFRC Label: All windows are not created equal. The National Fenestration Rating Council label helps you make an apples-to-apples comparison of a window's energy efficient qualities. (Courtesy of NFRC)

window screens were associated with storm windows and made out of sturdy aluminum screening that could actually take a fair amount of pressure before it would give out. Today, window screens are very, very light, almost flimsy, in fact, and designed only to keep the bugs out, not really part of the structure of the window.

If you have open windows, especially on second-floor bedrooms near children, add child safety bars on the inside of windows located on the second floor in or near kids' rooms. Make sure the child safety bars have quick-release features that can be easily opened in the event of an emergency. Child safety bars are not to be confused with security bars, which should be put on the outside of homes. If you put security bars on your home, you want to make sure that they also have a quick-release mechanism so that they, too, can be opened in the event of a fire.

For people who tend to avoid window screens because they obscure the view, Andersen Windows makes a virtually invisible screen called TruScene. Pella makes a similar product called Vivid View screen. Compared with a traditional screen, you will see a lot more of the great outdoors through both of these. Similarly, JELD-WEN offers Phantom Screens that disappear into the window frame. When you want the windows open and the screens in use, they're drawn to the center and held in place by magnets. When they're not in use, Phantom Screens simply retract, leaving an unobstructed view.

If you're wrapping up a Building Envelope adventure, you may already have another adventure waiting in the wings—in fact, it may actually have wings. Critters in the house and around the yard can threaten the survival of both you and your Money Pit, so prepare to check your phobias at the door and gain control in our next chapter.

Critter Control

As suburbia spreads further into forested territory, homeowners are meeting up with more and more of the critters and creepers who call it home. To you, they are pests, but in their world, they've each got a valid purpose. Termites, for example, have Mother Nature's assignment to get rid of dead wood and create fertilizer that helps more plants to grow. That's a beautiful circle of life, except when termites mistake your Money Pit for dead wood. Prevention and prompt response to infestations are keys to keeping critter levels under control.

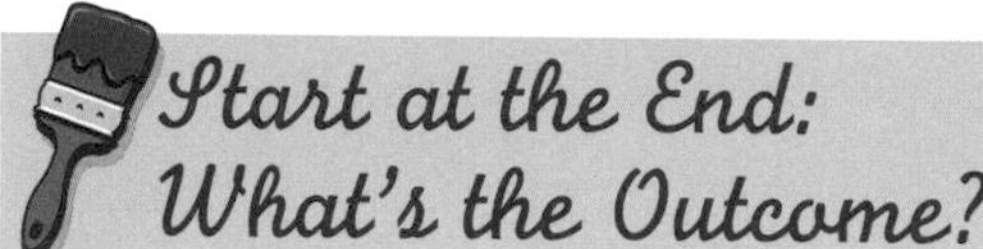

Start at the End: What's the Outcome?

A critter-free home is the goal here, along with avoidance of physical encounters with pests and attendant injuries, whether caused by a squirrel surprise or a crumbling structural support that has recently served as an all-you-can-eat bug buffet. If you're planning to put your home on the market sometime soon, pest control and abatement will be critical to the final sale.

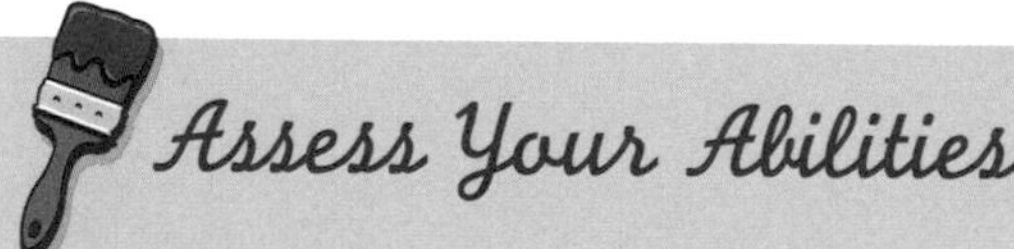

Assess Your Abilities

There's a lot you can do to prevent infestations and keep from creating exactly the environments that will attract pests. But when it comes to pest removal, never underestimate the power of a professional. Termites, for example, can literally destroy your house, and the fastest, most effective treatments are available only to licensed pros. Most people simply aren't capable of finding and controlling pest infestations, whether the invaders are termites, ants, or bees. Even over-the-counter pest-control products can be toxic when applied improperly or in excessive amounts. Pest-control pros have specialized knowledge to apply just the right product in just the right amount to eliminate the problem and keep your family safe.

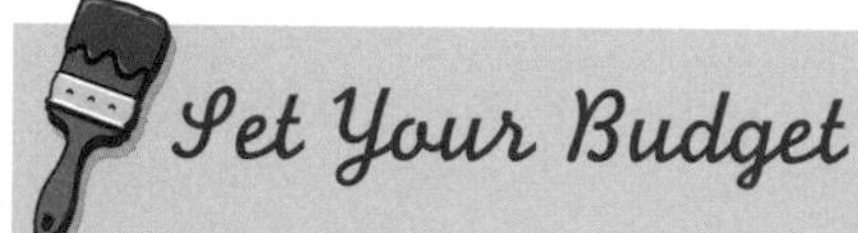

Set Your Budget

Time will be your biggest investment where pest-preventive measures are concerned, but eradication costs money. One way to manage costs associated with insect infestations is to invest in a monthly or quarterly maintenance plan with

Songs to Work By:

Tunes to help you get through your projects.

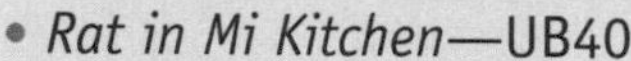

- *Rat in Mi Kitchen*—UB40
- *Ben*—Michael Jackson
- *Purple People Eater*—Sheb Wooley
- *The Bug*—Dire Straits or Mary Chapin Carpenter
- *Bugs*—Bobbie Gentry
- *Bugs*—Smashing Pumpkins
- *Feed Me—Little Shop of Horrors*
- *Ants Marching*—Dave Matthews Band
- *Hold That Critter Down*—Riders in the Sky
- *La Cucaracha*—Liberace
- Anything by the Boomtown Rats

a pest management firm. Often, professional exterminators will provide a service plan that includes smart annual inspections. Not only will maintenance treatments keep bugs in check, pest-control pros can spot budding infestations before they become full-blown homesteaders. Treatments are so effective today that the chance of pests returning is fairly small, but with such upkeep, you're not going to run into the offenders on your own if they do make a comeback.

Battling the Wood-Destroyers: Termites, Carpenter Ants, and Carpenter Bees

Nothing literally brings a house down like a party of wood-munching pests, so don't take shortcuts in preventing their presence. If you do meet up with one of the following species, call in a professional for their immediate removal.

Termites

Termites cause billions of dollars in damage each year, driving many in our Money Pit audience on home pest quests. Like us on Thanksgiving, termites especially love two things: plenty to eat and plenty of time to devour it.[105]

So you think it can't happen to you? As a home inspector, Tom toured over 6,000 homes in the Mid-Atlantic and Northeast regions, finding termite activity in about a third of them. Termites live in nests deep in the soil under your home. Their day planners include hours of munching madness in the territory of some unsuspecting homeowner, followed by a return to the soil for water.

To keep your abode off the menu, have a professional treat it with an effective undetectable liquid such as Termidor. Applied directly to the soil, this kind of chemical can't be seen or smelled by hungry termites, who very happily take it back to the nest to pass on to the rest of the community. As a result, termites disappear from your property and don't return.

Additional commonsense tips include:

Wood away. Keep all firewood and wood products away from your foundation and off the ground. Keep fence slats and any wood trim around your house up off the soil.

Stay dry. Keep your house dry, and check gutters and downspouts to ensure that water drains away from the foundation.

Elevate. Remove all wood, cardboard, and paper from crawl spaces and basement floors. If storage

They're Called "Bug Bombs" for a Reason

Insect foggers, more commonly known as "bug bombs," are an over-the-counter way of controlling a wide variety of insects. But some folks operate under the principle that if one bug bomb is good, more must be better. According to the California Department of Pesticide Regulation (DPR), flames from a gas pilot light ignited 18 foggers in a small San Diego apartment, ripping open the ceiling and tearing kitchen cabinets from the walls. In another incident, a Los Angeles woman sustained burns when 30 foggers exploded in her home, blowing off the roof! In addition to explosions, the DPR documented almost 50 cases of injuries due to the misuse of foggers including respiratory, eye, or skin irritation from overexposure to fumes.

105.) When you ask, they tell you they can't believe they ate the whole thing.

Termite Trouble

> **Termites or Carpenter Ants?**
> *Figuring out which wood predators have helped themselves to a home-cooked meal is the first step to determining how to treat for them. The differences between carpenter ants and termites are subtle, since they can be similar in size, but easy to see. First, a termite has a two-segmented body (head and torso); ants have three. Termites also have straight antennae, while an ant's antennae are bent.*

is necessary, make sure it's well above floor surfaces to avoid attracting insects.

Homes with concrete slab foundations can have an extra-high risk of termite infestations, as they offer the pests' preferred environment and are the most difficult to inspect. Regardless of the type of home you have, we recommend a preventive termite treatment and regular inspections by qualified pros to make sure infestations are spotted early enough to reduce the risk of serious damage.

Carpenter Ants

Carpenter ants don't actually eat wood but do plenty of deconstruction work by chewing through it to create nests big enough to house thousands of family members and friends.[106] You'll only see the occasional forager on the surface or flying around nearby, a sign that they've been building their own dangerous Money Pit deep inside yours.

The warm spring and summer months are the most common season for carpenter ant infestations, and these dastardly pests make frequent appearances in the Pacific Northwest and Northeast, as well as along the East Coast all the way down to Florida. They nest in both moist and dry wood, but the former is their preference. As a result, you'll find them (or their handiwork) most often in damp areas, such as spaces around sinks, tubs, poorly sealed door and window frames, roof leak locations, poorly flushed chimneys, behind dishwashers, and even inside hollow porch columns. Carpenter ants tend to do most of their work at night, so if you see only a few hanging around during daylight hours, don't assume the problem is minimal. After they've started digging in, they'll leave piles of sawdust on nearby surfaces such as windowsills and countertops, and at that point, you'll have no doubt as to who's moved into the wood.

Over-the-counter treatments don't do nearly enough to abate these creeping carpenters, so call in the professionals. Like termites, ants can be treated using a new category of pest-control prod-

106.) And you thought you had a lot of house guests.

ucts called undetectable liquids, which are able to take best advantage of ants' social natures through application where the ants are getting to work. The ants then unwittingly carry the chemical around with them, sharing the substance with their nestmates until the whole colony is wiped out.

To prevent a carpenter ant work site from being established anywhere near your home, here are some things you can do:

Trim landscape. Outdoors, keep bushes and any creeping ivy vines well trimmed and away from exterior surfaces. Ivy may look charming, but those lush leaves often hide a carpenter ant fantasyland. Keep firewood stored away from the exterior walls of your home.

Reduce moisture. Carpenter ants need water to survive. Eliminate standing water around your property, especially at the perimeter of the foundation.

Seal cracks. Further reduce the risk of moisture buildup by sealing any cracks and leaks in pipes and faucets. Ensure that doors and windows have secure screens, and seal all cracks and crevices around these openings.

Carpenter Bees

These low-flying attack helicopters are very aggressive, and just about the size of bumblebees. They may strafe in your general direction, but they won't bite or sting. Instead, they're equipped to drill into wood, usually the softer species of trim woods used for fascia, soffits, and fences. Carpenter bees drill nearly perfect ³/₈-inch-wide holes in surfaces[107] and wood end-grain, drop their eggs inside, and work their way back out again before you know what they've done. For these clever offenders, get professional help with removal and prevention of future landings. Also consider replacing favored carpenter ant snack foods like fascia, soffits, and other soft trim with cellular PVC trim boards, such as AZEK. These look and cut like wood, but are unaffected by insects.

Powder Post Beetles

The powder post beetle is another wood dweller, tunneling through and leaving crumbling orange-tinted powder in its wake. Little pinholes of about a sixteenth to an eighth of an inch in diameter are also left behind on wood surfaces, and taking a close look at the area around them is the way to tell whether or not the infestation is active. A ring of dust around a hole means a beetle is moving in and out, bringing the dust it's creating inside to the outside as it exits the wood; no dust around a hole means the beetle has already done damage and is long gone.

Powder post beetles love damp places, so monitor at-risk areas such as crawl spaces. Infestations can sometimes be treated with surface chemicals, but in serious cases a larger-scale professional fumigation is often needed.

Warm-Blooded Pests: Mice, Rats, Moles, and Squirrels

They can leap off tall buildings in a single bound, pass through seemingly solid walls, and may even be able to smell nuclear fallout.[108] They're not superheroes, but something far less welcome: rodents.

Just as the arrival of cold weather sends people looking for the comfort of a heated place, so too with mice and rats, who seek out the relative comfort of your basement or crawl space, or even

107.) Let's see you do that. 108.) True, according to a study conducted by the International University of Health and Welfare in Japan, although Homeland Security hasn't recommended adding mice to duct tape supply for emergencies.

the rooms in which you live. Cohabitating with these quickly breeding creatures isn't just frightening, it's a potentially serious health threat.

If you've ever thought you could mouse-proof your house by sealing up small gaps around the outside, forget it. Mice can squeeze through spaces as small as a nickel, and rats need a space only twice that size to find their way into your home. They're great climbers and jumpers, too: mice can leap 12 inches into the air and hop down from the same height without injury, and rats can leap 36 inches vertically and jump off a 50-foot-tall building without a scratch.

In addition to these frightening feats, rodents indiscriminately leave droppings that can get more dangerous by attracting molds, and mice are carriers of potentially allergen-producing insects like mites and carpenter beetles. They also release allergens in the forms of urine and dander that have been found to be contributing factors to childhood asthma, and contaminate food in their quest for sustenance.

Fortunately, there are a number of ways you can make your house a much less welcoming place for mice and rats, beyond the obvious advice of buying a cat.

Avoid creating nesting sites. Stacks of newspapers, cardboard boxes, firewood, lumber, and other storage encourage nesting. Keep all storage off the ground or floor at the inside and outside foundation perimeters of your home, and make sure all bushes, hedges, and other plantings are trimmed back and well away from the foundation.

Secure storage. Mice can squeeze through spaces as small as nickel, so seal up potential entrances with sheet metal, steel wool, or cement. Pay particular attention to the spaces around pipes, vents, and ducts. Store any loose dry foods in sealed plastic containers, especially pet foods.

Keep a clean house. Wash dishes and cooking utensils immediately after use. Keep counters and floors free of soiled food, and clean the insides of cabinets and pantries frequently to avoid feeding furry creatures.

Use rodenticides. Poisons designed to eliminate rodent infestations are safe and highly effective if used in accordance with label instructions. If exposure to children or pets is a concern, use lockable bait stations; with these, the poison is secured inside a container that has holes small enough for only a rodent to enter.

Green Scene: Mother Nature's Pest Control

A lawn loaded with grubs is a dining and digging invitation for moles, and though chemical treatments are effective in turning them away, there are green steps you can take as well. A healthy lawn is among the best defenses, so maintain thick, lush growth through overseeding and avoid blending-in weak-rooted mixes like Kentucky bluegrass. Attracting grub-eating birds such as blue jays, blackbirds, European starlings, and robins to your yard is another help, and if you raise the deck on your lawn mower more spiders and ants will stick around to control the grass-dwelling population. Parasitic nematodes and milky spore will also help to break down and dismiss grub colonies; check with your local garden center or extension office for sources and applications of these treatments.

Moles

We get a fair number of calls from folks suffering the sight of lawns that are being absolutely ravaged by moles. They don't come into your yard just to undo the landscaping, but rather are searching your lawn for the insects (especially beetle larvae, otherwise known as grubs) that they love to dine on. As dumb as their digging patterns may seem, they're smart enough to steer around traps and sonar-style repellent systems, so the best mole control is to treat the lawn directly to remove the insects they're seeking. Check out your local garden center for over-the-counter treatments, or consult with a pro if you've got a larger area or complicated infestation to clear.

Squirrels

When they're not leaping up and across exterior surfaces, flying their way from roof to roof, or chasing Boris and Natasha, squirrels can nest in the darnedest indoor spaces. This can be dangerous as well as annoying, as Tom has discovered during home inspections where a squirrel's nest has been found blocking a flue or other important outlet, causing carbon monoxide to back up into living spaces.

Besides keeping such areas clear of nests through regular checks and, where appropriate, applying screening and other barriers that prevent entry, humane traps such as those made by Havahart can help reduce squirrels' interest in your abode. Instead, they'll be attracted by the snack you're serving within the trap, and its doors will shut once they're well inside it. From there, you can release the squirrel into a more hospitable, far-from-your-home corner of the great outdoors.

Vampire Varmints: Mosquitoes, Ticks, and, Yes, Bats

In the late spring and summer, the outside of your Money Pit puts you in contact with some of nature's biggest pests—the kind that go way beyond bugging you to spreading dangerous diseases. In 2006 alone, the Centers for Disease Control and Prevention received reports of over 4,200 documented human cases of mosquito-borne West Nile virus. And the California Environmental Protection Agency has reported that Lyme disease is the leading tick-borne illness in the U.S. Take the following precautions to ensure that you enjoy your time outdoors without being pestered.

Mosquitoes

Time and standing water: a recipe for mosquito passion and rapid reproduction in as little as a few days. We think of mosquitoes as breeding in large wet areas like swamps, but smaller bodies of water that can appear around your property, can present infestations just as big. Here are a few ways to discourage their presence.

Clean gutters. Gutters clogged with debris allow stagnant water to form perfect "landing zones" for mosquito eggs. Gutters should be cleaned at least four times a year, and leaf guards can also be installed to help keep gutters dry.

Collect containers. Survey your yard for anything that holds water, looking for empty flowerpots, buckets, jars, wheelbarrows, and old tires. Drill holes in the bottoms of trash cans and recycling buckets to allow them to drain. Check kids' stuff like wading pools and sandboxes, and make sure any items covered by plastic tarps aren't becoming water-catchers. Also make a point of regularly draining air-conditioner drip pans, and flush birdbaths with clean water at least once a week.

Prevent puddles. Water puddles that last for even a few days can allow mosquitoes to hatch, so fill low areas in your yard where water tends to collect. Use clean fill dirt to build up these areas, and then cover with topsoil and a layer of grass seed, sod, or mulch.

Stay away. Perhaps the simplest way to avoid mosquitoes is to stay inside at dusk and dawn. Those are the times when females have a biological drive to seek a "host" (a.k.a. you!) from which to get blood to fertilize their eggs. By staying inside for the dawn and dusk hours, you'll be staying off the mosquitoes' menu and out of their sex lives.

Also keep in mind that among the several advertised and rumored mosquito repellents, there are few that actually work. Bug zappers do kill a lot of insects, but only a fraction of them are mosquitoes; the same goes for bats, the natural zappers of the outdoor zone. And handheld electronic devices that rely on high-frequency sound to repel mosquitoes don't do the job either, so save your money.

Ticks

Over the last century, nationwide deer populations have grown from 500,000 to over 28 million. And as deer have moved in on populated areas, they've brought the risk of deer ticks and Lyme disease along with them. When you head outdoors, whether at home or in a nearby recreation area, be wise about preparations and remain alert to tick dangers.

Dress smart. Wear long pants, sleeves, and socks, and tuck pants cuffs into boots or socks (yes, even in summer). Light colors are best, since they help you to spot ticks more easily.

Stay on track. Stay to the center of hiking paths, and avoid grassy and marshy woodland areas. Ticks can't jump; they simply hang out on brush and tall grasses waiting for you to pass and rub up against them.

Inspect daily. Inspect yourself and your children for clinging ticks after being outdoors. Deer ticks are hard to see, with nymphs being dot-sized and adults smaller than a sesame seed. If you discover a tick attached and feeding, don't panic—studies indicate that an infected tick doesn't usually transmit the spirochetes bacteria associated with Lyme disease during the first 24 hours. Remove the tick immediately using fine-tipped tweezers, and monitor your health closely after a bite, being alert for any signs and symptoms of a tick-borne illness.

Use repellent. When in a tick-infested area, use of insect repellent is a good preventive measure; however, consider using a product designed to be applied to clothing rather than your skin.

Deer ticks are most active from April through October, so use caution when venturing into tick country. If you suspect Lyme disease or its symptoms, contact your doctor immediately.

Bats

Bats in your belfry, attic, or elsewhere aren't just a creepy, pseudo-Transylvanian invasion, but a real threat to structures and your health. Bats need only up to a half inch of space to access your home's darkest, quietest interiors, and once inside, their droppings damage surfaces and give off gases that are harmful to humans. Sealing such gaps is the best prevention, but if bats get inside before you can do so, call your local animal control department for assistance with removal.

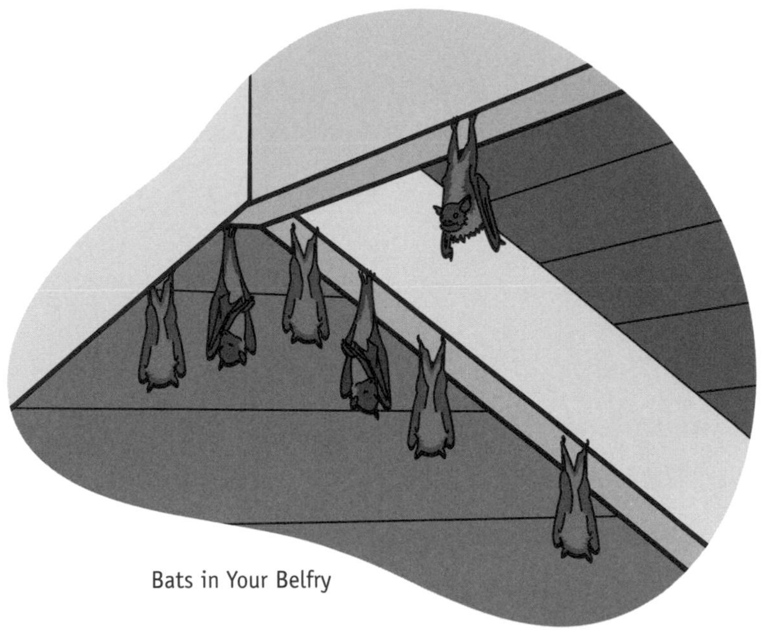

Bats in Your Belfry

Link Up:
Bats in Your Belfry, er . . . Attic?

For great tips and advice on how to eliminate bats from your home, check out the website for Bat Conservation International at www.Batcon.org. The site offers tips and advice on how to humanely remove bats, including step-by-step instructions for constructing a one-way bat door that allows bats to get out and not get back in.

Critters in Flight: Woodpecker and Pigeon Proofing

Are our fine feathered friends making themselves at home in your Money Pit? We can help you shoo away those uninvited house guests for good.

Sending Woodpeckers Packing

With the obvious exception of brick, just about all forms of siding like wood shingles, shakes, clapboard, synthetic stucco, and even vinyl over wood can be attractive to woodpeckers who, being slowly but surely pushed out of their natural environments, find your home a welcome place to carve out a spot to nest or hunt for yummy insects. Woodpeckers can be 7 to 15 inches tall and have short, strong legs and sharp-clawed toes, enabling them to be quite comfortable as they peck away at your house.

Fortunately, there are a number of humane, homemade control methods that can nudge Woody to a safe alternative neighborhood. Take two or three 12-inch-diameter tin or aluminum pie plates and hang them in the area of infestation, allowing them to blow freely in the wind. Mirrors, like the inexpensive 9-inch-diameter round magnifying shaving style, are also effective; affix one or two near the favored drilling spot. Both of these methods frighten woodpeckers away as the reflections fool them into thinking that predators are near.

Another effective method is to cut strips of black plastic (such as from a large plastic garbage bag) about 2 inches wide and 2 to 3 feet long, and tack them around the infestation zone, again letting them blow freely in the breeze.

Once the woodpeckers clear out, you can remove the woodpecker-proofing decorations and store them in case of any future visits. Then be sure to repair any holes they've created or seal up any voids they could possibly return to nest in.

Pigeon Proofing

Besides woodpeckers, we're often asked about pesky pigeons, known fondly in New York and other big cities as flying rats. As is done in the city, you can humanely deter their activity by installing plastic or metal bird spikes on areas where they like to land. This deterrent won't harm them; it just firmly encourages them to seek alternate landing zones.

Managing the wildlife around your Money Pit is not always the most enjoyable part of money pit maintenance. But just like a slightly over-the-hill Hollywood starlet, who doesn't enjoy a good facelift? Up next, 40 fabulous facelifts to improve your façade—with no anesthesia required.

CHAPTER 14

40 Fabulous Facelifts to Improve Your Façade

When it comes to your home, you can judge a book by its cover. Projects to improve your home's curb appeal deliver a terrific return on both your emotional and financial investments. Here's list of favorites that will perk up your property.

1. **Be Bold:** Go out on a limb and paint your front door the happiest color you know. Bright reds, deep ocean blues, or glossy greens create a standout feature. Wait for a warm day and take the door off the hinges and lay it flat across two sawhorses. Then lightly sand, prime, and paint each side, as well as the edges. If you are planning to sell your house any time soon, rumor has it that a yellow door will help do the trick!

2. **Shape Up:** Start with what you've got. Trim, shape, prune your existing landscaping. You might be surprised by the treasure you find in that overgrown nightmare. Add a few plants, trees, or shrubs where they will make the most impact for a fresh new look, such as at the walkway that leads to your front door, selecting smaller to larger sized shrubs as you get closer to the building.

3. **Hang Out:** Hanging baskets make a happy and welcoming addition to homes with covered porches. Place baskets in between each set of posts for an evenly spaced look. Plant the baskets with the same type of hearty flowers and greenery for an overflowing cascading effect. Then show them the love with a daily dose of water.

4. **Go Boxy:** Whether your home is in suburbia or the city, window boxes are a simple way to add architectural and natural appeal to your home's façade. Store bought or homemade, window boxes can create instant depth and a focal point for your windows. Paint or stain the window boxes to match your home's shutters or front door. Keep them full year-round with seasonal blooms and greenery for a colorful

Songs to Work By:

Tunes to help you get through your projects.

- *Start of Something New*—*High School Musical*
- *Facelift*—Joni Mitchell
- *Strawberry Fields Forever*—The Beatles
- *Waiting in the Weeds*—Eagles
- *Pushing Up Daisies*—Garth Brooks
- *Losing My Ground*—Fergie
- *Trampled Rose*—Robert Plant/Alison Krauss
- *Picture Perfect*—Chris Brown
- *It's A Beautiful Day in the Neighborhood*—Mr. Rogers
- Anything by the Rolling Stones

view or plant herbs like lavender, basil, parsley, or thyme for an aromatic experience that is hard to beat.

5. **Trim Touch-up:** Add a decorative edge to the exterior of your home as well as around windows and doors. Paint the trim in a new color that complements your home's façade. If you are lacking inspiration, then head to your local paint store for suggestions on exterior color groupings to match your home's style.

6. **Under Pressure:** Give your home a good scrubbing. Once a year, pressure wash your home's exterior for a good-as-new glow. Be careful to not set your pressure washer too high or you may just blast a hole right through! Hard to clean areas can more safely be handled with a bleach and water solution applied with a stiff brush. Next, extend the pressure cleaning to your walks to strip away dirt and deliver a brighter path to your door.

7. **Step it Up:** Add appeal to plain concrete steps by facing them with brick, slate, or natural stone. This creates a more earthy and interesting look to a once very plain entrance. For the best results, use good quality mastic and work on a warm and dry day to make sure your new face stays put.

8. **Overhead Attractions:** Give visual interest to your garage by creating an arbor that rises on each side of your garage doors and then spans the distance between. Train climbing plants[109] and vines to cover the arbor to add instant appeal to an otherwise boring view.

9. **Beautiful Borders:** Separate the driveway from the yard with a border of evergreens. They will look lively all year long and will create two distinct areas.

10. **Welcome Walkways:** Add a walkway to your home's front entrance to draw visitors in. Straight or sweeping, your walkway can be created from pavers, flagstone, stamped concrete, or even aggregate within a border. Finish it off with a row of low-voltage lights for impact and safety.

11. **Dressed-up Doorways:** Add architectural appeal to dreary doors by creating an overhang to your home's front entry. Plan the overhang to mimic your home's architectural style and existing roof line to create a welcoming area to guide visitors to your front door and keep them dry while they wait for your friendly face.

109.) Which is just as hard as training your children, but at least they don't talk back.

12. **Fence Feats:** Create a more inviting side- or backyard by adding a fence. While it might seem you are doing the opposite, fencing in your space can create a cozier feel and serve as the backdrop for all your future backyard beautification projects. Choose natural building materials that best suit your home's style and remember that neighborhood manners[110] dictate that you should always place the good side out.

13. **Great Gates:** Even if you go fenceless, simply adding a gate to your front entrance creates a stately welcome for your visitors. Tall wrought iron–styled gates work well with nicely landscaped bushes and flowerbeds surrounding the posts. Or, construct masonry columns out of brick or stone and hinge the gates off those columns for a more massive feel.

14. **Light Your Landscape:** Why let gardens be enjoyed only in the daytime? Add lighting to your flowerbeds, walkways, and planted areas so they can be enjoyed and appreciated after dusk. Use a combination of up-lighting, down-lighting, and side lighting for the best, most professional looking effect.

15. **Green Lights:** Solar light fixtures have come a long way in their design and the light that they cast is now a more even and natural-looking glow. Their eco-friendly marvels can be added to walkways, patios, landscaped area, and even as table lamps for your favorite picnic spots. So keep your energy bills down and let Mother Nature do the work.

16. **Add Some Bling:** Change all the hardware from door knobs and hinges to knockers and kick plates to a bright brass to add instant shine. This subtle but stylish change will deliver a big impact.

17. **Big Paint Projects:** Painting is the least expensive way to deliver dramatic change without dramatic costs. If your home is due for a new hue, refresh its outlook with a new coat of paint. Choose several hues of the same tone to add dimension to the entire façade. If you don't want to play decorator by yourself, most paint manufacturers offer color collections that do the matching for you by selecting complementary colors for siding, trim, and accents. When painting exteriors, don't skip the priming steps to make sure your paint job lasts through the ages.

18. **Support Style:** Dress up wood or steel support columns on your porch or other outdoor area by wrapping them with an architectural column. (This also works for columns in your carport, garage, and basement as well.) Available in many styles from tapered craftsman to gothic styling, most are constructed of cellular PVC or another

110.) And building code.

maintenance-free synthetic and made to withstand the elements. They come in two to four pieces and are easily installed by wrapping around the existing support.

19. **Driveway Do-overs:** Breathe new life into a tired blacktop driveway on your own by applying a filler and topcoat sealer. Resealing is a quick way to instantly revive your driveway's appearance on a budget. Many new sealer formulations are latex, making them easy to apply with just a squeegee, and are long-lasting.

20. **Invisible Fence:** If you want the protection a fence can offer but don't like the aesthetics, black fences are a great solution that offers near invisible security. Made from wrought iron or aluminum, black metal fences are far less obvious to the eye than white metal or PVC fences, as well as wood fences. Continue the illusion by adding a row of green bushes in front of the fence line and watch it magically disappear. Black fencing is a great choice around pools, for example, where fences are absolutely necessary but somewhat unattractive.

21. **Luscious Lawns:** Are you losing the battle of the weeds and having a hard time getting your lawn to grow? Then throw in the towel and start from scratch. Sod is a great way to quickly achieve a lush green lawn and has become increasingly more affordable. Treat it right, and it will love you for a lifetime.

22. **Luscious Lawns 2:** Another option is a Roundup restoration. Best done in the fall, a pro can spray down your existing weed-infested lawn using Roundup or a similar weed and grass killer, and then reseed the lawn a short time later. As the old lawn dies out, the new seed takes root and results in a brand-new lawn next spring. We will warn you though, for a short time your entire lawn will be brown, leaving your neighbors to wonder whether a dreaded disease struck your entire yard!

23. **Luscious Lawns 3:** After several years of drought and hauling garden hoses around his yard, Tom decided to finally install a sprinkler system to keep his lawn looking great. Murphy's Law being what it is, installing the sprinkler system cured the drought, but years later he was glad to have a system in place. When installing your system, use plenty of zones and target each head accurately. Remember that the only thing that grows when sprinklers land on sidewalks and driveways is the size of your water bill.

24. **Shed New Light:** Change out existing porch light fixtures that are dated or just don't work with your home's design with new ones. Besides being more energy efficient, new finishing technologies on these fixtures mean brass won't tarnish and

paint stays put much longer. Look for fixtures designed for compact fluorescent bulbs with built-in dawn-to-dusk sensor technology. Select fixtures to match the architectural style of your home.

25. Garage Door Makeover: Replacing an old, worn-out garage door is not only a design choice but a smart safety decision as well. Choose a door that complements the architecture of your home to add style and modern safety features that will keep you and your family safe. Garage doors are available as either tilt-ups, with a single panel that tilts to open, or the more typical roll-up design with sections that roll up overhead as the door is opened. Complement you new door with an opener, as newer models have more safety features than even those a few years old.

26. **Trim Tips:** Adding new decorative trim elements such as muntins, mullions, and shutters around boring windows can create a whole new look. Made from synthetic materials and available in a wide variety of sizes and styles, these low-maintenance additions bring depth and detail to your otherwise plain panes.

27. **Siding Solutions:** Changing your home's siding can bring about a major change. Choose from stone veneer, cedar shake shingles, vinyl siding, stucco, or fiber cement to create a whole new façade. Mixing materials is a great way to create design flair on a budget. Use more costly materials such as synthetic stone on the front and save the budget-conscious materials like vinyl for the sides and rear.

28. **Wired for Holidays:** When doing any electrical work to your home's exterior, take the opportunity to add extra outlets around the building's exterior and the front yard to handle holiday lighting needs. When the holidays roll around, you'll need fewer extension cords and have enough power to create a display that can even be seen from space.

29. **Easy Window Washing:** While it might not be your favorite chore, sparkly clean windows can make a house shine like new. A mixture of white vinegar and water can make this job much easier. Mix one tablespoon of vinegar to a quart of water and apply with a spray bottle. Then wipe down the windows with newspaper, black and white sections only, and you'll find the windows quickly become shiny and absolutely streak-free.

30. **Crisp Edges Count:** A clean crisp manicured landscaped edge at sidewalks and driveways will provide a clear transition between the two materials and make everything seem larger. An edger is a great and fun tool to tackle this project. Neatness also counts when it comes to maintaining curb appeal and sharp edges make sure your home stays in total focus.

31. Put Your Trees to Bed: Trees make a beautiful addition to a home's property, but the shade they create makes planting under them a challenge. The solution is to select greenery that thrives in the shade like hostas, a hardy and beautiful plant that is available in many shades of greens and variegated greens, some of which even flower in the summer.

32. **Stained Glass Style:** Have stained-glass panels made to match the size of your front windows or choose a great vintage find on your next antiquing adventure. Hang them just inside for privacy and style. Lights inside your house in the evening will make them magically sparkle.

33. **Painted Patios:** Dull gray concrete patios can be spruced up with new epoxy paints. These two-part mix-it-yourself marvels are available from several manufacturers and can add pizzazz to your patio that will last a really long time. For added impact, use readily available stencils to paint a brick or flagstone pattern on top that looks close to the real thing.

34. **Focus on the Front Door:** Add depth, dimension, and focus to your front entryway by creating an outdoor foyer in front of your door. Smaller than a porch yet larger than a stoop, an outdoor foyer can have just enough room for a bench or chair, as well as space for a bit of container gardening, and creates a warm welcome for visitors.

35. **Retaining Walls:** Retaining walls can help owners of hilly properties reclaim valuable land for gardens or recreation. Today, a variety of modular materials like interlocking concrete blocks makes constructing retaining walls easier than ever before. This project requires a high degree of heavy lifting, but the result is more useable space as well as an attractive terraced look for your property.

36. **Deck Do-Over:** If your deck has lots of cracked, splintery boards, here's a quick trick for a smooth finish. Using a "cat's paw,"[111] a handy curved nail puller, carefully remove the badly split deck boards and flip them over. Since the underside of the board was not exposed to the sun, you'll find that it is usually as smooth as the day it was first installed. Renail the boards with this side up and you'll be able to walk barefoot once again.

111.) Note to pet lovers: No cats are ever harmed in the manufacture of cat's paws.

37. Artful Awnings: If your deck or patio becomes an unusable hot spot every summer, consider installing a retractable awning. These attach to the siding above the deck and can be operated manually or automatically with the addition of an electrical connection.

38. **Porch Protection:** Unless you are one of the lucky few who live in a mosquito-free zone, screening in your porch is a DIY project that can take a bite out of many a summer evening. If your porch is an open design with columns that support the roof overhead, plan to build floor-to-ceiling screened panels that can be easily installed for the buggy season and then taken down to enjoy a wide open space for the rest of the year.

39. **Perfect Paths:** Is there an area around your yard that that is frequently trampled due to foot traffic to and from? This could be a perfect place to create a garden path. There's a simple way to build a walkway without ordering a cement truck: just head out to your local landscape supply store and pick up sections of slate or precast concrete slabs made to look like brick. Install these by excavating only the area beneath each one and check to make sure it is level and firm before moving on to the next. By leaving space between each step, you'll allow the grass to grow around your walk while encouraging friends and family to step where they'll do no harm.

40. **Go Virtual:** Can't decide what improvements will make your home look its best? Take a photo of your home and print it up as an 8x10 on your home computer and printer. Now you can lay tracing paper over the image to see what changes will create the home of your dreams—without ever lifting a hammer or brush!

In the last part of our Money Pit adventure, we're going to look closer at important need-to-knows like security, stormproofing, and hiring professionals.

Hiring Help: If Do-It-Yourself Will Do You In, Don't Do It at All

Hiring home improvement professionals is just a bit lower on the stress scale than hiring a babysitter.[112] *We know the horror stories about contractors—we've even told a few in this book, like the one about so-called basement waterproofing companies. The truth is, however, that the vast majority of home improvement professionals are talented and honorable when it comes to getting the most out of your Money Pit adventures. Every study we've ever seen shows that the vast majority of homeowners are happy with the outcome of their project and the professionals they hired.*

The purpose of this chapter is to make sure you are in that majority. Your Money Pit is emotional to you, but the process of hiring and working with a home improvement professional shouldn't be. To quote Michael Corleone in The Godfather, *"it's just business."*

Types of Home Improvement Professionals

Corleone was smart about knowing who to hire, and you should be, too. As you go through the planning process we laid out for each home improvement project in this book, you'll be making decisions about what to outsource, so it helps to know the options.

Building/Home Service Trades

Contractors specializing in your home's mechanical systems are the most common hire for Money Pit adventures, so you're likely to work with them eventually. Even seasoned DIYers like us hire professionals for services related to heating, air conditioning, critter control, electricity, roofing, and natural gas.

As you've seen, we also hire specialized pros for convenience and to save time, especially for detail-oriented jobs that will drive us crazy if they aren't done just so. You may also be considering painters, carpenters, and plumbers to save time instead of doing it yourself.

Trade professionals are typically educated at technical schools and through apprenticeships in the field; some are subject to state and local licensing. They tend to be mom-and-pop businesses—literally—with Mom answering the phones and paying bills and Pop out on sales and service calls. When we see conflicts arising in these relationships, it's often because trade professionals can be more skilled at their craft than at other business management skills, including customer service. Communication breakdowns tend to occur when there are mismatched expectations for the project, such as homeowners not really

112.) For your first child.

Songs to Work By:

Tunes to help you get through your projects.

- *Changes*—David Bowie
- *What Cha Gonna Do for Me*—Chaka Khan
- *Waiting in Vain*—Bob Marley
- *I'll Be There*—The Jackson Five
- *One Thing Leads to Another*—The Fixx
- *Lean on Me*—Bill Withers
- *A Question of Time*—Depeche Mode
- *Patience*—Guns N' Roses
- *Help Me*—Joni Mitchell (and k.d. lang)
- *I Want It That Way*—The Backstreet Boys
- Anything by Men at Work

knowing what to expect before, during, and after the installation.[113] In those cases, conflicts can be easily resolved with cool heads, often forming the basis of a decades-long relationship between your contractor and your Money Pit.

Remodelers

Remodelers can specialize in an area (such as decks or kitchens) or operate as generalists, doing a variety of interior and exterior renovations. The advantage of specialists is that they tend to be better-educated partners in helping you navigate the jungle of product and design choices. The trade-off can come in higher rates, but it's often a great value.

Remodelers acting as general contractors—the coordinator of the projects—can work with you to create a plan or work from a plan created by an architect or designer. Some remodelers offer design/build or "turnkey" services for major projects, from the design right through to installation.

Architects/Designers

Architects and designers may own or work for design/build "turnkey" firms, or you may hire their expertise to design the space and deliver an accurate set of "specs" (professional shorthand for "specifications") for you or a contractor to install. We strongly recommend these professionals when it comes to large projects, structural changes, and assuring that expansion fits the character of your neighborhood.

Architects and designers are good partners in solving tricky space problems, as well as bringing an aesthetic sensibility to projects such as additions, where the value of your home may depend on the curb view of the outcome. There are some who specialize in the intricacies of kitchen and bathroom remodeling.

Education and training can vary widely, as can local licensing requirements. Good explanations about the differences can be found at the websites of the American Institute of Architects (www.aia.org) and the American Society of Interior Designers (www.asid.org). Learn more about the training for kitchen and bathroom designers through the National Kitchen & Bath Association (www.nkba.org).

Green Scene: We ❤ Green Remodelers

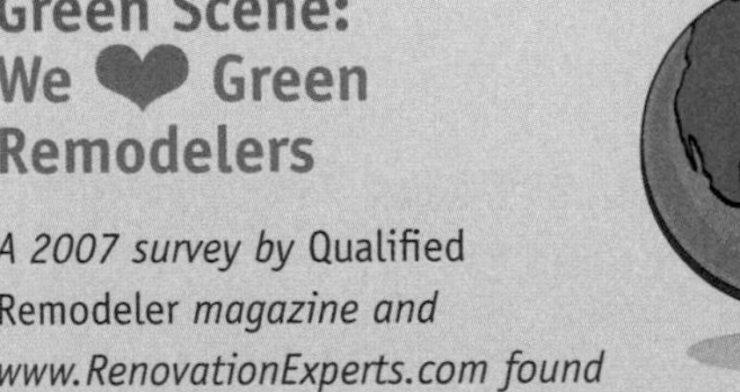

A 2007 survey by Qualified Remodeler *magazine and www.RenovationExperts.com found that 34 percent of remodeling contractors surveyed used earth-friendly or "green" products in their projects. On average, homeowners who worked with green remodelers had higher rates of satisfaction with the project outcome than other homeowners.*

113.) What a great idea for a book!

Landscapers, Landscape Designers, and Landscape Architects

Confusion sometimes reigns about these terms, although all of them can improve your curb appeal. Landscapers are professionals who plan and execute small-scale landscaping projects and maintain the grounds of a private residence or a business. Landscape designers work with landscapers or landscape architects to help design a layout for flowerbeds, pathways, water features, tree lines, and seasonal foliage.

According to the Council of Landscape Architectural Registration Boards, the term "landscape architect" is specific to professionals licensed in the jurisdiction where they work. Besides basic plant designs, landscape architects are typically involved in larger-scale earth-moving projects like the construction of freestanding retaining walls and drainage systems for properties, or designs for decks, patios, or pergolas.

As with interior design professionals, exterior design professionals can manage everything for your landscaping or provide a plan for you to follow. Their services can save research time, as they can develop a plan according to the local climate and the amount of sunlight on your property.

Retailers/Dealers

Major retailers offer professional services on everything from maintenance to remodeling, while thousands of smaller dealers sell and install everything from flooring to lighting to complete kitchens.

Stores and showrooms allow you to touch, feel, and often experience the products you've been dreaming about. If you work with a professional who doesn't operate from a retail location or showroom, chances are they will send you to trusted suppliers where you can see before you sign on the bottom line.

With the rise of the home improvement retailers came the advent of BIYers (or buy-it-yourselfers), meaning the homeowner would go buy products themselves and hire a contractor to install them. This setup can work out beautifully so long as the professional you want to work with is comfortable. In some cases, contractors will only warrant their work if they purchase as well as install the products. Also make absolutely sure you know what you're doing. It won't be the contractor's fault if the stove you ordered doesn't fit the space between the cabinets. Plus, if the contractor's crew is standing around because you ordered the wrong-handed door, any BIY savings can be quickly eaten up in additional labor charges.

The best of any retailer is its people. Trust us when we say your Money Pit will know no greater friend than a long-term relationship with a knowledgeable local salesperson. Don't hesitate to ask around for recommendations.

Due Diligence: What to Look For, and How to Hire

Once you narrow down the types of pros you want to work with, the tried-and-true method of getting recommendations from friends, neighbors, and family members is still the best. Angie's List (www.angieslist.com), a consumer site dedicated to helping homeowners find the best pros, is another great resource for both finding contractors and reviewing reports from other consumers about the quality of their work. Other good resources are building inspectors and even your friends at the local hardware store. Be aware that some stores may feel uncomfortable recommending one contractor customer over another, so you may just get a list. But it's likely to be a list of top pros.

We also recommend trade association websites—there is pretty much at least one association serving professionals for every room inside and outside the home. Many offer testing and certification, requiring ongoing education. As you probably know from your own career, folks who are active in their business associations tend to be dedicated to their craft. Few fly-by-nights invest the time for ongoing learning.

Alphabet Soup of Professional Certifications

Do you need a CR, a CGR, a CKD, or a CAPS? Were you looking for a NATE or an NCIDQ professional?

The home improvement industry has a lot of acronyms. Many are related to specialized training and testing, similar to certified public accountants (CPA) and board-certified surgeons. If you don't understand the designations on a professional's business card, ask. He or she will be thrilled to explain the process they went through. Alternately, you can look up the requirements on the Web.

Here are a few you might come across:

***CR** (Certified Remodeler), a program of education and testing from the National Association of the Remodeling Industry (NARI, www.nari.org).*

***CGR** (Certified Graduate Remodeler), a similar program offered through the National Association of Home Builders (NAHB, www.nahb.org), which also offers the CAPS (Certified Aging in Place Specialist) designation and several others.*

***CKD** (Certified Kitchen Designer), offered through the National Kitchen & Bath Association (www.nkba.org), as is Certified Bath Designer (CBD) and several others.*

***NATE** (North American Technician Excellence), a training and testing program for heating and air-conditioning technicians.*

***ASID**, a professional member of the American Society of Interior Designers (who, by the way, must pass a national qualifying examination administered by the National Council for Interior Design Qualification or NCIDQ [see www.asid.org].*

Good Interview Questions

Once you've narrowed the field of recommended pros to two or three, the interviewing begins in earnest. According to the National Association of the Remodeling Industry (NARI), their contractor members say these are the most common questions they get from homeowners:

- When can you start?
- When will you be finished?
- What time will you knock on my door each morning?
- What time will you quit for the day?
- Are you going to work every day?
- Can you finish before (insert any major holiday or significant family event)? How much will it cost per square foot?

NARI says these are the questions homeowners should actually be asking contractors:

- How long have you been in business?
- Who will be assigned as project supervisor for the job?
- Who will be working on the project? Are they employees or subcontractors?
- Does your company carry workers compensation and liability insurance? (Always verify this information by calling the agency. A copy

of an insurance certificate does not let you know if the policy is still current. Even if the certificate has an expiration date, you cannot tell if the insurance has been canceled by either party. If licensing is required in your state, also ask if the contractor is licensed and call to verify compliance with the law. Not all states offer or require licensing. Check with your local or state government agencies.)

- What is your approach to a project such as this?
- How many projects like mine have you completed in the past year?
- May I have a list of references from those projects?
- May I have a list of business referrals or suppliers?
- What percentage of your business is repeat or referral business?
- Are you a member of a national trade association?
- Have you or your employees been certified in remodeling or had any special training or education?

In summary, you want the basics: the professional's permanent place of business, telephone number, tax identification number, and business license. Obtain copies of the contractor's license, liability and worker's comp insurance; then confirm the standing of the license with your state's contractor board. On insurance, check the term of coverage and confirm that it extends through the expected duration of your project.

Ask what type of training the contractor's team has received in the products you've selected. Improper installations can void warranties (see below) and worse. A so-so installation can cut a 20-year roof down to 10 years of service, sinking the return on your coverage accordingly.

Check with the Better Business Bureau to confirm that there are no complaints or suits against the pro. Then actually call the references provided. NARI helpfully provides that list of questions, too:

- Were they able to communicate well with the contractor?
- Were they satisfied with the quality of work?
- Were they satisfied with the contractor's business practices?
- Did the crew show up on time?
- Were they comfortable with the tradespeople the contractor subcontracted to?
- Was the job completed on schedule?
- Did the contractor fulfill his or her contract?
- Did the contractor stay in touch throughout the project?
- Were the final details finished in a timely manner?
- Would you use the contractor again without hesitation?

Link Up: How to Check Licensing

In a perfect world, all the contractors working on your Money Pit would be licensed by a governing agency that established performance standards and provided consumers recourse if a job went wrong. Politics being what it is, licensing programs vary dramatically from state to state, county to county, and sometimes even city to city. To get the lay of the land for your part of the country, contact your local building inspection department. You may also find your state licensing board's contact information at www.contractors-license.org.

Evaluating Bids

Among the most frequently asked questions on *The Money Pit* is how to tell the difference between two project estimates that are thousands of dollars and seemingly worlds apart in language.

In some cases, it's the difference between the operating costs to run a trustworthy firm (with up-to-date licenses, insurance, and ongoing training) versus the classic guy-in-a-pickup low-balling disaster-waiting-to-happen.

In other cases, you really are looking at apples and oranges,[114] due to misunderstandings and miscommunication, which can lead to much bigger problems than confusing estimates.

For this reason we always recommend you ask contractors to create an itemized bid, listing out each element of the project you are being charged for. For simple projects, write out your own "specs" for the contractors you're considering, including the products you plan to replace and any changes to the existing footprint. Your "specs" may change as various professionals weigh in, so keep it consistent and updated for best results. For major remodels and additions, hire an architect or designer to create the specs, paying them what is sometimes called a design fee or design retainer. Regardless of the size of your project, having all pros bid on the same specs is the only way you can begin to sort out who is best suited to do the job.

Contracting with Your Contractor

The contracts, change orders, project guarantees, and product warranties consumers must deal with when starting a home improvement project all have one thing in common: the goal of customer satisfaction. But what do all these documents really mean and how do you use them to make sure your job comes on track, on time, and on budget?

Written contracts are the absolute bare minimum required for all home improvement projects. The written contract is the tool that spells out everyone's expectations and responsibilities for the project. They protect each party's rights, reflect a trust between the parties, and should demonstrate a thorough understanding of the budget, project details, and what the homeowner hopes to accomplish through the work being done.

A standard project contract includes sections that describe:

- the scope of work, materials, and equipment;
- the work and payment schedules;

Change Your Mind? You've Got Time!

The Federal Communication Commission (FCC) requires contractors to give homeowners three business days to cancel a contract for any transactions of $25 or more made at your home. This "cooling off" period is designed to give you time to reflect on your decision and not feel pressured by a contractor who may still be sitting in your living room!

114.) Neither of which are particularly helpful in home improvement.

- confirmation of the contractor's ability to provide proof of all required insurance; and
- confirmation that all written warranties on materials and products will be delivered to the homeowner.

While we recommend written contracts be used in all home improvement projects, smaller projects may be suited by a letter of understanding between the parties. Say, for example, that you and the plumber agree that he'll install a new toilet for you next week for $500. You can document that with a quick email to that effect.

Change Orders and Punch Lists

Just as important as the initial contract are related documents like change orders and punch lists. A change order is a notice describing a change to the project contract. Say your kitchen is underway, and you see the range you absolutely must have, which is not the same one you ordered. A good contractor will get that change in writing from you, through a change order. Change orders should include a description of the task to be performed as well as the resulting labor and materials costs. If the project completion date is impacted by the change order, it should also list the newly agreed-to date.

We can't emphasize enough how important change orders are. Since many home improvement project disputes result from a lack of communication between the contractor and customer, use of change orders is an important tool to avoid misunderstandings that can later result in serious disagreements.

A punch list is not a list of people you need to get even with in your office. Used as a project nears completion, it is a checklist of all items to be finished or fixed before a project can be regarded as complete. Usually generated via a walk-through by the homeowner and contractor, punch list items should be resolved and signed by both parties before the final project payment is issued.

Can This Relationship Be Saved?

Mars and Venus, husbands and wives, homeowners and contractors. Just to prove that there are always two sides to every story, Kimberly-Clark surveyed homeowners and contractors about their unmet needs and unspoken[115] desires. Their press release reported the following findings:

For Homeowners

- *Worst Nightmares: Contractors who make romantic advances, break things, talk all day, or even use the bathroom without flushing.*
- *Top Complaints: Work isn't started on time, the price of the job is increased after it's been started or completed, contractors who leave a mess and don't clean up.*

For Contractors

- *Worst Nightmares: Customers who try to get them to do more work without additional compensation.*
- *Top Complaints: Customers who continually ask for work to be changed or redone, and customers who don't pay on time. Contractors also mentioned customers who talk too much, who ask for work that doesn't conform to building codes, and those who threaten to sue.*

Warranties, Guarantees, and Service Contracts

Manufacturers' warranties are the assurance from manufacturers that their products will work as intended under the circumstances prescribed for use. Longer warranties can signal a manufacturer's confidence in their technology, especially if they compare favorably to competitor warranties.

115.) Until the deposition.

In general, these warranties only cover the replacement materials, not the labor costs to make the replacements. And they won't cover problems caused by improper installation, which is why we always recommend buying from pros who have been trained on the material they are about to administer to your Money Pit, or using experienced pros to install materials you've purchased yourself.

Some professionals, home improvement retailers, and contractor referrals services offer project guarantees, although they are relatively new on the home improvement scene. Other specialists, including heating and air-conditioning contractors, will offer guarantees if you stay current on service agreements.

Such ongoing agreements make sense for your home's mechanical systems, but that's about it. We generally don't recommend buying into other extended warranty contracts.

When Experts Battle: What to Do When Two Pros Disagree

Here's one example of an actual caller trying to figure out conflicting advice from two contractors competing for his business:

I'm in the process of talking to some contractors about putting some vinyl siding on my home. I've received a couple of conflicting messages from the contractors and I was just wondering if you might be able to answer some questions. I've got natural cedar shakes on my 37-year-old house. Both contractors agree to rip the shakes, wrap it with Tyvek, and put blue insulation on. Problem is, one guy is trying to tell me that insulation bonded to the vinyl is good. Another guy says no. Who's right?

—Jim in New Jersey

You definitely need a third party expert to sort through these claims, and we'd be thrilled to have you do just what Jim in New Jersey did and call us.[116] If it's not calling us, check in at a trusted retailer, search online forums (although verify those findings, too) or visit the manufacturer's website to confirm the claims.

We could write another whole book about how to get along with your contractor, but we can probably sum up most conflicts with everything we learned in kindergarten: play fair, play nice, and don't tattle unless someone is about to get seriously hurt. In most cases, a time-out works better than a lawyer, but in all cases, a good contract, clear communications, and common sense seem to work best.

Practice Safe Pets

Don't overlook your furry friends in planning either the space or the remodel. It's not your contractor's responsibility to feed, walk, or otherwise manage Rover. That goes double when it comes to protecting your pets. Yes, Fluffys have been drywalled accidentally, and everything from electric wiring to solvents can make pets sick. Projects also require a lot of comings and goings, so if your pet is an escape artist, it's up to you to keep him safe during the project.

Now that you've improved your home, let's take on the task of keeping it that way. Protecting your Money Pit from fire and burglary.

116.) Because Tom solved it by advising Jim that he didn't need the insulated siding in addition to the house wrap. Question answered and money saved!

Protecting Your Money Pit, Part 1: Homeland Security

Securing the home front is serious business these days, far from our youth in suburbia where we didn't even lock the doors all the time. Keeping your Money Pit safe from break-ins and dangerous breakdowns takes ongoing vigilance—especially when you're not around.

Fired-up Fire Protection

In the next two hours, someone in the United States will die in a fire, and the National Fire Protection Association says 80 percent of these deaths will occur in the home. Thus, there are two nonnegotiable thou shalts for every Money Pit owner:

I. Thou shalt have smoke detectors on every floor and in bedrooms occupied by children and elderly family members, as they often have the hardest time waking. Thou shalt immediately replace batteries, not tomorrow when you get home from work or this weekend. Right now, thou.

II. Thou shalt have ABC-rated fire extinguishers in each of the following: kitchens, workshops, laundry room, and near any fireplaces or wood-burning stoves. Thou shalt read and understand how they work, not tunest them out like you doeth with flight attendants before takeoff.[117]

Make a Plan

The best defense being a good offense, planning for fire is critical. Draw a floor plan of your home; then meet with the entire family to talk about how you might get out depending on the location of a fire. "Move" the fire around and plan alternate escape routes on paper.

We know this sounds scary—and it should: Live the fire in your mind from every room in your house. Go to each room, close your eyes and find the exit, then find a second exit in case the first one is not available. Imagine what furnishings or other room landmarks you would

Songs to Work By:

Tunes to help you get through your projects.

- *Electrical Storm*—U2
- *I'm on Fire*—Bruce Springsteen
- *Gimme Shelter*—Rolling Stones
- *Steal Away*—Ozzy Osbourne
- *Steal Away*—Robbie Dupree
- *Brand New Key*—Melanie
- *Shelter from the Storm*—Bob Dylan
- *Wrapped*—George Strait
- *House on Fire*—Boomtown Rats
- *Great Balls of Fire*—Jerry Lee Lewis
- Anything by Steely Dan

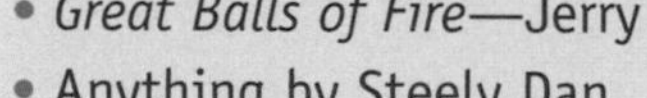

117.) Which you shouldn't doeth either, but statistically, your odds of fire are higher.

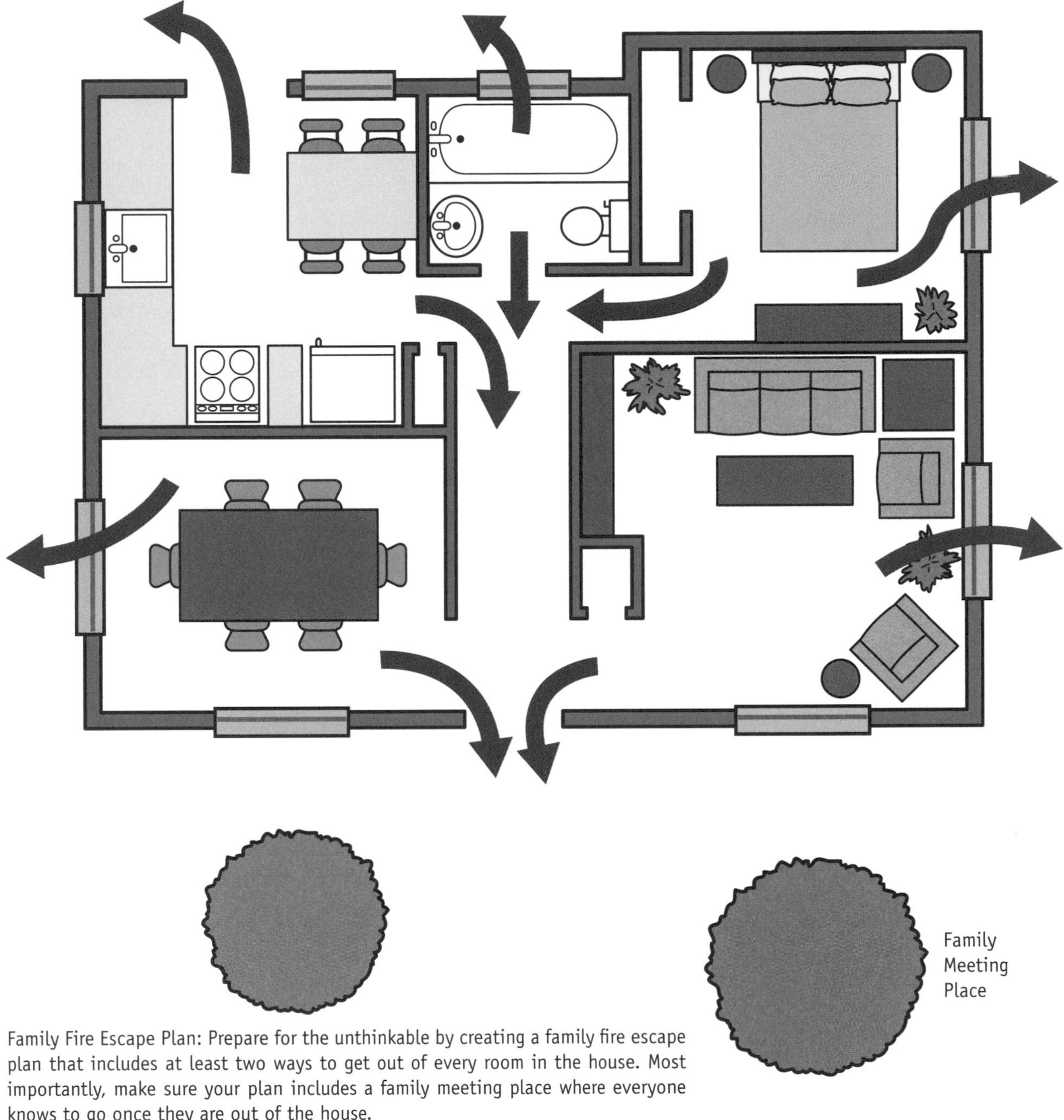

CHAPTER 16

Family Fire Escape Plan: Prepare for the unthinkable by creating a family fire escape plan that includes at least two ways to get out of every room in the house. Most importantly, make sure your plan includes a family meeting place where everyone knows to go once they are out of the house.

have to feel for to determine whether or not you were headed toward a room's exit in the event of a fire. Remember that smoke makes it hard to see as well as breathe.

Identify gear that might help, like escape ladders permanently mounted under your windows (not tucked away in the back of a closet—try finding *that* in a smoke-filled room while holding your breath). Figure out where the flashlights will go in every room. Use this powerful moment of visualizing fire to explain to your kids why the flashlight always has to stay there, and that it can't disappear into adventures or be used casually to give the cat something to chase.

When Dryer Lint Can Kill

No, it's not a movie on the SciFi Channel—nor is it even a joke. Lint is highly combustible. To prevent a fire risk, clean the lint trap every time you use the dryer. Vacuum behind the dryer as part of your regular housekeeping chores.

Most importantly, look behind your dryer to make sure the exhaust duct is metal, not plastic. Plastic dryer exhaust ducts were the norm for many years, but now we know that metal is safer and easier to keep clean. If you still have a plastic duct, remove and replace it with a metal duct; this is a simple job that can be accomplished with usually just a screwdriver to loosen the clamp that holds the duct to the back of the dryer and to the exhaust port in the wall.

Clean out the dryer exhaust duct from the back of the dryer all the way to where it exits your home at least twice a year. Professionals can do it, or you can do it yourself with a tool that's actually fun and easy to use, the LintEater(www.linteater.com). LintEater is a handy and effective brush mounted firmly at the end of an expandable fiberglass rod that snakes safely through the duct system for a strangely satisfying experience. Be prepared! The first time you do this vital—and, we think, fun—task, you'll be amazed at the amount of lint that ends up spilling out.

Closed-Door Policy

Make a habit of sleeping with bedroom doors closed. Closed doors help to slow down and even prevent the spread of fire, while open doors allow potentially fatal entry of toxic gases and smoke.

Make Sure to Maintain

If you have a fireplace or woodstove, have the flue cleaned well before heating season. Keep electrical appliances in good repair, and store matches and combustible liquids well out of the reach of children.

Get Smart on Security

The FBI reports that a home is broken into every 15 seconds.[118] At that rate, the risk for household break-ins is very real, no matter where you live. A home's security is only as good as its most vulnerable point of entry, so pay attention to the little things that could extend a big invitation to intruders.

The cost of installing a good-quality alarm system has come down in recent years due to increased competition and technology that makes installations simpler and quicker. In fact, some companies even offer to install "free" systems if you hire them to do monthly monitoring. Most home security systems connect your telephone to the company's central monitoring station so that if the alarm goes off, the station can alert police or fire officials.

One of the most common complaints about home security systems is excessive false alarms caused by malfunctions. If your alarm goes off all the time, neighbors and police may not take the alarm seriously if a real emergency exists. Police and fire services may even send you a bill. So check references of alarm companies carefully to make sure you'll be catching bad guys, not heck from your neighbors.

Tom knows this all too well. As we were on the phone in one of the many conference calls we had during the writing of this book, his cleaning crew was busy working on the second floor bath-

118.) Cue the *Dragnet* opening.

- *A burglary occurs every 14.4 seconds*
- *66.2 percent of all burglaries are residential*
- *63.1 percent occur during the day*
- *The average loss per burglary is $1,834*

Source: U.S. Department of Justice Uniform Crime Report

room in his home. Leaving the bath door open and the shower running with hot water full blast, the steam reached the detector outside the bathroom door, setting off the fire alarm. This signaled the monitoring company to call the fire department, resulting in a chagrined Tom apologizing to the local fire captain who showed up in minutes, failing to appreciate the rich irony of the situation!

Some security system add-ons are worth the investment, including freeze and leak alarms, as well as carbon monoxide, heat, and moisture detectors.

Bright Lights

Crime experts agree that a well-lit home is much less likely to be broken into. Keep the exterior of your home illuminated on all sides. One of the best ways to do this is to install motion-detector spotlights, which have built-in sensors that automatically turn the lights on when movement is detected in the area. Thieves really hate it when spotlights fire up their faces—they are generally not ready for their close-up.

Indoors, use timer switches on lights. These simple devices cost only a few dollars each, yet can create the appearance of activity inside your house 24 hours a day. Use at least one timer per floor, usually in the living room and bedroom. Set the living room light to stay on from dusk until about midnight. In the bedroom, set the timer to keep the light on from about 9 P.M. through 1 or 2 in the morning. Any criminal watching your home will think twice about breaking into a house that looks occupied.

Low-Lying Landscape

Dark houses surrounded by tall trees or high bushes give burglars plenty of cover to do their dirty work. Keep trees cut away from the house and make sure the bushes are trimmed low. Thugs can hide in bushes while breaking in or even lie in wait there, ready to attack the first person to arrive home.

Who Has Keys to Your Home?

According to a study by Master Lock, that's a question that nearly two out of every three American homeowners should consider closely:

- *A majority (64 percent) of American homeowners have knowingly circulated their house keys outside of their immediate family.*
- *Nearly 20 percent of homeowners have given a key to workers in their home—including contractors, painters, and servicemen. Twelve percent have also given keys to cleaning workers; and 10 percent to boyfriends or girlfriends.*
- *Nearly half (49 percent) of the survey respondents realized that relatives or acquaintances they've given a key to may inadvertently allow other people they do not know to gain access to that key.*

In each case, these homes become more and more vulnerable to a potential invasion with every key their owners allow to wander.

Durable Doors

Make your doors as strong as possible to deter break-ins, starting with a good-quality deadbolt. Doors with handle locks can be broken into with only a plastic credit card; deadbolts, on the other hand, require hammer force to break in. Make sure you buy a deadbolt with a key on the outside and a thumb latch on the inside. Locks that require keys to be used on the inside can be dangerous. If the house were on fire, for example, it could be difficult to find the key in time to get out safely.

The best lock is only as strong as the door itself, and the weakest part is usually the area around the lock. Wooden doors are especially vulnerable, but decorative door reinforcement plates are available for about $10, and can make this area more secure.

Sliding patio doors have let in many a bad guy in the movies—and in real life. Usually located in the rear (less-visible) areas of the building, patio doors have typically weak locks and older doors can even be lifted right out of their tracks. Purchase a specially made patio bar for about $25 to prevent the inside door from being slid open or pried off if the lock is broken. If your door is newer, you may be able to get away with a length of 2x4 cut to fit in the track between the sliding door and the wall. Newer doors can't be lifted out of their tracks, and the wood blocks will keep the door from opening if the lock is pried off.

If you don't have window panels on your front door, install a peephole—preferably a wide-angle (200-degree) model so that you can see who's come knocking before you open the door.

Secure Keys

The idea of handing your house key to a burglar may seem ridiculous, but that's exactly what you could be doing every time you send a spare floating among family, friends, and service personnel. The key holders themselves may be trustworthy, but you can't control the paths they may cross and the situations in which your key may be exposed to the risk of duplication. So be smart about issuing spares, and take care when you're carrying your master set through everyday routines, such as valet drop-offs and auto shop visits. And don't ever hide spare keys in "secret" places outside your home, because smart snoops can tell the fake stones from the real ones.

Weak Windows

Windows are usually the weakest link in home security. While there are many security devices to choose from, it's important to always keep in mind that windows must be easily opened by occupants for emergency exit in the event of a fire. Therefore, the security device you choose should not lock you in the building, but only keep burglars out.

Sash locks come installed on most new windows. These can be improved by drilling a hole from front to back where the top and bottom windows overlap and installing a long nail in the hole. If a thief breaks the lock, the nail will stop the windows from sliding open. The nails can be easily removed if you need to get out quickly. Sash locks are sometimes replaced with key-operated locks, but these can be very dangerous. As with the double-keyed deadbolts, it can be difficult, if not impossible, to find these seldom-used keys in an emergency.

Security bars installed over windows can also prevent intruder access. But these must be fitted with quick-release mechanisms to allow them to be opened if someone in the building needs to get out fast; otherwise, a home can become a deadly burning cage in a fire situation.

Beyond the structural security points of windows, make sure the view to the inside is properly screened by blinds and curtains, and that valuables are always out of sight.

Plan a Retreat

No system is foolproof, so prepare for the worst-case scenario. Plan as a family where you will go in the event of a home invasion while you're in it. Keep an extra cordless or charged cell phone in the room so that you can easily contact authorities should the unthinkable ever occur.

Vacation Protection for Your Home

At other times, your Money Pit needs protecting when you're not in it. In Tom's home inspector days, he once saw a home that had been left vacant over the Christmas holidays by owners who came back to find 4 feet of water in their living room.

As it happens, vacation times tend to coincide with temperature extremes: the holidays and summer vacation. Drastic temperature changes and idle systems can wreak havoc on an unattended home. In addition, there's a greater chance an invader will try to break in when you're away, so vacation-proofing needs to include all of the following.

Automate for safety. Home automation systems and features can also contribute to security and comfort, incorporating everything from surveillance cameras to automatic window shutter shutting. If you're planning a new build or major renovation, such super-customizers can be installed during construction where you can basically call your Money Pit and have it do what you want, something you really can't get from your kids.

Plumbing system. During prolonged absences from your home, shut off the water inside and out—there's no need for it to be on while you're away, and you'll greatly reduce the chances of damage resulting from cold-weather pipe breaks. Locate and turn off the main water valve, which is usually found on the front, street-facing side of a home's lower level (it may be located in the crawl space; if it's difficult to get to, a plumber can add an extension to put it within reach).

Tom's Tip: Tag Your Valves

Using index cards or tags with strings, make labels for each important valve in your home so that it will be easy to identify in an emergency. These include the main water valve, hose-bib valves, water heater valve, dishwasher valve, and icemaker valve.

While you're out and about, make sure all hose bibs are turned off at their inside valves, and leave faucets open to drain away any lingering water that could freeze and break the fixture later. Inside your home, drain all toilets and tanks, and pour a small amount of nontoxic marine antifreeze into toilet bowls and drains to prevent frost breaks.

Easy giveaways. Even the dumbest criminals know that piles of mail or newspapers around your front door are a sure sign that no one is watching the house. Make arrangements for deliveries to be discontinued while you're away from home or ask a neighbor to collect your mail and papers as well as keep an eye on things and check the house periodically. Don't forget the phone—turn off the ringer, and keep your everyday message in play (no "I'm away on vacation . . . " messages, please).

Inquire at your local police department about their vacant-house watch services. Many departments keep a list and make daily drive-bys and on-site checks to make sure your home is secure. Police officials should be informed as to which neighbors are collecting the mail and keeping a car in your driveway, and must be able to read your house numbers clearly from the street so as not to waste precious moments in the event of an emergency.

Don't spark electrical fires. Fires can develop in electrical circuits, as well as from appliances, even if they're not turned on. To prevent trouble, identify and carefully mark all nonessential (anything other than your heating system, security system, and outdoor lighting) circuit breakers in your home's electrical box. Tip: Use small colored dot stickers to mark the breakers. Then, with these carefully marked nonessential breakers as a guide, turn them off before you go away. Unplug appliances large and small, and in winter, adjust the heat to a minimum of 62 degrees to maintain proper interior humidity and prevent the development of molds and mildew. In the summer, you can set your air conditioner to 80 degrees or shut it down entirely if you'll be gone for an extended period of time.

In the next part of protecting your Money Pit, we look at its exposure to Mother Nature, and how to defend against the woes of wind, water, and wild weather.

CHAPTER 17

Protecting Your Money Pit, Part 2: Earth, Wind, and Fire

Regardless of where you live, disasters can happen. According to the Federal Emergency Management Agency (FEMA), every state in the country has been hit by flooding, wildfires, or destructive high winds, and 41 states have a significant earthquake hazard.

Half the battle with Mother Nature is knowing what to expect.[119] *There's a risk/reward benefit that is always weighed. Need new windows? Shatter-proof glass is available as an option, but at twice the cost of a standard window. That may make sense in hurricane and high-wind zones. Volcano insurance in Manhattan, on the other hand, may be overkill.*

Preparation varies by the type of disaster as well as by geographic area, so start by learning your climatology and other data from your local Red Cross chapter, or the National Oceanic and Atmospheric Administration (NOAA), and FEMA (for Web addresses, see "Link Up").

Homeowners insurance is meant to protect you when disaster strikes, but the kind of natural phenomena covered can vary depending on the policy. The most common policy type is homeowners-3 (form HO-3), and it usually covers damage to both structures and personal property from a wide variety of causes. Take time now to confirm your coverage, making sure you have enough to rebuild your home at today's prices, and get reacquainted with its inclusions and exclusions so that you're in the know before the next storm arrives.

Creating a Plan

The next step is planning for the likely scenarios. What would you do if you lost phone service: land lines and cell phones? How long can you go without your water, gas, or electricity? Are you ready right now to leave your Money Pit on a moment's notice? Here are tips from FEMA and the American Red Cross that can help with your planning.

1. Develop disaster plans. Find out about disaster plans where you work, at your children's school, and other places where your family spends time. Then hold a family meeting to create your own at-home plan. This should include evacuation routes from your house and two meeting places: one right outside of your home in case of a sudden emergency like a fire, and the other in another town. Make sure your family knows the phone number and address of this second meeting place.

2. Make contact. Determine the number and address of a friend or family contact outside your state, since it's sometimes easier to make long-distance calls during an emergency. Family members should call the designated out-of-stater who makes sure everyone is present and accounted for, even if you can't get physically together in a crisis.

119.) The other half is not trying to fool her.

Songs to Work By:

Tunes to help you get through your projects.

- *Hurricane*—Bob Dylan
- *Riders on the Storm*—The Doors
- *Ring of Fire*—Johnny Cash
- *I Feel the Earth Move*—Carole King
- *Stormy Weather*—Lena Horne
- *Hurricane Eye*—Paul Simon
- *Don't Fence Me In*—Asleep at the Wheel
- *No Shelter*—Rage Against the Machine
- *Pale Shelter*—Tears for Fears
- *Shelter in the Rain*—Stevie Wonder
- Anything by Earth, Wind & Fire

3. **Consider special needs.** Think through how you'll care for pets, elderly relatives, and others with special needs.

4. **Practice.** Make sure each family member knows how to turn off water, gas, and electricity at the main valves/switches, and how to operate fire extinguishers stationed in the kitchen, garage, and other areas of the home. Stock up on emergency supplies, including at least a gallon of clean water per person, and change them every six months.

5. **Document contents.** Having an accurate inventory of your home's contents is a critical first step in getting back on your feet, so maintain both a visual and written record of all of your household possessions, including any model and serial numbers. An easy way to do this is by videotaping each room in your home, making sure to open every drawer and closet as you go. This will remind you just what your home had in it if you need to file a claim. Several computer software programs are available that can help you record your home's contents quickly and easily, and even allow you to prepare formatted claim reports for submission to your insurance carrier.

6. **Find safe storage.** Store records such as this inventory and all other critical documents in a safe zone, either off-site in a safe deposit box, or at least in a fireproof box. Videotapes and computer discs require a special type of fireproof box called a media safe, made to protect the film, tape, and discs that can melt at a lower temperature than paper burns.

7. **Check insurance.** Floods, the most common form of natural disaster, are not covered by homeowners' insurance policies. However, flood insurance is available through the government-backed National Flood Insurance Program and typically includes Increased Cost of Compliance (ICC) coverage which pays homeowners in high-risk areas up to $30,000 for improvements to make homes less susceptible to flooding. Make sure the limits for the coverage are enough to rebuild the house.

8. **Know what to pack.** In the event of evacuation, take the following items in a bag or large container: flashlight and battery-powered radio with extra batteries, first-aid kit, prescriptions, eyeglasses, at least a gallon of clean water and a change of clothes for each person, nonperishable foods, sleeping bags, area maps, checkbook, cash, credit cards, driver's license and ID, insurance policies, wills, deeds, and other important papers.

Link Up: Disaster Planning

For more disaster planning information, visit www.fema.gov, www.nws.noaa.gov, and www.redcross.org.

Storm-Tossed: Secure Your Home Against the Tide

New homes are more disaster-resistant than ever, thanks to modern building codes. But even if your house is more than a few years old, you can still reduce your risk of severe storm damage with a few strategic additions.

Hurricane tie-downs. Roofs often go first in severe storms, and simple metal "tie-down" straps can keep roof rafters tied to the top wall of the house and prevent uplift during high winds. Straps can also secure walls to floors and keep floors tied tight to foundations. While this improvement takes some specialized skills, it's simple and inexpensive to accomplish, even with professional help. Add foundation bolts to prevent high winds, floods, or earthquakes from forcing a house off its foundation.

Garage doors. More homes are blown up in storms than blown down. The reason? Weak garage doors are often blown into the house, and when this happens, wind pressure fills the house with air and causes severe damage. Investing in a sturdy garage door may make sense. For a quick reinforcement when storms approach, secure two 2x4s across the inside of the garage door tracks or attach them to the inside jambs of the garage door opening in the exterior wall.

Window shutters. If you live along the coast, homemade plywood shutters are a must when storms are imminent. Buy 1/2-inch exterior-grade plywood (stamped "CDX") and cut sheets to fit the outside of each window. Pre-drill 1/8-inch holes every 12 inches and secure to windows with

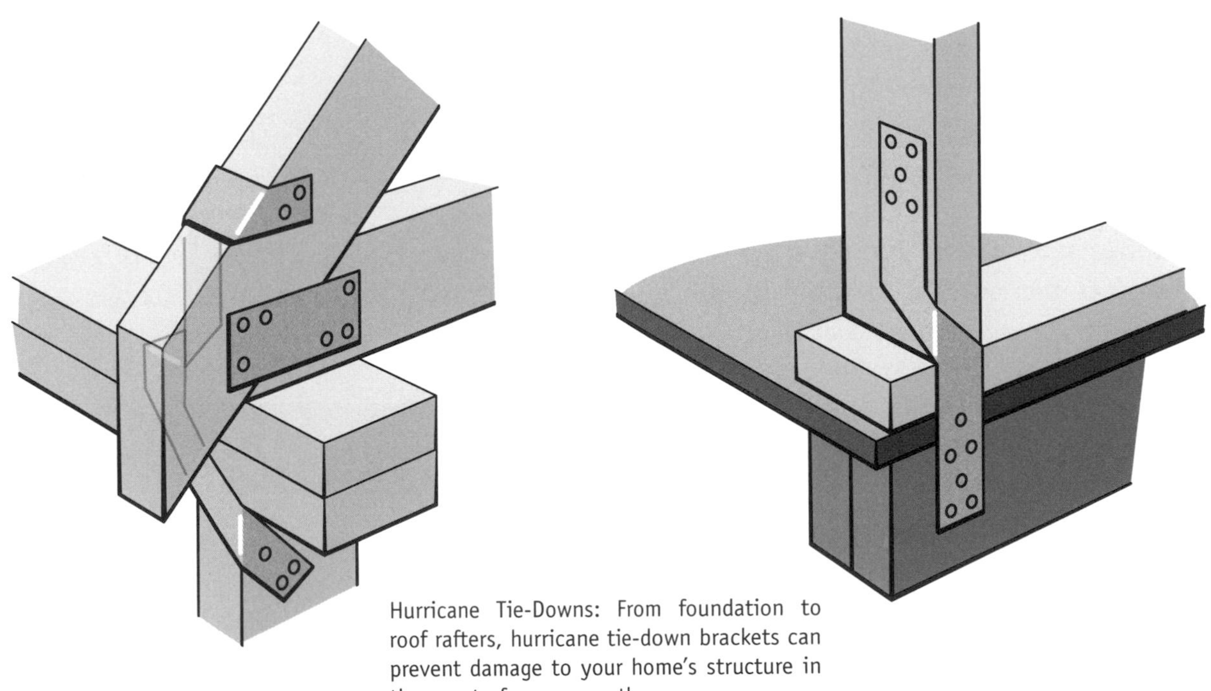

Hurricane Tie-Downs: From foundation to roof rafters, hurricane tie-down brackets can prevent damage to your home's structure in the event of severe weather.

screws. To minimize cosmetic damage, mark where each shutter goes; next time, you'll be able to use the same screw holes and have fewer repairs to fix after the storm passes.

Flood-proof basements. Basements and crawl spaces flood when the volume of water in the soil builds to the point where walls can no longer hold it back. To avoid this, act now and remove obstructions from gutters, extend downspouts, and eliminate low-lying areas of soil, which allow water to run back into foundations. By keeping water away from the foundation, flooding can be minimized or avoided completely. Check sump pump operation by filling the sump with a garden hose. The pump should come on before the sump overflows.

Trimmed trees. Survey your yard for weak tree branches that extend within crashing distance of your home and trim them away before a storm does it for you. You can also avoid the uprooting of larger trees by strategically trimming branches to allow high winds to flow through. If the project at hand is too big or too high up, even too heavy, definitely take advantage of the services of a professional arborist or tree surgeon to tackle the job. They may also be able to help you identify an infestation or fungus that is creating a dangerous situation for your tree and your house!

Sewer back-flow valves. Installing sewer back-flow valves can prevent dangerous, unsanitary conditions caused by municipal sewer backups during severe flooding. These valves can be costly and should be installed by a professional to be sure they work correctly.

Appliance strapping. Water heaters, fuel tanks, and appliances that fall or spill during an earthquake or flood can cause contamination and fires. Metal strapping is available at home centers and hardware stores to secure these components and prevent falling.

Need more specific storm-proofing advice? Hiring a building inspection professional to conduct a pre-disaster check of your home is also a smart way to uncover simple repairs that could save your house from serious damage if tragedy strikes. In fact, the American Society of Home Inspectors (ASHI) has forged agreements with major insurance companies so homeowners can receive discounts on insurance if an ASHI-certified inspector deems their home storm resistant. To find an ASHI inspector in your area, go to www.ashi.org.

Pick Up Projectiles

Every item left outside of your home in a storm can become a dangerous projectile when hurled by high winds. When a storm is predicted, remove all outside furniture, garbage cans, toys, flowerpots, and any other piece of personal property you can move.

Lightning Protection

Thunder and lightning storms are fairly common occurrences in the U.S.—maybe every day where you live. With the impressive show they put on, it can be easy to forget their dangers and the damage they do. Every year around 25 million storm-associated cloud-to-ground lightning strikes occur in this country, and they're second only to floods among weather-related threats to

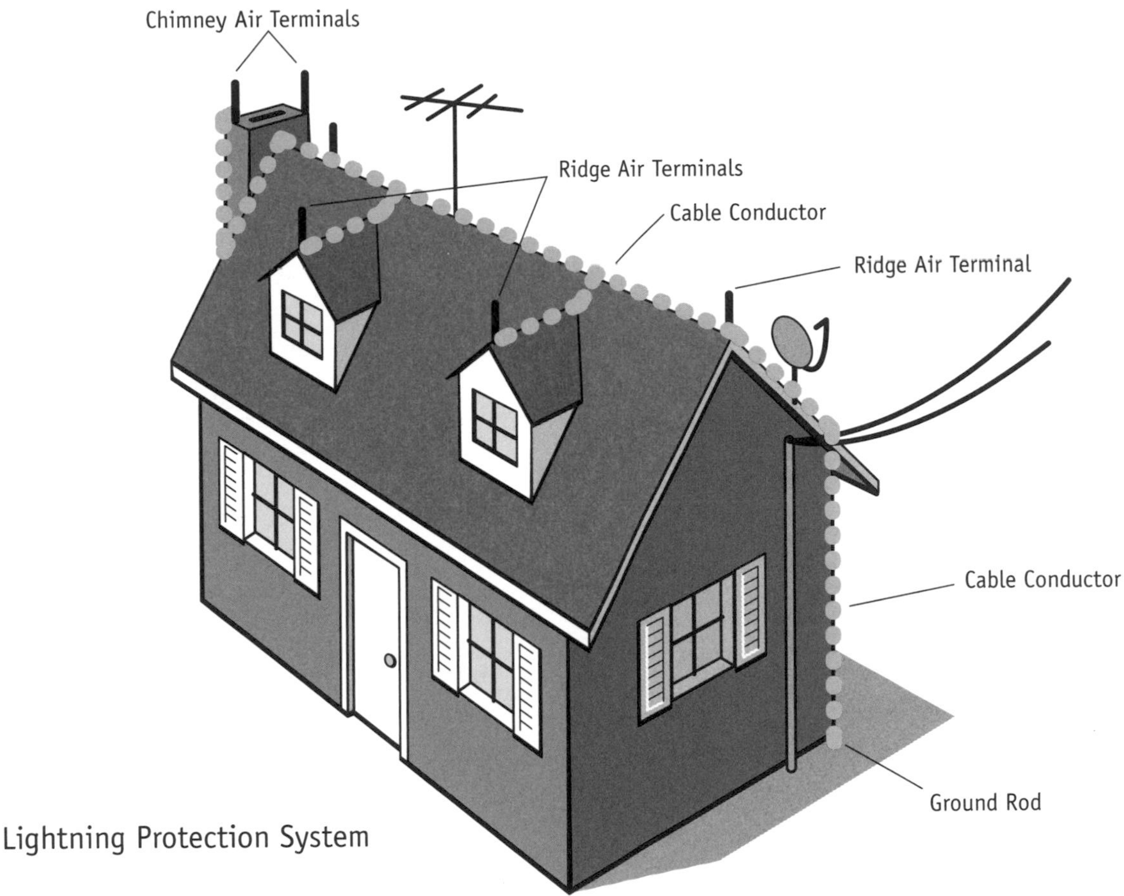

Lightning Protection System

life and limb. Lightning is also responsible for about $5 billion in annual economic impact resulting from the property and systems damage it causes.

Founding father and inventor Ben Franklin is credited with the beginnings of modern lightning protection systems (LPS). Franklin observed that lightning tends to strike elevated objects, and that a network of conductors and grounding electrodes can carry lightning currents safely away from structures and into the earth to dissipate. Over 200 years later, such systems still do the job, and are all the more vital since contemporary structures contain far more conductive material than those built in Ben's day.

The three main LPS components are air terminals, conductors, and ground electrodes. Air terminals, also known as lightning rods, are placed at intervals on a home's roof and any high points projecting from it, and are designed so that lightning strikes them instead of the building. Conductors are the cables that run from among the air terminals to the ground electrodes, where lightning's charge is sent safely into the earth.

For thorough lightning protection, you'll also need a complete network of connections which could include vent fans, gutters, water pipes, home electrical systems, phone lines, and other vital connections. Between this and the tricky rooftop LPS installation requirements, it's best to get the help of an experienced installer to set up your system.

Lightning protection systems may be costly to install but could be an especially good investment if your home is in an area prone to strikes. In addition, some homeowners insurance companies offer discounts that may offset costs.

Pros are also needed to install surge arrestors, which protect your wiring and electrical equipment should a lightning-induced power surge travel down a power line toward your home. Surge arrestors are installed either outside where the electric service enters a building or at the inside service entrance, supplying a ground so that a power surge can't enter the structure.

Once you have a lightning protection system in place, you may think you're safely indoors ahead of the storm. Not quite—lightning can wreak havoc inside, too.

- Shut down your air conditioner, as a lightning-induced power surge can overload and damage its compressor.
- Avoid using the telephone (especially the corded variety) unless it's an emergency.
- Avoid contact with electrical equipment or cords, and unplug any equipment possible before the thunderstorm arrives (if you're going to be away from home during thunderstorm weather, unplug all unnecessary equipment before you go).
- Avoid any tasks that involve contact with pipes or running water that means no use of sinks or showers, and no laundry chores.
- Don't lie on concrete floors or lean against concrete walls.
- Stay off your porch or deck, and steer clear of windows and doors while you're inside the house.
- Draw blinds and shades over windows so that if windblown objects hit and break them, shattering glass won't scatter into your home.
- Bring all pets indoors to safety before a storm. Remember that outdoor doghouses aren't lightning-safe shelters.

Power Protection: Avoiding Sags, Surges, and Spikes

Beyond lightning storms, power disruptions brought on by severe storms can range from complete blackouts to fluctuations in the amount of power delivered to a home's electrical system. Such fluctuations usually occur either as sags, also known as "brownouts," or surges. With sags, the startup demands of electrical appliances pull more power from the utility company than it can resupply to the home, potentially causing serious damage to appliances like computers, which need very steady sources of electricity to function. Surges occur when high-powered electrical motors, such as those in air conditioners and household appliances, are switched off and cause extra voltage to dissipate through the power line. Computers and other sensitive electronic equipment can also become damaged by surges.

Spikes form another damaging disruption as instantaneous and sometimes dramatic increases in voltage, and can be caused by an event like a lightning strike or a car accident involving a utility pole. During a spike, huge amounts of voltage can instantly spread throughout centrally wired electronic equipment like telephones or televisions. Spikes are the most damaging of all power problems and can completely destroy these appliances.

Set up backup systems to protect mission-critical appliances from damage and destruction.

Start with an installation of the lightning rods and whole-house surge arrestors described in the section above, and add surge suppressors as the second stage of an interior defense system. Most suppressors resemble power strips with outlets, and protect equipment that's particularly sensitive to modern surges (such as computers, televisions, and audio/video systems).

Home stand-by generators are another vital component of your backup system; they run on natural gas or liquid propane, and when properly wired through a transfer switch, can quickly re-power most of your home's critical systems within a short time of an outage. Unlike portable generators, home stand-by generators are permanently installed and an important addition to your home's electrical system. Finally, make sure your computer has a battery backup: known as an uninterruptible power supply (UPS), these small devices will not only protect your sensitive data from surges or spikes, but can instantly restore power to your computer long enough to allow you to safely save your work and shut down the system properly.

Storm-Ready Toolbox

Here's what to have on hand in the event of a weather emergency:

- ***Hammer.*** *Buy a 16-ounce straight-claw hammer. Straight claws are better than curved claws, as they can be used as a wrecking tool for pulling damaged lumber apart.*
- ***Crowbar.*** *If serious damage is done, this is an essential extraction tool that can even help save lives.*
- ***Battery-operated power tools.*** *You'll need a circular saw, a drill with a Phillips bit extension and a reciprocating saw. Keep these tools charged ahead of time in case the power goes out before a storm.*
- ***Staple gun and plastic sheeting.*** *Useful to slow down major leaks through windows or doors or to protect belongings if the rain gets inside.*
- ***Caulking gun with silicone caulk.*** *Also useful to stave off leaks. Silicone can be applied even when the surface is wet.*
- ***Chain saw and fresh fuel.*** *Unless a stabilizer has been added, gasoline goes bad after just 30 days. Keep 5 gallons fresh at all times.*
- ***Leather gloves, safety glasses, and dust masks.*** *Protect yourself from injury so that you can protect your family.*
- ***Assortment of nails and screws.*** *Double-headed scaffold nails and case-hardened drywall screws are handy to have around as they can be easily pulled out after the storm.*

Blackout Safety Tips: What to Do When the Lights Go Out

When a power outage occurs, life as you know it can take some twists and turns. Here are some things to keep in mind so that you get through it safely:

- ***Drive with care.*** *Traffic lights won't be working, so slow down and consider every intersection a four-way stop.*
- ***Power down.*** *Turn off appliances and don't restart them until the electricity has been restored for at least 30 minutes; that way, the utility company can stabilize the power grid and avoid another blackout.*
- ***Keep food cold.*** *Avoid opening your refrigerator during a power outage to keep the cool inside. Eat food from the refrigerator first and the freezer next, as frozen items can last for several days.*
- ***Prevent poisoning.*** *To avoid becoming a victim of carbon monoxide poisoning, never run a gas-powered generator indoors or in an open garage. Avoid cooking with charcoal or propane in any enclosed area.*
- ***Use safe lights.*** *To avoid fire risks, don't use candles. Instead, invest in a few good-quality flashlights and replace the batteries often.*

After the Storm

If you've had a storm like this pass through your area, it's wise to check the house carefully for any damage that may have occurred and promptly report damage to your homeowners insurance company. Obvious damage, like a broken window, is easy to spot. But if you don't look closely, little problems can be missed and develop into big repair bills later. Contaminants in the water can cause serious damage to sensitive electrical components. Besides malfunctioning, they could even result in electrical fires. If your heating system has been flooded out, have it checked by an expert heating and cooling contractor or home inspector. In many cases, individual parts can be changed without it becoming necessary to replace the entire unit.

Basement Blues

If your basement has flooded from the storm, don't panic. Severe weather can cause even the driest basement to turn into an indoor swimming pool. Remove damaged belongings and dry the basement with fans. Then avoid future problems by checking outside for loose or disconnected gutters and fix any that you find. Look for washed-out soil along the foundation walls, and regrade affected areas by adding clean fill dirt and sloping it away from the house.

Windward Woes

Winter winds can rip through the outer skin of your house and cause damage in many areas. Examine every side of your house from the ground up, checking for loose siding, metal trim, and loose soffits. If these parts are loose or missing, leaks can develop. Also look for cracked, loose, or broken window panes and fix any you find.

Wind can cause shingles to blow off and roof antennas to collapse. Even the best roofs can leak under extreme conditions: driving rain can "push up" under the roof shingles and result in major leaks. If this has happened to your home, repairs may not be necessary unless the shingles have been damaged (these leaks are not likely to reoccur with normal rainfall). Also, look for loose flashing around the chimney and plumbing vents; wind can loosen the flashing and cause leaks if it's not tight.

Cleaning Up

When cleaning up after the storm, be sure to use a good-quality disinfectant on all floor and wall surfaces. Floodwaters can be contaminated with all sorts of bacteria that are unwelcome guests in a home. When using commercial disinfectants, make sure you ventilate the house or use an environmentally safe mix of one cup of borax in a bucket of hot water.

If you've been affected by a flood and find that recovery of your home is more than you can handle, reach out for help. The American Red Cross has offices in virtually every county, and their number is in the phone book. Red Cross workers are experts in disaster relief and can provide guidance as well as access to many programs designed to help you get back on dry land.

Products That Protect

As you seal your home against future storms, shop wisely for products to help you do the job. Here are a few options to consider.

Storm Panels and Shutters

Installed on windows and at entries, these devices can protect and prevent glass breakage during a storm, and offer shade, noise reduction, and UV protection the rest of the time. Panels are available for DIY installation before a storm hits and removal after it passes; shutters come in such configurations as traditional, roll-down, and accordion, and are permanently installed (some products are motorized for easy operation).

Flashing for Windows and Doors

Raindrops don't always fall on your head; sometimes wind-driven rain pounds against the side of your home and leaks into small, vulnerable cracks around the frames of your windows and doors. These leaks can spread as quickly and cause as much damage as any leak in your roof, so ensuring that your windows and doors are properly flashed is important. Grace Vycor V40 is a great product to install, specifically designed to meet the federal code for weather-resistive barriers. It works in severe winter climates as well as coastal areas where wind-driven rain is common. Compatible with wood, plywood, concrete, and masonry, it fully adheres to the substrate to prevent water from passing through. Grace also offers VYCORners to complement its flashing products and provide extra protection to the corners of doors and windows.

Durable Doors

A main entry that doesn't welcome storms and their ravages is easy to find these days, thanks to improved technologies in fiberglass door construction. Impervious to the factors that can create damage in natural wood and metal doors, fiberglass also does a great imitation of the look of those natural materials while fending off the elements. Therma-Tru (www.thermatru.com), for example, has expanded its array of such durable doors with a system called Tru-Defense, which meets and exceeds code requirements in coastal regions as well as other areas of the country with extreme weather conditions. High-performance components such as a steel plate under the fiberglass skin and Lip-Lite impact-rated glass add up to a unit with an air, water, and structural performance rating of DP-40 or higher, assuring that it can structurally withstand 150-MPH winds and 8 inches of wind-driven rain per hour.

Portable Power

A portable generator makes sense for any homeowners, but it's almost a must-have in high-wind zones. Choices are a do-it-yourself or professional-grade model. The latter typically has bells and whistles you won't need, so it's okay to get the DIY type and invest part of the savings in a powerful engine. Factors to consider are rated and surge wattage. Rated watts represent the amount of electricity your appliance needs to keep it running. Surge watts stand for the amount of electricity needed to start the appliance's motor. For example, a refrigerator requires 500 watts to run, but it needs 1,000 to 2,000 watts to get its motor started, not unlike you on many mornings. So you'll probably need at least 5,000 rated watts to power for basic survival appliances like the fridge, a sump pump, freezer, television, and lights.

Remember to keep plenty of generator fuel

on hand. It can be hard to get in an emergency situation when your neighbors are shopping for the same fuel. Generators with a 5-gallon tank will generate around 10 hours of electricity. Also, be sure stored gasoline is treated with a fuel stabilizer, an inexpensive additive available at auto parts stores that can extend its usable life from 30 days to more than a year.

Permanent Power

For more permanent power protection, install a home stand-by generator. Unlike portable generators, a home stand-by generator is permanently installed alongside your home and wired to a transfer switch that is connected to your main electrical panel. Should your electricity go out, the stand-by generator comes on automatically, usually in less than 30 seconds, and can re-power your entire home. Best of all, stand-by generators run on natural gas or propane, the supply of which would not be impacted by a community-wide power outage. With today's aging power grids and the constant threat of storm-based power outages, installing a home stand-by generator is a smart move that will deliver convenience, safety, and security while adding value to your home.

If you're a serial renovator, someone that just loves to work and work and work on their Money Pit until all possible home improvement projects have been successfully completed, this next chapter is for you! Learn how to sell your Money Pit so you can move on to new projects in a new home.

Home Selling Tips and Advice

Throughout this book, we've given you every trick of the trade we know for the care and feeding of your Money Pit. But just like a parent that raises a child, the time may come when you have to let go. Yes, we know it's painful! We know it's emotional! We also know we can write a whole book on this topic too!

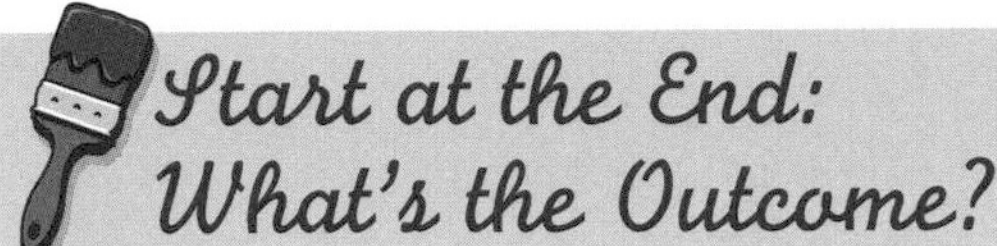

Start at the End: What's the Outcome?

This is probably the easiest outcome to determine: You want to sell your home for the highest possible price in the shortest possible time. Accomplishing this requires the strategic coordination of everything from market forces to mortgages to master plumbers. Selling a home is a three-ring circus with you under the big top taming lions in one ring while juggling pie plates in another.

Most people wouldn't think twice about putting out their junk on their front lawn with a "for sale" sign and have at it. But this isn't a lawn sale. It is a major financial transaction, probably one of the biggest you'll ever make in your life, unless your last name is Trump.

Most home sellers don't think of themselves as fierce competitors in a market of high-priced products. But make no mistake, in any given city, there are hundreds from which buyers can choose. The best way to make certain your home sells high is to make sure it's "dressed for success," both inside and out.

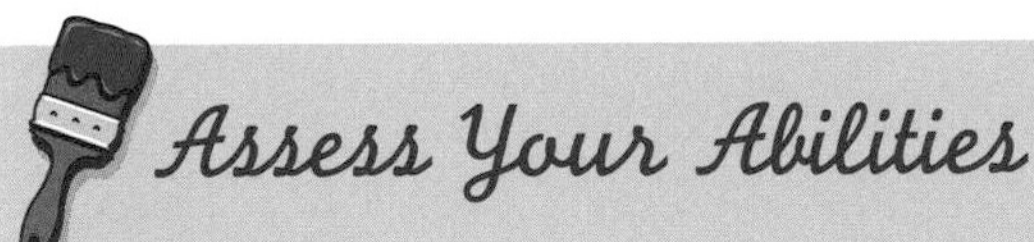

Assess Your Abilities

You've probably heard the old saying that a lawyer who represents himself has a fool for a client, and without proper preparation, the same can be said about the homeowner who serves as her own real estate agent. Saving the dollars you would spend on an agent's 6- to 7-percent commission may sound appealing, but in our opinion, you're getting a lot of value in the services rendered for that price.

In the present inventory-heavy housing market, you can't afford to not be honest with yourself about the money and time you're willing to spend on marketing, selling, and closing, and your ability to successfully represent yourself and your home. Nonetheless, if you have the chops for a for-sale-by-owner or FSBO (FIZ-bow) adventure, here's the 411.

Songs to Work By:

Tunes to help you get through your projects.

- *Signed, Sealed, Delivered, I'm Yours*—Stevie Wonder
- *Go Your Own Way*—Fleetwood Mac
- *Get Ready*—Rare Earth
- *People Get Ready*—Jeff Beck and Rod Stewart
- *So Long, It's Been Good to Know You*—Woody Guthrie
- *Got to Give It Up*—Marvin Gaye
- *Prepared*—Eisley
- *Ready to Rock*—Whitesnake
- *I'm Ready*—Bryan Adams
- *Be Prepared*—The Boy Scouts
- Anything by The Motels

Not-So-Magic Marketing

There's much more to marketing your property than simply sticking a "for sale" sign on the front lawn. Detailed, descriptive fact sheets need to accompany that sign, be posted elsewhere, and then be replenished as your neighbors scarf them up. You'll have to invest in advertising online, local newspapers, real estate circulars, and other promotional tools to reach your target buyer. One thing's for sure: this isn't anything like selling your old set of golf clubs. It takes savvy to promote your home's best assets in a sea of competition, and commitment to stay on task in unpredictable circumstances. It also takes money, so, just as the pros do, you'll need to add home marketing costs into your monthly budget.

Accessibility for the Sale

The best time to sell a home is when the buyer is in the mood to buy, which may or may not suit your personal plans and schedule. It's possible to designate show days and times, but you really need to be flexible in order to welcome opportunity when it literally comes knocking. Remember, you're a salesperson now.

Touring the Digs

Also consider your comfort level with actually showing your home to potential buyers. As excited as you may be over the move you and your family are making, your current abode has a lot of memories, sentiment, and life experience tied into it—all things that have to stay out of the conversation during a sales pitch. You may be selling a home, but the buyer is shopping for a property, and the more objective their tour guide, the better.

Paperwork, Paperwork, Paperwork

The sale of a home involves an important array of documentation, from contracts to disclosure forms, and as a FSBO, you'll be in charge of sourcing and assembling every last bit of it. To avoid pitfalls, employ the services of a real estate attorney to help clarify complicated jargon and processes, interpret local and state laws involved in the transaction, or handle the closing process. Regardless of the assistance you get, you must have a clear understanding of all requirements to properly organize and manage the paperwork process.

Writing the Price Tag

You may have big dreams about the profits you'll reap by selling on your own, but before they come true, you've got to set an asking price that's based on a number of factors, including reality.[120] You'll need to research sales data for comparable homes in your area. Start with online home valuation tools like those at AOL Real Estate (www.realestate.aol.com) or www.Zillow.com. But before you finalize your price, get a review by an independent real estate appraiser to make sure you are hitting the mark. Also consider a dollar range in which you're willing to negotiate, keeping in mind that the commission an agent would receive should be incorporated into the total price (no discounts for the buyer just because you're the agent here).

Finally, in addition to the monetary costs of the sales process, consider the value of your own time. You'll have to invest a lot of it if you decide to be your own agent. And, consider the costs of making a mistake. Inexperience can lead to errors, which can lead to lawsuits when transactions go awry. Still think you want to be a FSBO?

> **Real Estate Agent or Realtor?**
>
> *Realtor is a professional trademark of the National Association of Realtors (NAR). A real estate agent who belongs to NAR has the legal right to call him- or herself a Realtor.*

120.) Which can bite.

Hiring a Home Selling Pro

If you do decide to hire a professional real estate agent, choose carefully. On the surface, all real estate agents seem alike. They all charge about the same fee, 6 percent of the sales price, and most agencies offer similar services. But, in reality, differences can be huge. Consumers who don't do their homework can wind up getting bad advice that could cost thousands. To pick yourself a top-notch professional, do the following.

As with hiring a home improvement professional, the best way to find a good real estate professional is by asking friends for referrals. Do an informal search of the properties in the neighborhood. If the same name pops up on lots of signs, you've probably found someone who specializes in that particular area. This can be a real plus, since the agent will probably be well versed in the homes, schools, municipal services, and other important information that buyers will want to know.

Once you've narrowed down the list, make an appointment to meet with the agent at your house. Before you start talking about what they might do for you, find out as much as you can about the agent, information like:

- **How long have they been licensed as an agent.** For the most part, you want to look for somebody who has at least five years of experience. Getting licensed is relatively easy. Staying with the business for at least five years isn't and shows a strong commitment to the profession.

- **Whether the agent is part-time or full-time.** While all agents have to start somewhere, you're not obliged to make it your Money Pit. Part-time agents can have other commitments that can get in the way of giving you full-time attention, or may simply not be successful enough to have developed business adequate to support a full-time commitment.

- **How accessible the agent will be.** Does he or she maintain office hours? Can you call them at home? By cell? Email? Text message? Buying real estate can be a traumatic experience. With lots of surprises along the way, you'll want an agent who's easily accessible if you need to reach them.

Styled to Sell

Regardless of whether you ultimately decide to sell your home yourself or get a pro to do it for you, preparing a home for sale requires seeing it with new eyes—a bit of a challenge when you've lived in and loved a space for years. You've grown accustomed to its ins and outs and learned how to step around undone repairs, but a prospective buyer brings a completely different view to the scene. Though they're aware your home isn't brand-new, they're looking for a like-new space that reflects care, quality, and cleanliness.

This is where home staging, the art of styling your home for the buying audience, comes in. Industry surveys show that staged homes sell faster and at higher prices than those that aren't, so the effort and minor expense invested in the process

Styled to Sell: As shown here, in this before and after example, simple reorganization and a bit of decorating is all it took to convert this kitchen into an attractive selling point for this home.

can definitely put dollars in your pocket at closing time. Real estate agents often include the services of a professional stager in their marketing package, and this can be invaluable in gaining an objective view of a home and grooming it for sale. To give you an idea of what's involved as well as a head start in preparing your own home:

Drive by. Grab a pad and pen, hop into your car, and do a drive-by viewing of your home's exterior. What do you notice first: a haphazard collection of family bikes scattered across lawns and walks, or a welcoming, tidy façade? Make notes on what needs to be cleared away, cleaned up, repaired, and repainted.

Inspect. Follow with an interior tour of your home, taking a step back from your usual traffic patterns to note the dominant features of every room, planning touch-ups to make the best shine.

Be nosy. If you've been home-shopping yourself, do a little research during visits to open houses and model homes. Take note of what's displayed and what's not, the extent of furnishings used, and how architectural elements are highlighted.

Clear clutter. Begin by clearing away the personal clutter, including everything from paperwork to photos to collections. Remember that the potential buyer needs to visualize themselves in the space, and your particular brand of "lived-in" may not match up with theirs (you could also end up making a negative connection by reminding them of the clutter cleanup that awaits them back at their current home).

Check furniture flow. Edit furnishings for the kind of just-right balance that would suit Goldilocks. There needs to be enough in place to suggest proper scale and capacity within each room, but not so much that traffic flow is hindered and architectural elements are obscured.

Reduce art. Limit wall decorations to fewer and larger pieces of artwork, again keeping a subtle, neutral look in mind (this is no time for dramatic artistic statements). Also include a few strategically placed mirrors to expand the space and reflect its best assets.

Accessorize sparingly. When re-accessorizing rooms with pared-down selections from your collection, remember the rule of threes to create pleasing, uncluttered groupings of items. A few plants placed within main living areas can also add welcome vitality.

Tidy up. Clean, clean, clean! Ensure that every inch of your home sparkles for a fresh, welcoming appearance, from ceiling cobweb hideaways to windows to floors. After all, soap is cheap, even if haggling with your kids about clutter every morning will get old really fast.

Clean smell. As part of your cleaning program, address and banish odors resulting from pets, cooking, smoking, and the like. Anything offensive or even the least bit memorable will override all your efforts in the visual department, so don't underestimate a buyer's sense of smell.

Tone down. Neutralize walls and floors to create a backdrop for buyer imagination. Replace patterned wall coverings with off-white paint, and install low-grade tan wall-to-wall carpet. It's easier to imagine a new baby's room when you're looking at cleanly painted neutral walls, instead of the Day-Glo orange left by the teenager that last lived there.

Fix up. Touch up interior trim, repair or replace

inoperable hardware, and make sure all light fixtures are clean and loaded with brand-new bulbs.

All systems go. Inside the home, give your mechanical systems an honest assessment. If your heating and cooling system hasn't been recently inspected and serviced, do it now. If you are aware of any minor plumbing or electrical repairs that need to be done, get them done way before the inspection takes place. Leaky toilet fill valves, drippy faucets, or electrical outlets that don't work might seem minor, but fixing them now not only means you'll have less to worry about when the home inspection is done, it also shows both the inspector and the buyers that you've taken good care of your home.

Clear garage. Garages are a big "bonus space" for new-home buyers, so make sure yours can be seen. Clear away corner cobwebs, sweep floors, dust surfaces, and pack up any straggling tools and project materials.

Green scene. Lush landscaping is one of your home's best exterior assets at selling time, and according to the Professional Landcare Network, it can add as much as 15 percent to property value. So get out the mower, fertilize all turf and plantings, weed diligently, and add seasonal color to flowerbeds.

Gardens. While you're in the garden, apply the same staging eye you did indoors to any outdoor accessories. Large, idiosyncratic sculptures can be off-putting, and too many garden ornaments can add up to clutter rather than whimsy. Also ensure that water features are clean and operable, as their look and soothing sound will contribute positively to exterior impressions.

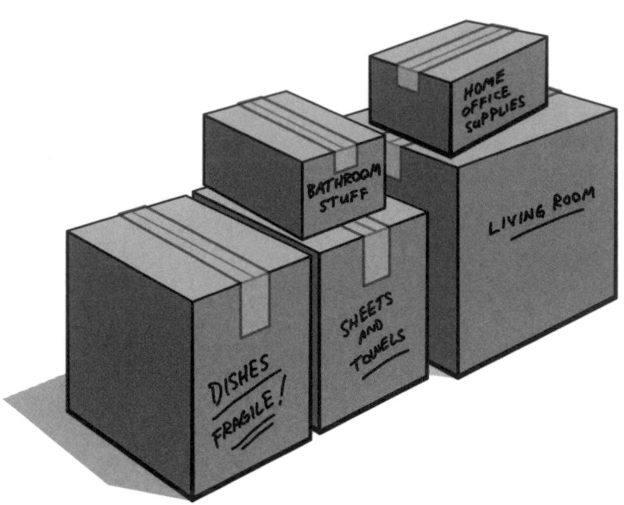

Do-It-Yourself Packing Tips

If you want to save some money, moving yourself is always an option. Besides having plenty of friends and family on hand to help pack, load, and unload, consider these packing tips from professional movers:

- ***Pack light.*** *Avoid putting more than 40 pounds into a box. Overloaded boxes tend to explode during transit.*
- ***Mark each box.*** *Note the contents and what room it should be deposited in upon arrival.*
- ***Stacking.*** *Pack the heaviest items on the bottom, cushioned with newspaper and lighter items on top.*
- ***Built-in boxes.*** *Use container furniture—hampers, laundry baskets, benches, and drawers—to pack linens and other soft goods.*
- ***Don't pack important papers.*** *Make sure to keep important paperwork with you during the move, such as your child's school and medical records as well as your pets' vet records.*
- ***Start early.*** *Reserve a van or truck about six weeks before your move date. When you pick up the van, spend a few minutes getting comfortable driving the vehicle.*

Pack up. Stow away all athletic equipment, gardening implements, and surplus furniture, and neatly coil and rack hoses.

Touch up. Touch up trim and other exterior surfaces as needed, and repair any loose or damaged shutters and ornamentation.

Clean up. Clean windows and operable, sparkling lighting fixtures will both reflect positively on your home, so make sure they're on your to-do list. Soak up any driveway oil stains, and sweep away grass clippings and other debris.

First impressions. Finally, create a grand and welcoming entrance with a perfectly swept walk, freshly painted door and trim, polished hardware, and address numbers, tidy doormat, and a few pots of colorful blooms on the front porch.

Remember that people aren't buying a home, they're buying a lifestyle. If they can't imagine themselves in the home because it's cluttered, dirty, or in poor mechanical condition, the home becomes much harder to sell.

Home Inspection Survival

Selling your home involves a lot more than finding the right buyer. Once you have the buyer under contract, that contract will allow the buyer to get a home inspection done to assess property condition. Here is where it can get really interesting.

A home inspection can be like a scene from a reality television show. Strangers arrive at your front door and dive into every nook and cranny of your personal space. For hours on end they open closets, crawl through your belongings, turn on every faucet in the house, flush toilets, fire up your oven, and run your washer, dryer, or any other appliance they can find. Then, they climb your roof, wander through your basement, and seemingly trounce over every square inch of your yard. Your challenge, as the contestant in this show, is to remain pleasant, cheerful, and completely accommodating while these personal invaders tear through your home.

But if you survive the harrowing ordeal without blowing a fuse, the payoff can be big: a windfall of hundreds of thousands of dollars from the sale of your home.

According to a joint study by the American Society of Home Inspectors (ASHI) and the National Association of Realtors (NAR), nearly four out of every five homes sold in the nation are evaluated by a professional home inspector before they are sold. Hired by the home buyer, these inspections are designed to protect the buyers from investing in a home that turns out to be a real-life money pit. NAR reports that realtors recommend buyers get a home inspection nearly 99 percent of the time. Most buyers heed that advice, requesting home inspections in 84 percent of all transactions.

For sellers, understanding the inspection process and preparing your home for the inevitable evaluation not only helps to ensure that the transaction goes through, but can often translate into getting a top-dollar selling price as well.

How It Works

Nearly all purchase contracts for homes sold today include an inspection contingency clause, a provision to allow the buyers to hire a home inspector of their choosing to thoroughly evaluate the home for any major problems.

Once the contract has been signed, inspections usually happen quickly. After an appointment is made with the seller, the home inspector arrives with buyer in tow, and goes through the entire house. A typical home inspection will take two to three hours. According to American Society of Home Inspectors (ASHI), a basic home inspection includes an evaluation of 10 different areas of the home: structure, exterior, roofing system, plumbing system, electrical system, heating system, air-conditioning system, interior, insulation and ventilation, and fireplaces. Inspectors may also do tests for radon gas, check for wood-destroying insects, or perform other services requested by the buyer.

When the home inspection is complete, the inspector will issue a report to the home buyer detailing what was found. Inspectors will report on problems needing immediate attention, as well as conditions that can lead to more serious defects down the road.

So Now What?

What happens next is usually detailed in the inspection contingency clause. Typically, there will be additional negotiation between buyer and seller if problems are found. In most cases, the difference between what a buyer expected going into the transaction and what was actually uncovered by the inspection defines the scope of what they might ask the seller to fix.

For example, the buyers may have known the roof is old, so a report detailing a roof in need of replacement might not raise eyebrows. However, if they expected to get through their first winter without buying a brand-new furnace and learn otherwise through the inspection, sellers can expect a request to toss one into the transaction.

In a best-case scenario, resolving these disputes is best done by sharing the expense. After all, the seller didn't promise a home with a brand-new furnace, and the buyer wasn't expecting to go 20 years without replacing the existing one. Splitting the cost in a case like this is a fair and reasonable way to resolve the issue.

> **Link Up: Finding a Home Inspector**
>
> *To find a qualified inspector in your area, use the "Find an Inspector" locator on the ASHI website at www.ashi.org. Inspectors listed here have met rigorous testing and experience requirements and are among the most qualified in the nation.*

What's Good for the Goose Is Good for the Gander

If you can afford it, one of the smartest things you can do to get your home ready for sale is to hire your own home inspector to go through it before it goes on the market. Doing this will provide several distinct advantages.

First, it is likely to avoid "surprises," like when the buyer's inspector proclaims your electrical panel needs to be replaced. By the time the contract price is agreed to, most sellers have negotiated down as far as they want to go and the buyers have also offered up the most they want to spend, so finding a costly problem at this late stage can send the transaction into a tizzy.

Secondly, if problems are discovered, you have the time and the ability to either repair these on your own schedule or to disclose them up front to the buyer, eliminating the possibility that the buyer will demand you make repairs later. Plus, if repairing the problem is your choice, you can do so without the buyer looking over your shoulder, second-guessing every decision you make.

Finally, once the buyer hires his own inspector, you'll have a good baseline by which to compare the new report. While inspection reports will rarely match item for item, major differences are few and far between among qualified and experienced inspectors. Your home inspector can even become your advocate by looking over and dissecting the buyer's inspector's report.

Link Up:
Virtual Home Inspection Offers Peek at the Inspection Process

The experience of a real home inspection is just a few clicks away at www.ashi.org, the website for the American Society of Home Inspectors. ASHI's Virtual Home Inspection tool takes consumers through each of 10 different areas ASHI inspectors must check, explaining what is looked for along the way. By using the tool, both home buyers and sellers can gain a good understanding of what inspectors search for, before anyone sets foot on the real property.

Seller Disclosure Can Reduce Liability

Some years ago Tom got an assignment from a television station to do a home inspection that would be aired live across New Jersey. To do this, he needed a house and a willing owner. Initially, he saw this as no problem, figuring he'd just offer a free professional home inspection to anyone willing to participate.

Not so. After calling several real estate agents and lining up several prospects, one-by-one most backed out. Why? Home sellers were afraid if Tom found something wrong, they would have to disclose the problem to a potential buyer. In short, they were trying to avoid "seller disclosure."

Seller disclosure, the obligation of a home seller to tell any potential buyer about problems in the property, is only mandatory in several states. But it is an absolute necessity if you are selling your home. The reason is simple: disclosure reduces liability. If a home buyer knows about a problem up front, then they can't later claim you hid it from them. A buyer can file a consumer fraud suit that can cost you three times as much as taking care of the problem in the first place. Avoiding disclosure is like crossing the street with your eyes closed—eventually you will get hit.

Seller disclosure not only includes a duty to disclose problems you know about, but it also includes responsibility to disclose problems you should have known about. That is why sellers are smart to have a professional home inspection done when their house is listed. Home inspectors can identify problems, provide solutions, and offer suggested improvements that can actually help you sell your home more quickly.

If there is a problem, it's always better to find out now, rather than later, when a buyer is involved. This way you can elect to either fix the problem or disclose it. If you choose to make repairs, you can bet it will always be less expensive to do this before a buyer is involved. Buyers will usually want the top-of-the-line repair when an average-quality job is good enough.

Also, most home buyers will eventually get an inspection before finalizing a sale, so having one done ahead of time will give a seller some idea of what to expect. There's nothing worse than bargaining down the price of your house to your bottom dollar, only to find out that the furnace is shot and the buyer wants a new one.

As the old football phrase goes—the best defense is a good offense. Identifying and disclosing the condition of your house will not only help sell it faster, it will allow you to move on to your new Money Pit adventure with far fewer worries.

By now you've realized that if you take care of your Money Pit, your Money Pit will take care of you! But Money Pit maintenance does not have to be a full-time job. That's why in the final chapter of our home improvement adventure, we highlight 30 home maintenance projects you can do in less than 30 minutes. So roll up your sleeves, and turn the page!

CHAPTER 19

30 Under 30: Best Maintenance in Under 30 Minutes

Got 30 minutes? Take a nap! Got another 30 minutes? Here's a rundown of the best things you can do for your Money Pit in less than a half hour.

1. **Locate and label important valves.** Imagine that a pipe broke in your ceiling and water is now leaking through every electric light fixture onto your brand-new carpet. Got that mental picture? Locate and label every important water valve in your house including the main water valve, hose valves, icemaker valve, and water heater valve. If that unthinkable level of leak ever really did happen, you'd now be all of 30 seconds away from stopping the flow.

2. **Leak check.** Put your sinks and tubs and shower pans through their paces to find small leaks before the ceiling caves in:

   - **Sinks.** Turn each faucet on and run it full blast for a minute or two. Then, with a bright flash-light, inspect the drain under the sink. If no leak is spotted, close the stopper and let the sink fill up until it hits the overflow (do not walk away during this part, as some faucets can fill a sink faster than the overflow can drain it!). After the water has been running through the overflow for another minute or two, check the drain under the sink again. If no leak is spotted, your sink is good to go. Move on to the next sink and repeat the procedure.

Songs to Work By:

Tunes to help you get through your projects.

- *Dirty Deeds Done Dirt Cheap*—AC/DC
- *My Next Thirty Years*—Phil Vassar
- *Thirty Thousand Pounds of Bananas*—Harry Chapin
- *Thirty Days to Come Back Home*—Ernest Tubb
- *16 Shells from a Thirty-Ought Six*—John Hammond
- *Time Is on My Side*—Rolling Stones
- *Thirty Days*—Gary Moore
- *Backside of Thirty Years*—John Conlee
- *Sixty-Minute Man*—Billy Ward and His Dominoes
- *The Cheap Seats*—Alabama
- Anything by Quicksilver

- **Tubs.** Similar to sinks, run the tub for a few minutes and then go downstairs, or to the crawl space or basement and check the area where the tub drain is for leaks. If none are spotted, go back to the tub, close the stopper, and this time fill it all the way up to the overflow. Then open the stopper and check beneath once again for any leaks.

- **Shower pans.** If you have a tiled shower pan that is more than a few years old, it is important that it be tested for leaks. Pans can crack below the tile and rot away the subfloor and floor joists below before you know it. Grab a washcloth or one of those rubber jar openers and block the drain. Then run the shower and fill the pan up with 3 to 4 inches of water, being very careful not to let the water overflow the pan. Then, check the area below the pan for leaks. If none are found, leave the shower pan plugged for another 30 minutes and check it again. If leaks are spotted, your shower pan may be cracked and needs to be replaced—a big job that will exceed our 30-minute rule here for sure and is best left to a pro.

3. Caulk a tub. Bathtubs are the closest thing in a home to a boat, and that proximity to water wears on the caulk, which must be replaced. Remove the old caulk and clean the lip of the tub with a 1:4 solution of bleach and water to kill any mold or mildew that may have been left behind. Fill the tub with water and recaulk. Yes, you read that right, so take off those shoes, roll up your pants, and step in. When the caulk dries, drain the tub. As the water drains, the tub will come back up and compress the new caulk so it won't fall out. Clever, no?[121]

4. Check toilet for leaks. Toilet flush and fill valves can break down over time, wasting lots of water. As we pointed out in the Bathroom chapter, a running toilet or one that "ghost flushes" all by itself needs new valves. Another easy way to tell if flush valves leak is to add food coloring to the toilet tank, wait 30 minutes, and then check the bowl. If the food coloring has leaked into the bowl, the flush valve is leaking and should be replaced, a job that can easily be done in less than 30 minutes and for only a few dollars. Toilets can also develop leaks at their base where a wax seal makes the connection between the toilet and the floor. An easy way to check this is to gently press your foot against the floor to the immediate right and then the left side of the toilet. If the floor feels spongy, the wax seal may be leaking and the toilet should be reset.

121.) More than 30 minutes, no? OK, yes, maybe a little longer, but worthwhile. You'll be amazed at how it brightens your whole bathroom.

5. **Clean faucet aerators and showerheads.** Slow-flowing faucets or showerheads are typically caused by blockage from debris or mineral deposits that get stuck there. To free up the flow, unscrew and disassemble the aerators or faucet heads and soak them in a solution of white vinegar and water. Then reassemble and enjoy new vigor in your shower or sinks!

6. **Drain water heater.** Water heaters can build up sediment on the boot that makes them less efficient. To keep yours running at peak efficiency, use the tank's drain valve to carefully let a few gallons of water [122] out of the tank every six months.

7. **Exercise your circuit breakers and ground fault circuit interrupters (GFCIs).** Exercise is good for you and your circuit breakers! About every six months, turn each breaker off and back on again. Every month, push the test button on the GFCI to make sure it stays flexible and strong—just like you after a good workout!

8. **Check outside walls, windows, and doors for drafts.** Be a draft detective and save on energy bills all year long. Using the back of your hand, carefully run it along the top, bottom, and sides of windows and doors. The skin on the top of your hand is much more temperature sensitive than your palm, and if there's a draft, you'll pick it up right away. Also check outlets and light switches along the exterior walls. If you pick up a draft, grab your caulking gun or weather-stripping and seal away.

9. **Lubricate locks and hinges.** Grab a can of WD-40 and use the straw attachment to squirt lubricant in all your exterior door locks and hinges. WD-40 will both clean and lubricate the metal all at the same time.

10. **Free-up a stuck window.** Have an old double-hung window that's stuck in place? Usually this happens when it has been painted in place for a long time. Grab a putty knife and work it around the entire frame to break the paint seal. If it needs more convincing, take a block of wood and place it on the top of the lower window sash at the corner. Give the block of wood a few downward quick taps with a hammer. This will help break any remaining part of the paint seal you haven't been able to get to with the putty knife, and the window should open right up.

122.) Captain Obvious says: The water in the water heater is HOT. So be careful!

11. **Clean dryer exhaust ducts.** Dryer fires happen when ducts get clogged with lint. Keep your dryer safe by cleaning the entire exhaust duct from the dryer to the exterior vent using a dryer duct-cleaning brush, available at home centers or hardware stores. Also check to make sure your exhaust duct behind the dryer is not plastic, which is unsafe and should be replaced with a metal duct.

12. **Check bath exhaust fans.** Bath exhaust fans that discharge into the attic instead of outside dump moisture where it can cause damage. Damp insulation won't insulate, and that same moisture can condense on roof sheathing and cause rot. Test yours by turning on the fan and then going outside to make sure you see the flapper door on the exhaust fan vent spring open. Also take a look in the attic to make sure the duct that goes from the fan to that vent is free flowing and has as short a distance to travel as possible.

13. **Check HVAC ducts for good supply and return airflow.** Good airflow is a key to the efficiency of any forced-air heating and cooling system. To check yours, turn your fan to the "on" position and then check airflow at every supply and return duct with a tissue. If you find any that are blocked, contact your heating and cooling contractor to track down the cause. Ducts can get disconnected or inadvertently turned off.

14. **Bleed excess air from hot-water radiators.** Air sometimes gets trapped at the top of old cast-iron radiators and prevents the radiator from fully heating. Turn your heat up and check each radiator in your home. If you find one that is cold at the top, bleed the excess air from it using a bleeding key (small thumbscrew-shaped wrench, available at any home center or hardware store). Open the bleed valve about half a turn until you hear air hissing out. When the air stops hissing and water dribbles out, the air has been drained and the radiator should fully heat up.

15. **Replace HVAC filters.** If you use disposable fiberglass filters in your heating and cooling system, they need to be replaced once per month. The filter will be at or near the blower compartment in the furnace or at a return duct. Remove and replace, keeping the airflow in mind. Fiberglass filters have an arrow on their side pointing in the direction of airflow. Make sure you follow the arrow when replacing yours, or the filter won't work nearly as well. For a more permanent solution, consider having your HVAC contractor install a whole-house electric air cleaner. These are far more efficient, and you can cut back your maintenance to once per year.

16. Clean or replace filter on kitchen exhaust fan. Kitchen "recirculating" exhaust fans are in the "better than nothing" category as far as an air-cleaning appliance is concerned, but that doesn't mean they should not be kept at their limited but peak efficiency. Remove both the metal and charcoal filters in the exhaust fan. Soak metal screens and replace charcoals filters every six months. Wipe any grease from the underside of the hood and replace the lightbulb.

17. **Test your air conditioner's cooling power.** Wondering if your A/C is performing up to snuff? Here's a quick way to test it without calling in a pro. Take a thermometer and measure the airflow at the supply and return duct nearest the blower. The temperature difference should be between 12 and 20 degrees. If it's not, your system is not running efficiently and probably needs refrigerant, which can easily be added by your local HVAC pro.

18. **Clean and reverse ceiling fans.** Ceiling fans need to run in a different direction based on the season, and have a small reversing switch on the side of the motor to do just that. In the summer, fans should "pull" cooler air up from the floor; in the winter, they should "push" warm air from the ceiling downward. Check your fan, reverse the spin if necessary, and clean the blades every six months.

19. **Test smoke and carbon monoxide detectors.** These detectors monitor your air 24/7/365 and need to be maintained. Use the device's test button to check its function once a month, and replace batteries at least twice a year or in accordance with manufacturer's directions. It's also a good idea to vacuum them to reduce dust accumulation.

20. **Clean refrigerator coils and drain pans.** Coils on the back side of your refrigerator must stay clean for the refrigerator to run efficiently. Pull the refrigerator away from the wall and vacuum every six months. Also if you have a vintage refrigerator with a drain pan underneath, be sure to pull that out and clean it frequently to avoid mold growth.

21. **Clean humidifier.** If they are not maintained, humidifiers can get clogged and stop working or, worse yet, distribute mold or bacteria through your house. Clean your humidifier as recommended by the manufacturer. One trick of the trade is to

soak the evaporator pad in a white vinegar and water solution. Humidifiers often get clogged by the mineral salts that are left behind as water evaporates and the vinegar melts that salt. Be sure to rinse well, though—or your home might start to smell like an antipasto.[123]

22. **Check for roof leaks.** Inside your home, the area where roof leaks are most likely to show up is fairly predictable. Most roofs leak under protrusions like where chimneys or plumbing vent pipes go up through the roof. The next time you have a heavy rain, check these areas carefully with a flashlight to spot small leaks that can be fixed before they become bigger flows. Outside the home, check the same areas using a pair of binoculars. If you spot loose flashing or missing shingles, get them fixed before the next downpour.

23. **Inspect your deck.** Decks take a lot of punishment from sun and snow alike. Check yours for rot or cracks at least yearly. Your deck check should include the floor joists beneath, as well as posts, columns, girders, and decking. Most importantly, check its attachment point with the house. If you spot cracked or rotted beams or any rusty hardware, get it repaired before your next big family blowout.

24. **Repair cracked sidewalks.** Cracks in sidewalks can worsen quickly and cause the sidewalk to lift or heave if they are not fixed. Small cracks can be fixed quickly with silicone caulk. For larger ones, we'd recommend an epoxy patching compound.

25. **Caulk windows and doors.** Caulk joints around windows and doors should be checked yearly to prevent drafts and leaks. If yours are looking a bit tattered, scrape out the old caulk and replace with a good quality window/door caulk. At the same time, check windowsills and trim for rot, which can be easily detected by tapping horizontal areas with a screwdriver.

26. **Clean air-conditioning compressor.** In order to run efficiently, the central air-conditioning compressors need to be kept clean. Inspect coils and wash them down with a hose to free up loose dirt. Also be sure that all bushes are trimmed to allow at least 12 inches of space around the compressor. Any closer, and the unit can't cool properly and will have to run longer to cool your house, lowering efficiency and increasing costs.

123.) Not a top-selling potpourri scent yet.

27. Caulk chimney crown. One common weak link in a masonry chimney is the crown, the cement area between the outside edge of the brick and the terra-cotta clay chimney liner. When the crown cracks, water leaks down into the chimney, causing bricks to freeze and break, therefore driving up repair costs. Inspect and caulk chimney crowns yearly to help maintain the chimney's structural integrity.

28. **Kitchen cabinet checkup.** Clean and lubricate drawers and hinges on kitchen cabinets. Replace any catches that have stopped working.

29. **Clean screens.** Give your window screens a bath. Remove all the screens, and mix up some household cleaner like Spic And Span. Apply with a gentle brush, rinse with a garden hose, and reinstall.

30. **Handrail safety check.** Check inside and outside handrails to make sure they are secure. Repair any loose railings, posts, or spindles. Loose wood spindles inside your house can be repaired by wedging a wooden toothpick dipped in glue where the spindle goes into the handrail. Let the glue dry, then break the toothpick off in place or trim it with a utility knife.

APPENDIX 1:
Home Improvements by Number

You've probably heard it said dozens of times before: "They don't build 'em like they used to." Well, it's true—and sometimes that's a good thing! While home construction has changed quite dramatically over the years, every era of home construction had its strengths and weaknesses. For example, old homes offer character and charm that is rarely reproduced in modern construction. But, old homes are also drafty and leaky. Newer homes might offer energy efficiency, but they go up so quickly that workmanship often falls by the wayside.

In the 20 years Tom spent as a professional home inspector before hosting *The Money Pit,* he developed an uncanny ability to predict what might be wrong with a home without even setting foot in the door. This wasn't a parlor trick but the result of having done thousands of home inspections and seeing the same problems over and over again. Once you know the age of a home, the construction shortcomings are fairly consistent.

To help you understand what you may be up against in your home, here's Tom's year-by-year checklist of what typically goes wrong.

1900–1940

- **Green lumber.** Ever wonder why old houses have so many unusual twists and turns? Much of this is the result of "green lumber," wood that was never kiln-dried. Between 1900 and 1920, it was common to use lumber that came right from the sawmill as the kiln-drying process had not been developed. As a result, this lumber shrank, twisted, and turned, resulting is some pretty interesting wall and floor shapes. The good news is that this is mostly a cosmetic defect. Think of it as house personality!

- **Knob-and-tube wiring.** Around 1920, it became standard practice to install electrical wiring in homes. This wiring was called "knob-and-tube" because it was strung alongside wooden framing on ceramic knobs and run through lumber via ceramic tubes. If you spot some of this in your home, get rid of it. Knob-and-tube wiring is unsafe for a bunch of reasons and should be completely replaced.

- **Steel water supply pipes.** Used from 1900 until around 1940, steel plumbing pipes worked well for the first 20 years or so; then they began to rust shut, much like a clogged artery. If the reduced water pressure doesn't force you to change them, the bursting pipes will. If you spot steel pipes in your house, you might notice white spots on the outside. Don't touch them. The white stuff is a mineral salt deposit that got left behind by the leak, which you'll soon discover once the mineral "scab" falls away!

- **Balloon-framed walls.** Old homes were commonly built with studs that were two stories. This was known as balloon framing. The downside is fire. In a balloon-framed wall, fire can rush up through two stories in no time. The solution is to install "fire blocks," short pieces of 2x4 lumber installed horizontally between wall studs. This slows the fire and buys precious time to get out.

- **Uninsulated walls.** Before 1940, insulated exterior walls were a rarity. Insulating the attics wasn't much better. If you had any insulation at all, it was usually just an inch or two. Today, blown-in insulation is a good option. By drilling a small hole in each wall cavity, a pro can blow-in insulation that fills the space and warms your home.

- **Unlined chimneys.** Between 1900 and 1920, chimneys were commonly made of brick and had no terra-cotta clay liners. If you look up your old house chimney and see just brick, it might be very dangerous to use to burn wood, and it might even be unsafe to use to vent your gas or oil furnace. The solution: get it relined or build a new one.

- **Plaster on wood lath.** Plaster walls, constructed by attaching thin pieces of wood to wall studs and then covering them with several layers of wet plaster, was the standard up until around 1935. The problem with these walls today is that they are weak and usually badly cracked. The solution is to either completely remove or replace the plaster with drywall, or to skin them by nailing new drywall over the old walls.

- **Asbestos heating pipes and ducts.** Unfortunately, asbestos was the insulation of choice for heating systems up until the 1940s. On hot water systems, a version that looks much like corrugated cardboard was wrapped around straight pipes and a wet plaster-like concoction was packed around the elbows. This stuff can be downright dangerous. If you still have asbestos on your old heating pipes, contact a pro to get it removed, then reinsulate with a nontoxic product. Whatever you do, don't do it yourself! Asbestos fibers are so fine, you could easily contaminate your entire house with these cancer-causing fibers.

1940–1960

- **Undersized electrical systems.** Although the wiring of the 1940s was a bit safer than knob-and-tube wiring of the 1920s, it was still plagued by lots of problems. Have you ever wondered why your old house wiring dims the lights from time to time? It's because back then, it was common to put all the electrical needs of one room, or even a couple of rooms, on the same circuit. With kitchens, for example, this would cause the lights to dim every time the compressor in the refrigerator kicked on. Small electrical systems of less than 100 amps were also common, as were two-prong ungrounded outlets. If you have some of this wiring still running parts of your home, add upgrades to the "to do" list for your local electrician.

- **Leaky, drafty windows.** Inefficient steel and aluminum windows were common in this era. While seen at the time as a modern upgrade to iron-weighted wood windows that swelled and rotted, time has proven these windows to be just as problematic. Steel windows rust badly and unless they have rusted shut, are probably very drafty. If you are still nursing some of these antiques, they should be replaced, as I can guarantee you they won't become more valuable over time!

- **Asbestos ceiling tile and textured ceilings.** Remember those old 12x12 ceiling tiles that you may have grown up with? Chances are they contained asbestos. The same goes for textured ceilings that were from this same period. If you still see these in your house today, it's a good idea to have them tested by a lab to make sure they are asbestos-free before removing them.

- **Vermiculite.** Vermiculite is a lightweight brownish-gold mineral that was used as insulation in attics. While it seemed like a good idea at the time, it also loaded with asbestos and needs to be removed by a pro.

1960–1980

- **Decorating's "dark era."** The 1960s were certainly an odd time for decorating trends. Wall paneling, dark kitchen cabinets, carpet in kitchens and bathrooms, and poor lighting were all the norm. Remember the "Early American" trend? It was popular in my house growing up, and I swear if I saw just one more badly drawn picture of a bald eagle I would just choke! If some of these decorating archives adorn your walls, get out the paintbrush or crowbar and start swinging!

- **Aluminum wiring.** In 1962, a new era of electrical code made homes a lot safer than they had ever been before, with one single lapse in judgment. This same code allowed for aluminum branch circuit wiring. Used between 1964 and 1973, this wiring had the nasty little habit of catching on fire and took many a home down before it was pulled out of service. If your home was built in these years, have an electrician check to determine if you have any aluminum branch circuits. If so, there is a modification approved by the Consumer Product Safety Commission called COPALUM that can make the wiring safe.

- **Fire-retardant plywood.** Millions of condominiums were constructed from the late 1970s on that used a material in their roofs known as fire-retardant plywood. In principle, this stuff was supposed to slow the spread of fire between adjoining units. Unfortunately, it had design flaws that caused the wood to disintegrate. Most has already been replaced, but if you ever look up in the attic of your condo or townhouse and notice that the wood nearest the next unit looks more like shredded wheat, you might still have a roof repair on your hands.

- **Inadequate roof vents.** In the 1960s and through to the mid-'70s, attics typically did not have enough ventilation. As a result, moisture buildup over all those years caused the roof sheathing to eventually rot away. If you own a home in this era, your best bet is to add more. Continuous ridge-and-soffit venting works best. This system will flush warm or moist air out of the attic 24/7, leaving the structure in good shape while keeping both heating and cooling costs in check.

- **Fogged window and door glass.** Insulated glass was becoming the norm as energy prices rose in the '70s. Unfortunately, manufacturers didn't quite have it down right just yet, and as a result, the seals between the glass often failed, leaving windows and doors fogged. If you spot old windows around your home that have bad seals, replace them to restore energy efficiency.

- **Composite siding.** For some silly reason, a bunch of manufacturers thought hardboard would make a fine siding product. For those of you that don't know what this is, it's compressed paper. During the years I spent as a professional home inspector, I would tell my clients that they shouldn't expect a single problem with their hardboard siding—as long as they painted it every day before going to work! There is not much chance you still have this on your home now, as most of it has melted away, and taken some wall structures with it.

- **Speed-built homes.** If you really want to draw a line when homes began to be built poorly, my vote would be to set that mark at around 1970. When the Vietnam War and government spending stimulated high inflation, President Nixon instituted price controls that really hurt builders. Costs were going up, interest rates were sky high, and the only thing that helped builders recoup was getting homes built as fast as possible. Also around this time, builders stopped paying employees hourly for work and began paying by the task. The faster the kitchen was installed or the deck got built, the more that particular contractor would make for his day's wage. As a result, workmanship really took a nosedive.

- **Tight houses.** As energy costs rose in the '70s, homes began to be constructed tighter than ever. But, tight homes are a good thing, right? Not necessarily. Homes that are overly tight don't breathe and, as a result, suffer from indoor air pollution and worse—toxic mold. If you suspect your home might not be ventilated properly, you can install an air-to-air heat exchanger. During cold winters, this device brings fresh air into your home without wasting heat.

1980–Present

- **Old appliances.** Many house components have life cycles that run from 15 to 20 years. These include appliances like furnaces, water heaters, washers, dryers, and dishwashers. By plotting the age of your appliances, you'll have a good idea when replacement should be expected.

- **Cathedral ceilings.** Oversized cathedral ceilings that did not heat or cool well were common in this era. If you have one that looks good but wreaks havoc on your heating or cooling bills, you may be able to install ceiling fans that would blow hot air down in the summer and pull cold air up in the winter.

- **Fiberglass shingles.** Around 1980 or so, roofing manufacturers began changing the way they made roof shingles by replacing the organic mat that held the asphalt with a fiberglass mat. Originally, this seemed like a good idea, but once many of these fiberglass shingles got to be 5 to 10 years old, they began to crack, rip, and tear and needed to be replaced. If you have a home with fiberglass shingles, have it periodically inspected. The best way to do this is from a ladder at the roof edge, as the cracks are hard to spot from the ground.

- **Synthetic stucco.** One of the more modern construction goofs in my opinion is synthetic stucco. Technically known as an Exterior Insulated Finish System or "EIFS," this material creates an attractive finish to home exteriors that looks very much like a masonry stucco. There is only one problem: it leaks. And, it can leak very, very badly, causing water to get behind it and rot away the exterior wall structure. Manufacturers claim the most recent applications have improved it by adding draining channels, but as a home inspector friend of mine once said, this stuff was leaking on the drawing board. If your home has EIFS, you'd better watch it carefully for leaks and keep a caulking gun always at the ready.

Yes—they don't build them like they used to. But if you know when your house was built, this will give you a good idea of what to watch out for.

APPENDIX 2:
Best Return on Investment

When you decide to take on a home improvement project, how do you know you'll get a return on that investment? That's a question the folks at *Remodeling* magazine have been accurately answering for 20 years in their annual *Remodeling Cost vs. Value Report*. The report compares the cost-to-construct for a selection of common remodeling projects with the added value those projects bring at resale, a question home improvers should be asking themselves before committing big bucks to a project.

The data below, excerpted from the 2007 *Remodeling Cost vs. Value Report,* points out both the percent of the project that can be recouped at resale, as well as the cost per dollar to construct the project. Take vinyl siding, for example: Add that to your house, and you can expect better than an 83-percent return on the investment when it comes time to sell. The real installation cost, though, is only 17 cents on the dollar, not counting the fact that you'll be enjoying that siding until it comes time to sell.

	2007 National Averages		
Project Description	**Job Cost**	**Value at Sale**	**% Cost Recovered**
Attic Bedroom—Mid-range	$46,691	$35,771	76.6%
Backup Power Generator	$13,357	$7,748	58.0%
Basement Remodel—Mid-range	$59,435	$44,661	75.1%
Bathroom Addition—Mid-range	$37,202	$24,553	66.0%
Bathroom Addition—Upscale	$73,145	$50,442	69.0%
Bathroom Remodel—Mid-range	$15,789	$12,366	78.3%
Bathroom Remodel—Upscale	$50,590	$34,588	68.4%
Deck Addition—Wood	$10,347	$8,835	85.4%
Deck Addition—Composite	$15,039	$11,672	77.6%
Family Room—Mid-range	$78,989	$54,148	68.6%
Garage Addition—Mid-range	$53,897	$37,461	69.5%
Garage Addition—Upscale	$82,108	$53,056	64.6%
Home Office Remod.—Mid-range	$27,193	$15,498	57.0%
Maj. Kitch. Remod.—Mid-range	$55,503	$43,363	78.1%
Maj. Kitch. Remod.—Upscale	$109,394	$81,096	74.1%
Master Suite—Mid-range	$98,863	$68,172	69.0%
Master Suite—Upscale	$220,149	$141,120	64.1%
Minor Kitch. Remod.—Mid-range	$21,185	$17,576	83.0%
Roofing Replacement—Mid-range	$18,042	$12,166	67.4%
Roofing Replacement—Upscale	$33,151	$21,769	65.7%
Siding Replacement (Vinyl)—Mid-range	$9,910	$8,245	83.2%
Siding Replacement (Foam-Backed Vinyl)—Mid-range	$12,132	$9,668	79.7%
Siding Replacement (Fiber Cement)—Upscale	$13,212	$11,633	88.1%
Sunroom—Mid-range	$69,817	$41,231	59.1%
Two-Story Addition—Mid-range	$139,297	$103,010	73.9%
Window Replacement (Wood)—Mid-range	$11,384	$9,241	81.2%
Window Replacement (Wood)—Upscale	$17,383	$13,784	79.3%
Window Replacement (Vinyl)—Mid-range	$10,448	$8,290	79.3%
Window Replacement (Vinyl)—Upscale	$13,479	$10,913	81.0%

APPENDIX 3:
Life Expectancy of Home Components

By any reckoning, a home is expected to last many years and serve several successive generations. But what about all the individual components that make up the house? How many years of service can a homeowner reasonably expect from a roof or a door, a window, or a whirlpool tub?

A study sponsored by Bank of America Home Equity and conducted by the National Association of Home Builders takes some of the mystery out of the subject.

While numerous factors, including use, maintenance, climate, advances in technology, and your own preferences can have a dramatic effect on how long a product lasts, the following can provide you a valuable alert on when to expect to have to replace various components of your home.

Appliances

The life expectancy of a typical appliance depends to a great extent on the use it receives. Moreover, appliances are often replaced long before they are worn out because changes in styling, technology, and consumer preferences make newer products more desirable. Of the major appliances in a home, gas ranges have the longest life expectancy: 15 years. Dryers and refrigerators last about 13 years. Some of the appliances with the shortest life span are compactors (six years), dishwashers (nine years), and microwave ovens (nine years).

Cabinetry and Storage

Kitchens are becoming larger and more elaborate, and together with the family room, modern kitchens now form the "great room." Great rooms are not only a place to cook, but also a space where people gather to read, eat, do homework, surf the internet, and pay bills. Kitchen cabinets are expected to last up to 50 years, medicine cabinets for 20+ years, and garage/laundry cabinets for 100+ years. Closet shelves are expected to last for a lifetime.

Concrete and Masonry

Masonry is one of the most durable components of a home. Chimneys, fireplaces, and brick veneers can last a lifetime, and brick walls have an average life expectancy of more than 100 years.

Countertops

Natural stone countertops, which are less expensive than a few years ago, are gaining in popularity and are expected to last a lifetime. Cultured marble countertops have a life expectancy of about 20 years.

Decks

Because they are subject to a wide range of conditions in different climates, the life expectancy of wooden decks can vary significantly. Under ideal conditions and with proper maintenance, they have a life expectancy of about 20 years.

Doors

Exterior fiberglass, steel, and wood doors will last as long as the house exists, while vinyl and screen doors have a life expectancy of 20 and 40 years, respectively. Closet doors are expected to last a lifetime, and French doors have an average life of 30 to 50 years.

Electrical and Lighting

Copper-plated wiring, copper-clad aluminum, and bare copper wiring are expected to last a lifetime, whereas electrical accessories and lighting controls are expected to last 10+ years.

Engineered Lumber

Floor and roof trusses and laminated-strand lumber are expected to last a lifetime, and engineered trim is expected to last 30 years.

Faucets and Fixtures

Kitchen sinks made of modified acrylic will last 50 years, while kitchen faucets will work properly for about 15 years. The average life of bathroom shower enclosures is 50 years. Showerheads last a lifetime, while shower doors will last about 20 years. Bath cabinets and toilets have an unlimited life span, but the components inside the toilet tank do require some maintenance. Whirlpool tubs will function properly for 20 to 50 years, depending on use.

Flooring

All-natural wood floorings have a life expectancy of 100 years or more. Marble, slate, and granite are also expected to last for about 100 years, but can last a shorter time due to a lack of maintenance. Vinyl floors last up to 50 years, linoleum about 25 years, and carpet between 8 and 10 years (with appropriate maintenance and normal traffic).

Footings and Foundations

Poured as well as concrete block footings and foundations last a lifetime, assuming they were properly built. Termite-proofing of foundations will last about 12 years if the chemical barriers put in place during construction are left intact. Waterproofing with bituminous coating lasts 10 years, but if it cracks it is immediately damaged. Concrete or cast-iron waste pipes are expected to last 100 years or more.

Framing and Other Structural Systems

Framing and structural systems have extended longevities: poured-concrete systems, timber-frame houses, and structural insulated panels will all last a lifetime. Wall panels and roof and floor trusses will similarly last a lifetime. Softwood, hardboard, and plywood last an average of 30 years, while OSB and particleboard are expected to function properly for 60 years.

Garages

Garage door openers are expected to last 10 to 15 years, and light inserts for 20 years.

Heating, Ventilation, and Air Conditioning (HVAC)

Heating, ventilation, and air-conditioning systems require proper and regular maintenance in order to work efficiently, but even in the best-case scenarios most components of such systems only last 15 to 25 years. Furnaces on average last 15 to 20 years, heat pumps 16 years, and air-conditioning units 10 to 15 years. Tankless water heaters last more than 20 years, while an electric or gas water heater has a life expectancy of about 10 years. Thermostats usually are replaced before the end of their 35-year life span due to technological improvements.

Home Technology

Home technology systems have various life expectancies. While a built-in audio system will last 20 years, security systems and heat/smoke detectors have life expectancies of 5 to 10 years. Wireless home networks and home automation systems are expected to work properly for more than 50 years.

Insulation and Infiltration Barriers

As long as they are not punctured, cut, or burned and are kept dry and away from UV rays, the cellulose, fiberglass, and foam used in insulation materials will last a lifetime. This is true whether the insulation was applied as loose fill, house wrap, or batts/rolls.

Jobsite Equipment

Ladders are expected to last a lifetime, and life expectancy of lifts is about 8 to 10 years.

Molding and Millwork

Custom millwork will last a lifetime, and all stairs—circular and spiral stairs, prebuilt stairs, and attic stairs—are expected to last a lifetime.

Paint, Caulks, and Adhesives

Both interior and exterior paints can last for 15 years or longer; however, homeowners often paint more frequently.

Panels

Hardboard panels and softwood panels are expected to last 30 years, while oriented-strand board (OSB) and particleboard have a life expectancy of 60 years. Wall panels are expected to last a lifetime.

Roofing

The life of a roof depends on local weather conditions, proper building and design, material quality, and adequate maintenance. Slate, copper, and clay/concrete roofs have the longest life expectancy—over 50 years. Roofs made of asphalt shingles last for about 20 years, while roofs made of fiber cement shingles have a life expectancy of about 25 years, and roofs made of wood shakes can be expected to last for about 30 years.

Siding and Accessories

Outside materials typically last a lifetime. Brick, vinyl, engineered wood, stone (both natural and manufactured), and fiber cement will last as long as the house exists. Exterior wood shutters are expected to last 20 years, depending on weather conditions. Gutters have a life expectancy of more than 50 years if made of copper and 20 years if made of aluminum. Copper downspouts last 100 years or more, while aluminum ones will last 30 years.

Site and Landscaping

Most landscaping elements have a life expectancy of 15 to 25 years. Sprinklers and valves last about 20 years, while underground PVC piping has a life span of 25 years. Polyvinyl fences are designed to last a lifetime, and asphalt driveways should last between 15 and 20 years. Tennis courts can last a lifetime if recoated; most coatings last 12 to 15 years. The concrete shell of a swimming pool is expected to last over 25 years, but the interior plaster and tile have life expectancies of about 10 to 25 years.

Walls, Ceilings, and Finishes

Walls and ceilings last the full life span of the home.

Windows and Skylights

Aluminum windows are expected to last between 15 and 20 years, while wooden windows should last upwards of 30 years.

Reprinted with permission of National Association of Home Builders. None of the above information should be interpreted as a representation, warranty, or guarantee regarding the life expectancy or performance of any individual product or product line. Readers should not make buying decisions and/or product selections based solely on this information.

INDEX

Italicized page references indicate illustrations. Footnotes are indicated with "n" followed by the endnote number.